JOINT AND SEVERAL LIABILITY IN EU COMPETITION LAW

Contribution claims in antitrust are controversial and under-researched in the legal literature. This book provides the first comprehensive analysis of contribution claims in EU competition law. By drawing on the historical and current practice of EU and national courts, as well as national laws of major EU jurisdictions, it explains contribution claims in antitrust law in concrete and practical terms. It also provides much-needed clarity on the relationship between competition law and joint and several liability, as well as guiding those concerned by contribution claims through the issues that are likely to arise. Topics examined include the requirements competition law sets for contribution claims; the criteria for dividing antitrust liability between individual co-infringers; the impact of EU Directive 2014/10; and whether liability-sharing agreements can resolve the problems joint and several liability brings to EU competition law.

DR. KATARZYNA SADRAK is an associate at Covington & Burling, Brussels. She has advised clients in several high-stakes European Commission investigations and merger cases with a focus on the tech and digital sectors. In her academic career, she has been affiliated with Heidelberg University, Harvard Law School and Jagiellonian University.

Global Competition Law and Economics Policy

This series publishes monographs highlighting the interdisciplinary and multijurisdictional nature of competition law, economics, and policy. Global in coverage, the series should appeal to competition and antitrust specialists working as scholars, practitioners, and judges.

Joint and Several Liability in EU Competition Law

KATARZYNA SADRAK

CAMBRIDGE
UNIVERSITY PRESS

CAMBRIDGE
UNIVERSITY PRESS

University Printing House, Cambridge CB2 8BS, United Kingdom

One Liberty Plaza, 20th Floor, New York, NY 10006, USA

477 Williamstown Road, Port Melbourne, VIC 3207, Australia

314–321, 3rd Floor, Plot 3, Splendor Forum, Jasola District Centre, New Delhi – 110025, India

103 Penang Road, #05–06/07, Visioncrest Commercial, Singapore 238467

Cambridge University Press is part of the University of Cambridge.

It furthers the University's mission by disseminating knowledge in the pursuit of education, learning, and research at the highest international levels of excellence.

www.cambridge.org
Information on this title: www.cambridge.org/9781108839310
DOI: 10.1017/9781108989794

First published 2022

A catalogue record for this publication is available from the British Library.

Library of Congress Cataloging-in-Publication Data
NAMES: Sadrak, Katarzyna, author.
TITLE: Joint and several liability in EU Competition Law / Katarzyna Sadrak, Geradin Partners (Brussels).
DESCRIPTION: Cambridge, United Kingdom ; New York, NY : Cambridge University Press, 2022. | SERIES: Global competition law and economics policy | Based on author's thesis (doctoral - Universität Heidelberg, 2021). | Includes bibliographical references and index.
IDENTIFIERS: LCCN 2021061940 (print) | LCCN 2021061941 (ebook) | ISBN 9781108839310 (hardback) | ISBN 9781108970600 (paperback) | ISBN 9781108989794 (epub)
SUBJECTS: LCSH: Antitrust law–European Union countries. | Correality and solidarity–European Union countries.
CLASSIFICATION: LCC KJE6530 .S23 2022 (print) | LCC KJE6530 (ebook) | DDC 343.240721–dc23/eng/20220531
LC record available at https://lccn.loc.gov/2021061940
LC ebook record available at https://lccn.loc.gov/2021061941

ISBN 978-1-108-83931-0 Hardback

To Ula, Piotr,
Aga and Thomas

Contents

List of Figures — *page* ix
List of Table — xi
Preface — xiii
Acknowledgements — xv
Table of Cases — xvii
Table of Legislation, Official Papers and Policy Documents — xxxi
List of Abbreviations — xxxv

1 **Introduction** — 1
- 1.1 Uncharted Waters of Joint and Several Liability — 1
- 1.2 Problems Raised by Joint and Several Liability in EU Competition Law — 2
- 1.3 A Note on Scope and Terminology — 4

2 **EU Competition Law and Its Impact on Contribution Claims** — 8
- 2.1 Joint and Several Liability in the EU Competition Law Enforcement System — 9
- 2.2 Interference between Contribution Claims and Joint and Several Liability in EU Competition Law — 48
- 2.3 Conclusions — 84

3 **Enforcing Contribution Claims under National Laws** — 85
- 3.1 Competition Law Context of the Dispute — 86
- 3.2 Does a Right to Claim Contribution Exist in National Legal Orders? — 88
- 3.3 Legal Basis and Types of Contribution Claims — 91
- 3.4 Addressees of Contribution Claims — 108
- 3.5 Legal Tests — 113

3.6 Criteria for Establishing Relative Shares of Liability 117
3.7 Competition Law–Specific Approach to Contribution Claims 158

4 **Modifications of Joint and Several Liability with Respect to Certain Groups of Entities** 162
4.1 Entities Engaged in Consensual Dispute Resolution 162
4.2 Immunity Recipients 179
4.3 Small and Medium Enterprises 197
4.4 Conclusions 205

5 **Liability Sharing Agreements** 207
5.1 Are Liability Sharing Agreements Allowed in EU Competition Law? 208
5.2 Precautions That Need to Be Considered While Concluding Liability Sharing Agreements 223
5.3 Conclusions 225

6 **Conclusions and Recommendations** 227
6.1 Conclusions De Lege Lata 227
6.2 Conclusions De Lege Ferenda 229
6.3 Looking Ahead 231

Bibliography 233
Index 257

Figures

2.1 Frequency of applying joint and several liability in Commission decisions *page* 16
4.1 Scenarios for leniency consideration 189

Table

3.1 Choice of criteria for dividing competition law liabilities *page* 156

Preface

Contribution claims are on the eve of being broadly enforced in the context of EU competition law. The private enforcement reform has led to an increasing number of antitrust damages claims. The truck cartel alone influenced nearly nine out of ten trucks manufactured in Europe for fourteen years, giving the owners of approximately thirty million trucks a right to claim damages. Each of such claims, if enforced, can be followed by a claim for contribution to settle the internal division of liability between antitrust infringers who are jointly and severally liable for antitrust debts. Contribution litigation is thus likely to appear in the coming years. This is, however, a novel and undiscovered kind of litigation for EU competition law.

This book provides the first comprehensive analysis of contribution claims in EU competition law. By drawing on the historical and current practice of EU and national courts, as well as national laws of major EU jurisdictions, it explains contribution claims in antitrust law in concrete and practical terms. It also provides much-needed clarity on the relationship between competition law and joint and several liability, as well as guiding those concerned by contribution claims through the issues that are likely to arise. The following questions are examined: (i) What requirements does competition law set for contribution claims? (ii) Which legal framework applies to contribution litigation in the competition law context? (iii) Which modifications to joint and several liability are introduced with Directive 2014/104 EU? (iv) Can liability sharing agreements resolve the problems that joint and several liability brings to EU competition law?

The law is stated as of 6 October 2021.

Acknowledgements

The book is based on a thesis defended at the University of Heidelberg in March 2021. It would not have been possible without the support and guidance of numerous people. I am incredibly grateful for the extraordinary direction of Professor Dr Christoph A. Kern. The book has greatly benefited from his excellent knowledge, academic rigour and valuable critique. I would also like to thank Professor David Rosenberg for the thought-provoking debates on key points of my research and for his invaluable insight into US law. My thanks also go to Professor Louis Kaplow for inspiring discussions on the economic analysis of law. I am also thankful to Nicholas Bridgland for fruitful conversations on UK law, Ben Bornemann for lending his knowledge on private enforcement, Professor Francesco Martucci for his academic guidance, Dr John Sorabji, Professor Dr Dr h.c. Thomas Pfeiffer and Dr Leonhard Hübner. I would also like to thank Harvard Law School for hosting me as a visiting researcher and providing me with an inspirational working environment. My gratitude also goes to the Fulbright Program and the Friedrich Naumann Foundation for their financial assistance. I also had first-rate editing assistance from Melissa Sheridan and Cambridge University Press.

On a more personal note, I would like to express my greatest thanks to Thomas Lymes. Not only was he the first – and multiple – reader of this book, but he also provided me with unconditional encouragement along the way. I would also like to thank Ula, Piotr and Aga Sadrak for their love, a lifetime of support and advice on various aspects of this book. I also thank Anne and Thierry Lymes for making it possible for me to write some parts of this book surrounded by the gorgeous Breton landscape.

Table of Cases

EUROPEAN UNION

COURT CASES (CHRONOLOGICAL ORDER)

COURT OF JUSTICE

Joined cases 40–48, 50, 54–56, 111, 113 and 114/73, Coöperatieve Vereniging "Suiker Unie" UA and others v. Commission of the European Communities, ECLI:EU: C:1975:174 19, 23
Case 33/76, Rewe-Zentralfinanz AG and Rewe-Zentral AG v. Landwirtschaftskammer für das Saarland, ECLI:EU:C:1976:188 59
Case 28/77, Tepea BV v. Commission of the European Communities, ECLI:EU: C:1978:133 214
Case 22/78, Hugin Kassaregister AB and Hugin Cash Registers Ltd v. Commission of the European Communities, ECLI:EU:C:1979:138 14
Case 68/79, Hans Just I/S v. Danish Ministry for Fiscal Affairs, ECLI:EU:C:1980:57 59
Case 199/82, Amministrazione delle Finanze dello Stato v. SpA San Giorgio, ECLI: EU:C:1983:318 59
Case 319/82, Kerpen and Kerpen, ECLI:EU:C:1983:374 225
Case 170/83, Hydrotherm Gerätebau GmbH v. Compact del Dott. Ing. Mario Andreoli and C. Sas, ECLI:EU:C:1984:271 15
Case C-41/90, Klaus Höfner and Fritz Elser v. Macrotron GmbH, ECLI:EU: C:1991:161 17
Case C-9/93, IHT Internationale Heiztechnik GmbH and Uwe Danzinger v. Ideal-Standard GmbH and Wabco Standard GmbH, ECLI:EU:C:1994:261 214
Case C-326/96, B.S. Levez v. T.H. Jennings (Harlow Pools) Ltd, ECLI:EU: C:1998:577 59
Case C-126/97, Eco Swiss China Time Ltd v. Benetton International NV, ECLI: EU:C:1999:269 213
Case C-49/92 P, Commission of the European Communities v. Anic Partecipazioni SpA, ECLI:EU:C:1999:356 23, 24

Case C-78/98, Shirley Preston and Others v. Wolverhampton Healthcare NHS Trust and Others and Dorothy Fletcher and Others v. Midland Bank plc, ECLI:EU:C:2000:247 59
Case C-248/98 P, NV Koninklijke KNP BT v. Commission of the European Communities, ECLI:EU:C:2000:625 23
Case C-344/98, Masterfoods Ltd v. HB Ice Cream Ltd, ECLI:EU:C:2000:249 79
Case C-453/99, Courage Ltd v. Bernard Crehan and Bernard Crehan v. Courage Ltd and Others, ECLI:EU:C:2001:465 11
Case C-196/199, Siderúrgica Aristrain Madrid SL v. Commission of the European Communities ECLI:EU:C:2002:537 21, 25
Joined cases C-204/00 P, C-205/00 P, C-211/00 P, C-213/00 P, C-217/00 P and C-219/00 P, Aalborg Portland A/S, Irish Cement Ltd, Ciments français SA, Italcementi – Fabbriche Riunite Cemento SpA, Buzzi Unicem SpA and Cementir – Cementerie del Tirreno SpA v. Commission of the European Communities, ECLI:EU:C:2004:6 23
Case C-289/04 P, Showa Denko KK v. Commission of the European Communities ECLI:EU:C:2006:52 200
Joined cases C-295/04 to C-298/04, Vincenzo Manfredi v. Lloyd Adriatico Assicurazioni SpA, Antonio Cannito v. Fondiaria Sai SpA and Nicolò Tricarico, and Pasqualina Murgolo v. Assitalia SpA, ECLI:EU:C:2006:461 11, 12, 62, 81
Case C-280/06, Autorità Garante della Concorrenza e del Mercato v. Ente tabacchi italiani – ETI SpA and Others and Philip Morris Products SA and Others v. Autorità Garante della Concorrenza e del Mercato and Others, ECLI:EU:C:2007:775 23
Case C-8/08, T-Mobile Netherlands BV, KPN Mobile NV, Orange Nederland NV and Vodafone Libertel NV v. Raad van bestuur van de Nederlandse Mededingingsautoriteit, ECLI:EU:C:2009:343 19
Case C-97/08 P, Akzo Nobel NV and Others v. Commission of the European Communities, ECLI:EU:C:2009:536 18, 20, 21
Case T-24/05, Alliance One International, Inc., formerly Standard Commercial Corp. and Others v. European Commission, ECLI:EU:T:2010:453 18, 25
Joined cases 201/09 P, 216/09 P, ArcelorMittal Luxembourg SA v. European Commission and European Commission v. ArcelorMittal Luxembourg SA and Others, ECLI:EU:C:2011:190 20
Case T-191/06, FMC Foret, SA v. European Commission, ECLI:EU:T:2011:277 76
Joined cases 144/07, 147-150/07 and 154/07, ThyssenKrupp Liften Ascenseurs NV and Others v. European Commission, ECLI:EU:T:2011:364 20
Joined cases C-89/10 and C-96/10, Q-Beef NV v. Belgische Staat and Frans Bosschaert v. Belgische Staat, Vleesgroothandel Georges Goossens en Zonen NV and Slachthuizen Goossens NV, ECLI:EU:C:2011:555 59
Case C-521/09 P, Elf Aquitaine SA v. European Commission, ECLI:EU:C:2011:620 19
Case C-199/11, Europese Gemeenschap v. Otis NV and Others, ECLI:EU:C:2012:684 60, 61, 62, 80, 81
Case C-508/11 P, Eni SpA v. European Commission, ECLI:EU:C:2013:289 21
Case C-536/11, Bundeswettbewerbsbehörde v. Donau Chemie AG and Others Donau Chemie, ECLI:EU:C:2013:366 12, 193

Case C-440/11 P, European Commission v. Stichting Administratiekantoor Portielje and Gosselin Group NV, ECLI:EU:C:2013:514 21, 75
Joined cases C 231/11 P, C 232/11 P and C 233/11 P, Siemens Österreich and Others, Siemens Transmission and Distribution Ltd, Siemens Transmission and Distribution SA and Nuova Magrini Galileo SpA v. European Commission, ECLI:EU:C:2013:578 and ECLI:EU:C:2014:256 15, 28, 48, 52, 53, 55, 56, 58, 60, 67–72, 75, 7, 79, 83, 86, 104, 110, 116, 118, 128, 150, 211
Case C-58/12, Groupe Gascogne v. European Commission, ECLI:EU:C:2013:770 27
Case C-557/12, Kone AG and Others v. ÖBB-Infrastruktur AG, ECLI:EU:C:2014:1317 193
Case C-67/13 P, Groupement des cartes bancaires (CB) v. European Commission, ECLI:EU:C:2014:2204 81
Joined cases C-93/13 P and C-123/13 P, European Commission v. Versalis SpA and Eni SpA and Versalis SpA and Eni SpA v. European Commission, ECLI:EU:C:2015:150 27
Case C-194/14 P, AC-Treuhand AG v. European Commission, ECLI:EU:C:2015:350 and ECLI:EU:C:2015:717 214
Case C-724/17, Vantaan kaupunki v. Skanska Industrial Solutions Oy and Others, ECLI:EU:C:2019:100 and ECLI:EU:C:2019:204 12, 13, 31, 32, 44, 62, 71, 73, 83, 110, 111
Case C-435/18, Otis Gesellschaft m.b.H. and Others v. Land Oberösterreich and Others, ECLI:EU:C:2019:1069 60, 61, 62, 80, 81
Case C-882/19, Sumal, S.L. v Mercedes Benz Trucks España, S.L., ECLI:EU:C:2021:800 12, 13, 17, 18, 22, 27, 32, 33, 57, 62, 71, 72, 73, 74, 110, 111

GENERAL COURT

Case T-134/94, NMH Stahlwerke GmbH v. Commission of the European Communities, ECLI:EU:T:1999:44 23
Joined cases T-25/95, T-26/95, T-30/95, T-31/95, T-32/95, T-34/95, T-35/95, T-36/95, T-37/95, T-38/95, T-39/95, T-42/95, T-43/95, T-44/95, T-45/95, T-46/95, T-48/95, T-50/95, T-51/95, T-52/95, T-53/95, T-54/95, T-55/95, T-56/95, T-57/95, T-58/95, T-59/95, T-60/95, T-61/95, T-62/95, T-63/95, T-64/95, T-65/95, T-68/95, T-69/95, T-70/95, T-71/95, T-87/95, T-88/95, T-103/95 and T-104/95, Cimenteries CBR and Others v. Commission of the European Communities, ECLI:EU:T:2000:77 23
Case T-9/99, HFB Holding für Fernwärmetechnik Beteiligungsgesellschaft GmbH and Co. KG and Others v. Commission of the European Communities, ECLI:EU:T:2002:70 24
Joined cases T-71/03, T-74/03, T-87/03 and T-91/03, Tokai Carbon Co. Ltd, Intech EDM BV, Intech EDM AG and SGL Carbon AG v. Commission of the European Communities, ECLI:EU:T:2005:220 76
Case T-43/02, Jungbunzlauer AG v. Commission of the European Communities, ECLI:EU:T:2006:270 21
Joined cases T-259/02 to T-264/02 and T-271/02, Raiffeisen Zentralbank Österreich AG and Others v. Commission of the European Communities ECLI:EU:T:2006:396 26
Case T-405/06, ArcelorMittal Luxembourg SA, ArcelorMittal Belval and Differdange SA and ArcelorMittal International SA v. Commission of the European Communities ECLI:EU:T:2009:90 15

Case T-40/06, Trioplast Industrier AB v. European Commission ECLI:EU:T:2010:388 33
Case T-117/07 and T-121/07, Areva and Others and Alstom v. European Commission ECLI:EU:T:2011:69 22, 23, 55
Joined cases T-122/07 to T-124/07 Siemens AG Österreich and VA Tech Transmission and Distribution GmbH and Co. KEG, Siemens Transmission and Distribution Ltd and Siemens Transmission and Distribution SA and Nuova Magrini Galileo SpA v. European Commission ECLI:EU:T:2011:70 22, 27, 51, 52, 54, 55
Case T-377/06, Comap SA v. European Commission ECLI:EU:T:2011:108 76
Case T-385/06, Aalberts Industries NV and Others v. European Commission ECLI:EU:T:2011:114 76
Case T-185/06, L'Air liquide, société anonyme pour l'étude et l'exploitation des procédés Georges Claude v. European Commission ECLI:EU:T:2011:275 19
Joined cases T-141/07, T-142/07, T-145/07 and T-146/07, General Technic-Otis and Others v. Commission, ECLI:EU:T:2011:363 21
Case T-54/06, Kendrion NV v. European Commission ECLI:EU:T:2011:667 21, 76, 104
Case T-360/06, Heijmans NV v. European Commission ECLI:EU:T:2012:490 15
Case T-27/10, AC-Treuhand AG v. European Commission, ECLI:EU:T:2014:59 214
Case T-541/08, Sasol and Others v. European Commission, ECLI:EU:T:2014:628 18, 171
Case T-419/14, The Goldman Sachs Group, Inc. v. European Commission, ECLI:EU:T:2018:445 21

COURT CASES (ALPHABETICAL ORDER)

Aalberts Industries NV and Others v. European Commission (Case T-385/06) ECLI:EU:T:2011:114 76
Aalborg Portland A/S, Irish Cement Ltd, Ciments français SA, Italcementi – Fabbriche Riunite Cemento SpA, Buzzi Unicem SpA and Cementir – Cementerie del Tirreno SpA v. Commission of the European Communities (Joined cases C-204/00 P, C-205/00 P, C-211/00 P, C-213/00 P, C-217/00 P and C-219/00 P) ECLI:EU:C:2004:6 23
AC-Treuhand AG v. European Commission (Case C-194/14 P) ECLI:EU:C:2015:350 and ECLI:EU:C:2015:717 214
AC-Treuhand AG v. European Commission (Case T-27/10) ECLI:EU:T:2014:59 214
Akzo Nobel NV and Others v. Commission of the European Communities (Case C-97/08 P) ECLI:EU:C:2009:536 18, 20, 21
Alliance One International, Inc., formerly Standard Commercial Corp. and Others v. European Commission (Case T-24/05) ECLI:EU:T:2010:453 18, 25
Amministrazione delle Finanze dello Stato v. SpA San Giorgio (Case 199/82), ECLI:EU:C:1983:318 59
ArcelorMittal Luxembourg SA v. European Commission and European Commission v. ArcelorMittal Luxembourg SA and Others (Joined cases 201/09 P, 216/09 P) ECLI:EU:C:2011:190 20

ArcelorMittal Luxembourg SA, ArcelorMittal Belval and Differdange SA and ArcelorMittal International SA v. Commission of the European Communities (Case T-405/06) ECLI:EU:T:2009:90 15
Areva and Others and Alstom v. European Commission (Case T-117/07 and T-121/07) ECLI:EU:T:2011:69 22, 23, 55
Autorità Garante della Concorrenza e del Mercato v. Ente tabacchi italiani – ETI SpA and Others and Philip Morris Products SA and Others v. Autorità Garante della Concorrenza e del Mercato and Others (Case C-280/06) ECLI:EU:C:2007:775 23
B.S. Levez v. T.H. Jennings (Harlow Pools) Ltd (Case C-326/96) ECLI:EU:C:1998:577 59
Bundeswettbewerbsbehörde v. Donau Chemie AG and Others Donau Chemie (Case C-536/11) ECLI:EU:C:2013:366 12, 193
Cimenteries CBR and Others v. Commission of the European Communities (Joined cases T-25/95, T-26/95, T-30/95, T-31/95, T-32/95, T-34/95, T-35/95, T-36/95, T-37/95, T-38/95, T-39/95, T-42/95, T-43/95, T-44/95, T-45/95, T-46/95, T-48/95, T-50/95, T-51/95, T-52/95, T-53/95, T-54/95, T-55/95, T-56/95, T-57/95, T-58/95, T-59/95, T-60/95, T-61/95, T-62/95, T-63/95, T-64/95, T-65/95, T-68/95, T-69/95, T-70/95, T-71/95, T-87/95, T-88/95, T-103/95 and T-104/95) ECLI:EU:T:2000:77 23
Comap SA v. European Commission (Case T-377/06) ECLI:EU:T:2011:108 76
Commission of the European Communities v. Anic Partecipazioni SpA (Case C-49/92 P) ECLI:EU:C:1999:356 23, 24
Coöperatieve Vereniging "Suiker Unie" UA and others v. Commission of the European Communities (Joined cases 40–48, 50, 54–56, 111, 113 and 114/73) ECLI:EU:C:1975:174 19, 23
Courage Ltd v. Bernard Crehan and Others (Case C-453/99) ECLI:EU:C:2001:465 11
Eco Swiss China Time Ltd v. Benetton International NV (Case C-126/97) ECLI:EU:C:1999:269 213
Elf Aquitaine SA v. European Commission (Case C-521/09 P) ECLI:EU:C:2011:620 19
Eni SpA v. European Commission (Case C-508/11 P) ECLI:EU:C:2013:289 21
European Commission v. Stichting Administratiekantoor Portielje and Gosselin Group NV (Case C-440/11 P) ECLI:EU:C:2013:514 21, 75
European Commission v. Versalis SpA and Eni SpA and Versalis SpA and Eni SpA v. European Commission (Joined cases C-93/13 P and C-123/13 P) ECLI:EU:C:2015:150 27
Europese Gemeenschap v. Otis NV and Others (Case C-199/11) ECLI:EU:C:2012:684 81
FMC Foret, SA v. European Commission (Case T-191/06) ECLI:EU:T:2011:277 76
General Technic-Otis and Others v. Commission (Joined cases T-141/07, T-142/07, T-145/07 and T-146/07) ECLI:EU:T:2011:363 21
Groupe Gascogne v. European Commission (Case C-58/12) ECLI:EU:C:2013:770 27

Groupement des cartes bancaires (CB) v. European Commission (Case C-67/13 P) ECLI:EU:C:2014:2204 81
Hans Just I/S v. Danish Ministry for Fiscal Affairs (Case 68/79) ECLI:EU:C:1980:57 59
Heijmans NV v. European Commission (Case T-360/06) ECLI:EU:T:2012:490 15
HFB Holding für Fernwärmetechnik Beteiligungsgesellschaft GmbH and Co. KG and Others v. Commission of the European Communities (Case T-9/99) ECLI:EU:T:2002:70 24
Hugin Kassaregister AB and Hugin Cash Registers Ltd v. Commission of the European Communities (Case 22/78) ECLI:EU:C:1979:138 14
Hydrotherm Gerätebau GmbH v. Compact del Dott. Ing. Mario Andreoli and C. Sas (Case 170/83) ECLI:EU:C:1984:271 15
IHT Internationale Heiztechnik GmbH and Uwe Danzinger v. Ideal-Standard GmbH and Wabco Standard GmbH (Case C-9/93) ECLI:EU:C:1994:261 214
Jungbunzlauer AG v. Commission of the European Communities (Case T-43/02) ECLI:EU:T:2006:270 21
Kendrion NV v. European Commission (Case T-54/06) ECLI:EU:T:2011:667 21, 76, 104
Kerpen and Kerpen (Case 319/82) ECLI:EU:C:1983:374 225
Klaus Höfner and Fritz Elser v. Macrotron GmbH (Case C-41/90) ECLI:EU:C:1991:161 17
Kone AG and Others v. ÖBB-Infrastruktur AG (Case C-557/12) ECLI:EU:C:2014:1317 193
L'Air liquide, société anonyme pour l'étude et l'exploitation des procédés Georges Claude v. European Commission (Case T-185/06) ECLI:EU:T:2011:275 19
Masterfoods Ltd v. HB Ice Cream Ltd (Case C-344/98) ECLI:EU:C:2000:249 79
NMH Stahlwerke GmbH v. Commission of the European Communities (Case T-134/94) ECLI:EU:T:1999:44 23
NV Koninklijke KNP BT v. Commission of the European Communities (Case C-248/98 P) ECLI:EU:C:2000:625 23
Otis Gesellschaft m.b.H. and Others v. Land Oberösterreich and Others (Case C-435/18) ECLI:EU:C:2019:1069 60, 61, 62, 80, 81
Q-Beef NV v. Belgische Staat and Frans Bosschaert v. Belgische Staat, Vleesgroothandel Georges Goossens en Zonen NV and Slachthuizen Goossens NV (Joined cases C-89/10 and C-96/10) ECLI:EU:C:2011:555 59
Raiffeisen Zentralbank Österreich AG and Others v. Commission of the European Communities (Joined cases T-259/02 to T-264/02 and T-271/02) ECLI:EU:T:2006:396 26
Rewe-Zentralfinanz AG and Rewe-Zentral AG v. Landwirtschaftskammer für das Saarland (Case 33/76) ECLI:EU:C:1976:188 59
Sasol and Others v. European Commission (Case T-541/08) ECLI:EU:T:2014:628 18, 171
Shirley Preston and Others v. Wolverhampton Healthcare NHS Trust and Others and Dorothy Fletcher and Others v. Midland Bank plc (Case C-78/98) ECLI:EU:C:2000:247 59
Showa Denko KK v. Commission of the European Communities (Case C-289/04 P) ECLI:EU:C:2006:52 200
Siderúrgica Aristrain Madrid SL v. Commission of the European Communities (Case C-196/199) ECLI:EU:C:2002:537 21, 25

Siemens AG Österreich and VA Tech Transmission and Distribution GmbH and Co. KEG, Siemens Transmission and Distribution Ltd and Siemens Transmission and Distribution SA and Nuova Magrini Galileo SpA v. European Commission (Joined cases T-122/07 to T-124/07) ECLI:EU:T:2011:70 22, 27, 51, 52, 54, 55

Siemens Österreich and Others, Siemens Transmission and Distribution Ltd, Siemens Transmission and Distribution SA and Nuova Magrini Galileo SpA v. European Commission (Joined cases C 231/11 P, C 232/11 P and C 233/11 P) ECLI:EU:C:2013:578 and ECLI:EU:C:2014:256 15, 28, 48, 52, 53, 55, 56, 58, 60, 67–72, 75, 7, 79, 83, 86, 104, 110, 116, 118, 128, 150, 211

Sumal, S.L. v. Mercedes Benz Trucks España, S.L., ECLI:EU:C:2021:293 (Case C-882/19) ECLI:EU:C:2021:293 13, 18, 22, 31, 32, 71, 72, 73, 74, 111, 132

Sumal, S.L. v Mercedes Benz Trucks España, S.L., ECLI:EU:C:2021:800 (Case C-882/19) 12, 13, 17, 18, 22, 27, 32, 33, 57, 62, 71, 72, 73, 74, 110, 111

Tepea BV v. Commission of the European Communities (Case 28/77) ECLI:EU:C:1978:133 214

The Goldman Sachs Group, Inc. v. European Commission (Case T-419/14) ECLI:EU:T:2018:445 21

ThyssenKrupp Liften Ascenseurs NV and Others v. European Commission (Joined cases 144/07, 147-150/07 and 154/07) ECLI:EU:T:2011:364 20

T-Mobile Netherlands BV, KPN Mobile NV, Orange Nederland NV and Vodafone Libertel NV v. Raad van bestuur van de Nederlandse Mededingingsautoriteit (Case C-8/08) ECLI:EU:C:2009:343 19

Tokai Carbon Co. Ltd, Intech EDM BV, Intech EDM AG and SGL Carbon AG v. Commission of the European Communities (Joined cases T-71/03, T-74/03, T-87/03 and T-91/03) ECLI:EU:T:2005:220 76

Trioplast Industrier AB v. European Commission (Case T-40/06) ECLI:EU:T:2010:388 33

Vantaan kaupunki v. Skanska Industrial Solutions Oy and Others (Case C-724/17) ECLI:EU:C:2019:100 and ECLI:EU:C:2019:204 12, 13, 31, 32, 44, 62, 71, 73, 83, 110, 111

Vincenzo Manfredi v. Lloyd Adriatico Assicurazioni SpA, Antonio Cannito v. Fondiaria Sai SpA and Nicolò Tricarico, and Pasqualina Murgolo v. Assitalia SpA (Joined cases C-295/04 to C-298/04) ECLI:EU:C:2006:461 11, 12, 62, 81

DECISIONS (CHRONOLOGICAL ORDER)

Commission decision of 18 August 1969 in Case IV.22.548 – Cristiani and Nielsen Den Haag, OJ 1969 No. L165/12 18

Commission decision of 14 December 1972 in Case IV/26.911 – ZOJA/CSC – ICI, OJ 1972 No. L299/51 14, 22

Commission decision of 8 December 1977 in Case IV/29.132 – Hugin/Liptons, OJ 1978 No. L22/23 14

Commission decision of 25 November 1980 in Case IV/29.702 – Johnson and Johnson, OJ 1980 No. L377/16 14, 26

Commission decision of 24 July 1991 in Case IV/31043 – Tetra Pak II, OJ 1992 No. L72/1 141

Commission decision of 13 July 1994 in Case IV/C/33.833 – Cartonboard, OJ 1994 No. L243/1 15

Commission decision of 21 October 1998 in Case IV/35.691/E-4 – Pre-Insulated Pipe Cartel, OJ 1999 No. L24/ 23, 24

Commission decision of 20 September 2000 in Case COMP/36.653 – Opel, OJ 2001 No. L59/1 15
Commission decision of 29 June 2001 in Case COMP/F-2/36.693 – Volkswagen, OJ 2001 No. L262/14 78–9
Commission decision of 5 December 2001 in Case COMP/E-1/36.604 – Citric acid, OJ 2002 No. L239/18 22
Commission decision of 11 December 2001 in Case COMP/E-1/37.027 – Zinc phosphate, OJ 2003 No. L153/1 24
Commission decision of 20 December 2001 in Case COMP/E-1/36.212 – Carbonless paper, OJ 2004 No. L115/1 24
Commission decision of 11 June 2002 in Case COMP/36.571/D-1 – Austrian banks – “Lombard Club”, OJ 2004 No. L56/1 26
Commission decision of 30 October 2002 in Case COMP/35.587 – PO Video Games, COMP/35.706 PO Nintendo Distribution and in Case COMP/36.321 – Omega – Nintendo, OJ 2003 No. L255/33 27
Commission decision of 20 October 2004 in Case COMP/C.38.238/B2 – Raw tobacco – Spain, OJ 2007 No. L102/14 21, 25
Commission decision of 3 May 2006 in Case COMP/F/C.38.620 – Hydrogen Peroxide and Perborate, OJ 2006 No. L353/54 23, 173
Commission decision of 21 February 2007 in COMP/E-1/38.823 – PO/Elevators and Escalators, OJ 2008 No. C75/19 22
Commission decision of 24 January 2007 in Case COMP/F/38.899 – Gas Insulated Switchgear, C(2006) 6762 final 22, 51
Commission decision of 20 November 2007 in Case COMP/38.432 – Professional Videotape, C(2007)5469 final 27
Commission decision of 11 March 2008 in Case COMP/38.543 – International removal services, C (2008) 926 final 75, 77
Commission decision of 28 January 2009 in Case COMP/39406 – Marine Hoses, not published yet 24, 75
Commission decision of 22 July 2009 in Case COMP/39.396 – Calcium carbide and magnesium-based reagents for the steel and gas industries, C(2009) 5791 final 49
Commission decision of 7 October 2009 in Case COMP/39.129 – Power Transformers, C(2009) 7601 final 131
Commission decision of 30 June 2010 in Case COMP/38.344 – Prestressing Steel, C (2010) 4387 final 80, 81
Commission decision of 19 June 2013 in Case AT.39226 – Lundbeck, C(2013) 3803 final 76, 147
Commission decision of 27 November 2013 in Case AT.39633 – Shrimps, C(2013) 8286 final 147
Commission decision of 2 April 2014 in Case AT.39610 – Power Cables, C(2014) 2139 final 25
Commission decision of 15 July 2014 in Case AT.40098 – Blocktrains, C(2015) 4646 final 81
Commission decision of 15 October 2014 in Case AT.39523 – Slovak Telekom, C (2014) 7465 final 27, 73
Commission decision of 27 January 2016 in Case AT.40028 – Alternators and Starters, C(2016) 223 final 81
Commission decision of 8 February 2017 in Case AT.40018 – Car battery recycling, C(2017) 900 final 143

Commission decision of 22 November 2017 in Case AT.39881 – Occupant Safety Systems supplied to Japanese Car Manufacturers, C(2017) 7670 final 13, 20, 143
Commission decision of 21 February 2018 in Case AT.39920 – Braking Systems, C (2018) 925 final 143
Commission decision of 21 February 2018 in Case AT.40113 – Spark Plugs, C(2018) 929 final 143

DECISIONS (ALPHABETICAL ORDER)

Alternators and Starters (Case AT.40028) Commission decision of 27 January 2016, C(2016) 223 final 81
Austrian banks – "Lombard Club" (Case COMP/36.571/D-1) Commission decision of 11 June 2002, OJ 2004 No. L56/1 26
Blocktrains (Case AT.40098) Commission decision of 15 July 2014, C(2015) 4646 final 81
Braking Systems (Case AT.39920) Commission decision of 21 February 2018, C (2018) 925 final 143
Calcium carbide and magnesium-based reagents for the steel and gas industries (Case COMP/39.396) Commission decision of 22 July 2009, C(2009) 5791 final 49
Car battery recycling (Case AT.40018) Commission decision of 8 February 2017, C (2017) 900 final 143
Carbonless paper (Case COMP/E-1/36.212) Commission decision of 20 December 2001, OJ 2004 No. L115/1 24
Cartonboard (Case IV/C/33.833) Commission decision of 13 July 1994, OJ 1994 No. L243/1 15
Citric acid (Case COMP/E-1/36.604) Commission decision of 5 December 2001, OJ 2002 No. L239/18 22
Cristiani and Nielsen Den Haag (Case IV.22.548) Commission decision of 18 August, OJ 1969 No. L165/12 18
Gas Insulated Switchgear (Case COMP/F/38.899) Commission decision of 24 January 2007, C(2006) 6762 final 22, 51
Hugin/Liptons (Case IV/29.132) Commission decision of 8 December 1977, OJ 1978 No. L22/23 14
Hydrogen Peroxide and Perborate (Case COMP/F/C.38.620) Commission decision of 3 May 2006, OJ 2006 No. L353/54 23, 173
International removal services (Case COMP/38.543) Commission decision of 11 March 2008, C (2008) 926 final 75, 77
Johnson and Johnson (Case IV/29.702) Commission decision of 25 November 1980, OJ 1980 No. L377/16 14, 76
Lundbeck (Case AT.39226) Commission decision of 19 June 2013, C(2013) 3803 final 76, 147
Marine Hoses (Case COMP/39406) Commission decision of 28 January 2009, not published yet 24, 75
Occupant Safety Systems supplied to Japanese Car Manufacturers (Case AT.39881) Commission decision of 22 November 2017, C(2017) 7670 final 13, 20, 143
Opel (Case COMP/36.653) Commission decision of 20 September 2000, OJ 2001 No. L59/1 15

PO/Elevators and Escalators (COMP/E-1/38.823) Commission decision of 21 February 2007, OJ 2008 No. C75/19 22
PO Video Games (Case COMP/35.587), Nintendo Distribution (Case COMP/35.706 PO) and Omega – Nintendo (Case COMP/36.321) Commission decision of 30 October 2002, OJ 2003 No. L255/33 27
Power Cables (Case AT.39610) Commission decision of 2 April 2014, C(2014) 2139 final 25
Power Transformers (Case COMP/39.129) Commission decision of 7 October 2009, C(2009) 7601 final 131
Pre-Insulated Pipe Cartel (Case IV/35.691/E-4) Commission decision of 21 October 1998, OJ 1999 No. L24/ 23, 24
Prestressing Steel (Case COMP/38.344) Commission decision of 30 June 2010, C (2010) 4387 final 80, 81
Professional Videotape (Case COMP/38.432) Commission decision of 20 November 2007, C(2007)5469 final 27
Raw tobacco – Spain (Case COMP/C.38.238/B2) Commission decision of 20 October 2004, OJ 2007 No. L102/14 21, 25
Shrimps (Case AT.39633) Commission decision of 27 November 2013, C(2013) 8286 final 147
Slovak Telekom (Case AT.39523) Commission decision of 15 October 2014, C(2014) 7465 final 27, 73
Spark Plugs (Case AT.40113) Commission decision of 21 February 2018, C(2018) 929 final 143
Tetra Pak II (Case IV/31043) Commission decision of 24 July 1991, OJ 1992 No. L72/1 141
Volkswagen (Case COMP/F-2/36.693) Commission decision of 29 June 2001,OJ 2001 No. L262/14 78–9
Zinc phosphate (Case COMP/E-1/37.027) Commission decision of 11 December 2001, OJ 2003 No. L153/1 24
ZOJA/CSC – ICI (Case IV/26.911) Commission decision of 14 December 1972, OJ 1972 No. L299/51 14, 22

FRANCE

Cass. Req., 15.01.1878: S. 1878 I 152 38
Cass. Req., 24.02.1886: S. 1886 I 460 123
Civ., 11.07.1892: S. 1892 I 505 29
Civ., 21.12.1943: JCP 1945 II 2779 38
Crim., 21.05.1959: JCP 1959 IV 85 103
Civ. II, 05.02.1960: D. 1960, 365 146
Civ. I, 16.05.1960: D. 1960, 737 note Tunc 132
Civ. II, 16.02.1962: Bull civ. II 208 123
Civ. I, 14.12.1964: D. 1965, 95 212
Civ. I, 07.07.1965: JCP G 1965 II 14376 96
Crim., 12.01.1966 and 22.02.1966: Gaz. Pal. 1966 I 425 103
Civ. III, 08.07.1971: Bull. Civ. III 448 96
Civ. I, 19.06.1973: Bull. Civ. I 208 82
Civ. II, 22.10.1975: Bull. Civ. II 235 82

Civ. II, 17.11.1976: D. 1977 IR 29 123
Civ. I, 7.06.1977: JCP 1978 II 19003 95, 96
Civ. III, 22.06.1977: D. 1977 IR 472 115
Civ. II, 08.05.1978: Gaz. Pal. 1978 II 262 123
Civ. I, 06.02.1979: Bull. Civ. I 45 115
Civ. II, 18.01.1984: Gaz. Pal. 1984 I 125 123
Civ. II, 02.04.1997: Bull. Civ. II 112 146
Civ. II, 14.01.1998: JCP 1998 II 10045 132
Civ. I, 04.04.2001: JCP 2002 I 134 96
Civ. II, 25.01.2007: JurisData n° 2007-037038 123
Civ. I, 24.09.2009: JurisData n° 2009-049535 123
Civ. I, 24.09.2009: JurisData n° 2009-049537 123
Civ. I, 28.01.2010: JurisData n° 2010-051305 123
Civ. II, 13.01.2011: Bull. Civ. II 8 123
Tribunal de commerce de Grenoble, 18.12.2009, 2007J00528 50, 51

GERMANY

BGH, NJW 1963, 1873 103
BGH, NJW 1966, 1262 132
BGH, NJW 1969, 789 121
BGH, NJW 1971, 752 132
BGH, NJW 1972, 1802 119
BGH, NJW 1973, 1077 103
BGH, NJW 2006, 896 121
BGH, BeckRS 2015, 00033 50, 68–70, 102–3, 122, 125, 152, 154
OLG Stuttgart, ZIP 94, 201 122
OLG Hamm, NJW 2002, 1054 122
OLG München, BeckRS 2012, 8896 50, 69, 103, 122, 125
LG Düsseldorf, WuW 2007, 520 185
LG Düsseldorf, BeckRS 2013, 22380 185
LG München I, BeckRS 2013, 10095 49, 50, 69, 103, 122, 125

NETHERLANDS

The Hague District Court, judgment of 21 September 2016 in Case C/09/414499 / HA ZA 12-293, *CDC Project 14 SA v. Shell Petroleum N.V. and Others* 171

POLAND

Judgment of the Supreme Court from 16.10.1958, III CR 81/58, OSPiKA 1960, nr 1, poz. 6 35, 97
Ruling of the Supreme Court from 25.04.1962, I CR 469/61, OSNC 1963, nr 3, poz. 75 97, 122
Judgment of the Supreme Court from 17.03.1970, II PR 659/68, OSNCP 1970, nr 12, poz. 231 77
Judgment of the Supreme Court from 07.03.1978, III CZP 14/178, not published 109

Judgment of the Supreme Court from 27.02.2009, II CNP 117/08, LEX nr 599749 122
Judgment of the Supreme Court from 15.10.2010, v. CSK 78/10, LEX nr 677911 122

SPAIN

Audiencia Provincial de Barcelona, request for a preliminary ruling of 3 December 2019 in Case C-882/19, Sumal, S. L. v. Mercedes Benz Trucks España, S. L. 32

UNITED KINGDOM

Brook's Wharf and Bull Wharf Ltd. v. Goodman Bros [1937] 1 KB 534 CA 103
Craythorne v. Swinburne [1807] 14 Ves. Jun. 160, 33 ER 482 119
Development Ltd. v. ABB AB [2018] EWHC 2616 (Ch) 80
Downs v. Chappel [1997] 1 WLR 426, CA; [1996] 3 All ER 344; [1996] CLC 1492 121, 124
Dubai Aluminium Co. Ltd. v. Salaam [2003] 2 AC 366; [2002] 3 WLR 1913; [2003] 1 All ER 97; [2002] UKHL 48 121, 124, 132
Duncan, Fox and Co. v. North and South Wales Bank [1880] 6 App Cas 1 HL, All ER Rep Ext 1406 97, 104
Gray v. Fire Alarm Fabrication Services Ltd. [2006] All ER (D) 133; [2006] EWCA Civ 1496 121
Merryweather v. Nixan [1799] 8 TR 186, 101 ER 1337 37, 89
Royal Mail Group Limited v. DAF Trucks Ltd. and Others [2020] CAT 7 80
Schott Kern Ltd. v. Bentley [1991] 1 QB 61, CA 121
Smith v. Bray [1939] 56 TLR 200 121
South Australia Asset Management Co. v. York Montague Ltd. and Banque Bruxelles Lambert SA v. Eagle Star Insurance Co. Ltd. [1997] AC 191; [1996] 3 WLR 87; [1996] 3 All ER 365; [1996] UKHL 10 135
The Koningin Juliana [1974] 2 Lloyd's Rep. 353, CA 124
UK Trucks Claim Ltd. v. Fiat Chrysler Automobiles NV and Others and DAT Trucks NV and Others and Road Haulage Association Ltd. v. MAN SE and Others and Daimler AG [2019] CAT 26 1, 173, 175
Weaver v. Commercial Process Co. Ltd. [1947] 63 TLR 466 121
Weld-Blundell v. Stephens [1920] AC 956 89
WH Newson Holdings Ltd. v. IMI Plc. [2017] Ch 27; [2016] 3 WLR 1595; [2016] EWCA Civ 773 173, 175
Whitby v. Burt Boulton and Hayward Ltd. [1947] KB 918 132
Whitham v. Bullock [1939] 2 All ER 310, 316, CA 6, 92, 97
Wolseley UK Limited and Others v. Fiat Chrysler Automobiles N.V. and Others [2019] CAT 12 173, 175
Yuille v. B & B Fisheries (Leigh) Ltd. and Bates (The Radiant) [1958] 2 Lloyd's Rep 596 78

UNITED STATES

American Society of Mechanical Engineers, Inc. v. Hydrolevel Corporation, 102 S. Ct. 1935, 1945 (1982) 44

Cimarron Pipeline Constr. v. Nat'l Council on Comp. Ins., Civ.-89-822-T, 1992 U.S. Dist. LEXIS 18560 (W.D. Okla. 1992) 208
Illinois Brick Co. v. Illinois, 431 U.S. 720 (1977) 44, 208
In re "Agent Orange" Prod. Liab. Litig., 597 F. Supp. 740, 816-42 (E.D.N.Y. 1984), aff'd, 818 F.2d 145 (2nd Cir. 1987) 146
In re Brand Name Pharm. Antitrust Litig., MDL 997, 1995 WL 234521 (N.D. Ill. 1995) 208
Mahar v. Hanover House Indus., Inc., No. CA 880156, 1995 WL 1146188 (Mass. Super. Ct. Dec. 12, 1995) 146
Olson Farms, Inc. v. Safeway Stores, Inc., 649 F.2d 1370 (10th Cir. 1979) 40
Professional Beauty Supply v. National Beauty Supply, 594 F.2d 1179 (8th Cir. 1979) 40
Russo v. Material Handling Specialties Co., No. 9101209, 1995 WL 1146853 (Mass. Super. Ct. Aug. 29, 1995) 146
Sindell v. Abbott Labs., 607 P.2d 924, 925, 927 (Cal. 1980) 146
Texas Indus. v. Radcliff Materials, 451 U.S. 630 (1981) 1, 2, 39, 40, 44, 46

Table of Legislation, Official Papers and Policy Documents

EUROPEAN UNION

Charter of Fundamental Rights of the European Union, OJ 2012 No. C326/391 60

Commission Green Paper – Damages actions for breach of the EC antitrust rules, SEC(2005) 1732, COM/2005/0672 final 12

Commission Guidelines on the method of setting fines imposed pursuant to Article 23(2)(a) of Regulation No 1/2003, OJ 2006 No. C210/2 9, 10, 46, 130, 140, 141, 143, 153, 154, 155, 200

Commission Notice on immunity from fines and reduction of fines in cartel cases, OJ 2002 No. C45/3 183

Commission Notice on immunity from fines and reduction of fines in cartel cases, OJ 2006 No. C298/17 68, 183

Commission Notice on the conduct of settlement procedures in view of the adoption of Decisions pursuant to Article 7 and Article 23 of Council Regulation (EC) No 1/2003 in cartel cases, OJ 2008 No. C167/1 45

Commission Notice on the definition of relevant market for the purposes of Community competition law, OJ 1997 No. C372/5 146

Commission Recommendation 2003/361/EC of 6 May 2003 concerning the definition of micro, small and medium-sized enterprises, OJ 2003 No. L124/36 202

Commission Regulation (EC) No 622/2008 of 30 June 2008 amending Regulation (EC) No 773/2004 as regards the conduct of settlement procedures in cartel cases, OJ 2008 No. L171/3 45

Commission Staff Working Document, Impact Assessment Report. Damages actions for breach of the EU antitrust rules. Accompanying the proposal for a Directive of the European Parliament and of the Council on certain rules governing actions for damages under national law for infringements of the competition law provisions of the Member States and of the European Union, SWD(2013) 203 final 31

Commission Staff Working Paper accompanying the White Paper on Damages actions for breach of the EC antitrust rules, SEC(2008) 404 192

Commission Staff Working Paper, Annex to the Green Paper Damages actions for breach of the EC antitrust rules, SEC(2005) 1732 179, 190, 191
Commission White Paper on damages actions for breach of the EC antitrust rules, 2.4.2008, COM(2008) 165 final 11, 12, 29, 30, 179, 196
Communication from the Commission on quantifying harm in actions for damages based on breaches of Article 101 or 102 of the Treaty on the Functioning of the European Union, 2013/C 167/07 140
Communication from the Commission to the Council, the European Parliament, the European Economic and Social Committee and the Committee of the Regions – "Think Small First" – A "Small Business Act" for Europe, COM/2008/0394 final 199
Communication from the Commission to the European Parliament, the Council, the European Economic and Social Committee and the Committee of the Regions Entrepreneurship 2020 Action Plan Reigniting the entrepreneurial spirit in Europe COM/2012/0795 final 199
Communication from the Commission, Guidelines on the applicability of Article 101 of the Treaty on the Functioning of the European Union to horizontal co-operation agreements, OJ 2011 No. C11/1 21
Communication from the Commission, Notice on agreements of minor importance which do not appreciably restrict competition under Article 101(1) of the Treaty on the Functioning of the European Union (De Minimis Notice), OJ 2014 No. C291/1 146
Consolidated version of the Treaty on European Union, OJ 2012 No.C 326/13 xxxvi
Consolidated version of the Treaty on the Functioning of the European Union, OJ 2012 No. C326/47 4, 9, 17, 18, 32, 44, 50, 61, 72, 79, 136, 214, 215, 223, 225
Directive 2011/7/EU of the European Parliament and of the Council of 16 February 2011 on combating late payment in commercial transactions, OJ 2011 No. L48/1 199
Directive 2014/104/EU of the European Parliament and of the Council of 26 November 2014 on certain rules governing actions for damages under national law for infringements of the competition law provisions of the Member States and of the European Union, OJ 2014 No. L349/1 3, 5, 12, 28–9, 31, 45, 48, 53, 60, 62, 71, 73–4, 83, 86–7, 96, 99, 101, 106–7, 118–20, 124, 155, 159, 162–3, 166, 168, 174, 177, 179, 181, 185, 188–92, 194–5, 197–8, 201, 203, 205, 211, 216, 219, 228, 231
European Competition Network (ECN), Resolution of the Meeting of Heads of the European Competition Authorities, Protection of leniency material in the context of civil damages actions (23 May 2012) available at https://ec.europa.eu/competition/ecn/leniency_material_protection_en.pdf 192
European Parliament resolution of 25 April 2007 on the Green Paper on damages actions for breach of the EC antitrust rules (2006/2207(INI)) 30
European Parliament resolution of 26 March 2009 on the White Paper on damages actions for breach of the EC antitrust rules (2008/2154(INI)) 191
Regulation 1/2003 of 16 December 2002 on the implementation of the rules on competition laid down in Articles 81 and 82 of the Treaty, OJ 2003 No. L1/1 17, 27, 30, 50, 61, 72, 76, 79, 128

FRANCE

Code civil des français: édition originale et seule officielle, Paris: L'Imprimerie de la République. XII. 1804 38

Code civil, Version consolidée au 1 octobre 2018 (English translation: John Cartwright, Bénédicte Fauvarque-Cosson, Simon Whittaker, *The Law of Contract, The General Regime of Obligations, and Proof of Obligations*, available at https://textes.justice.gouv.fr/art_pix/Translationrevised2018final.pdf 34, 90, 95, 96, 103, 108, 114, 212
Code de commerce, Version consolidée au 1 janvier 2019 (English translation: own) 96, 99, 102–3, 108, 120, 159–60
Code pénal, Version consolidée au 25 novembre 2018 130
Ordonnance n° 2016-131 du 10 février 2016 portant réforme du droit des contrats, du régime général et de la preuve des obligations, Journal officiel de la république française n°0035 du 11 février 2016 texte n° 26 90

GERMANY

Bürgerliches Gesetzbuch (BGB) in der Fassung der Bekanntmachung vom 2. Januar 2002 (Bundesgesetzblatt I, 42, 2909; 2003 I, 738), das zuletzt durch Artikel 4d des Gesetzes vom 18. Dezember 2018 (Bundesgesetzblatt I, 2651) geändert worden ist (English translation: Langenscheidt Translation Service, *German Civil Code BGB* (Saarbrücken, juris, 2009)) 29, 34, 37, 69, 94, 98, 100, 102, 106–8, 114, 119, 121–2
Gesetz gegen Wettbewerbsbeschränkungen (GWB) in der Fassung der Bekanntmachung vom 26. Juni 2013 (Bundesgesetzblatt I, 1750, 3245), das zuletzt durch Artikel 10 des Gesetzes vom 12. Juli 2018 (Bundesgesetzblatt I, 1151) geändert worden ist (English translation: Language Service of the Bundeskartellamt in cooperation with Renate Tietjen, available at https://gesetze-im-internet.de/englisch_gwb/englisch_gwb.html#p0252 28, 94, 96, 100, 102, 107, 163, 171, 180, 181, 198, 199
Neuntes Gesetz zur Änderung des Gesetzes gegen Wettbewerbsbeschränkungen vom 1. Juli 2017 (Bundesgesetzblatt I (33) 1416) (9. Novelle) (English translation: Language Service of the Bundeskartellamt in cooperation with Renate Tietjen, available at https://gesetze-im-internet.de/englisch_gwb/englisch_gwb.html#p0252) 100, 102, 107
Strafgesetzbuch (StGB) in der Fassung der Bekanntmachung vom 13. November 1998 (Bundesgesetzblatt I, 3322), das zuletzt durch Artikel 14 des Gesetzes vom 18. Dezember 2018 (Bundesgesetzblatt I, 2639) 130

POLAND

Rozporządzenie Prezydenta Rzeczypospolitej z dnia 27 października 1933 r. Kodeks zobowiązań, Dz.U. 1933 nr 82 poz. 598 90
Ustawa z dnia 23 kwietnia 1964 r. Kodeks cywilny, Dz.U. 1964 nr 16 poz. 93 (English translation: available at https://supertrans2014.files.wordpress.com/2014/06/kodeks-cywilny-pol-ang.docx) 34, 92, 97–8, 100, 102, 106, 108, 114, 120, 122, 181, 198, 199
Ustawa z dnia 6 czerwca 1997 r. Kodeks karny, Dz. U. 1997 nr 88 poz. 553 130
Ustawa z dnia 21 kwietnia 2017 r. o roszczeniach o naprawienie szkody wyrządzonej przez naruszenie prawa konkurencji, Dz.U. 2017 poz. 1132 (English translation: own) 96, 99, 100, 163, 171, 180, 181, 198

UNITED KINGDOM

Law Reform (Married Women and Tortfeasors) Act 1935 [Ch. 30] 38, 89
The Civil Liability (Contribution) Act 1978 [Ch. 47] 38, 88–9, 92, 97, 100–1, 106, 211
The Claims in respect of Loss or Damage arising from Competition Infringements (Competition Act 1998 and Other Enactments (Amendment)) Regulations 2017, [2017 No. 385] 96, 100, 119, 163, 171, 180–1, 198

UNITED STATES

Antitrust Criminal Penalty Enhancement and Reform Act of 2004, 15 U.S.C. 1, Public Law 108-237, 22 June 2004, 118 Stat. 661 187–8, 216
Uniform Contribution among Tortfeasors Act, 12 U.L.A. 60 (1975) 38
United States Department of Justice, Corporate Leniency Policy of 10 August 1993, available at https://justice.gov/sites/default/files/atr/legacy/2007/08/14/0091.pdf 187

OTHER

Act LVII of 1996 on the Prohibition of Unfair and Restrictive Market Practices (Hungarian Competition Act) 191–2
London Court of International Arbitration Rules 2014 (1 October 2014) 167
Maltese Police Act As changed by Act IV of 2014: The Various Law (Criminal Matters) (Amendment) Act 2014 (An Act further to Amend Various Laws related to Criminal Matters) 191
Singapore International Arbitration Centre Rules 2013 (1 April 2013) 167
The United Nations Commission on International Trade Law (UNCITRAL) Ad Hoc Rules 2013 (16 December 2013) 68/109 167

Abbreviations

ACPERA	Antitrust Criminal Penalty Enhancement and Reform Act
AG	Advocate General
BGB	Bürgerliches Gesetzbuch (German Civil Code)
BGH	Bundesgerichtshof (German Federal Supreme Court)
Cass. Req.	Chambre des requêtes de la Cour de cassation (French Supreme Court, Requests Division)
CC	Code Civil (French Civil Code)
CEE	Central and Eastern Europe
CEPR	Centre for Economic Policy Research
CEPS	Centre for European Policy Studies
Civ.	Chambre civile de la Cour de cassation (French Supreme Court, Civil Division)
CJEU	Court of Justice of the European Union
CLES	Centre for Law, Economics and Society
Commission	European Commission
Crim.	Chambre criminelle de la Cour de cassation (French Supreme Court, Criminal Division)
DG	Directorate-General of the European Commission
DG COMP	Directorate-General for Competition
EEA	European Economic Area
EU	European Union
GCEU	General Court of the European Union
GWB	Gesetz gegen Wettbewerbsbeschränkungen (German Competition Act)
k.c.	Kodeks Cywilny (Polish Civil Code)
LG	Landesgericht (German Regional Court)

LSA	liability sharing agreement
OECD	Organisation for Economic Co-operation and Development
OFT	Office of Fair Trading
OJ	*Official Journal*
OLG	Oberlandesgericht (German Higher Regional Court)
PETL	Principles of European Tort Law
SME	small and medium enterprise
TEU	Treaty on European Union
TFEU	Treaty on the Functioning of the European Union
TILEC	Tilburg Law and Economics Center

1

Introduction

1.1 UNCHARTED WATERS OF JOINT AND SEVERAL LIABILITY

The recent truck cartel has certainly drawn a lot of public attention, with the cartel comprised of MAN, Volvo Group, Daimler, Iveco and DAF Trucks[1] being fined nearly EUR 3.8 billion. Similarly, record damages are currently in litigation in several jurisdictions, including the UK, the Netherlands, Germany, Spain and France. In the UK alone, a single lawsuit brought forward by the UK Truck Cartel (UKTC) amounts to GBP 14 billion.[2] The financial stakes certainly make this litigation interesting to follow. But the application of joint and several liability is even more intriguing. UKTC decided not to make claims against all cartelists but addressed its claims only to Iveco and Daimler.[3] It relied on joint and several liability and the resulting right to choose from whom to claim damages. While joint and several liability is certainly beneficial for UKTC as it can recover the entirety of the damages from just a few chosen entities, it leads to severe consequences for Iveco and Daimler. They risk being held liable for GBP 14 billion in damages, whereas their competitors and co-conspirators could theoretically get a free ride.

This would be an expected turnaround in the United States, where antitrust law prohibits infringers to internally divide antitrust liabilities and to request contribution for the payment of damages from each other.[4] This is explained by the deterrent function of private law antitrust liability: '[n]o-contribution rule among antitrust co-conspirators is rationally related to achievement of purpose of antitrust laws to preserve and promote public interest in competition by insuring existence of open

1 European Commission, 'Antitrust: Commission Fines Truck Producers € 2.93 Billion for Participating in a Cartel' (19 July 2016) IP/16/2582; European Commission, 'Antitrust: Commission Fines Scania €880 Million for Participating in Trucks Cartel' (27 September 2017) IP/17/3502.

2 *UK Trucks Claim Ltd v. Fiat Chrysler Automobiles* [2019] CAT 26 ('*UKTC*').

3 Ibid.

4 *Texas Indus. v. Radcliff Materials*, 451 U.S. 630 (1981) ('*Texas Industries*').

and free market'.[5] The crucial question is whether a similar policy is implemented by EU competition law, and consequently whether and how joint tortfeasors can claim contribution from each other in order to internally divide the burden of the liability they have borne by paying fines and compensation for competition law violations.

UKTC v. Iveco and Daimler and other lawsuits for antitrust damages[6] demonstrate that there is an urgent need for guidance on the relationship between joint and several liability and EU competition law. While joint and several liability for fines has been applied for at least 50 years, it is currently increasingly applied, especially in private courts. This means that disputes on contribution are turning from a rare phenomenon into a regular part of competition law litigation. To get a sense of magnitude, let us consider that there are 30 million potential claims in the truck cartel and each of them may trigger a dispute on contribution between violators of EU competition law.[7] Berto Winters, a lawyer of DAF, said that '[w]e're talking about "hundreds of cases"' and continued that '[t]he first batch of claims involved 2,000–3,000 parties while the second group involved 4,000–5,000'.[8] What Berto Winters has not mentioned so far is that after dealing with claims for damages, DAF will need to consider how to settle accounts for compensation paid in each of these cases with MAN, Volvo Group, Daimler and Iveco. The disputes on contribution between antitrust infringers are, however, both a controversial and undiscovered area of EU competition law.

Against this background, this book provides the first comprehensive analysis of contribution claims in EU competition law. By drawing on the historical and current practice of EU and national courts, as well as national laws of major EU jurisdictions, it explains contribution claims in EU competition law.

1.2 PROBLEMS RAISED BY JOINT AND SEVERAL LIABILITY IN EU COMPETITION LAW

The following chapters unpack the relationship between joint and several liability and discuss contribution litigation. Chapter 2 investigates the interference between the imposition of liability and its internal apportionment. The ability of antitrust infringers to internally divide their liability *prima facie* influences the effective enforcement of competition law. For instance, the European Commission

[5] *Texas Industries*, Publisher's Remarks, para. 9.

[6] For a review of private law disputes in the truck cartel, see *Mlex*, Case file, 'Antitrust – MAN – Iveco'.

[7] Commissioner Margrethe Vestager quoted by the European Commission, 'Antitrust: Commission Fines Truck Producers'.

[8] Andrew Boyce, 'Truck Makers and AkzoNobel, Unilever, Others Dispute Damage Claim Time-Frame in Dutch Court' (13 March 2020), *Mlex*, available at https://mlex.com/GlobalAdvisory/DetailView.aspx?cid=1170341&siteid=244&rdir=1.

('Commission')'s decision to hold several entities liable for an antitrust infringement can potentially be circumvented if an entity escapes liability by successfully claiming contribution. In light of this, Chapter 2 asks whether contribution claims are permitted in general and what impact competition law has on their enforcement. The general conclusion is that EU competition law allows for contribution claims; however, it influences a number of elements of contribution litigation – the addressees of contribution claims, the application of a 10 per cent turnover cap and the establishment of antitrust infringement.

Chapter 3 asks how contribution claims can be concretely enforced. Contribution claims are brought forward pursuant to national laws in compliance with EU law and the principles of effectiveness and equivalence. Until now, there have been hardly any rules on contribution specific to competition law and contribution has needed to be claimed by relying on a traditional framework for joint and several liability that homogeneously applies to car accidents, construction failures or labour law liabilities. Competition law brings many challenges to this framework. Uncertainty remains as to the grounds on which contribution can be claimed, available types of action, addressees of contribution claims and criteria for granting contribution. The aim of Chapter 3 is to guide readers through these problems and explain the practicalities of contribution litigation. The discussion concentrates on the criteria to divide antitrust liability, which is an essential litigation point. There are multiple possible options – relative blamefulness, causation, illicit gains, values of sales, market shares or individual fines – each leading to a different outcome and each suitable for specific competition law infringements.

Directive 2014/104/EU[9] introduces some special regimes for joint and several liability that are a source of further complications. The aim of Directive 2014/104/EU is to encourage settlements, to guarantee the effectiveness of leniency programmes and to protect small and medium enterprises (SMEs). It therefore introduces some modifications to joint and several liability. Chapter 4 asks how joint and several liability applies to these groups and whether the modifications introduced are justified. The treatment of leniency programs by Directive 2014/104/EU raises particular controversy. While a modified joint and several liability regime shields immunity recipients from a massive wave of claims for antitrust damages, it is questionable whether it provides them with sufficient incentive to keep leniency programs effective. In addition, Directive 2014/104/EU has created a very complex liability system, whereby antitrust infringers are liable to a different degree vis-à-vis their direct and indirect providers and purchasers, providers and purchasers of other cartelists and those who sustained the so-called umbrella damage. This complexity

9 Directive 2014/104/EU of the European Parliament and of the Council of 26 November 2014 on certain rules governing actions for damages under national law for infringements of the competition law provisions of the Member States and of the European Union, OJ L 349, 5.12.2014, p. 1–19 ('Directive 2014/104/EU' or 'Directive').

similarly concerns those concluding settlements and small and medium enterprises. As a result, Chapter 4 investigates the special regimes for joint and several liability in detail and makes recommendations for law making in this area.

Finally, liability sharing agreements can be considered a potential tool for dealing with contribution. Given the multitude of contribution claims, the lack of competition law–specific framework for claiming contribution and the complexity of the current rules, antitrust infringers may wish to divide their antitrust liability contractually. Liability sharing agreements are in fact already a common and established element of US antitrust enforcement. The question is whether they can also become a part of EU competition law practice. Chapter 5 asks whether such agreements are allowed under national laws, whether they are acceptable from the standpoint of competition law and if so, under which conditions they can be concluded. The book makes a positive case for liability sharing agreements and encourages the exploitation of their potential.

With the various shortcomings of existing rules on joint and several liability in mind, Chapter 6 takes a policy angle and proposes several modifications to account for the antitrust context of disputes. This includes a proposal on how to settle the relationship between competition law and the rules on contribution, which types of contribution claims should be available, what criteria should be decisive in dividing liability in antitrust cases and which exceptions to the general rules on joint and several liability should be maintained.

1.3 A NOTE ON SCOPE AND TERMINOLOGY

Before examining the above-described problems in detail, it is important to bear in mind a few general points. This scrutiny concentrates on EU competition law, which is treated holistically, including both the Commission's fining decisions ('public enforcement') and national courts' judgments establishing competition law violations ('private enforcement'). A special focus is placed on infringements of Article 101 TFEU given that the notion of 'agreement' pre-supposes the involvement of more than one entity and leads to a regular application of joint and several liability.[10]

Whenever necessary, the book makes a reference to substantive national laws. This is done in a comparative fashion and on the basis of EU jurisdictions that represent various legal traditions – England and Wales (common law), Germany (Germanic legal orders), France (Napoleonic legal orders) and Poland (Central and Eastern European legal orders) – so as to demonstrate different solutions to joint and

[10] The book sometimes refers to broader terms such as 'competition law' and 'antitrust law' for the reasons of brevity. The book also deals with the post-Directive 2014/104/EU reality and does not deal with specific intertemporal questions that may arise before the Directive is fully applied.

several liability in the European Union.[11] Due to Brexit, there is doubt whether to continue investigating the laws of England and Wales in relation to EU competition law. This research is believed to be nonetheless valuable as the UK maintains laws of EU origins (e.g. Directive 2014/104/EU implemented per Competition Act 1998 and Other Enactments (Amendment) Regulations 2017, 2017 No. XXXX), and most importantly, there is still a significant private enforcement practice in the UK for damages claims from across Europe.[12] The law of England and Wales is also an example of a common law of which investigation could also be relevant for Ireland, Cyprus and globally.

The term 'joint and several liability' is used as established under substantive[13] English law. However, it is meant to also cover corresponding rules in other jurisdictions: *gesamtschuldnerische Haftung* in Germany,[14] *solidarité* and *obligation*

[11] The book is limited to these four national legal orders, although more general terms are sometimes used, for instance, 'EU legal orders' and 'national civil laws'. For the same reason, only the term 'England' is used to refer to the law of England and Wales. The book is also focused on substantive national laws and does not dwell on procedural aspects, which are explained in great detail by standard textbooks on joint and several liability.

[12] For more on this topic, see, for instance, Niamh Dunne, 'Competition Law and Policy after Brexit' (2017) 24 *LSE Law Policy Briefing Series*, Brexit Special 4, 2; Gelmini Francesca, 'Brexit: The Future of Private Antitrust Enforcement in the UK' (20 December 2017) *EuropeanFuture*, available at https://europeanfutures.ed.ac.uk/brexit-the-future-of-private-antitrust-enforcement-in-the-uk/; Farin Harrison, 'The Practical Antitrust Implications of Tomorrow: Brexit Day', (30 January 2020) *Kluwer Competition Law*, available at https://competitionlawblog.kluwercompetitionlaw.com/2020/01/30/the-practical-antitrust-implications-of-tomorrow-brexit-day/.

[13] A caveat here is that the term 'joint and several liability' is used in this context only to express the concept of substantive law and does not cover procedural issues, which may be regulated differently in researched jurisdictions. On the liability for the entire debt, see Julia Körner, *Die Gesamtschuld im europäischen Kartellbußgeldrecht* (Köln: Carl Heymanns Verlag, 2016), 36; Carsten Krüger, *Kartellregress* (Baden-Baden: Nomos, 2010), 182; W. V. Horton Rogers, 'Multiple Tortfeasors under English Law' in W. V. Horton Rogers (ed.), *Unification of Tort Law: Multiple Tortfeasors* (Den Haag: Kluwer Law International, 2004), 65–68; Mirosław Nesterowicz and Ewa Bagińska, 'Multiple Tortfeasors under Polish Law' in W. V. Horton Rogers (ed.), *Unification of Tort Law: Multiple Tortfeasors* (Den Haag: Kluwer Law International, 2004), 153. On the freedom of choosing a defendant, see Antonia Hösch, *Der schadensrechtliche Innenausgleich zwischen Kartellrechtsverletzern* (Baden-Baden: Nomos, 2015), 216; Marine Ranouil, *Les recours entre coobligés* (Paris: Bilbliothèque de l'IRJS – André Tunc, 2014), 93; Rogers, 'Multiple Tortfeasors', 65; Nesterowicz and Bagińska, 'Multiple Tortfeasors', 154. Joint and several liability is frequently contrasted with the regime of proportional liability. Under this scheme, each debtor is liable only for its own part of the debt and the creditor needs to individually address debtors for their relevant parts; see Christian von Bar and Eric M. Clive (eds.), *Principles, Definitions and Model Rules of European Private Law. Draft Common Frame of Reference (DCFR). Full Edition*, 6 vols. (München: Sellier European Law Publishers, 2009), vol. I, 975.

[14] For joint and several liability in Germany, see, for instance, Sonja Meier, *Gesamtschulden* (Tübingen: Mohr Siebeck, 2010); Florian Bentele, *Gesamtschuld und Erlass* (Tübingen: Mohr Siebeck, 2006); Götte Wulf, *Gesamtschuldbegriff und Regressproblem* (Bonn: Ludwig Rührscheid, 1974).

in solidum in France[15] and *odpowiedzialoność solidarna* in Poland.[16] Joint and several liability contrasts with 'proportional liability', which is used to cover German *Teilschuld*, French *responsabilité proportionnelle* and Polish *odpowiedzialność proporcjonalna*.[17]

The same applies to the term 'contribution claims', which is used as defined in English law but also refers to equivalent claims in other researched legal orders: German *Ausgleichsklagen*, French *recours en contribution* (also referred to as *recours*) and Polish *roszczenia regresowe* (also known as *regres*). The term 'contribution' is meant to also cover claims for 'indemnity'. English law distinguishes these two types of claims based on the quantum of recovery sought: recovery of a part of the debt paid is contribution; recovery of the entire debt paid is indemnity.[18] Since this distinction is not made in other jurisdictions,[19] this study uses in principle a single term for these two types of claims.

The book analyses a three-party constellation, in which a competition authority or a private party that sustained antitrust damages ('the creditor'), respectively, enforces a fine or damages ('the debt') against an infringer of competition law ('the claimant', 'the debtor') that seeks contribution from a co-infringer of EU competition law ('the defendant', 'the debtor').[20]

[15] Recently, there has been a theory to treat *solidarité* and *obligation in solidum* together as *obligation au tout/au total*, see Marine Ranouil, *Les recours entre coobligés*, 31 *et seq.*; Marc Mignot, *Les obligations solidaires et les obligations in solidum en droit privé français* (Paris: Dalloz, 2002), 25 *et seq.*; Patrick Maistre du Chambon, 'Régime de la réparation. Action en réparation. Parties à l'instance' (2016) *JurisClasseur Civil Code*, 220, para. 140; Marc Mingot, 'Régime général des obligations. Pluralité de sujets de l'obligation. Principe de division' (2017) *JurisClasseur Civil Code*, 10, paras. 4–5. For joint and several liability in France, see, for instance, Marc Mignot, *Les obligations solidaires*; Noël Dejean de la Bâtie, 'Responsabilité délictuelle. Tome VI-2' in André Ponsard and Ibrahim Fadlallah (eds.), *Aubry et Rau, Droit Civil Français* (Paris: Librairies Techinques, 1989).

[16] For joint and several liability in Poland, see, for instance, Biruta Lewaszkiewicz-Petrykowska, *Wyrządzenie szkody przez kilka osób* (Warszawa: Wydawnictwo Prawnicze, 1978); Alfred Klein, 'Istota solidarności biernej a stosunki prawne odpowiedzialności' in Zbigniew Radwański (ed.), *Studia z prawa zobowiązań* (Warszawa and Poznań: Polskie Wydawnictwo Naukowe, 1979).

[17] For English law explanation of these terms, see Glanville Llewelyn Williams, *Joint Torts and Contributory Negligence* (London: Stevens & Sons Limited, 1951), 1–3; Charles Mitchell, *The Law of Contribution and Reimbursement* (Oxford: Oxford University Press, 2002), 160–161, 170–173. For German law, see above note 14. For French law, see note 15. For Polish law, see note 16.

[18] For further explanation of these terms, see Mitchell, *The Law of Contribution*, 9–11;Williams, *Joint Torts*, xli.

[19] Even in England it is expressed that these two claims are similar; see, for instance, *Whitham v. Bullock* [1939] 2 K.B. 81, 87. In France, a difference between these two claims is sometimes expressed in linguistic terms as *le recours total* (indemnity) and *le recours divisé* (contribution); see Ranouil, *Les recours entre coobligés*, 233–234.

[20] On the debtor side, there may be more than two entities. It should be assumed that the term 'claimant' refers to all debtors seeking competition, and the term 'defendant' to all entities against which contribution is sought.

The analysis is both pragmatic and critical. While it discusses contribution litigation, which might be particularly interesting for legal practitioners, it also points out shortcomings in the current legal framework and proposes reforms that are necessary to provide a simple and efficient framework for contribution claims in antitrust.

2

EU Competition Law and Its Impact on Contribution Claims

The objective of this chapter is to bring conceptual clarity to the intersection between contribution claims and EU competition law, as well as to determine the practical influence of competition law on contribution claims. The key questions raised are whether contribution claims are allowed in EU competition law and what requirements competition law sets for contribution litigation.

In order to answer them, it is worth investigating the role that joint and several liability plays in a broader context of competition law enforcement. The relationship between joint and several liability and competition law is essentially a part of the competition law enforcement policy. The more rights that are given to antitrust infringers as to how they can shape their antitrust liability, the more doubts appear as to whether competition law is effectively enforced. The question of whether the contribution rule exists or not is thus a matter of policy. Section 2.1 analyses various policy stakes and reveals the stance of EU legislation, which is ultimately to allow for contribution claims in EU competition law.

The interplay between joint and several liability and competition law is relevant not only for the availability of contribution claims but also for other elements of contribution litigation. Dogmatic, historic and policy arguments continue to be decisive factors in the extent to which competition law impacts contribution claims. As Section 2.2 explains, different solutions can be chosen depending on whether joint and several liability is considered to be strictly intertwined with competition law or not. Contribution claims might lie in EU law and use competition law–specific criteria to settle the allocation of antitrust liability, or they might lie in national laws and use traditional civil law criteria. The discussion about the intersection between joint and several liability and EU competition law therefore does not only have policy-related and academic interests but is also relevant in litigation. The chapter closes with conclusions and recommendations (Section 2.3).

2.1 JOINT AND SEVERAL LIABILITY IN THE EU COMPETITION LAW ENFORCEMENT SYSTEM

Joint and several liability is commonly used in EU competition law, being present in 88 per cent of Commission decisions adopted in the last fifteen years.[1] Joint and several liability is always applied when a private person claims damages resulting from antitrust violations committed by multiple entities.[2] This section provides the background to these statements by presenting the place of joint and several liability in a broader framework for competition law enforcement, its functions and whether contribution claims are capable of jeopardising them.

2.1.1 *EU Competition Law Enforcement*

Joint and several liability is applied in two basic situations: when the European Commission adopts infringement decisions and when antitrust violators are held liable by victims of their infringements in private law.

2.1.1.1 Public Enforcement of EU Competition Law

The European Commission is the guardian of competition law enforcement under Article 105(2) of TFEU.[3] Its principal power is to 'impose fines on undertakings and associations of undertakings where, either intentionally or negligently: ... they infringe Article [101] or Article [102] of the Treaty'.[4]

The core of public enforcement is the Commission's power to conduct administrative proceedings and establish infringements. The Commission reviews complaints from market participants about potential market abuses and conducts its own inquiries to identify violations of EU competition law. The Commission's investigations most commonly end with a decision finding a competition law violation and imposing fines.[5]

The principle upon which the fines are set and that public competition law enforcement follows is deterrence.[6] In general, deterrence is achieved by creating a

1 Between 2006 and 2020. Own calculations, see Figure 2.1.

2 See Article 11(2) of Directive 2014/104/EU.

3 See, for instance, Philip Lowe, Mel Marquis and Giorgio Monti, *European Competition Law Annual 2013: Effective and Legitimate Enforcement of Competition Law* (Oxford and Portland, OR: Hart, 2016), lxxi.

4 Article 23(2) of Regulation 1/2003 of 16 December 2002 on the implementation of the rules on competition laid down in Articles 81 and 82 of the Treaty, OJ L 1, 4 January 2003, pp. 1–25 ('Regulation 1/2003').

5 See, for instance, Michael Frese, *Sanctions in EU Competition Law: Principles and Practice* (Oxford and Portland, OR: Hart, 2014), 184–191.

6 Guidelines on the method of setting fines imposed pursuant to Article 23(2)(a) of Regulation 1/2003, OJ C 210, 1 September 2006, pp. 2–5 ('Guidelines on Fines'), para. 3. On deterrence, see also Kai-Uwe Opper, *Die gesamtschuldnerische Bußgeldhaftung für Kartellverstöße innerhalb eines Konzerns* (Baden-Baden: Nomos, 2016), 35–37; Hösch, *Der schadensrechtliche Innenausgleich*, 44–45; Janine

situation in which disadvantages resulting from antitrust infringement are higher than advantages derived from it.[7] Deterrence can be understood in general terms as a signal to all enterprises that antitrust violations will be condemned (*general deterrence*) and, in individual terms, as a way to discourage concrete companies from committing antitrust infringements again (*individual deterrence*).[8]

Guidelines on fines specify that fines are set based on the gravity and the duration of the infringement[9] and are capped at 10 per cent of the infringer's turnover.[10] The Guidelines also give the Commission several tools to ensure deterrence. First, the Commission may impose a special deterrence increase for undertakings that have a particularly large turnover.[11] Second, the fine may be increased with the so-called *entry fee* to cover illicit gains.[12] Lastly, the Commission may deviate from the usual way of setting fines for the sake of deterrence.[13] This allows the Commission to impose very high fines on undertakings,[14] such as its recent EUR 4.34 billion fine against Google.[15]

Weinhold, *Der Gesamtschuldnerausgleich zwischen den Kartellmitgliedern* (Frankfurt am Main: PL Academic Research, Europäische Hochschulschriften, 2015), 29 *et seq.*; Wouter P. J. Wils, 'The Relationship between Public Antitrust Enforcement and Private Actions for Damages' (2009) 32 *World Competition*, 6–11. Some authors argue the high amounts indicate their penal nature; see Opper, *Die gesamtschuldnerische Bußgeldhaftung*, 33–35; Tobias Bieber, *Die gesamtschuldnerische Haftung für die Zahlung von Kartellbußen im EU-Recht* (Köln: Carl Heymanns Verlag, 2014), 57–59; Christian Heinichen, *Unternehmensbegriff und Haftungsnachfolge im Europäischen Kartellrecht* (Baden-Baden: Nomos, 2010), 148; Körner, *Die Gesamtschuld im Kartellbußgeldrecht*, 14–17; Hösch, *Der schadensrechtliche Innenausgleich*, 43–44. Since the line between deterrence and penalization is difficult to set and Regulation 1/2003 expressively mentions only deterrence, this book takes as a starting point only the deterrent function of the public enforcement of EU competition law.

7 Wils, 'The Relationship', 7. This will usually also mean that fines are aimed at depriving the infringer of illicit gains. Kai-Uwe Opper and Christian Heinichen consider it a specific function of fine setting; however, it is believed here that this constitutes part of deterrence. See Opper, *Die gesamtschuldnerische Bußgeldhaftung*, 38–39; Heinichen, *Unternehmensbegriff und Haftungsnachfolge*, 138–140.

8 Guidelines on Fines, para. 4.

9 Ibid., para. 19.

10 Article 23(4) of Regulation 1/2003 and Guidelines on Fines, paras. 32–33.

11 Ibid., para. 30.

12 Ibid., para. 31; Wils, 'The Relationship', 8–9.

13 Ibid., para. 37.

14 See, for instance, Marco Mansdörfer, 'Das Modell der Verbandshaftung im europäischen Kartellbußgeldrecht' (2011) *Europäische Zeitschrift für Wirtschaftsrecht*, 214, available at: https://books.google.be/books?id=m_eeDwAAQBAJ&pg=PA294&lpg=PA294&dq=Das+Modell+der+Verbandshaftung+im+europ%C3%A4ischen+Kartellbu%C3%9Fgeldrecht&source=bl&ots=ZG435wjXLq&sig=ACfU3UoFkMX_76zfcGvAAJPmoXoZ8Z-kgQ&hl=en&sa=X&ved=2ahUKEwi54rWL7cX2AhVPjokEHah1BmIQ6AF6BAgEEAM#v=onepage&q=Das%20Modell%20der%20Verbandshaftung%20im%20europ%C3%A4ischen%20Kartellbu%C3%9Fgeldrecht&f=false; https://books.google.be/books?id=HF54DwAAQBAJ&pg=PA481&lpg=PA481&dq=Das+Modell+der+Verbandshaftung+im+europ%C3%A4ischen+Kartellbu%C3%9Fgeldrecht&source=bl&ots=Oibpvpm6qR&sig=ACfU3U3EUqkRS4eQ1qFQFwjVQ33EtpFkww&hl=en&sa=X&ved=2ahUKEwi54rWL7cX2AhVPjokEHah1BmIQ6AF6BAgDEAM#v=onepage&q=Das%20Modell%20der%20Verbandshaftung%20im%20europ%C3%A4ischen%20Kartellbu%C3%9Fgeldrecht&f=false.

15 European Commission, 'Antitrust: Commission Fines Google €4.34 Billion for Illegal Practices Regarding Android Mobile Devices to Strengthen Dominance of Google's Search Engine' (18 July 2018) IP/18/4581.

The discretion that the Commission has in setting the fines makes some commentators wonder whether public competition law also has a punitive role.[16] For the analysis of joint and several liability, it suffices to treat deterrence as a bottom line of public enforcement.

2.1.1.2 Private Enforcement of EU Competition Law

A significant problem with the enforcement of EU competition law was posed because individual victims of antitrust violations had no remedies available.[17] The problem with fines imposed by the Commission is that they cannot remedy the wrong to the factual victims of antitrust violations.[18] Private remedies are necessary to bring justice to those who suffered due to competition law violations.

The EU Courts noticed this flaw and expressed in *Courage* and *Manfredi* that EU law gives individuals a right to claim compensation for the antitrust damage.[19] According to the CJEU's case law, every individual can claim compensation for the damage suffered as a result of a competition law violation.[20] Every individual may thus become an antitrust enforcer. This has led to defining private actions for antitrust damages as the private enforcement of EU competition law.

[16] See, for instance, Frese, *Sanctions in EU Competition Law*; Wouter P. J. Wils, 'Optimal Antitrust Fines: Theory and Practice' (2006) 29 *World Competition*, 2, 183.

[17] For a summary, see Krüger, *Kartellregress*, 28–33; see also Section 1.1 of the White Paper on damages actions for breach of the EC antitrust rules, 2 April 2008, COM(2008) 165 final ('White Paper').

[18] See, for instance, Niamh Dunne, 'The Role of Private Enforcement within EU Competition Law' (2014) 16 *Cambridge Yearbook of European Legal Studies*, 149–150; Robert H. Lande, 'The Role of Private Enforcement within EU Competition Law' in Albert A. Foer and Jonathan W. Cuneo (eds.), *The International Handbook on Private Enforcement of Competition Law* (Cheltenham and Northampton: Edward Elgar, 2010), 7–8; more broadly Christoph Kern, 'Private Law Enforcement versus Public Law Enforcement' (2007) 12 *Zeitschrift für Zivilprozess International*, 370.

[19] CJEU, Case C-453/99, *Courage Ltd* v. *Bernard Crehan and Bernard Crehan* v. *Courage Ltd and Others*, ECLI:EU:C:2001:465 ('*Courage*'), para. 26; CJEU, Joined cases C-295/04 to C-298/04, *Vincenzo Manfredi* v. *Lloyd Adriatico Assicurazioni SpA, Antonio Cannito* v. *Fondiaria Sai SpA and Nicolò Tricarico, and Pasqualina Murgolo* v. *Assitalia SpA*, ECLI:EU:C:2006:461 ('*Manfredi*'), para. 95. For more on the historic development of claims for antitrust damages, see Dorota Leczykiewicz, 'Private Party Liability in EU Law: In Search of the General Regime' in Catherine Barnard and Okeoghene Odudu (eds.), *The Cambridge Yearbook of European Legal Studies. Volume 12, 2009–2010* (Oxford and Portland, OR: Hart, 2010), 257–282; Robert Stefanicki, 'Civil Law Remedies for Violation of Competition Law' (2012) 4 *European Review of Contract Law*, 400–419; Wolfgang Wurmnest, 'Zivilrechtliche Ausgleichsansprüche von Kartellbeteiligten bei Verstößen gegen das EG-Kartellverbot' (2003) 12 *Recht der internationalen Wirtschaft*, 896–900; Hösch, *Der schadensrechtliche Innenausgleich*, 21–26; Krüger, *Kartellregress*, 31–39.

[20] CJEU, Case C-453/99, *Courage Ltd* v. *Bernard Crehan and Bernard Crehan* v. *Courage Ltd and Others*, ECLI:EU:C:2001:465 ('*Courage*'), para. 26; CJEU, Joined cases C-295/04 to C-298/04, *Vincenzo Manfredi* v. *Lloyd Adriatico Assicurazioni SpA, Antonio Cannito* v. *Fondiaria Sai SpA and Nicolò Tricarico, and Pasqualina Murgolo* v. *Assitalia SpA*, ECLI:EU:C:2006:461 ('*Manfredi*'), para. 95.

Directive 2014/104/EU has gone a step further in providing a legal framework for private antitrust enforcement. Its aim has been to strengthen the position of those who suffered damage as a result of competition law violation and allow them to bring claims for damages more easily.[21] It guarantees easier access to evidence, the binding force of the Commission's and national competition authorities' decisions, reasonable limitation periods, standing of indirect purchasers and passing-on defence.

Thanks to these improvements, private antitrust damages are currently increasing across Europe, turning private enforcement into an important pillar of EU competition law. In Germany alone, there were 119 judgments concerning claims for antitrust damages up until the end of 2018, and since then, 650 cases have been pending.[22] Germany is not an exception. The Netherlands and the UK are also growing to become major venues for private antitrust litigation.[23]

The compensatory nature of private enforcement is undisputable and has been the reason for judicial and legislative activity in this area.[24] Yet, the nature of claims for antitrust damages is a hotly debated topic. The idea of punitive double damages proposed in the Green Paper has come under heavy criticism due to the usual compensatory functions of EU Member States' tort laws.[25] Article 3 of the Directive has expressly rejected the repressive function of damages: 'Full compensation under this Directive shall not lead to over compensation, whether by means of punitive, multiple or other types of damages'. Recent *Skanska* and *Sumal* judgments, on the contrary, promote the deterrent and even the punitive function of private enforcement: 'actions for damages for infringement of EU competition rules are an integral part of the system for enforcement of those rules, which are intended to punish

[21] Recital 4 of Directive 2014/104/EU; Section 1.2 of the White Paper. This is in line with many CJEU cases; see CJEU, Case C-536/11, *Bundeswettbewerbsbehörde* v. *Donau Chemie AG and Others Donau Chemie*, ECLI:EU:C:2013:366, para. 32; CJEU, *Courage*, para. 26; CJEU, *Manfredi*, para. 60. See also Christian Kersting, 'Die neue Richtlinie zur privaten Rechtsdurchsetzung im Kartellrecht' (2014) 6 *Wirtschaft und Wettbewerb*, 567; Gerald Mäsch, 'Private Ansprüche bei Verstößen gegen das europäische Kartellverbot – "Courage" und die Folgen' (2003) 5 *Zeitschrift Europarecht*, 829–830.

[22] Lukas Rengier, 'Cartel Damages Actions in German Courts: What the Statistics Tell Us' (2019) 11 *Journal of European Competition Law and Practice*, 1, 1.

[23] Matthijs Kuijpers et al., 'Actions for Damages in the Netherlands, the United Kingdom, and Germany' (2015) 6 *Journal of European Competition Law and Practice*, 2 *et seq*.

[24] See, for instance, Grangeon Julie, 'La directive relative aux actions en réparation à la suite d'une pratique anticoncurrentielle: révolution ou évolution du private enforcement dans l'Union?' (2015) 101 *Revue Lamy droit des affaires*, 59; Wouter P. J. Wils, 'Private Enforcement of EU Antitrust Law and Its Relationship with Public Enforcement: Past, Present and Future' (2017) 40 *World Competition*, 1, 25; Wils, 'The Relationship', 11–12.

[25] See, for instance, Monique Hazelhorst, 'Private Enforcement of EU Competition Law: Why Punitive Damages Are a Step Too Far' (2010) 4 *European Review of Private Law*, 757 *et seq*.; Wolfgang Wurmnest, 'Schadensersatz wegen Verletzung des EU-Kartellrechts. Grundfragen und Entwicklungslinien' in Oliver Remien (ed.), *Schadensersatz im europäischen Privat- und Wirtschaftsrecht* (Tübingen: Mohr Siebeck, 2012), 52.

anticompetitive behaviour on the part of undertakings and to deter them from engaging in such conduct'.[26]

Advocate General (AG) Nils Wahl justifies this position by the potential of actions for damages to support public enforcement. Claims for antitrust damages can indeed reinforce the deterrence of rules on competition in a unique way, as they increase the chance of detecting anticompetitive practices and are a threat to potential infringers given the number of potential private claims that can be brought forward against them.[27]

In line with the most recent case law, the book will therefore assume both the compensatory and deterrent functions of private enforcement. For a more detailed discussion, the reader is referred to the main EU competition law textbooks.[28]

2.1.2 *Imposition of Joint and Several Liability in the Area of Competition Law*

Joint and several liability is used in both public and private law enforcement. In the context of public enforcement, it appears in infringement decisions when the amount of the fine is specified and addressed to a concrete company. The recent decision condemning the cartel in *Occupant Safety Systems* illustrates a typical deployment of joint and several liability:

> For the infringement referred to in Article 1, the following fines are imposed: (...) (c) on Autoliv, Inc. and Autoliv Japan Ltd., *jointly and severally*: EUR 265 000.[29]

In private enforcement, joint and several liability is applied pursuant to national laws implementing Article 11(1) of Directive 2014/104/EU:

> undertakings which have infringed competition law through joint behaviour are *jointly and severally liable* for the harm caused by the infringement of competition law.

[26] CJEU, Case C-724/17, *Vantaan kaupunki* v. *Skanska Industrial Solutions Oy and Others*, ECLI:EU:C:2019:204 ('*Skanska*'), para. 45; see also CJEU, Case C-882/19, *Sumal, S.L.* v. *Mercedes Benz Trucks España*, S.L., ECLI:EU:C:2021:800 ('*Sumal*'), para. 37; Opinion of AG Pitruzzella, Case C-882/19, *Sumal, S.L.* v. *Mercedes Benz Trucks España*, S.L., ECLI:EU:C:2021:293 ('*Sumal*'), para. 67.

[27] CJEU, Case C-724/17, *Vantaan kaupunki* v. *Skanska Industrial Solutions Oy and Others*, ECLI:EU:C:2019:204 ('*Skanska*'), paras. 28, 45–48; Please also refer to AG Wahl, Case C-724/17, *Vantaan kaupunki* v. *Skanska Industrial Solutions Oy and Others*, ECLI:EU:C:2019:100 ('*Skanska*'), para. 80.

[28] See, for instance, Christopher H. Bovis and Charles M. Clarke, 'Private Enforcement of EU Competition Law' (2015) 36 *Liverpool Law Review*, 49; Frese, *Sanctions in EU Competition Law*; Hazelhorst, 'Private Enforcement', 757; Agata Jurkowska-Gomułka, *Publiczne i prywatne egzekwowanie zakazów praktyk ograniczających konkurencje: w poszukiwaniu zrównoważonego modelu współistnienia* (Warszawa: Wydawnictwo Naukowe Wydziału Zarządzania Uniwersytetu Warszawskiego, 2013); Christoph Kern, 'Restrukturierung als "private enforcement"' in Boris Paal, Dörte Poelzig and Oliver Fehrenbacher (eds.), Festschrift für Werner F. Ebke (Münich: C.H. Beck 2021)

[29] Commission Decision of 22 November 2017 in Case AT.39881 – *Occupant Safety Systems Supplied to Japanese Car Manufacturers*, C(2017) 7670 final, Article 5.

The following paragraphs identify the reasons for applying joint and several liability in these two contexts and ask whether the role of joint and several liability varies in public and private enforcement.

2.1.2.1 Public Enforcement

THE COMMISSION'S PRACTICE OF IMPOSING JOINT AND SEVERAL LIABILITY The history of using joint and several liability in antitrust cases testifies to the Commission's pragmatic application of joint and several liability in order to guarantee effective antitrust enforcement.[30] Three key types of case stand out.

Enterprises with their corporate seats outside of the European Union are the first major field. The first case in which joint and several liability was used was the *Commercial Solvents* (CSC) case of 1972.[31] CSC was a New York company that was a monopolist in manufacturing nitropropane and aminobutanol. It operated in Europe via an Italian subsidiary, Istituto Chemioterapico Italiano (ICI). When CSC refused to supply nitropropane and aminobutanol to its European downstream competitor, the Commission described the behaviour of CSC and ICI uniformly as the 'CSC-ICI-Group' and fined them jointly and severally.[32] This decision seems to have been taken due to the fact that CSC did not have its headquarters in the European Union. Given the uncertain enforcement of its decision,[33] the Commission also attributed the liability to its subsidiary present in the European Union.[34]

The Commission expanded its practice of fining more companies jointly and severally to situations where the antitrust infringer had limited assets.

[30] For the historic development, see Nada Ina Pauer, *The Single Economic Entity Doctrine and Corporate Group Responsibility in European Antitrust Law* (New York: Wolter Kluwer Law and Business, 2014); Heinichen, *Unternehmensbegriff und Haftungsnachfolge*, 141–147; Körner, *Die Gesamtschuld im Kartellbußgeldrecht*, 38–48; Bieber, *Die gesamtschuldnerische Haftung*, 18–53; Georg-Klaus de Bronett, 'Gesamtschuldnerische Geldbußen nach EU-Kartellrecht für Personen, die wettbewerbswidrig handelnden "wirtschaftlichen Einheiten" angehören' (2015) 3 *Europäisches Wirtschafts- und Steuerrecht*, 123 *et seq.*; Christoph von Laufenberg, *Kartellrechtliche Konzernhaftung* (Berlin: Duncker and Humblot, 2018), 28 *et seq.*; Braun, *Das Konzept der gesamtschuldnerischen Verantwortlichkeit*, 59 *et seq.*

[31] Commission Decision of 14 December 1972 in IV/26.911 – *ZOJA/CSC – ICI*, OJ L 299, 31 December 1972, pp. 51–58.

[32] Ibid., Article 3(1).

[33] Bieber, *Die gesamtschuldnerische Haftung*, 24–26; Heinichen, *Unternehmensbegriff und Haftungsnachfolge*, 142; Körner, *Die Gesamtschuld im Kartellbußgeldrecht*, 42–43.

[34] A similar rationale was used by the Commission to impose joint and several liability in Commission Decision of 8 December 1977 in IV/29.132 – *Hugin/Liptons*, OJ L 22, 27 January 1978, pp. 23–35 (repealed by the CJEU on reasons different than joint and several liability, see CJEU, Case 22/78, *Hugin Kassaregister AB and Hugin Cash Registers Ltd v. Commission of the European Communities*, ECLI:EU:C:1979:138, para. 26) and Commission Decision of 25 November 1980 in IV/29.702 – *Johnson and Johnson*, OJ L 377, 31 December 1980, pp. 16–27. For a detailed analysis of these cases, see Bieber, *Die gesamtschuldnerische Haftung*, 20–27.

In *Finnboard*,[35] the Commission conducted an inspection in the premises of carton board producers, which led to a discovery of a cartel.[36] The Commission observed that the carton board producers were represented in the meetings by Finnboard, a commonly owned sales organisation, which was fined.[37] Given that Finnboard had limited assets,[38] the Commission held its members jointly and severally liable for the fine.[39]

Finally, joint and several liability is increasingly utilised to address corporate groups. This occurred in the *Opel* case.[40] Opel Nederland BV violated EU competition law by obstructing exports of new motor vehicles from the Netherlands to other EU countries. General Motors, the mother company of Opel Nederland BV, was held jointly and severally liable for this infringement.[41] The Commission had already fined the mother company and its subsidiary when some of the companies were not based in the European Union.[42] The novelty of the *Opel* case was, however, that all fined companies had their corporate seats in the European Union.

Despite the criticism,[43] the CJEU approved the use of joint and several liability.[44] In *Siemens Österreich*, the CJEU prominently stated:

> the Commission has been recognised as having [the power to impose joint and several liability] by case-law, as joint and several liability constitutes an additional legal device arising from the need to guarantee the effectiveness of the action taken by the Commission to ensure that the implementation of EU competition rules and the pursuit of infringements of those rules are effective.[45]

Consequently, joint and several liability has become considered a *normal consequence* of antitrust infringements.[46] This is visible in the statistics. In the last fifteen

35 Commission Decision of 13 July 1994 in IV/C/33.833 – *Cartonboard*, OJ L 243, 19 September 1994, pp. 1–78.
36 Ibid., para. A.
37 Ibid., para. 175.
38 Ibid., para. 174.
39 Ibid.
40 Commission Decision of 20 September 2000 in COMP/36.653 – *Opel*, OJ L 59, 28 February 2001, pp. 1–42.
41 Ibid., para. 172.
42 See notes 31 and 35.
43 Hartmut Hamman, *Das Unternehmen als Täter im europäischen Wettbewerbsrecht* (Pfaffenweiler: Centaurus, 1992), 53; Heinichen, *Unternehmensbegriff und Haftungsnachfolge*, 142.
44 See, for instance, CJEU, Case 170/83, *Hydrotherm Gerätebau GmbH* v. *Compact del Dott. Ing. Mario Andreoli and C. Sas*, ECLI:EU:C:1984:271; GCEU, Case T-405/06, *ArcelorMittal Luxembourg and Others* v. *Commission*, ECLI:EU:T:2009:90, para. 117; GCEU, Case T-360/06, *Heijmans NV* v. *European Commission*, ECLI:EU:T:2012:490, para. 50.
45 CJEU, *Siemens Österreich*, para. 52.
46 Bieber, *Die gesamtschuldnerische Haftung*, 44; Körner, *Die Gesamtschuld im Kartellbußgeldrecht*, 46.

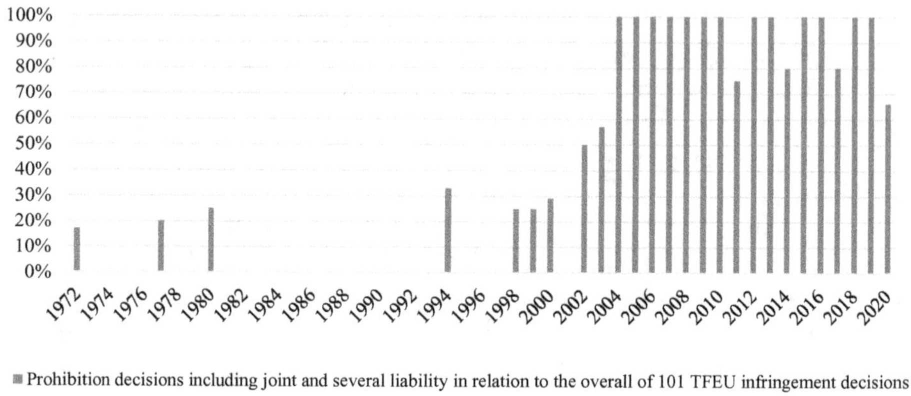

FIGURE 2.1 Frequency of applying joint and several liability in Commission decisions
Source: Own calculations.[47]

years, joint and several liability appeared in 88 per cent of the Commission's decisions (see Figure 2.1).

LEGAL BASIS FOR THE IMPOSITION OF JOINT AND SEVERAL LIABILITY Following the increased reliance on joint and several liability, the Commission started to support this practice with legal arguments such as the notion of *undertaking*, the doctrine of the *single economic entity* and the concept of *economic continuity*. Joint and several liability has been perceived as a consequence of applying these three concepts.

The Notion of Undertaking The Commission's competence to use joint and several liability has been most frequently inferred from the notion of undertaking.[48] The stance of EU law is that the legal status of an entity committing antitrust infringement is not dispositive as to whether it is considered an undertaking. Notably, several companies may constitute one undertaking in the meaning of EU competition law. In the case of violation, the companies forming such an undertaking are held jointly and severally liable for it.

[47] Commission's infringement decisions relating to Article 101 of TFEU (with preceding provisions) between 1 January 1972 and 31 December 2020, not including the re-adaptions. Joint and several liability is counted when it is imposed with respect to at least one undertaking. The number of times when joint and several liability was imposed in one decision is not reflected in the statistics.

[48] Observing the use of joint and several liability in this context, Körner, *Die Gesamtschuld im Kartellbußgeldrecht*, 148–149; Lukas Aberle, *Sanktionsdurchgriff und wirtschaftliche Einheit im deutschen und europäischen Kartellrecht* (Köln: Carl Heymanns Verlag, 2013), 124; Éric Barbier de La Serre and Eileen Lagathu, 'The Law on Fines Imposed in EU Competition Proceedings: On the Road to Consistency' (2014) 5 *Journal of European Competition Law and Practice*, 6, 414.

European Union law justifies its position by referring to the fact that EU competition law is directed at undertakings.[49] Article 101 of TFEU refers to the actions of undertakings. Also, secondary legislation names undertakings as those liable for antitrust infringements (see, for instance, Article 23(2) of Regulation 1/2003 and Article 1(1) of Directive 2014/104/EU). According to the case law of the CJEU, this notion needs to be understood broadly and is capable of covering several companies. The CJEU stated in *Höfner*:[50] '[t]he concept of an undertaking encompasses *every entity* engaged in an economic activity, regardless of the legal status of the entity and the way in which it is financed'.[51] This view has been firmly confirmed by the CJEU in *Sumal*:

[49] Okeoghene Odudu and David Bailey, 'The Single Economic Entity Doctrine in EU Competition Law' (2014) 51 *Common Market Law Review*, 1742; Christian Bürger, 'Die Haftung der Konzernmutter für Kartellrechtsverstöße ihrer Tochter nach deutschem Recht' (2011) 1 *Wirtschaft und Wettbewerb*, 131; Wouter P. J. Wils, 'The Undertaking as Subject of E.C. Competition Law and the Imputation of Infringements to Natural or Legal Persons' (2000) 25 *European Law Review*, 99–100.

[50] The legal definition of undertaking appears in Article 1 of the Protocol 22 to the EEA Agreement and provides that 'an "undertaking" shall be any entity carrying out activities of a commercial or economic nature'. This definition applies only among EFTA countries. EU law lacks a legal definition of the undertaking, see Heinichen, *Unternehmensbegriff und Haftungsnachfolge*, 35; Körner, *Die Gesamtschuld im Kartellbußgeldrecht*, 9; Opper, *Die gesamtschuldnerische Bußgeldhaftung*, 29; Bieber, *Die gesamtschuldnerische Haftung*, 6; Aberle, *Sanktionsdurchgriff*, 53; Wils, 'The undertaking', 100. This is not without a reason. Since EU competition law aims at protecting competition on the internal market and such protection shall be effectively guaranteed, the catalogue of addressees of EU competition law provisions shall be possibly wide. On the concept of undertaking, also see Pauer, *The Single Economic Entity Doctrine*, 5 *et seq.*; Christian Kersting, 'Die Rechtsprechung des EuGH zur Bußgeldhaftung in der wirtschaftlichen Einheit' (2014) 12 *Wirtschaft und Wettbewerb*, 64, 1157; Opper, *Die gesamtschuldnerische Bußgeldhaftung*, 27–29; Bieber, *Die gesamtschuldnerische Haftung*, 6; Heinichen, *Unternehmensbegriff und Haftungsnachfolge*, 35–80; Körner, *Die Gesamtschuld im Kartellbußgeldrecht*, 18–24; Dominik Braun and Manuel Kellerbauer, 'Das Konzept der gesamtschuldnerischen Verantwortlichkeit von Konzerngesellschaften bei Zuwiderhandlungen gegen das EU-Wettbewerbsrecht – Teil 1' (2015) *Neue Zeitschrift für Kartellrecht*, 175 *et seq.*; Günter Bauer and Nina Reisner, 'Erweiterte Zurechnung des Verhaltens Dritter bei der Festsetzung von Geldbußen im EG-Kartellrecht?' (2007) 8 *Wirtschaft und Wettbewerb*, 738; Dieter Zandler, 'Die wirtschaftliche Einheit als Normadressat im Kartellbußgeldrecht' (2016) *Neue Zeitschrift für Kartellrecht*, 98; Philipp Voet van Vormizeele, 'Die EG-kartellrechtliche Haftungszurechnung im Konzern im Widerstreit zu den nationalen Gesellschaftsrechtsordnungen' (2010) 9 *Wirtschaft und Wettbewerb*, 1009–1011; Bürger, 'Die Haftung der Konzernmutter', 131; Karl Hofstetter and Melanie Ludescher, 'Fines against Parent Companies in EU Antitrust Law: Setting Incentives for "Best Practice Compliance"' (2010) 33 *World Competition*, 1, 62–63; Alison Jones, 'The Boundaries of an Undertaking in EU Competition Law' (2012) 8 *European Competition Journal*, 2, 315 *et seq.*; Wils, 'The undertaking', 99 *et seq.*; Laufenberg, *Kartellrechtliche Konzernhaftung*, 34 *et seq.*; Helmut Köhler, 'EU-Kartellgeldbußen gegen Mutter- und Tochtergesellschaft: Gesamtschuldnerische Haftung und Ausgleich im Innenverhältnis' (2011) 3 *Wettbewerb in Recht und Praxis*, 278; Braun, *Das Konzept der gesamtschuldnerischen Verantwortlichkeit*, 110 *et seq.*

[51] CJEU, Case C-41/90, *Klaus Höfner and Fritz Elser v. Macrotron GmbH*, ECLI:EU:C:1991:161, para. 21.

> EU competition law, in targeting the activities of undertakings, enshrines as the decisive criterion the existence of unity of conduct on the market, without allowing the formal separation between various companies that results from their separate legal personalities to preclude such unity for the purposes of the application of the competition rules.[52]

The decisive criterion for finding that several companies constitute a single undertaking is their 'unity of conduct on the market', which should be interpreted in economic terms, meaning that companies together undertake the same economic activity.[53]

However, the reference to *companies* as legal forms in which undertakings operate is also present in EU competition law. The Commission's decisions are addressed to the companies and not undertakings. This is for enforcement reasons. Pursuant to Article 299(2)(1) of TFEU, the enforcement of the Commission's decisions is made under national civil procedures.[54] As most national laws only recognise the entities having legal standing, the Commission has decided to procedurally address its decisions to companies.[55]

There are therefore two subjects of competition law decisions. On the one hand, there are undertakings in a material sense, which are the subject of antitrust law. On the other hand, there are companies in the formal sense who are addressees of the Commission's decisions enforcing competition rules.[56] Joint and several liability is the tool that allows these two concepts to be reconciled. Such a role of joint and several liability was expressively confirmed by the General Court (GCEU) in the *Sasol* case.[57]

The Notion of the Single Economic Entity Joint and several liability is also used following the concept of the single economic entity,[58] which complements the definition of undertaking. It takes into account the assumption that each

[52] CJEU, *Sumal*, para. 41.

[53] *Ibid.*, AG Pitruzzella, *Sumal*, para. 26

[54] GCEU, Case T-24/05, *Alliance One International, Inc., formerly Standard Commercial Corp. and Others v. European Commission*, ECLI:EU:T:2010:453 ('*Alliance One*'), para. 125; CJEU, Case C-97/08 P, *Akzo Nobel NV and Others v. Commission of the European Communities*, ECLI:EU:C:2009:536 ('*Akzo*'), para. 57; Christian Heinichen, *Unternehmensbegriff und Haftungsnachfolge*, 133–135, 154–158.

[55] Ibid., 154–155.

[56] Opper, *Die gesamtschuldnerische Bußgeldhaftung*, 32; Odudu and Bailey, 'The Single Economic Entity Doctrine', 1742; Heinichen, *Unternehmensbegriff und Haftungsnachfolge*, 35 *et seq.* and 121 *et seq.* In the same line also Bieber, *Die gesamtschuldnerische Haftung*, 17; Körner, *Die Gesamtschuld im Kartellbußgeldrecht*, 18–24; Braun and Kellerbauer, 'Das Konzept der gesamtschuldnerischen Verantwortlichkeit – Teil 1', 175–176.

[57] GCEU, Case T-541/08, *Sasol and Others v. European Commission*, ECLI:EU:T:2014:628 ('*Sasol*'), para. 460.

[58] The notion of the single economic entity was first applied in Commission Decision of 18 August 1969 in IV. 22.548 – *Cristiani and Nielsen Den Haag*, OJ L 165, 5.7.1969, pp. 12–14. On the notion of the single economic entity, see Opper, *Die gesamtschuldnerische Bußgeldhaftung*, 30, 69–91; Bieber, *Die gesamtschuldnerische Haftung*, 6–18; Heinichen, *Unternehmensbegriff und Haftungsnachfolge*, 81–102; Körner, *Die Gesamtschuld im*

undertaking must be able to decide about its behaviour, which means that it is also to compete with other undertakings, to be subjected to EU competition law. The single economic entity doctrine requires each undertaking to be capable of determining its business activity and strategy independently.[59] If some companies are unable to do this, they are believed to form a single economic entity with the companies that have control over them and joint and several liability is applied.

In practice, the Commission and the CJEU associate single economic entities with corporate groups. From an economic standpoint, a single economic entity is adopted when some companies do not decide about their activity independently but follow the instructions of other companies in the corporate group.[60] From a legal standpoint, a company that is the majority shareholder of another company is

Kartellbußgeldrecht, 19–24, 50–54; Stefan Thomas, 'Die Gesamtschuld im EU-Kartellbußgeldrecht – die Kommission als "juristischer Pascha"?' in Stefan Bechtold, Joachim Jickeli, Mathias Rohe (eds.), *Recht, Ordnung und Wettbewerb – Festschrift zum 70. Geburtstag von Wernhard Möschel* (Baden-Baden: Nomos, 2012), 678; Odudu and Bailey, 'The Single Economic Entity Doctrine', 1725 *et seq.*; Stefan Thomas, 'Konzernprivileg und Gemeinschaftsunternehmen – Die kartellrechtliche Beurteilung konzerninterner Wettbewerbsbeschränkungen mit Gemeinschaftsunternehmen' (2005) 3 *Zeitschrift für Wettbewerbsrecht*, 238 *et seq.*; 'Das Konzept der gesamtschuldnerischen Verantwortlichkeit – Teil 1', 175 *et seq.*; Marco Mansdörfer, 'Verbandshaftung', 215; Daniel J. Zimmer and Thomas Paul, 'Kartellbußgeldrechtliche Haftung und Haftungsbefreiung im Konzern' (2007) 9 *Wirtschaft und Wettbewerb*, 971–972; Bauer and Reisner, 'Erweiterte Zurechnung des Verhaltens Dritter', 738; Zandler, 'Die wirtschaftliche Einheit', 98 *et seq.*; Aberle, Sanktionsdurchgriff, 16 *et seq.*; Wolfgang Bosch, 'Verantwortung der Konzernobergesellschaft im Kartellrecht' (2013) 277 *Zeitschrift für das gesamte Handels- und Wirtschaftsrecht*, 456; Ahrens Börries, 'Gemeinschaftsunternehmen als wirtschaftliche Einheit' (2013) *Europäische Zeitschrift für Wirtschaftsrecht*, 899; Juliane Kokott and Daniel Dittert, 'Die Verantwortlichkeit von Muttergesellschaften für Kartellvergehen ihrer Tochtergesellschaften im Lichte der Rechtsprechung der Unionsgerichte' (2012) 7–8 *Wirtschaft und Wettbewerb*, 672; Hofstetter and Ludescher, 'Fines against Parent Companies', 57 *et seq.*; Jones, 'Undertaking in EU Competition Law', 301, 305 *et seq.*; Jens Koch, 'Der kartellrechtliche Sanktionsdurchgriff im Unternehmensverbund' (2007) 171 *Zeitschrift für das gesamte Handels- und Wirtschaftsrecht*, 556 *et seq.*; Hauke Brettel and Stefan Thomas, 'Unternehmensbußgeld, Bestimmtheitsgrundsatz und Schuldprinzip im novellierten deutschen Kartellrecht' (2009) 1 *Zeitschrift für Wettbewerbsrecht*, 53–54; Laufenberg, *Kartellrechtliche Konzernhaftung*, 39 *et seq.*; Köhler, 'EU-Kartellgeldbußen', 278; Braun, *Das Konzept der gesamtschuldnerischen Verantwortlichkeit*, 130 *et seq.*

59 See, for instance, CJEU, Joined cases 40–48, 50, 54–56, 111, 113 and 114/73, *Coöperatieve Vereniging "Suiker Unie" UA and others v. Commission of the European Communities*, ECLI:EU:C:1975:174 ('*Suiker Unie*'), para. 173; CJEU, Case C-8/08, *T-Mobile Netherlands BV, KPN Mobile NV, Orange Nederland NV and Vodafone Libertel NV v. Raad van bestuur van de Nederlandse Mededingingsautoriteit*, ECLI:EU:C:2009:343, para. 32.

60 GCEU, Case T-185/06, *L'Air liquide, société anonyme pour l'étude et l'exploitation des procédés Georges Claude v. European Commission*, ECLI:EU:T:2011:275, para. 67–80 and GCEU, Case C-521/09 P, *Elf Aquitaine SA v. European Commission*, ECLI:EU:C:2011:620, paras. 60–68. See also Patrick Hubert and Marie-Laure Combe, '*Total SA and Elf Aquitaine SA*: A Missed Opportunity to Shed More Light on Joint and Several Liability' (2015) 6 *Journal of European Competition Law and Practice*, 9, 653–655.

capable of exercising decisive influence over its market behaviour, which makes them form together a single economic entity.[61]

The liability of Autoliv Japan Ltd. and Autoliv, Inc. in the *Occupant Safety Systems* cartel is a good illustration of this reasoning. The Commission explained that these companies are jointly and severally liable for the infringement because

> Autoliv Japan Ltd. directly participated in cartel contacts. (. . .) During the periods of [i]nfringements (. . .) Autoliv Japan Ltd. was *wholly owned* by the ultimate parent company of the group [legal assessment], Autoliv, Inc. Therefore, Autoliv, Inc. is presumed to have exercised decisive influence over Autoliv Japan Ltd. Autoliv, Inc. also clearly and unequivocally *acknowledged liability for the conduct of this subsidiary.* [economic assessment].[62]

The Commission's use of joint and several liability is enhanced by the fact that EU law gives much room for the application of the single economic entity doctrine. In *Akzo Nobel*, the CJEU stated that it can be presumed that a company holding 100 per cent shares in its subsidiary excludes the decision-making independence of the subsidiary.[63] Since the threshold for rebutting this presumption is high, the

[61] See, for instance, GCEU, Joined cases 201/09 P, 216/09 P, *ArcelorMittal Luxembourg SA v. European Commission and European Commission v. ArcelorMittal Luxembourg SA and Others*, ECLI:EU:C:2011:190, paras. 97–98; GCEU, Joined cases 144/07, 147–150/07 and 154/07, *ThyssenKrupp Liften Ascenseurs NV and Others v. European Commission*, ECLI:EU:T:2011:364, paras. 96–97. See also Aitor Montesa and Angel Givaja, 'When Parents Pay for Their Children's Wrongs: Attribution of Liability for EC Antitrust Infringements in Parent-Subsidiary Scenarios' (2006) 29 *World Competition*, 4, 555 *et seq.*; Opper, *Die gesamtschuldnerische Bußgeldhaftung*, 72 *et seq.*; Odudu and Bailey, 'The Single Economic Entity Doctrine', 1727 *et seq.*; Heinichen, *Unternehmensbegriff und Haftungsnachfolge*, 87; Körner, *Die Gesamtschuld im Kartellbußgeldrecht*, 52–54; Zandler, 'Die wirtschaftliche Einheit', 99 *et seq.*; Aberle, *Sanktionsdurchgriff*, 45 *et seq.*, 101–105; Wolfgang Bosch, 'Haftung für kartellrechtswidriges Handeln der Tochtergesellschaft – Neue Rechtslage nach dem Urteil in der Rechtssache Elf Aquitaine/Kommission?'(2012) 3 *Zeitschrift für Wettbewerbsrecht*, 368 *et seq.*; Ahrens, 'Gemeinschaftsunternehmen', 900 *et seq.*; Kokott and Dittert, 'Die Verantwortlichkeit von Muttergesellschaften', 673; van Vormizeele, 'Die EG-kartellrechtliche Haftungszurechnung', 1011; Bernd Meyring, 'Uferlose Haftung im Bußgeldverfahren?' (2010) 2 *Wirtschaft und Wettbewerb*, 165; Hofstetter and Ludescher, 'Fines against Parent Companies', 58 *et seq.*; Jones, 'Undertaking in EU Competition Law', 310 *et seq.*; Bosch, 'Kartellrechtswidriges Handeln der Tochtergesellschaft', 368 *et seq.*

[62] Commission decision of 22 November 2017 in Case AT.39881 – *Occupant Safety Systems supplied to Japanese Car Manufacturers*, C(2017) 7670 final, para. 94.

[63] CJEU, *Akzo*, paras. 60–61. On the presumption, see also Pauer, *The Single Economic Entity Doctrine*, 92 *et seq.*; Kersting, 'Die Rechtsprechung', 1163 *et seq.*; Montesa and Givaja, 'Parent-Subsidiary Scenarios', 561 *et seq.*; Opper, *Die gesamtschuldnerische Bußgeldhaftung*, 79–91; Manuel Kellerbauer and Olaf Weber, 'Die gesamtschuldnerische Haftung für Kartellgeldbußen und ihre Grenzen: Das Urteil Siemens VA Tech' (2011) 17 *Europäische Zeitschrift für Wirtschaftsrecht*, 689; Odudu and Bailey, 'The Single Economic Entity Doctrine', 1749–1753; John Temple Lang, 'How Can the Problem of the Liability of a Parent Company for Price Fixing by a Wholly-owned Subsidiary Be Resolved?' (2014) 37 *Fordham International Law Journal*, 5, 1481 *et seq.*; Bieber, *Die gesamtschuldnerische Haftung*, 9 *et seq.*; Heinichen, *Unternehmensbegriff und Haftungsnachfolge*, 95 *et seq.*; Körner, *Die Gesamtschuld*

single economic entity doctrine is applied frequently. As a result, a number of companies may be held liable for their subsidiaries' antitrust infringements, for instance, private equity investors, holding companies, foundations[64] or even sister companies.[65]

im Kartellbußgeldrecht, 53–54; Emmanuelle Claudel, 'L'essor des sanctions en droit de la concurrence. Quelle efficacité? Quelles garanties?' (2014) 6 *Contrats Concurrence Consommation*, 13, para. 44; Laurance Idot, 'Responsabilité des sociétés mères' (2016) 8–9 *Europe*, 11 *et seq.*; Thomas, 'Konzernprivileg', 242–244; Braun and Kellerbauer, 'Das Konzept der gesamtschuldnerischen Verantwortlichkeit – Teil 1', 177 *et seq.*; Mansdörfer, 'Verbandshaftung', 215; Zimmer and Paul, 'Kartellbußgeldrechtliche Haftung', 971; Bauer and Reisner, 'Erweiterte Zurechnung des Verhaltens Dritter', 739; Josefa F. Peter and Dominique S. Wagener, 'Anmerkung' (2013) 7 *Europäische Zeitschrift für Wirtschaftsrecht*, 268–269; Hanns Peter Nehl, 'Anmerkung' (2013) 14 *Europäische Zeitschrift für Wirtschaftsrecht*, 554–555; Aberle, *Sanktionsdurchgriff*, 61 *et seq.*, 103–104; Bosch, 'Verantwortung der Konzernobergesellschaft', 456; Georg-Klaus de Bronett '"Unternehmen" als Wiederholungstäter im EU-Kartellrecht vor und nach der Akzo Nobel-Rechtsprechung des EuGH zum Unternehmensbegriff' (2014) 6 *Europäisches Wirtschafts- und Steuerrecht*, 313 *et seq.*; Kokott and ittert, 'Die Verantwortlichkeit von Muttergesellschaften', 673–675; van Vormizeele, 'Die EG-kartellrechtliche Haftungszurechnung', 1011–1012; Bürger, 'Die Haftung der Konzernmutter', 131–133; Meyring, 'Haftung im Bußgeldverfahren', 165–166; Mantas Stanevičius, '*Portielje*: Bar Remains High for Rebutting Parental Liability Presumption' (2014) 5 *Journal of European Competition Law and Practice*, 1, 24 *et seq.*; Jones, 'Undertaking in EU Competition Law', 312 *et seq.*; Laura La Rocca, 'The Controversial Issue of the Parent-company Liability for the Violation of EC Competition Rules by the Subsidiary' (2011) 2 *European Competition Law Review*, 6873*et seq.*; Koch 'Sanktionsdurchgriff im Unternehmensverbund', 557; Walter Frenz and Tanja Lülsdorf, 'Kontinuität und Zurechnung im Kartellrecht' (2012) 12 *Europäisches Wirtschafts- und Steuerrecht*, 504 *et seq.*; Georg-Klaus de Bronett, 'Gesamtschuldnerische Geldbußen nach EU-Kartellrecht für Personen, die wettbewerbswidrig handelnden "wirtschaftlichen Einheiten" angehören' (2015) 3 *Europäisches Wirtschafts- und Steuerrecht*, 127 *et seq.*; Bosch, 'Kartellrechtswidriges Handeln der Tochtergesellschaft', 371 *et seq.*

64 See, for instance, GCEU, Case T-54/06, *Kendrion NV v. European Commission*, ECLI:EU:T:2011:667 ('*Kendrion*'); GCEU, Case T-419/14, *The Goldman Sachs Group, Inc. v. European Commission*, ECLI:EU:T:2018:445 (investment companies); CJEU, Case C-440/11 P, *European Commission v. Stichting Administratiekantoor Portielje and Gosselin Group NV*, ECLI:EU:C:2013:514 (foundation); CJEU, Case C-508/11 P, *Eni SpA v. European Commission*, ECLI:EU:C:2013:289 (technical and financial coordinator); GCEU, Joined cases T-141/07, T-142/07, T-145/07 and T-146/07, *General Technic-Otis and Others v. Commission*,ECLI:EU:T:2011:363 (holding company). However, there are also cases in which it has been indicated that certain companies are unlikely to become liable for antitrust infringements; see Commission Decision of 20 October 2004 in COMP/C.38.238/B2 – *Raw tobacco* – Spain, OJ L 102, 19.4.2007, pp. 14–14, para. 376; Case C-550/07 P, *Akzo Nobel Chemicals Ltd and Akcros Chemicals Ltd v. European Commission*, ECLI:EU:C:2010:229, note 67. See also Hans Jürgen Meyer-Lindemann, Clemens Graf York von Wartenburg and Andreas Kafetzopoulos, 'Private Equity Investors Are Not Immune to Antitrust Risks in the European Union' (2014) 35 *European Competition Law Review*, 8, 367–368; Lang, 'The Liability of a Parent Company', 1496–1497; Braun, *Das Konzept der gesamtschuldnerischen Verantwortlichkeit*, 94 *et seq.*

65 Communication from the Commission, Guidelines on the applicability of Article 101 of the Treaty on the Functioning of the European Union to horizontal co-operation agreements, OJ C 11, 14.1.2011, pp. 1–72, para. 11. See also CJEU, Case C-196/99 P, *Siderúrgica Aristrain Madrid SL v. Commission of the European Communities*, ECLI:EU:C:2003:529, paras. 98 *et seq.*; CJEU, Case T-43/02, *Jungbunzlauer AG v. Commission of the European Communities*,

The liability for competition law infringements can be attributed in various constellations. The Commission most frequently holds parent companies liable for the wrongdoings of their subsidiaries (so-called parental liability, bottom-up liability). Besides them, the Commission exceptionally targets sister companies.[66] The Commission's discretion in choosing various companies within a single economic entity as addressees of its decisions also indicates that subsidiaries can be held liable for anticompetitive practices of their parent companies (so-called subsidiarial liability, top-down liability). In the historically first decision imposing joint and several liability, *Commercial Solvens*, the Commission fined a subsidiary in addition to the parent company, which was the immediate perpetrator.[67]

The Court of Justice of the European Union considered the two scenarios of 'bottom-up' and 'top-down' liability in the recent Sumal case. Unsurprisingly, it was confirmed that the top-down liability applies in a similar fashion to the bottom-up liabilityand in both cases it is essential that the parent company excercises decisive influence over the subsidiary. However, the CJEU also focused on the fact whether the parent company and the subsidiary are active in the same area (as discussed in relation to undertaking), and considered it as a condition for establishing top-down liability. (see further in Section 3.4.2.2).[68]

The Notion of Economic Continuity Another justification for joint and several liability is the so-called economic continuity doctrine.[69] This concept allows the

ECLI:EU:T:2006:270, paras. 102 *et seq*. See also Christian Kersting, 'Liability of Sister Companies and Subsidiaries in European Competition Law' (2020) 41 *European Competition Law Review*, 125.

66 See, for instance, Commission decision of 21 February 2007 in COMP/E-1/38.823 – *PO/ Elevators and Escalators*, OJ 2008 No. C75/19; Commission decision of 5 December 2001 in Case COMP/E-1/36.604 – *Citric acid*, OJ 2002 No. L239/18.

67 Commission Decision of 14 December 1972 in IV/26.911 – *ZOJA/CSC – ICI*, OJ L 299, 31.12.1972, pp. 51–58.

68 CJEU, *Sumal*; AG Pitruzzella, *Sumal*, paras 48–59.

69 See, for instance, GCEU, Case T-117/07 and T-121/07, *Areva and Others and Alstom v. European Commission*, ECLI:EU:T:2011:69 ('*Areva*'); GCEU, Joined cases T-122/07 to T-124/07 *Siemens AG Österreich and VA Tech Transmission and Distribution GmbH and Co. KEG, Siemens Transmission and Distribution Ltd and Siemens Transmission and Distribution SA and Nuova Magrini Galileo SpA v. European Commission* ECLI:EU:T:2011:70 ('*Siemens Österreich*'). See also Bieber, *Die gesamtschuldnerische Haftung*, 45–48; Heinichen, *Unternehmensbegriff und Haftungsnachfolge*, 109–114; Körner, *Die Gesamtschuld im Kartellbußgeldrecht*, 56–67; Braun and Kellerbauer, 'Das Konzept der gesamtschuldnerischen Verantwortlichkeit – Teil 2', 213 *et seq*.; Zimmer and Paul, 'Kartellbußgeldrechtliche Haftung', 975–978; Bauer and Reisner, 'Erweiterte Zurechnung des Verhaltens Dritter', 739–740; Aberle, Sanktionsdurchgriff, 27 *et seq*.; Wils, 'The undertaking', 114–115; Gianni de Stefano, 'General Court Rules on Successor Liability and Apportionment of Group Liability in the Gas Insulated Switchgear Cartel' (2011) 2 *Journal of European Competition Law and Practice*, 4, 344–346; Adrian Brown and Morris Schonberg, 'Widening the Net: the General Court Extends the Principle of Successor Liability in EU Competition Law' (2013) 34(1) *European Competition Law Review*, 1 *et seq*.

Commission to hold a legal successor liable for the infringement committed by its predecessor.

In principle, EU competition law relies on the personal liability regime by which only the undertaking that committed the breach of EU competition law can be held liable.[70] However, when the company ceases to exist,[71] or if it transfers assets to another company,[72] the Commission has expressed doubts that its fines will be enforced. In such situations, the Commission has decided to also hold the successor liable for antitrust infringement.[73] The CJEU expressed that

> in certain circumstances an infringement of the rules on competition may be imputed to the economic successor of the legal person responsible, so that the effectiveness of those rules will not be compromised owing to the changes to, inter alia, the legal form of the undertakings concerned.[74]

As a result, joint and several liability for violation of EU competition law may be imposed on the undertaking committing the antitrust breach and the successor of its economic activities.[75]

The Commission has paid particular attention to the transfer of business taking place within company groups,[76] which may be easily undertaken to avoid antitrust

[70] See, for instance, CJEU, Case C-49/92 P, *Commission of the European Communities v. Anic Partecipazioni SpA*, ECLI:EU:C:1999:356 ('*Anic*'), para. 145; Case C-280/06, *Autorità Garante della Concorrenza e del Mercato v. Ente tabacchi italiani – ETI SpA and Others and Philip Morris Products SA and Others v. Autorità Garante della Concorrenza e del Mercato and Others*, ECLI:EU:C:2007:775 ('*ETI*'), para. 39; CJEU, Case C-248/98 P, *NV Koninklijke KNP BT v. Commission of the European Communities*, ECLI:EU:C:2000:625, para. 7; GCEU, *Areva*, para. 65.

[71] See, for instance, CJEU, *Suiker Unie*; CJEU, *Anic*, para. 145; Joined cases T-25/95, T-26/95, T-30/95, T-31/95, T-32/95, T-34/95, T-35/95, T-36/95, T-37/95, T-38/95, T-39/95, T-42/95, T-43/95, T-44/95, T-45/95, T-46/95, T-48/95, T-50/95, T-51/95, T-52/95, T-53/95, T-54/95, T-55/95, T-56/95, T-57/95, T-58/95, T-59/95, T-60/95, T-61/95, T-62/95, T-63/95, T-64/95, T-65/95, T-68/95, T-69/95, T-70/95, T-71/95, T-87/95, T-88/95, T-103/95 and T-104/95, *Cimenteries CBR and Others v. Commission of the European Communities*, ECLI:EU:T:2000:77 ('*Cimenteries*'), para. 1340.

[72] See, for instance, CJEU, *ETI*, paras. 40, 48; CJEU, Joined cases C-204/00 P, C-205/00 P, C-211/00 P, C-213/00 P, C-217/00 P and C-219/00 P, *Aalborg Portland A/S, Irish Cement Ltd, Ciments français SA, Italcementi – Fabbriche Riunite Cemento SpA, Buzzi Unicem SpA and Cementir – Cementerie del Tirreno SpA v. Commission of the European Communities*, ECLI:EU:C:2004:6, paras. 355–358.

[73] See notes 71 and 73; see also Aitor Montesa and Angel Givaja, 'Parent-Subsidiary Scenarios', 559.

[74] GCEU, Case T-134/94, *NMH Stahlwerke GmbH v. Commission of the European Communities*, ECLI:EU:T:1999:44, para. 127.

[75] See, for instance, Commission Decision of 3 May 2006 in Case COMP/F/C.38.620 – *Hydrogen Peroxide and Perborate*, OJ L 353, 13.12.2006, pp. 54–59, para. 19 and Article 2(a). See also Commission Decision of 21 October 1998 in Case No IV/35.691/E-4 – *Pre-Insulated Pipe Cartel*, OJ L 24, 30.1.1999, pp. 1–70.

[76] See Heinichen, *Unternehmensbegriff und Haftungsnachfolge*, 309; Körner, *Die Gesamtschuld im Kartellbußgeldrecht*, 67–80.

liability.[77] In such situations, the principle of economic continuity is a concept that supports the finding that the companies constitute a single economic entity.[78]

The principle of economic continuity has, however, a wider scope and can encompass additional companies, such as new companies[79] or independent companies who acquired the infringing business.[80] In *Pre-Insulated Pipe Cartel*,[81] the Commission jointly and severally fined the company that infringed EU competition law and the parent company, which obtained the infringing business after the end of the infringement and before the issuing of the Commission's decision.[82] Although this decision was repealed by the CJEU,[83] the CJEU confirmed that the principle of economic continuity applies when the business transfer is undertaken with the intention to avoid antitrust fines.[84]

THE FUNCTION OF USING JOINT AND SEVERAL LIABILITY IN THE CONTEXT OF PUBLIC LAW ENFORCEMENT Various applications of joint and several liability encourage us to reflect upon its functions in public antitrust enforcement. This question is important in order to identify which aspects of competition law might be at stake in contribution litigation. There are three possible interpretations that could explain the reliance on joint and several liability in public competition law enforcement, namely, (i) ensuring the effectiveness of EU competition law, (ii) deterrence and (iii) depriving infringers of unlawful profits.

Effectiveness of EU Competition Law Precedent reveals that the predominant rationale for using joint and several liability is the principle of effective antitrust enforcement.[85] Effective antitrust enforcement underpins the use of joint and several liability in all of the identified cases.

[77] See, for instance, CJEU, *ETI*, para. 41.

[78] See, for instance, Commission Decision of 20 December 2001 in Case COMP/E-1/36.212 – *Carbonless paper*, OJ L 115, 21.4.2004, pp. 1–88, para. 360; Commission Decision of 28 January 2009 in Case COMP/39406 – *Marine Hoses*, not published yet, para. 370 in which the Commission justified the imposition of liability on the companies involved in intra group transfer of assets and shares by saying that they constitute the same undertaking. Similarly, Heinichen, *Unternehmensbegriff und Haftungsnachfolge*, 327.

[79] See, for instance, Commission Decision of 11 December 2001 in Case COMP/E-1/37.027 – *Zinc phosphate*, OJ L 153, 20.6.2003, pp. 1–39, paras. 22 and 243. See also Heinichen, *Unternehmensbegriff und Haftungsnachfolge*, 270 *et seq*.

[80] See, for instance, CJEU, *Anic*, paras. 6, 141 and 144.

[81] Commission Decision of 21 October 1998 in Case No IV/35.691/E-4 – *Pre-Insulated Pipe Cartel*, OJ L 24, 30.1.1999, pp. 1–70.

[82] Ibid., Article 3(d).

[83] GCEU, Case T-9/99, *HFB Holding für Fernwärmetechnik Beteiligungsgesellschaft GmbH and Co. KG and Others v. Commission of the European Communities*, ECLI:EU:T:2002:70, paras. 104–108.

[84] Ibid., para. 107.

[85] Bieber, *Die gesamtschuldnerische Haftung*, 54; Braun and Kellerbauer, 'Das Konzept der gesamtschuldnerischen Verantwortlichkeit – Teil 2', 215; Aberle, *Sanktionsdurchgriff*, 128;

Joint and several liability has been identified first as a tool to apply the EU law definition of undertaking. This tool serves the aim realised by the wide definition of undertaking, which is to effectively enforce competition law. The more the entities are capable of falling within the notion of undertaking, the wider the personal scope of competition law. A wide scope of application allows competition law to have the capacity to catch a multitude of situations in its net and thus effectively guarantee that the markets are competitive.

The single economic entity doctrine, which also leads to the application of joint and several liability, is adopted for similar reasons. This doctrine allows the Commission to address not only the company directly infringing competition law but also other entities that belong to the same corporate and economic structure. This ability allows the Commission to address all the companies that contributed to antitrust infringement and prevents them from escaping antitrust sanctions by building complex corporate structures.

Finally, the economic continuity doctrine also applies because of the effectiveness of EU competition law. It prevents companies from evading competition law liability by restructuring or transferring assets.[86] One could possibly imagine that companies create special-purpose vehicles to outsource and distance themselves from anticompetitive practices.

The argument that joint and several liability is used to ensure the effectiveness of EU competition law is also supported by the Commission's inconsistent use of the above-mentioned doctrines.[87] For instance, the Commission does not always apply the concept of undertaking. In *Raw tobacco – Spain*, the Commission refused to hold parent companies jointly and severally liable with their subsidiaries for the infringement because they were not *materially involved* in the violation.[88] Conversely, in other cases, the Commission decided to rely on parental liability, although the parent did not have a hand in the anticompetitive practice or even was not aware of it.[89]

Another demonstration of the Commission's discretion in applying joint and several liability is that the Commission pragmatically chooses the addressees of its decisions.[90] The Commission does not fine all companies constituting one

Wils, 'The undertaking', 113; Opper, *Die gesamtschuldnerische Bußgeldhaftung*, 92–93; Bosch, 'Kartellrechtswidriges Handeln der Tochtergesellschaft', 374. In this line also Bürger, 'Die Haftung der Konzernmutter', 135. On the definition of effectiveness, see Section 2.2.4.1.

86 Heinichen, *Unternehmensbegriff und Haftungsnachfolge*, 152; Aberle, *Sanktionsdurchgriff*, 122.

87 See, for instance, CJEU, *Alliance One*, paras. 133–147. For the exercise of the freedom of choice who to address the decision to, see Heinichen, *Unternehmensbegriff und Haftungsnachfolge*, 129–131; Körner, *Die Gesamtschuld im Kartellbußgeldrecht*, 81–85; Thomas, 'Die Gesamtschuld', 679; Mansdörfer, 'Verbandshaftung', 215; Bauer and Reisner, 'Erweiterte Zurechnung des Verhaltens Dritter', 742–743; Aberle, Sanktionsdurchgriff, 89 *et seq.*, 125–127; Wils, 'The undertaking', 113.

88 Commission Decision, *Raw tobacco – Spain*, para. 376.

89 See, for instance, Commission decision of 2 April 2014 in Case AT.39610 – *Power Cables*, C (2014) 2139 final.

90 See, for instance, CJEU, Case C-196/199, *Siderúrgica Aristrain Madrid SL v. Commission of the European Communities*ECLI:EU:C:2002:537, ('*Aristrain*'), paras. 106–107. See also Kai-Uwe

undertaking but only selects some of them, usually a subsidiary infringing competition law and its ultimate parent company. By fining a holding company, the Commission in fact effectively reaches the financial resources that are present in the corporate group.

Similar inconsistencies appear when the Commission applies the doctrine of economic continuity. In comparable situations, the Commission sometimes applies personal liability and sometimes the concept of economic continuity.[91] In *KNP BT*, the Commission held the former parent company liable for the violation of EU competition law,[92] while in *Austrian banks* it decided to hold only the successor liable.[93] Such a policy indicates that the choice of the companies fined is made upon the Commission's pragmatic idea of what would guarantee effective enforcement of EU law.

Deterrence Tobias Bieber asks whether joint and several liability serves other fining objectives, such as deterrence.[94] According to him, deterrence is realised by the ability to impose fines exceeding the regular 10 per cent turnover cap, which is allegedly possible due to joint and several liability.[95] Julia Körner adds that joint and several liability even has a punitive character in EU competition law. The reason is that it triggers many negative consequences for those held jointly and severally liable, such as an increase in the basic amount of fines, an increase of deterrence fee and higher probability of finding recidivism.[96] Both scholars perceive joint and several liability as a gateway to increasing the deterrent and punitive effect of competition law enforcement.

This argumentation is not entirely correct as it confuses the *reasons* for attributing joint and several liability with the *effects* it has.[97] The Commission has not expressed willingness to apply joint and several liability to impose more severe fines. Quite to the contrary, in *Johnson and Johnson*, the Commission rejected such an intention.[98]

Opper, *Die gesamtschuldnerische Bußgeldhaftung*, 95–96; Kellerbauer and Weber, 'Das Urteil Siemens VA Tech', 691; Odudu and Bailey, 'The Single Economic Entity Doctrine', 1747–1753; Heinichen, *Unternehmensbegriff und Haftungsnachfolge*, 129; Körner, *Die Gesamtschuld im Kartellbußgeldrecht*, 44–45, 81–85, 172–174; Thomas, 'Die Gesamtschuld', 679; Aberle, Sanktionsdurchgriff, 89 *et seq*.

91 See, for instance, GCEU, Joined cases T-259/02 to T-264/02 and T-271/02, *Raiffeisen Zentralbank Österreich AG and Others v. Commission of the European Communities*, ECLI: EU:T:2006:396, paras. 332 and 335. See also Heinichen, *Unternehmensbegriff und Haftungsnachfolge*, 221–222; Julia Körner, *Die Gesamtschuld im Kartellbußgeldrecht*, 59–67.

92 Commission decision of 13 July 1994 in Case COMP/IV/C/33.833 – *Carton*, OJ 1994 L 243, p. 1, paras. 145 and 149.

93 Commission decision of 11 June 2002 in Case COMP/36.571/D-1 –*Austrian banks – 'Lombard Club'*, OJ 2004 L 56, p. 1, paras. 473–481.

94 Bieber, *Die gesamtschuldnerische Haftung*, 54–56.

95 Ibid.

96 Körner, *Die Gesamtschuld im Kartellbußgeldrecht*, 124–139.

97 For a correct understanding of the imposition of joint and several liability as a *consequence* of the application of the single economic entity, see Opper, *Die gesamtschuldnerische Bußgeldhaftung*', 91–92.

98 Commission Decision, *Johnson and Johnson*, para. 48.

Also, in *Slovak Telecom*, the Commission paid special attention to determine fines separately for each company that was held jointly and severally liable as a part of a single undertaking, and consider aggravating circumstances specifically for each company.[99] In light of the above, one cannot consider the deterrence and, *a fortiori*, the repression as the reasons for using joint and several liability.

On the other hand, joint and several liability definitely has positive *effects* on deterrence. First, increased deterrence always occurs with the increased effectiveness of enforcement. Deterrence is achieved by two elements: the severance of the sanction and the probability of being condemned.[100] Effective enforcement increases the probability of being condemned and thus realises the second of the above-mentioned elements. Second, the European Commission does not always make the same effort as in *Slovak Telekom*, and the conditions for setting a fine are often considered jointly for all companies fined jointly and severally.[101] Most frequently, the Commission applies a 10 per cent turnover cap for fines with respect to the undertaking, which has much higher turnover than a single company. For instance, in *Groupe Gascogne*, the CJEU determined that 'when the undertaking to which the infringement is attributed heads a group which constitutes an economic unit, the turnover of the group as a whole must be taken into account when calculating the upper limit of the amount of the fine referred to in Article 23(2) of Regulation No 1/2003'.[102] The CJEU also concluded that aggravating circumnstances can apply to the single economic unit as a whole. For example, the aggravating factor of repeated infringement can concern a parent company, whose subsidiary violated competition law in the past, even though the parent itself did not commit any antitrust infringement.[103] As a result, joint and several liability frequently leads to a higher turnover cap[104] or to the application of some special fine additions.[105]

[99] Commission decision of 15 October 2014 in Case AT.39523 – *Slovak Telekom*, C(2014) 7465 final.

[100] See, for instance, Douglas H. Ginsburg and Joshua D.Wright, 'Antitrust Sanctions' (2010) 6 *Competition Policy International*, 3, 7; Wils, 'Optimal Antitrust Fines', 193 *et seq*.

[101] See, for instance, GCEU, *Siemens Österreich*, para. 134; GCEU, *Cimenteries*, para. 5040. See also Körner, *Die Gesamtschuld im Kartellbußgeldrecht*, 125; de Bronett, '"Unternehmen" als Wiederholungstäter', 319; Braun and Kellerbauer, 'Das Konzept der gesamtschuldnerischen Verantwortlichkeit – Teil 2', 213; Zimmer and Paul, 'Kartellbußgeldrechtliche Haftung', 971; Zandler, 'Die wirtschaftliche Einheit', 98.

[102] Case C-58/12, *Groupe Gascogne v. European Commission*, ECLI:EU:C:2013:770, para. 52.

[103] Joined cases C-93/13 P and C-123/13 P, *European Commission v. Versalis SpA and Eni SpA and Versalis SpA and Eni SpA v. European Commission*, ECLI:EU:C:2015:150, para. 91 *et seq.* CJEU, *Sumal*, para. 49.

[104] See, for instance, GCEU, *Siemens Österreich*, para. 134; GCEU, *Cimenteries*, para. 5040. See also Braun and Kellerbauer, 'Das Konzept der gesamtschuldnerischen Verantwortlichkeit – Teil 2', 214; Zandler, 'Die wirtschaftliche Einheit', 98; Aberle, *Sanktionsdurchgriff*, 129, 133–134; Jones, 'Undertaking in EU Competition Law', 309; Koch, 'Sanktionsdurchgriff im Unternehmensverbund', 557–558.

[105] See, for instance, Commission Decision, *Video Games*, para. 406; Commission Decision of 20 November 2007 in Case COMP/38.432 – *Professional Videotape*, C(2007)5469 final, paras.

Given such effects, the CJEU recognised in *Siemens Österreich* that deterrence plays a role in using joint and several liability. It considered deterrence and effective competition law enforcement the *dual objective* of joint and several liability.[106] This decides in favour of accepting the joint and several liability's role also in terms of deterrence.

Deprival of Unlawful Profits Tobias Bieber mentions that joint and several liability is also used to deprive infringers of unlawful profits as its application allows higher fines to be imposed.[107]

This idea cannot be accepted as joint and several liability does not allow this effect to be achieved. Tobias Bieber disregards that before the Commission enforces its fines, infringers can voluntarily pay them. It may thus happen that one of the companies would pay a fine in full, whereas the other would keep the profits from the infringement. Joint and several liability does not give the Commission any power to intervene in the payment voluntarily undertaken by the companies.

2.1.2.2 Private Law Enforcement

DIRECTIVE 2014/104/EU Contrary to public antitrust enforcement, Directive 2014/104/EU provides for a clear legal basis for applying joint and several liability. Wherever multiple undertakings violate competition law, they are jointly and severally liable for the damage caused by the violation, pursuant to the laws implementing Article 11(1) of Directive 2014/104/EU:

> undertakings which have infringed competition law through joint behaviour are jointly and severally liable for the harm caused by the infringement of competition law; with the effect that each of those undertakings is bound to compensate for the harm in full, and the injured party has the right to require full compensation from any of them until he has been fully compensated.[108]

243–246; Observing the fact that the use of joint and several liability contributes to increasing the levels of fines, Oduduand and Bailey, 'The Single Economic Entity Doctrine', 1755; Lang, 'The Liability of a Parent Company', 1486; Montesa and Givaja, 'Parent-Subsidiary Scenarios', 556–557.

[106] CJEU, *Siemens Österreich*, para. 60.

[107] Bieber, *Die gesamtschuldnerische Haftung*, 54–56.

[108] For England, see Section 3 of the Civil Liability (Contribution) Act of 1978 and Department for Business Innovation and Skills, 'Consultation: Implementing the EU Directive on damages for breaches of competition law' (January, 2016), available at https://assets.publishing.service.gov.uk/government/uploads/system/uploads/attachment_data/file/495757/BIS-16-6-consultation-implementing-the-EU-directive-on-damages-for-breaches-of-competition-law.pdf, Section 7.32. For Poland, see Article 441 of the k.c. and Aleksandra Milewska, 'Solidarna odpowiedzialność sprawców naruszenia prawa konkurencji przewidziana w projekcie ustawy o roszczeniach o naprawienie szkody wyrządzonej przez naruszenie prawa konkurencji z 7 lutego 2017 r. – aspekt podmiotowy' (2017) 1 *internetowy Kwartalnik Antymonopolowy i Regulacyjny*, 6, 60–61. For Germany, see para. 33d(1) of the GWB. For France, see Art. L. 481–9 of the Code de Commerce.

Applying joint and several liability in such a case is not a novel solution. It corresponds to the orthodox tort law, in which joint tortfeasors are jointly and severally liable for the damage. For instance, in England, joint and several liability applies under Section 3 of the Civil Liability (Contribution) Act 1978, in Germany under § 421 and § 840(1) of the Bürgerliches Gesetzbuch (BGB), in Poland under Article 441(1) of the Kodeks Cywilny (k.c.) and in France according to the judgment of the Cour de Cassation of 11 July 1892.[109] The solution provided in Article 11 of Directive 2014/104/EU is thus fully in line with traditional EU legal orders. Article 11 was also one of the least disputed proposals of Directive 2014/104/EU.[110]

Nevertheless, joint and several liability is controversial in light of the massive nature of antitrust damages.[111] Damage caused by cartels is usually dispersed and suffered by many economic entities. For instance, the discussed truck cartel influenced nearly nine out of ten trucks manufactured in Europe for fourteen years,[112] giving the owners of approximately 30 million trucks a right to claim damages.[113] Thanks to the rules on joint and several liability, every entity that sustained damage can claim compensation from the tortfeasors it wishes to address. The result may be that only some companies are held liable for antitrust infringement. This is because some entities are more likely to be sued. They may have a seat in a given jurisdiction, the infringement decision may become final for them or they may have large financial resources. This places the burden of paying compensation only on some tortfeasors. Directive 2014/104/EU observes this problem and decides to limit joint and several liability with respect to certain groups of tortfeasors –small and medium enterprises, immunity recipients and those engaged in consensual dispute resolution (see further in Chapter 4).

THE FUNCTION OF USING JOINT AND SEVERAL LIABILITY IN PRIVATE ENFORCEMENT In tort law, joint and several liability is used to improve the legal standing of those unlawfully damaged. This is achieved with two elements: by giving the creditor discretion with regards to who to claim the entire debt from

109 Civ. , 11.07.1892: S. 1892 I 505.

110 The imposition of joint and several liability was neither discussed within the Green and White Papers, nor in the course of the public consultations and the legislative decision-making process.

111 See Laura, 'I'm an Immunity Applicant, Get Me Out of Here: Joint and Several Liability Revisited' (2014) 7 *Global Competition Litigation Review*, 2, 100–101; Carsten Krüge *Private und öffentliche Kartellrechtsdurchsetzung* (Berlin: Duncker and Humblot, 2012), 79; Carsten Krüger, 'Der Gesamtschuldnerausgleich im System der privaten Kartellrechtsdurchsetzung' (2012) 1 *Wirtschaft und Wettbewerb*, 11–12. On antitrust damage, see, in particular, Frank Maier-Rigaud and Ulrich Schwalbe, 'Quantification of antitrust damages' in David Ashton and David Henry (eds.), *Competition Damages Actions in the EU Law and Practice* (Chelentham and Northampton: Edward Elgar Publishing, 2013), 212 *et seq*.

112 Commissioner Margrethe Vestager quoted by European Commission, 'Antitrust: Commission fines truck producers € 2.93 billion for participating in a cartel' (19 July 2016) IP/16/2582.

113 Ibid.

and by not requiring proof of proportional liability. Joint and several liability has the same function in private antitrust enforcement.[114]

Regarding the first element, in tort, the creditor has a right to choose the entity from which it believes it will be able to obtain compensation most conveniently. If the debt is not fully satisfied by the chosen debtor, the creditor can bring the claim against others until the moment of obtaining the entire sum.[115] This is sometimes called the legal Pascha (*juristischer Pascha*).[116] Directive 2014/140/EU also moves to improve the position of the creditor. It introduces a compensation mechanism that shifts the costs of enforcing claims for antitrust damage from the victims of anticompetitive practices to their authors.[117] For instance, by relying on joint and several liability, victims of antitrust infringements can engage in some forum shopping[118] and bring forward claims against the infringers established in their own jurisdiction and in this way avoid costly litigation abroad (e.g. foreign lawyers, translations, travel expenses). Such costs would in turn be paid by infringers, which would need to come back to all co-infringers with contribution claims regardless of their home jurisdictions. The convenience of joint and several liability does not end with savings; victims of antitrust infringements can also rely on laws that are claimant-friendly. This has already been realised within the competition law community, and claims for damages are typically brought forward in the UK, the Netherlands and Germany.[119] This would not be possible without the rules on joint and several liability.

Regarding the second element, joint and several liability releases the claimant from the burden of proving the proportion in which each of the violators

[114] See Recital F of European Parliament resolution of 25 April 2007 on the Green Paper on Damages actions for breach of the EC antitrust rules (2006/2207(INI)).

[115] See, for instance, Marine Ranouil, *Les recours entre coobligés*, 93. See also the literature referred to in note 13 in Chapter 1.

[116] Heck Philipp, *Grundriß des Schuldrechts* (Tübingen: Mohr, 1929), 492. See also Stefan Thomas, 'Die Gesamtschuld'; Horst Ehmann, *Die Gesamtschuld* (Heidelberg: Inaugural-Dissertation, 1971), 97–98; Götte, *Gesamtschuldbegriff und Regressproblem*, 69; Walter Schmidt, *Gesamtschuld und Gesamtschuldregress* (Köln: Inaugural-Dissertation, 1973), 15; Mitchell, *The Law of Contribution*, 172; Ranouil, *Les recours entre coobligés*, 40, 93; Mignot, 'Régime général des obligations. Pluralité de sujets d'obligation. Obligation solidaire' (2017) *JurisClasseur Civil Code*, 20, para. 66; Dorothée Cochet, 'La contribution à la dette des coobligés in solidum' (2004) 118 *Petites affiches*, 3, paras. 24–25; Nesterowicz and Bagińska, 'Multiple Tortfeasors', 153; W. V. Horton Rogers, 'Comparative Report on Multiple Tortfeasors' in W. V. Horton Rogers (ed.), *Unification of Tort Law: Multiple Tortfeasors* (Den Haag: Kluwer Law International, 2004), 273; Kit Barker and Jenny Steele, 'Drifting towards Proportionate Liability: Ethics and Pragmatics' (2015) 74 *Cambridge Law Journal*, 1, 50 *et seq.*; Paul Bargren, 'Joint and Several Liability: Protection for Plaintiffs' (1994) *Wisconsin Law Review*, 453 *et seq.*

[117] Section 1.2 of the White Paper.

[118] Marieke Bredenoord-Spoek and Rein Wesseling, 'Forum Shopping on the Dutch High Street. Jurisdiction Issues in Follow-on Litigation Cases' available at https://pure.uva.nl/ws/files/7171252/Paper_Wesseling_Bredenoord_Spoek_IBA_Competition_Law_Conference_Floren..pdfi *et seq.*

[119] See note 23.

contributed to the infringement.[120] By having a possibility to claim the entire damage from any of debtors, the creditor saves time, effort and money, which it would have needed to invest in claiming damages proportionally from each of the debtors.[121] This effect of joint and several liability should not be underappreciated as proving specific shares of liability and the roles that were played by each infringer can be very difficult if not impossible, as anticompetitive practices and their mechanisms are kept in strict confidence. In line with general tort law, Directive 2014/104/EU also relieves the creditor from the need to establish proportional liability.

This increases the effectiveness of EU competition law.[122] The easier it is to claim compensation by private entities, the more likely it is that such claims succeed, and the more frequently competition law is enforced. As mentioned by AG Wahl, claims for damages increase the potential for detecting anticompetitive behaviour, as those with first-hand knowledge can individually establish competition law infringements. Combined with a possible high number of such claims, this can deter potential antitrust violators.[123]

2.1.2.3 Consistent Application of Joint and Several Liability in Public and Private Enforcement

In sum, joint and several liability is applied in both areas of EU antitrust enforcement. In public enforcement, it allows the Commission to enforce EU competition law with better ease and effectiveness, which leads to increased antitrust deterrence. In private enforcement, it improves the legal position of those suffering damages and thus also contributes to more effective competition law enforcement and deterrence.

The consistent application of joint and several liability in public and private enforcement is also supported by the recent *Skanska* and *Sumal* judgments.[124] The *Skanska* case can be traced to 1994 when several Finnish asphalt producers

[120] Biruta Lewaszkiewicz-Petrykowska, *Wyrządzenie szkody przez kilka osób*, 22. See also the literature referred to in note 13 in Chapter 1.

[121] Ehmann, *Die Gesamtschuld*, 45.

[122] *Ibid.*; Section 2.1. of Commission Staff Working Document, Impact Assessment Report.

[123] AG Wahl, *Skanska*, para. 48. See also AG Pitruzzella, *Sumal*, para. 67.

[124] For a commentary on the *Skanska* judgment, see Wamel, 'Shining a Light on the Interface between EU and National Law'; Fasoula Vasiliki, 'Extending the Principle of Economic Continuity to Private Enforcement of Competition Law. What Lies Ahead for Corporate Restructuring and Civil Damages Proceedings after Skanska? Case Comment to the Judgment of the Court of Justice of 14 march 2019 Skanska Industrial Solutions and others (Case C-724/17)' (2019) *Yearbook of Antitrust and Regulatory Studies*, 20, 259; Krisadhikhun Tangdham, *The Potential Civil Liability of Innocent Subsidiaries as a Consequence of the Notion of Undertaking in EU Competition Law an Implication from the Recent Case Skanska* (Lund: Lund University, 2020); Hans-Markus Wagener, 'Follow-up to Skanska – The "Implementation" by National Courts So Far' (2019) 10 *Neue Zeitschrift für Kartellrecht*, 535; Tatiana Siakka, 'Case C-724/17 Vantaan kaupunkiv Skanska Industrial Solutions: Transposition of the Concept of an "Undertaking" into Civil Damages Actions' (2019) 10 *Journal of European Competition Law & Practice*, 8, 479.

set up a cartel to fix prices, share customers and divide tender contracts. The Finnish Administrative Supreme Court established the infringement of competition law in 2009 and imposed fines on the companies involved in the cartel and their successors. The judgment triggered a follow-on claim of an asphalt purchaser, the City of Vantaa, which – similarly to the Finnish Administrative Supreme Court – relied on the doctrine of economic continuity to hold successors of several cartelists liable. This raised the question of whether the doctrine of economic continuity applies in private actions for damages.

The Court of Justice of the European Union firmly established that the notion of economic continuity applies both in public and private enforcement. It started with an observation that the right to claim antitrust damages is the direct effect of Article 101 TFEU[125] and the determination of entities that are required to provide compensation for their infringement is directly governed by EU law.[126] The notion of undertaking, which covers the economic continuity principle, is present both in public and private enforcement (e.g. Article 101 TFEU, Article 1(1) of Directive 2014/104/EU).[127] It also emphasised that these two enforcement types form an integral part of the system of enforcement of EU competition rules, which requires that the notions of undertaking and economic continuity are applied in the same way in public and private enforcement.[128]

Not surprisingly, the CJEU followed the same reasoning in *Sumal*. The case concerned Sumal's claim against Mercedes Benz Trucks España SL ('Mercedes'), part of the Daimler AG Group, for damages arising from the truck cartel. Sumal's claim was not against Daimler AG ('Daimler'), which was found liable by the Commission for the violation, but against its Spanish subsidiary, Mercedes. Sumal argued that Mercedes constituted a single undertaking with Daimler, such that it was jointly and severally liable for Daimler's violation of EU competition law, and the lawsuit could be pursued in Spain. In line with the previous *Skanska* judgment, the CJEU confirmed that Sumal's claim is admissible, as the notion of undertaking applies in the same fashion in public and private enforcement.[129]

The same conclusion holds true for joint and several liability, which applies consistently to both types of competition law enforcement. Joint and several liability is part of the integral system of enforcement of EU competition rules in the same way as the notion of undertaking, single economic unit or economic continuity. It is an important mid-point connecting the identification of the perpetrator of the infringement and the imposition of liability, both in terms of administrative fines and civil damages. As a direct consequence of finding single economic unit or

[125] CJEU, *Skanska*, para. 24.
[126] Ibid., para. 28.
[127] Ibid., paras. 32–35.
[128] Ibid., para. 47.
[129] AG Pitruzzella, *Sumal*, paras 60–69.

economic continuity,[130] its aim is the same in both public and private enforcement: it enhances effective competition law enforcement. This is an important function as it ensures that competition law is respected, its breaches are addressed and markets remain competitive. The ultimate goal of competition law is to maintain the competitiveness of the EU market, and joint and several liability has its share in fulfilling this objective.

2.1.2.4 Internal and External Dimensions of Joint and Several Liability

Joint and several liability has two-fold effects that are traditionally divided into the external and internal ones.[131]

From the external standpoint, joint and several liability impacts the relationship between joint and several debtors and the creditor ('external dimension of joint and several liability'). As mentioned in the paragraphs above, the creditor can claim the entire amount of debt from any of the debtors, regardless of their proportional involvement in the misconduct. This is the principal effect of joint and several liability under tort laws of many EU Member States.[132] This is also stipulated in Article 11 of Directive 2014/104/EU, and this is the Commission's understanding of joint and several liability in public enforcement.[133]

From the internal standpoint, joint and several liability has an impact on the position of infringers *vis-à-vis* each other ('internal dimension of joint and several liability'). Joint and several liability makes each of them potentially liable for the entire amount of debt regardless of their direct contribution to its creation.[134] This contrasts with the regime of proportional liability, which is based on liability for the extent of debt caused by individual conduct.[135] The main question raised by the internal dimension of joint and several liability is whether infringers can claim against each other for the difference between the sum paid and their proportional liability. The tool to achieve this is known as contribution claims. These claims are subject to the investigation in the following section.

[130] CJEU, *Sumal*, para. 44.

[131] See the literature referred to in note 28.

[132] See the literature referred to in note 13 in Chapter 1; see also DCFR para. III-4:102(1); PETL Article 9:101(2); Christian von Bar and Eric M. Clive (eds.), *Principles, Definitions and Model Rules of European Private Law. Draft Common Frame of Reference (DCFR)* (München and Oxford: Sellier European Law Publishers and Oxford University Press 2009/2010), para. III-4:102(1); European Group on Tort Law, *Principles of European Tort Law: Text and Commentary* (Wien and New York: Springer, 2005), Article 9:101(2).

[133] See, for instance, GCEU, Case T-40/06, *Trioplast Industrier AB v. European Commission*, ECLI:EU:T:2010:388, para. 165.

[134] See the literature referred to in note 13 in Chapter 1; see also DCFR para. III-4:102(1); PETL Article 9:101(2); Christian von Bar and Eric (eds.), *DCFR*, para. III-4:102(1); European Group on Tort Law, *PETL*, Article 9:101(2).

[135] See the literature referred to in note 13 in Chapter 1.

2.1.3 *Contribution Claims in EU Competition Law*

2.1.3.1 Contribution Claims in Civil Law

Contribution claims reside in traditional civil laws. They are brought forward by one debtor against other co-debtors to recover sums paid to the creditor in excess of its individual liability share. If we look back to the example presented in the Introduction, Iveco and Daimler could bring forward a claim for contribution against their fellow truck cartelists and request a contribution towards the GBP 14 billion paid to UKTC, the organisation representing the victims of the truck cartel.

This interpretation of contribution claims is common to many jurisdictions. For instance, Section 1 of the English Contribution Act stipulates that 'any person liable in respect of any damage suffered by another person may recover contribution from any other person liable in respect of the same damage'. In France, Article 1346 of the Code Civil (CC) provides that the debtor can claim up to the entire sum paid to the creditor from the creditor's other debtors as if it were the original creditor, provided that its payment exceeds its own proportion in the global debt.[136] In Germany, § 426 (1) of the BGB provides that when the debtor pays the creditor compensation exceeding its own share of liability, it is entitled to contribution from other co-debtors.[137] A substantially similar provision is adopted in Polish Article 441(2) of the k.c.[138]

The function of contribution claims is disputed, depending on the understanding of joint and several liability adopted. One option is to explain contribution claims with reference to the exceptional nature of joint and several liability. According to this approach, joint and several liability is an exception to the general rule of

[136] Article 1346 of the Code Civil reads: '*La subrogation a lieu par le seul effet de la loi au profit de celui qui, y ayant un intérêt légitime, paie dès lors que son paiement libère envers le créancier celui sur qui doit peser la charge définitive de tout ou partie de la dette*'. ('Subrogation takes place by the sole operation of law in favour of a person with a legitimate interest in it who satisfies a debt provided that his satisfaction discharges as against the creditor another person who is subject to the final burden in respect of all or part of a debt').

[137] Paragraph 426(1) of the BGB first sentence reads: '*Die Gesamtschuldner sind im Verhältnis zueinander zu gleichen Anteilen verpflichtet, soweit nicht ein anderes bestimmt ist*'. ('The joint and several debtors are obliged in equal proportions in relation to one another unless otherwise determined').

[138] Article 441(2) of the k.c. reads: '*Jeżeli szkoda była wynikiem działania lub zaniechania kilku osób, ten, kto szkodę naprawił, może żądać od pozostałych zwrotu odpowiedniej części zależnie od okoliczności, a zwłaszcza od winy danej osoby oraz od stopnia, w jakim przyczyniła się do powstania szkody*'. ('If damage results from an action or omission of several persons, the one who remedies the damage may demand that the other persons reimburse a relevant part, depending on the circumstances, and especially on the fault of a given person and on the extent to which he contributed to the damage arising').

proportional liability.[139] For instance, some French scholars claim that joint and several liability is added atop proportionally divided debts.[140] In this context, contribution claims are a means to return to the natural state of proportional liability after having achieved the benefits brought by joint and several liability for the creditor.[141] The main drawback of this approach is that it is difficult to prove that proportional liability is the natural state of liability. According to Ernst von Caemmerer, joint and several liability also results from the nature of the matter (*Natur der Sache*).[142] Both proportional liability and joint and several liability are stipulated in national laws.[143] In common law, joint and several liability is actually sometimes considered to be a default rule.[144]

Contribution claims can also be explained with reference to the circumstances in which joint and several liability is imposed. Some commentators believe that contribution claims do not have an aim in themselves and their function is to support the aims determined by the legal relationship existing between the debtors and the creditor.[145] For instance, if a contribution claim follows a claim for damages,

139 See, for instance, Bentele, *Gesamtschuld und Erlass*, 6; Jacques Boré, 'Le recours entre coobligés in solidum' (1967) 1.2126 *La Semaine Juridique*, para. B; Mignot, *Les obligations solidaires*, 1, 3, 35 *et seq.*; Antoine Hontebeyrie, 'Pluralité de sujets : altération et complications' (2015) 249 *Droit et Patrimoine. Dossier*, 46, para. I.

140 See Sébastien Pimont and Eric Roux-Sibillon, 'Les dispositions du projet de réforme du droit des obligations relatives aux obligations plurales' (2015) 47 *La Semaine Juridique Notariale et Immobliere*, 1218, 23–24; Mignot, 'Principe de division', paras. 1 *et seq.*; Marc Mignot, 'Commentaire article par article de l'ordonnance du 10 fevrier 2016 portant réforme du droit des contrats, du régime general et de la preuve des obligations (VIII)' (2016) 80 *Petites affiches*, 4, para. 3; Didier R. Martin, 'Article 1310: l'obligation solidaire' (2015) 3 *Revue de contrats*, 799; Antoine Hontebeyrie, 'Pluralité de sujets', para. II; Laetitia Bougerol 'La réforme de la solidarité passive, illusions perdues et incertitudes' (2016) 2 *Revue de Droit bancaire et financier*, 9, para. 27.

141 Brigitte Keuk, 'BGB paras. 426, 633, 634, 635, 638, 242' (1972) 17 *Juristen Zeitung*, 528–531; Götte, *Gesamtschuldbegriff und Regressproblem*, 71, 126; Hösch, *Der schadensrechtliche Innenausgleich*, 174; Ehmann, *Die Gesamtschuld*, 100; Walter Selb, *Schadensbegriff und Regreßmethoden* (Heidelberg: Carl Winter Universitätsverlag, 1963), 90; Ernst von Caemmerer, (1968) 9 *Zeitschrift für Europarecht, Internationales Privatrecht und Rechtsvergleichung*, 86.

142 von Caemmerer, 85 *et seq.* See also Glaßer, *Der Gesamtschuldnerausgleich*, 32 *et seq.*; Pierre Catala, *Avant-projet de réforme du droit des obligations et de la prescription* (Paris: La Documentation française, 2006), 67.

143 See the literature referred to in note 13 in Chapter 1.

144 Barker and Steele, 'Drifting towards Proportionate Liability', 50; the same was proposed in Catala, *Avant-projet de réforme project*, 67.

145 Meier, *Gesamtschulden*, 47; Ehmann, *Die Gesamtschuld*, 105; Hösch, *Der schadensrechtliche Innenausgleich*, 39, 176–180; Krüger, *Kartellregress*, 192; Claus-Peter Fabian, *Schädigermehrheit und Regreß im internationalen Umwelthaftungsrecht unter besonderer Berücksichtigung des anglo-amerikanischen Rechts* (Frankfurt am Main: Peter Lang, 1999), 88; Lewaszkiewicz-Petrykowska, *Wyrządzenie szkody przez kilka osób*, 142; Adam Szpunar, 'Glosa do orzeczenia Sądu Najważniejszego z dn. 16.10.1958 r.' (1960) 1 *Orzecznictwo Sądów Polskich i Komisji Arbitrażowych*, 21 *et seq.*; Szpunar, 'Roszczenia regresowe Zakładu Ubezpieczeń' (1974) XII *Studia Prawno-Ekonomiczne*, 29 *et seq.*; Jan Kosik, 'Glosa do orzeczenia Sadu Najwyższego z

it should fulfil the objective of compensation; if a contribution claim follows a judgment issued in a criminal case, it should fulfil the objective of repression.[146] However, the majority view is that the external aspect of joint and several liability and its internal aspect constitute separate legal relationships.[147] While the external relationship has to support the aims justifying the imposition of liability, this is not the case for the internal one. The functions envisaged with joint and several liability are met the moment the creditor obtains the payment. The payment of the debt fulfils compensation, provides restitution and creates deterrence. Contribution has no influence on such principles.

Finally, contribution claims can be understood as having an independent function,[148] which is to provide for fairness.[149] Each joint and several debtor is liable for the entire debt. As a consequence, one of the debtors may be called to pay the entire debt,[150] while other co-debtors might not be called to pay it at all. The principle of equality calls for some form of redistribution of the payments made to the creditor in order to provide for a fair allocation of the liability between the co-debtors.[151] This theory seems to best reflect the function of contribution claims. The reliance on joint and several liability by creditors benefits them, but it also results in debtors

dn. 14.03.1964 r.' (1965) 5 *Orzecznictwo Sądów Polskich i Komisji Arbitrażowych*, 333–334; Mazeaud Henri, Mazeaud Léon, Mazeaud Jean and Tunc André, *Traité théorique et pratique de la responsabilité civile délictuelle et contractuelle*, 3 vols.(Paris: Montchrestien, 1958), vol. II, 836 *et seq*.

[146] Wojciech Marek, 'Roszczenia regresowe z art. 441 k.c.' (1974) 3 *Nowe Prawo*, 298–299.

[147] See the literature referred to in note 28.

[148] Stefan Grzybowski, 'Roszczenia zwrotne w prawie alimentacyjnym a problem nieprzenaszalności roszczeń alimentacyjnych' (1956) 1 *Nowe Prawo*, 55; Stefan Buczkowski, Z zagadnień regresu' (1952) 1 *Przegląd Ustawodawstwa Gospodarczego*, 43, 444; Stanisław Garlicki, 'Glosa do orzeczenia Sądu Najwyższego z dn. 21.11.1967 r.' (1969) 1 *Orzecznictwo Sądów Polskich i Komisji Arbitrażowych*, 342; Alfred Ohanowicz, 'Glosa do orzeczenia Sądu Najwyższego z dn. 23.01.2957 r.' (1958) 2 *Orzecznictwo Sądów Polskich i Komisji Arbitrażowych*, 142; Marek, 'Roszczenia regresowe', 295; Ernest Till, *Polskie prawo zobowiązań. Część ogólna. Projekt wstępny z motywami* (Lviv: Komisja Kodyfikacyjna Rzeczpospolitej Polskiej, 1923), 52–53.

[149] Fairness is defined by reference to equality. See Shozo Ota, 'The Fairness and the Efficiency of the Compensation System: An Economic Analysis of the Tort Theories' (1987) 7 *International Review of Law and Economics*, 230; Patrick Canin, *Les actions récursoires entre coresponsables* (Paris: Litec, 1996), 139–140; François Chabas 'Remarque sur l'obligation in solidum' (1967) *Revue trimestrielle de droit civil*, 334.

[150] Hösch, *Der schadensrechtliche Innenausgleich*, 173; Krüger, *Kartellregress*, 188; Maistre du Chambon, 'Régime de la réparation' para. 140; Cochet, 'La contribution', para. 17.

[151] Selb, *Schadensbegriff und Regreßmethoden*, 90; Ehmann, *Die Gesamtschuld*, 100–102; Schmidt, *Gesamtschuld und Gesamtschuldregress*, 124–125; Williams, *Joint Torts and Contributory Negligence*, 89; Chabas 'Remarque sur l'obligation in solidum', 320, 335; Gerard Bieniek, 'Pojęcie regresu w prawie cywilnym' (1972) 6 *Nowe Prawo*, 894–895; Ranouil, *Les recours entre coobligés*, 93–96, 254; Canin, *Les actions récursoires*, 103, 257; Cristina Corgas-Bernard, 'La pluralité de responsables en droit français et dans d'autres ordres juridiques nationaux' in G.R.E.R.C.A. (ed.), *Le droit français de la responsabilité civile confronté aux projets européens d'harmonisation* (Paris: Irjs editions, 2012), para. 31; Patrice Jourdain, 'Les recours en contribution' (2015) 9 *Responsabilité civile et assurance*, 16, para. 1.

being treated differently from one another. Contribution claims are a reaction to this state.[152] They are a tool that allows for redistributing the payments made to the creditor and satisfying general principles of law such as fairness and equal treatment. This understanding of contribution claims is revealed in historic sources, which evidence the reasons for introducing the right to claim contribution (see Section 2.1.3.2).

2.1.3.2 The Relationship between the Imposition of Joint and Several Liability and Contribution Claims

The crucial question is whether one can always imply the existence of contribution claims from the fact that joint and several liability applies. Historic development of joint and several liability proves that contribution claims do not always appear when joint and several liability applies. Even though joint and several liability has existed since Roman times, it has not been the case of contribution claims.[153] There were only four cases in which it was possible to divide tortious liability: between legal guardians, in case of co-owners' noxal-liability, in case of landowners' water-damages claims, in case of action *de effuses ve deiectis*. Also, in early common law, contribution claims were excluded in tort.[154] In England, this was based on the *Merryweather* doctrine and in Germany following the interpretation of Justinian's Novellea 99.[155] The change came starting from the nineteenth century.[156] In Germany, it was the legislative Commission for the BGB who decided to introduce such claims.[157] While it was recognised that there is no legal basis for contribution, 'practical considerations demand however ... another determination, namely, that unless differently established by law or by a legal transaction, ... joint and several debtors should be obliged in equal shares among each other'.[158]

[152] In the same line, Lewaszkiewicz-Petrykowska, *Wyrządzenie szkody przez kilka osób*, 139; Ranouil, *Les recours entre coobligés*, 93–96; Canin, *Les actions récursoires*, 7; Corgas-Bernard, 'La pluralité de responsables', para. 31; Roman Inderst and Stefan Thomas, *Schadensersatz bei Kartellverstößen* (Düsseldorf: Handerlsblatt Fachmedien, 2015), 400; Carsten Krüger, 'Überlegungen zur Gesamtschuld von Kartellmitgliedern im System der privaten Kartellrechtsdurchsetzung. Einer für alle, alle gegen einen?' in Peter Oberender (ed.), *Private und öffentliche Kartellrechtsdurchsetzung* (Berlin: Duncker and Humblot, 2012), 85.

[153] Meier, *Gesamtschulden*, 263 *et seq.* and 561–570. Sonja Meier names only four cases in which it was possible to divide tortious liability: between legal guardians, in case of co-owners' noxal-liability, in case of landowners' water-damages claims, in case of action *de effuses ve deiectis*. See also Florian Bentele *Gesamtschuld und Erlass*, 141 *et seq*; Körner, *Die Gesamtschuld im Kartellbußgeldrecht*, 104–106; Ehmann, *Die Gesamtschuld*, 46.

[154] The Law Commission, *Working Paper No 59 Contribution* (London: Her Majesty's Stationery Office, 1975), para. 7; *Merryweather v. Nixan* [1799] 8 TR 186.

[155] Sonja Meier, *Gesamtschulden*, 559.

[156] Ibid., 577.

[157] On the German codification and the reasons for introducing contribution claims, see Hösch, *Der schadensrechtliche Innenausgleich*, 172; Meier, *Gesamtschulden*, 584–590; Ehmann, *Die Gesamtschuld*, 90–97; Götte, *Gesamtschuldbegriff und Regressproblem*, 117–124.

[158] *Hervorh v. Verf.* quoted by Horst Ehmann, *Die Gesamtschuld*, 91–92: '*Praktische Erwägungen erheischen aber, wie auch der Vorgang der erwähnten grossen Gesetzgebungen zeigt, eine andere Bestimmung, nämlich, dass, soweit nicht aus Gesetz (z. B. §§ 338, 713, 1696) oder Rechtsgeschäft*

In France, the right to claim contribution was guaranteed under Article 1213 of Code Civil (old version) for *la solidarité* and under Article 1251(3) of Code Civil (old version) for *obligation in solidum*.[159] Today, Article 1317 spells this out even more clearly: 'As between themselves, the contribution of each joint and several debtor is limited to his own share. A debtor who has satisfied the obligation beyond his own share has a right of recourse against the others in proportion to their own shares.'[160]

In England, contribution claims appeared with the development of equity and common law[161] and their application was expanded with the 1935 Act[162] and with the Civil Liability (Contribution) Act 1978:[163] 'any person liable in respect of any damage suffered by another person may recover contribution from any other person liable in respect of the same damage (whether jointly with him or otherwise)'.

In the United States, contribution claims have been provided since 1925 at the state level[164] and at the federal level since the Uniform Contribution Among Tortfeasors Act 1939.[165]

The reasons for introducing contribution claims also demonstrate that such claims are a desired element of joint and several liability rather than a necessary one. In Germany, there was an intensive discussion over whether to introduce contribution claims.[166] As an argument against, it was claimed that, dogmatically, claims for contribution are not necessary.[167] It was argued that each joint tortfeasor committed a wrong for which it should be liable in its entirety.[168] The argument that decided in favour of introducing contribution claims was the willingness to remedy the so-called *roulette* of creditor's requests for payments.[169] Using the words of

ein Anderes sich ergibt, im Verhältnisse zu einander die Gesammtgläubiger als zu gleichen Antheilen berechtigt, die Gesammtschuldner als zu gleichen Antheilen verpflichtet gelten.'

159 In the nineteenth century, a separate type of liability – *obligation in solidum* – developed next to *la solidarité*, see Cass. Req., 15.01.1878: S. 1878 I 152. Article 1251(3) of the Code Civil (currently Article 1346 of the Code Civil) was believed to apply only to the second type of liability, *obligation in solidum*. However, later also Article 1213 of the Code Civil was considered to be the cause of action available in the case of *obligation in solidum* ; see Civ. , 21.12.1943: JCP 1945 II 2779. See also Götte, *Gesamtschuldbegriff und Regressproblem*, 113; Bieniek, 'Pojęcie regresu', 897; Ranouil, *Les recours entre coobligés*, 133.

160 See note 54 in Chapter 2.

161 The Law Commission, *Contribution*, para. 7. On the history of the no-contribution rule in the US, see Frank H. Easterbrook, William M. Landes and Richard A. Posner, 'Contribution among Antitrust Defendants: A Legal and Economic Analysis' (1980) 23 *The Journal of Law and Economics*, 2, 332–337.

162 Law Reform (Married Women and Tortfeasors) Act 1935 [Ch. 30] .

163 The Civil Liability (Contribution) Act 1978 [Ch. 47] .

164 Easterbrook, Landes and Posner, 'Contribution among Antitrust Defendants', 334–337.

165 Uniform Contribution among Tortfeasors Act, para. 1, 12 U.L.A. 60 (1975).

166 A similar discussion took place in French courts in connection with liability *in solidum*. See, for instance, Cour de cassation (Ch. Civ.), 21.12.1943, JCP 1945 II 2779. See also note 159.

167 Savigny Friedrich Karl von, *Das Obligationenrecht als Theil des heutigen Römischen Rechts*, 2 vols. (Berlin: Bei Zeit und Comp., 1851), vol. I, 227.

168 Ibid.

169 Reference to Friedrich Karl von Savigny's idea of *Glückspiel*. Ibid.

Friedrich Karl von Savigny, claims for contribution are not necessary; they are simply *just and recommended* in light of the right to fair treatment.[170] This means that contribution claims are not inherently linked with the imposition of joint and several liability.

The fact that there is no necessary connection between the imposition of joint and several liability and contribution claims has two principal consequences. First, claims for contribution do not automatically arise from the fact that joint and several liability is applied. The historical development of joint and several liability proves that the decision to introduce contribution claims is a policy choice. As a result, the existence of contribution claims cannot be presumed and such claims need to have their basis in law.

Second, the functions of the external aspect of joint and several liability are different from those of the internal one.[171] As Section 2.1.3.1 demonstrated, the role of contribution is to prevent inequalities in the way final liability burdens the debtors. Contribution claims are thus introduced to provide for fairness and equality. The role of contribution claims is thus different from the role of joint and several liability in its external dimension, which is to provide the creditor with a more convenient position for enforcing its rights and to enhance the objectives sought by its claim.[172]

2.1.3.3 Contribution Claims in EU Competition Law

Since a right to claim contribution cannot be derived from the mere fact that joint and several liability has been applied, it needs to be established whether contribution claims exist in EU competition law. The US experience shows that contribution claims should not be taken for granted and the very existence of the right to contribution may collide with the enforcement of rules on competition.

THE US DEBATE ON THE DESIRABILITY OF CONTRIBUTION CLAIMS IN ANTITRUST In US antitrust law, contribution claims are rejected.[173] A *no-contribution* system means that even though tortfeasors violating antitrust law are jointly and severally liable for the damage caused by their misconduct, they cannot claim contribution for the compensation paid to the creditor. So far in the United States, there has not been any legal act introducing claims for contribution in the field of

[170] Ibid., 229–230. See also Ehmann, *Die Gesamtschuld*, 25; Meier, *Gesamtschulden*, 916.

[171] Lewaszkiewicz-Petrykowska, *Wyrządzenie szkody przez kilka osób*, 139–140; Götte, *Gesamtschuldbegriff und Regressproblem*, 131, see also the literature referred to in note 28.

[172] See Section 2.1 and the literature referred to in note 13 in Chapter 1.

[173] United States Supreme Court, *Texas Industries*. See also Easterbrook, Landes and Posner, 'Contribution among Antitrust Defendants', 331–334; James F. Ponsoldt and Benjamin H. Terry, 'Contribution in Civil Antitrust Litigation: The Emerging Consensus in Legal Literature' (1981) 38 *Washington and Lee Law Review*, 2, 316.

antitrust law. In *Professional Beauty Supply*, the US Court of Appeals for the Eighth Circuit attempted to take a step forward and stated that 'under certain circumstances an antitrust defendant may be entitled to pro rata contribution from other joint tortfeasors'.[174]

Other courts of appeals, however, opposed such a development and claimed that contribution may decrease deterrence and cause procedural difficulties.[175]

In *Texas Industries*,[176] the Supreme Court resolved this conflict. It stated that on the one hand, fairness and equity speak in favour of allowing for contribution claims. On the other hand, introducing such claims might not be in line with the doctrine of *unclean hands* and *inpari delicto*; it could decrease the deterrent role of treble damages and lead to complex litigation. Eventually, the Supreme Court left the question of introducing contribution claims open and concluded that such claims are currently not available due to the lack of relevant legislative action:[177]

> [t]here is no statutory right of contribution provided under either the Sherman Act ... or the Clayton Act ... We do not, however, interpret this omission as evidence that Congress necessarily intended to deny contribution under antitrust laws.[178]

Although there has been a number of proposals for adopting relevant laws (bills introduced at 96th, 97th and 98th Congress Sessions, proposals of Antitrust Modernization Commission),[179] none of them has been realised so far and the dispute between opponents of contribution rules and their supporters continues.

Arguments against Introducing the Contribution Rule Opponents of contribution claims argue firstly that the deterrence factor of competition law would decrease if antitrust infringers were liable ultimately only for a proportion of the damage corresponding to their own share of liability.[180] The economic literature proves that

[174] *Professional Beauty Supply v. National Beauty Supply*, 594 F.2d1179 (8th Cir. 1979). For a commentary see Donald J. Polden and E. Thomas Sullivan, 'Contribution and Claim Reduction in Antitrust Litigation: A Legislative Analysis' (1983) 20(1) *Harvard Journal on Legislation*, 399–401.

[175] United States Supreme Court, *Texas Industries, Inc.*; *Olson Farms, Inc. v. Safeway Stores, Inc.*, 649 F.2d370 (10th Cir. 1979).

[176] United States Supreme Court, *Texas Industries*. For a commentary, see Polden and Sullivan, 'Contribution and Claim Reduction', 401–403; Edward D. Cavanagh, 'Contribution, Claim Reduction, and Individual Treble Damage Responsibility: Which Path to Reform of Antitrust Remedies?' (1987) 40 *Vanderbilt Law Review*, 1286–1287; Easterbrook, Landes and Posner, 'Contribution among Antitrust Defendants', 338.

[177] Ibid.

[178] United States Supreme Court, *Texas Industries*.

[179] Polden and Sullivan, 'Contribution and Claim Reduction', 403–408; Cavanagh, 'Contribution, Claim Reduction', 1314–1315; Antitrust Modernization Commission, 'Report and Recommendations', 244.

[180] See, for instance, W. Stephen Cannon, 'The Administration's Antitrust Remedies Reform Proposal: Its Derivation and Implications' (1986) 55 *Antitrust Law Journal*, 1, 120–121;

the introduction of contribution claims decreases the deterrence of the no-contribution rule for risk-averse companies.[181] In simple terms, a fine of USD 30 million deters a cartel between three companies, in which each cartelist earns USD 15 million, as each of them can face a potential liability of USD 30 million. However, with the same fine and contribution based on the *pro capita* allocation, the cartel is not deterred as each cartelist ultimately keeps USD 5 million.

Second, high financial liability for antitrust damages encourages violators to conclude settlements.[182] Treble damages in judicial proceedings encourage settlements in which the debtors can settle for less. The creditors are, however, unlikely to settle with the last debtor, as it can be held responsible for nearly all damages based on the rule that the damages are first calculated and trebled and only then the settlement amounts are accounted for.[183] These rules create significant pressure on debtors to settle early and avoid becoming the last one on the battlefield. Settlements are thus frequent. This relieves the judicial system from dealing with claims for antitrust damages and reduces the costs of such proceedings for the judicial system and the parties. Settlements are also helpful in terms of gaining access to evidence for court litigation with other infringers.[184] The introduction of contribution claims may jeopardise settlements and their positive effects since it will reduce the infringers' incentive to conclude them by reducing the threat of extremely high liability imposed on the infringer that does not escape the litigation.[185]

Third, claims for contribution are complex judicial disputes. Judges need to decide on the criterion to divide liability, analyse what the parties' positions are with respect to this criterion, weigh their relative liability and ultimately determine contribution sums. Arguably, the justice system should not deal with contribution claims as they concern only the interests of those that are already in breach of law at the expense of society as a whole.[186] Frank H. Easterbrook, William M. Landes and

Easterbrook, Landes and Posner, 'Contribution among Antitrust Defendants', 353; Cavanagh, 'Contribution, Claim Reduction', 1293 *et seq*.

181 See, for instance, Cavanagh, 'Contribution, Claim Reduction', 1306; A. Mitchell Polinsky and Steven Shavell, 'Contribution and Claim Reduction among Antitrust Defendants: An Economic Analysis' (1981) 33 *Stanford Law Review*, 3, 453; Easterbrook, Landes and Posner, 'Contribution among Antitrust Defendants', 351.

182 See, for instance, Cannon, 'Antitrust Remedies Reform Proposal', 103 *et seq*.; Easterbrook, Landes and Posner, 'Contribution among Antitrust Defendants', 353–368.

183 Antitrust Modernization Commission, 'Report and Recommendations', 252.

184 See, for instance, Morten Hviid and Andrei Medvedev, 'The Role of Contribution among Defendants in Private Antitrust Litigation' (2008) 8 *CCP Working Paper*, 3, 1 306.

185 See, for instance, Christopher R. Leslie, 'Judgment-Sharing Agreements' (2009) 58 *Duke Law Journal*, 747 *et seq*.

186 See, for instance, Easterbrook, Landes and Posner, 'Contribution among Antitrust Defendants', 340–341; Cavanagh, 'Contribution, Claim Reduction', 1295.

Richard A. Posner are blunt about this: 'the benefit of greater fairness inures to those who violated the law while the costs fall on society as a whole'.[187]

Fourth, some authors deny antitrust violators a right to distribute liability since wrongdoers should accept the results of their acts in their entirety.[188] All antitrust infringers risk being held liable for the infringement equally. Liability without the subsequent right to contribution is thus fair from the *ex-ante* standpoint.[189]

Arguments in Favour of Introducing the Contribution Rule Supporters of introducing contribution claims argue that it is not proven whether the risk of paying treble damages has deterrent effects.[190]As it is debated whether most companies are risk-averse or risk-neutral, the effects envisaged by the no-contribution rule are uncertain.[191] Supporters of contribution claims state that the deterrent effects of contribution and no-contribution rules are actually identical[192] or even that deterrence is higher for risk-seeking enterprises in the contribution regime.[193] In fact, contribution claims allow more antitrust infringers to be brought to justice and therefore increase deterrence. Finally, they state that the financial burden of compensation is already high when each of the co-tortfeasors pays a tripled compensation with respect to the proportion of damage caused by each of them only.[194] This ensures that damages are deterrent.

Many criticise the race to settle. The reason is that it allows some companies to conclude settlements that are far below their relative share of liability (the so-called whipsaw or sweetheart settlements).[195] Such settlements leave smaller companies in a difficult situation of paying high and disproportional damages.[196] The Antitrust

[187] Easterbrook, Landes and Posner, 'Contribution among Antitrust Defendants', 340.

[188] See, for instance, Easterbrook, Landes and Posner, 'Contribution among Antitrust Defendants', 339; Cavanagh, 'Contribution, Claim Reduction', 1296.

[189] See, for instance, Easterbrook, Landes and Posner, 'Contribution among Antitrust Defendants', 342–343; Section of Antitrust Law of the American Bar Association, *Contribution and Claim Reduction in Antitrust Litigation* (Chicago:American Bar Association Publishing, 1986), 9.

[190] See, for instance, Easterbrook, Landes and Posner, 'Contribution among Antitrust Defendants', 345 *et seq.*; Lewis A. Kornhauser and Richard L. Revesz, 'Sharing Damages among Multiple Tortfeasors' (1989) 98 *Yale Law Journal*, 5, 960 *et seq.*; Polinsky and Shavell, 'Contribution and Claim Reduction', 451 *et seq.*

[191] See, for instance, Easterbrook, Landes and Posner, 'Contribution among Antitrust Defendants', 351. See also William Breit and Kenneth G. Elzinga, 'Antitrust Penalties and Attitudes towards Risk: An Economic Analysis' (1973) 86 *Harvard Law Review*, 4, 704–706.

[192] See, for instance, Easterbrook, Landes and Posner, 'Contribution among Antitrust Defendants', 349.

[193] See, for instance, Cavanagh, 'Contribution, Claim Reduction', 1307.

[194] See, for instance, 1297; Larry S. Kaplan, 'From Contribution to Good Faith Settlements: Equity Where Are You?' (1984) 49 *Journal of Air Law and Commerce*, 771 *et seq.*

[195] See, for instance, Susan P. Koniak and George M. Cohen, 'Under Cloak of Settlement' (1996) 82 *Vanderbilt Law Review*, 1051 *et seq.*; Joseph Angland, 'Joint and Several Liability, Contribution, and Claim Reduction' (2008), available at https://papers.ssrn.com/sol3/papers.cfm?abstract_id=1528007, 2380 *et seq.*

[196] See, for instance, Easterbrook, Landes and Posner, 'Contribution among Antitrust Defendants', 365; Leslie, 'Judgment-Sharing Agreements', 759 *et seq.*; Cavanagh, 'Contribution, Claim

Modernization Commission concludes that the combination of the no-contribution rule and the settlement dynamics makes the current rules 'fundamentally unfair'.[197] In any event, should settlements deserve special treatment, the supporters of contribution demonstrate that it is possible to combine contribution claims with settlements. For instance, settlements are believed to not be discouraged if a claim reduction rule is introduced.[198]

Finally, according to some, the rules on contribution can operate in a simple way and can be linked with factors that are not difficult to prove.[199] For instance, the liability for the infringement may be shared according to the infringers' market shares on the market affected by their misconduct.[200] This would make the claims for contribution easy to enforce and not burdensome for the parties and the judicial system.[201] At worst, relative liabilities can be allocated *pro capita*, which would be child's play and still fairer than the no-contribution rule.

Since it is possible to create an acceptable contribution regime, the supporters of the contribution rule advocate for its introduction. The reason is that the contribution rule would make antitrust law fairer[202], and it would leave antitrust infringers with liabilities that correspond to their individual involvement in the wrongdoing.[203] The concept of fairness cannot be rejected just because antitrust infringers are wrongdoers, as stressed by McClory before the US Senate: 'there is an element of fairness always applied in our system of justice, including fairness to those charged with crime, even to illegal aliens and to others that do not have the status of citizens of our country'.[204]

THE US DEBATE IN THE EU CONTEXT It is interesting to ask whether the arguments present in the United States are also applicable to the EU context.[205] For instance,

Reduction', 1288–1292; Cannon, 'Antitrust Remedies Reform Proposal', 117; Bruce Hay and David Rosenberg, '"Sweetheart" and "Blackmail" Settlements in Class Actions: Reality and Remedy' (2000) 75 *Notre Dame Law Review*, 1377.

197 Antitrust Modernization Commission, 'Report and Recommendations' 252.

198 See, for instance, Polinsky and Shavell, 'Contribution and Claim Reduction' (1981), 459 *et seq*. For more details on claim reduction rule, see X.

199 Ibid., 464; Angland, 'Joint and Several Liability', 2393–2394.

200 Antitrust Modernization Commission, 'Report and Recommendations', 253.

201 Polden and Sullivan, 'Contribution and Claim Reduction', 413.

202 See, for instance, Harry M. Reasoner, 'Prepared Statement of Harry M. Reasoner' (14 July 2005), available at https://govinfo.library.unt.edu/amc/commission_hearings/pdf/Reasoner.pdf, 11; Polinsky and Shavell, 'Contribution and Claim Reduction', 449; Angland, 'Joint and Several Liability', 2371 *et seq*.; Kaplan, 'Good Faith Settlements', 771.

203 See, for instance, Reasoner, 'Prepared Statement', 11; Polinsky and Shavell, 'Contribution and Claim Reduction', 449; Angland, 'Joint and Several Liability', 2371 *et seq*.; Kaplan, 'Good Faith Settlements', 771.

204 United States Congress, 'Antitrust Damage Allocation', 24.

205 For a general comparison of US and EU antitrust enforcement, see Douglas H. Ginsburg, 'Comparing Antitrust Enforcement in the United States and Europe' (2005) 1 *Journal of Competition Law and Economics*, 3, 427 *et seq*.

Tobias Lettl endorses a view that the solutions present in the United States are also applicable in the European Union. He claims that the objectives of prevention and deterrence require contribution claims to be excluded between those who infringed Article 101 of TFEU. The infringers shall bear the risk that they can be targeted with antitrust claims for damages without having recourse to contribution from their co-infringers.[206] Such an automatic acceptance of the solutions present in the United States cannot be approved. It needs to be asked first whether US and EU competition law enforcement systems are comparable and then whether joint and several liability has the same functions in both legal orders.

Private Enforcement The US debate on contribution claims is only to some extent transposable to EU private antitrust enforcement. First, the prime objective of US private enforcement is deterrence.[207] The no-contribution rule is claimed to contribute to deterrence.[208] On the surface, EU private enforcement is also about deterrence.[209] The discrepancies, however, occur when we investigate how the principle of deterrence is implemented in US and EU private enforcement. In the United States, there is a great focus on the size of liability imposed on infringers of antitrust laws. Damages are trebled, so there is an evident element of penalty on top of compensation.[210] The main aim of the no-contribution is to prevent reducing the size of liability by allowing it to be shared between more entities. In the European Union, the focus is on detection as the size of liability is the crown jewel of public enforcement. Advocate General Wahl explains in *Skanska* that actions for damages increase the probability of identifying and holding competition law infringers liable.[211] Yet damages cannot exceed the actual damage sustained by those harmed by anticompetitive practices pursuant to Article 3(3) of Directive 2014/104/EU. The size of private law liability is therefore limited to compensation. The deterrent role of private enforcement in the European Union is therefore significantly more

[206] Tobias Lettl, 'Der Schadensersatzanspruch gemäß § 823 Abs. 2 BGB i. V. mit Art. 81 Abs. 1 EG' (2003) 167 *Zeitschrift für das gesamte Handels- und Wirtschaftsrecht*, 491 *et seq*.

[207] See, for instance, United States Supreme Court, *Texas Industries*; *American Society of Mechanical Engineers, Inc. v. Hydrolevel Corporation*, 102 S. Ct. 1935, 1945 (1982). See also Daniel A. Crane, 'Optimizing Private Antitrust Enforcement' (2010) 63 *Vanderbilt Law Review*, 2, 678 *et seq*.; United States Department of Justice, 'Public and Private Antitrust Enforcement in the United States'(11 February 2004) *Justice News*, available at https://justice.gov/atr/file/517756/download, 3. For the primary place of deterrence over compensation, see, for instance, *Illinois Brick Co. v. Illinois*, 431 U.S. 720 (1977); Roger D. Blair and D. DanielSokol, *The Oxford Handbook of International Antitrust Economics*, 2 vols. (New York: Oxford University Press, 2015), vol. I, 259.

[208] See, for instance, Cannon, 'Antitrust Remedies Reform Proposal', 120; Easterbrook, Landes and Posner, 'Contribution among Antitrust Defendants', 353; Cavanagh, 'Contribution, Claim Reduction', 1293 *et seq*.

[209] CJEU, *Skanska*, para. 45.

[210] Antitrust Modernization Commission, 'Report and Recommendations', 252.

[211] AG Wahl, *Skanska*, para. 48.

limited to that in the United States, and it is questionable whether no-contribution is required by EU competition law.[212]

Second, settlements in EU private enforcement do not have the same position as in the United States. In the European Union, settlements are generally not as prevalent as in the United States.[213] It is difficult to imagine that the situation of settlements would be much different for claims for antitrust damages. Even though Directive 2014/104/EU expressly encourages settlements, the incentives for their use remain relatively low. In the United States, the discount received with a settlement is high as treble damages are avoided. In Europe, it is small as the benchmarks for litigation and settlement are both single damages. In the European Union, settlements also have less to do with the discovery of evidence. Private enforcement takes place mainly in the form of follow-on claims that are reliant on the Commission's establishment of infringement.[214] Consequently, settlements in the European Union do not have two key features that decide their attractiveness in the United States, and their number is likely to remain moderate regardless of the rules on contribution.

The principle of deterrence and the protection of settlements are key arguments in the US discussion on the right to claim contribution. These elements, however, do not play the same role in the European Union as they do in the United States. This makes the US discussion hardly transposable to the European Union.

Public Enforcement The US debate on contribution claims is also barely transposable in the context of public enforcement. The European Commission and national competition authorities are responsible for such enforcement, and they use administrative tools to that end. The argument concerning settlements finds little application in administrative law.[215] Additionally, the reasoning about deterrence

[212] The divergence in antitrust enforcement objectives has been recognised also by Crane, 'Optimizing Private Antitrust Enforcement', 679, note 10. Contrary Weinhold, *Der Gesamtschuldnerausgleich*, 111–127; Krüger, *Kartellregress*, 209–231, 246–276.

[213] With regard to Italy, see David Nelken, 'Using the Concept of Legal Culture' (2004) 29 *Australian Journal of Legal Philosophy*, 18; with regard to England and Wales, see Oliver Cain and Danielle Carr, 'Litigation and Enforcement in the UK (England and Wales): Overview' (2018) available at https://uk.practicallaw.thomsonreuters.com/7-502-0631?transitionType=DefaultandcontextData=(sc.Default), Section 1.

[214] Matthijs Kuijpers, Stefan Tuinenga and et al., 'Actions for Damages', 1; Sebastian Peyer, 'Compensation and the Damages Directive' (2015) 15 *Centre for Competition Policy Working paper*, 10, 27.

[215] There is a settlement procedure before the European Commission; however, it is one of administrative procedures used to establish antitrust infringements. See Commission Notice on the conduct of settlement procedures in view of the adoption of Decisions pursuant to Article 7 and Article 23 of Council Regulation (EC) No 1/2003 in cartel cases, OJ C 167, 2.7.2008, pp. 1–6 and Commission Regulation (EC) No 622/2008 of 30 June 2008 amending Regulation (EC) No 773/2004 as regards the conduct of settlement procedures in cartel cases, OJ L 171, 1.7.2008, pp. 3–5. See also Flavio Laina and Aleko Bogdanov, 'The EU Cartel Settlement Procedure: Latest Developments' (2017) 8 *Journal of European Competition Law and Practice*, 5, 333 *et seq.*; Marc Barennes, 'The Role of the Settlement Procedure and

cannot apply in the case of public competition law enforcement. The US debate refers to the situation in which the risk of the high financial burden of paying treble damages decreases companies' incentives to engage in anticompetitive conduct and the no-contribution rule protects such a high financial burden. In the EU public enforcement system, the Commission enjoys many powers to make sure that its fines are deterrent (see Section 2.1.1.1). The Commission can apply a special bonus for deterrence or even completely deviate from the usually applied Guidelines on Fines. If the Commission imposes liability correctly, contribution claims have no effect on deterrence.

In sum, the only argument that seems transposable to the EU context is that contribution claims are complex and that they will be a burden on judicial resources. It is, however, doubtful whether this argument alone is sufficient for adopting the no-contribution rule.

EUROPEAN UNION POLICY CHOICES Difficulties in transposing the arguments present in the US debate to the European Union already demonstrate that the no-contribution rule is unlikely to be followed in the European Union. On the contrary, the existence of contribution claims in the majority of tort laws of EU Member States supports its use in EU competition law.[216] This is because civil laws are based on the principle of individual liability and avoid imposing liability for the events outside one's responsibility.[217] Contribution claims in antitrust are also backed by some general principles of EU law.

First, a right to claim contribution is consistent with the principle of proportionality.[218] According to its EU understanding, every legal measure must be supported by a legitimate aim (i), must be suitable to achieve such an aim (ii) and must be necessary and reasonable (iii).[219] No-contribution as a rule governing the internal aspect of joint and several liability fails to meet these conditions. There is no

Leniency Programme in the European Commission's Fight Against Cartels' in Vesna Tomljenović, Nada Bodiroga-Vukobrat, Vlatka Butorac Malnar and Ivana Kunda (eds.), *EU Competition and State Aid Rules. Europeanization and Globalization* (Berlin and Heidelberg: Springer, 2017), 131; Molly Kelly, 'Settling for Settlement: The European Commission's New Cartel Settlement Procedure' (2010) 9 *Washington University Global Studies Law Review*, 699 *et seq*.

216 For the common use of the contribution rule in Europe, see Section 2.1.3.

217 See, for instance, Biruta Lewaszkiewicz-Petrykowska, *Wyrządzenie szkody przez klika osób*, 5–6.

218 For the importance of the principle of proportionality in the EU contribution system, see Köhler, 'Kartellverbot und Schadensersatz' (2004) *Gewerblicher Rechtsschutz und Urheberrecht*, 101; Weinhold, *Der Gesamtschuldnerausgleich*, 133–137; Krüger, *Kartellregress*, 177.

219 For the principle of proportionality in EU law, see Paul P. Craig, EU *Administrative Law* (Oxford and New York: Oxford University Press, 2012), 590 *et seq*.; Nicholas Emiliou, *The Principle of Proportionality in European Law: A Comparative Study* (London and Cambridge MA: Kluwer Law International, 1996); Stefan Vogenauer and Stephen Weatherill, *General Principles of Law: European and Comparative Perspectives* (Oxford and Portland: Hart, 2017).

problem with the first condition of this test. The no-contribution rule increases deterrence, which is supported by both public and private enforcement. By deterring companies from entering into anticompetitive agreements, competition law is enforced without any action on the part of competition authorities or courts. This, however, does not help pass the suitability test, which is the second condition. The no-contribution rule is not a tool that helps increase deterrence in the public enforcement of EU competition law. As discussed above, companies are free to decide amongst themselves who pays the antitrust sanction, and the Commission has no power to intervene. In order to provide for individual deterrence, the Commission's tool is actually to set individual fines and use its powers to guarantee that the fine is sufficiently high (see Section 2.1.1.1). In private enforcement, the no-contribution rule is also incapable of increasing deterrence in terms of better detection of antitrust infringements. Quite to the contrary, the contribution rule allows those who avoided liability in actions for damages to be brought to justice. The no-contribution rule can increase deterrence in terms of increasing the liability of competition law infringers; however, this objective is questionable in private enforcement given an expressive prohibition for courts to impose punitive, multiple or similar damages.[220]

Second, the no-contribution rule is also difficult to accept due to the principle of equality, which requires entities to be treated in the same way in the same situation.[221] When companies jointly breach competition law, each of them is liable for the damage and fines imposed by the Commission. Thanks to joint and several liability, the Commission and the claimants have the choice to enforce their rights against only some infringers. This leads to those obligated to pay being treated in a different way to those infringers who were not called by the creditor.[222] This is remedied by contribution claims.[223] It may be argued that the principle of equality is not breached as in the moment of infringement all companies are equally liable (equality *ex-ante*).[224] This, however, does not mean that equality is maintained after the creditor has exercised its discretion as to who to claim the debt from (inequality *ex-post*). There is no reason why the principle of equality should apply only to the initial and not the subsequent situation.

As a result, contribution claims shall be supported in the European Union. Contribution claims are a desirable reaction to the effects that joint and several

[220] Article 3(3) of the Directive 2014/104/EU.

[221] Weinhold, *Der Gesamtschuldnerausgleich*, 137–140; Ota, 'The Fairness and the Efficiency', 230. For the principle of equality in EU law, see Lucia Serena Rossi and Federico Casolari, *The Principle of Equality in EU Law* (Cham: Springer International Publishing, 2017).

[222] For the division between the fairness *ex ante* and *ex post*, see, for instance, Krüger, *Kartellregress*, 203; Weinhold, *Der Gesamtschuldnerausgleich*, 140.

[223] In the same line, Weinhold, *Der Gesamtschuldnerausgleich*, 137–140; Krüger, *Kartellregress*, 177, 188–205; Canin, *Les actions récursoires*, 7; Dejean de La Bâtie 'Responsabilité délictuelle', 163.

[224] See note 190.

liability has in its external dimension. They aim to correct the unequal allocation of liability and spread the liability among the tortfeasors pursuant to a benchmark determined by law. This is desirable from the standpoint of the general principles of EU law. European Union policy thus points clearly in the direction of the contribution rule.

THE RIGHT TO CLAIM CONTRIBUTION Given that a right to claim contribution is wished from the standpoint of EU law, it is not surprising that EU legislators took a clear stance on allowing contribution claims in competition law.

In the context of public competition law enforcement, the right to claim contribution has been established in *Siemens Österreich*:

> where there is no contractual agreement as to the shares to be paid by those held jointly and severally liable for payment of the fine, it is for the national courts to determine those shares, in a manner consistent with EU law, by applying the national law applicable to the dispute.[225]

In the context of private enforcement, contribution claims can be brought forward based on laws implementing Directive 2014/104/EU into national legal orders.

Article 11(5) of the Directive guarantees the following:

> Member States shall ensure that an infringer may recover a contribution from any other infringer, the amount of which shall be determined in the light of their relative responsibility for the harm caused by the infringement of competition law.

In light of these clear rules, it is difficult to argue that a right to claim contribution does not exist in EU competition law. The discussion about the existence of contribution rights in EU competition law can be thus considered as settled in favour of the contribution rule.

2.2 INTERFERENCE BETWEEN CONTRIBUTION CLAIMS AND JOINT AND SEVERAL LIABILITY IN EU COMPETITION LAW

Although European Union law has allowed for contribution claims without hesitance, the interplay between joint and several liability and EU competition law is far from being settled. There are many points of contact between contribution claims and competition law, such as jurisdiction in which contribution claims should be enforced, the binding effect of decisions and judgments finding antitrust violations in subsequent contribution disputes or the alignment of the internal allocation of antitrust liability with the aims of EU competition law.

The key argument made by US antitrust scholars and practitioners – that contribution claims weaken competition law enforcement – resonates across all these

[225] CJEU, *Siemens Österreich*, para. 62.

areas and speaks in favour of keeping contribution litigation within the narrow frames defined by competition law enforcement. The concern that an antitrust infringer would be entirely released from liability following a successful dispute on contribution is also *prima facie* real in EU competition law[226]. On the other hand, the fact that EU law chose not to follow US no-contribution rule casts some doubt on whether the impact of contribution claims on competition law enforcement is comparable to that in the United States.[227]

2.2.1 *EU or National Right to Claim Contribution?*

Possibly the safest option for competition law enforcement is to keep contribution litigation within the ambit of competition law. If the division of liability between antitrust infringers is dealt with at the same time as antitrust liability is determined, there is virtually no chance of a discord between contribution and the enforcement of competition law. This can be achieved by conferring the jurisdiction to deal with the question of contribution upon the European Commission for public antitrust enforcement and upon the same judges that have decided on antitrust damages for contribution in private antitrust enforcement. In 2015, the CJEU had a perfect occasion to decide about this as there were two cases on this topic referred to it.

2.2.1.1 German Calcium Carbide Litigation

The *Calcium carbide* case[228] concerned a cartel in the market for calcium carbide and magnesium-based reagents. Having established the infringement of Article

[226] See, for instance, LG München I, 13.07.2011 – 37 O 20080-10, BeckRS 2013, 10095 ('*Calcium carbide*'); OLG München, 09.02.2012 – U 3283/11 Kart, BeckRS 2012, 8896 ('*Calcium carbide*'); BGH, 18.11.2014 – KZR 15/12, BeckRS 2015, 00033 ('*Calcium carbide*'); Thomas, 'Die Gesamtschuld', 684; Manuel Kellerbauer and Olaf Weber, 'Das Urteil Siemens VA Tech', 692.

[227] See Article 11(5) of Directive 20174/104/EU.

[228] Commission decision of 22 July 2009 in Case COMP/39.396 – *Calcium carbide and magnesium based reagents for the steel and gas industries*, C(2009) 5791 final ('*Calcium carbide*'). For other analyses of the *Calcium carbide* case, see Opper, *Die gesamtschuldnerische Bußgeldhaftung*, 170–192; Körner, *Die Gesamtschuld im Kartellbußgeldrecht*, 217–220; Ulrich Rust, 'Kartellverstoß und Gesamtschuld – Bestandsaufnahme und Ausblick' (2015) *Neue Zeitschrift für Kartellrecht*, 503–504; Johannes Pitsch, 'Kein Rückgriff der Muttergesellschaft gegen die Tochtergesellschaft wegen kartellrechtlicher Geldbuße (Calciumcarbid-Kartell)' (2011) *Gesellschafts- und Wirtschaftsrecht*, 192 *et seq.*; Gerald Mäsch, 'Innenausgleich bei gesamtschuldnerisch festgesetzter Kartellbuße der EU-Kommission – "Calciumcarbid"' (2012) *Gewerblicher Rechtsschutz und Urheberrecht Praxis im Immaterialgüter und Wettbewerbsrecht*, 268–269; Ines Bodenstein, 'Zurück zum bewährten Grundsatz: Wer handelt, haftet. Wegweisende Klärung zum Gesamtschuldnerausgleich bei Kartellgeldbußen durch den BGH in Sachen Calciumcarbid' (2015) *Neue Zeitschrift für Kartellrecht*, 143 *et seq.*; Braun and Kellerbauer, 'Das Konzept der gesamtschuldnerischen Verantwortlichkeit – Teil 2', 216; Kellerbauer and Weber, 'Das Urteil Siemens VA Tech', 666 *et seq.*; Alexander Böhlke, 'Die gesamtschuldnerische Verantwortlichkeit im EU-Wettbewerbsrecht' (2011) *Europäische Zeitschrift für Wirtschaftsrecht*, 781 *et seq.*; von Laufenberg, *Kartellrechtliche*

101 of TFEU, the Commission imposed a fine of around EUR 13.3 million on three companies jointly and severally: Gigaset, Arques and SKW.[229] These companies belonged to the same corporate group: SKW was a subsidiary of Gigaset and Arques was their holding company.[230]

Shortly after the infringement took place, Gigaset sold all shares in SKW to Arques. Arques paid a part of the fine to the Commission. At the same time, it appealed the decision and filed a lawsuit before the Landesgericht (LG) München to recover the amount paid to the Commission from SKW and Gigaset. Arques argued that as a holding company it was not liable for the infringement and was completely unaware of it. This was not the case of SKW, which was directly involved in the anticompetitive practice, and Gigaset, which was aware of the infringement and failed to prevent it.[231]

The LG München's first question was whether it has jurisdiction to deal with the claim that directly relates to the fines imposed by the Commission. The LG München, supported later by the Oberlandesgericht (OLG) München, concluded that claims for contribution should be dealt before national courts.[232] This was backed by two arguments. First, there is no rule that gives the Commission power to internally allocate the liability between those held jointly and severally liable for the fine.[233] Second, Regulation 1/2003 explicitly provides that national laws deal with contribution in another situation related to the distribution of liability between joint and several debtors. Recital 30 of Regulation 1/2003 states that claims for recovery of sums paid as fines between the companies belonging to an association violating competition law are resolved according to national rules.[234]

The Bundesgerichtshof (BGH) seemed not to be entirely convinced by this argumentation and asked the CJEU for a preliminary reference. The question was generally whether the internal allocation of fines is a task of national courts or EU Courts and under which conditions national courts shall distribute the fine in order to be in line with EU law.[235]

2.2.1.2 French Siemens Österreich Case

Around the same time, a similar question appeared before the Tribunal de commerce de Grenoble in the *Siemens Österreich* case. The matter concerned an

Konzernhaftung, 239 *et seq.*; Braun, *Das Konzept der gesamtschuldnerischen Verantwortlichkeit*, 425 *et seq.*

229 Commission decision, *Calcium carbide*, Article 2(f).

230 Ibid., paras. 25–33.

231 LG München, BeckRS 2013, 10095, Section *Tatbestand.*

232 Ibid., Section I; OLG München, BeckRS 2012, 8896, Section II(1).

233 LG München, BeckRS 2013, 10095, Section II(1)(a)(bb).

234 OLG München, BeckRS 2012, 8896, Section II(1).

235 BGH, Vorlage von Fragen an den Gerichtshof der Europäischen Union zur Auslegung des Unionsrechts darüber, ob und wie bei der Verhängung einer Geldbuße gegen mehrere Personen als Gesamtschuldner entschieden werden muss, in welchem Verhältnis die Geldbuße intern auf die einzelnen Gesamtschuldner aufzuteilen ist (2013) 38 *Wertpapier-Mitteilungen* 1820.

anticompetitive agreement to allocate GIS projects and to fix market shares of undertakings at their historical levels.[236] The Commission imposed a fine on three companies jointly and severally: Schneider Electric SA, Siemens Transmission and Distribution SA, and Nuova Magrini Galileo S.p.a. Schneider Electric SA was a mother company of the two latter companies.[237]

Although Schneider Electric SA paid the entire fine, it claimed that only its subsidiaries were liable for the infringement. As a consequence, it filed a claim for indemnity against them before the Tribunal de commerce de Grenoble.[238] The French court asked the same question as the German courts: do national courts have jurisdiction to deal with contribution claims?[239]

The Tribunal de commerce de Grenoble reached a contrary conclusion to the one adopted in Germany.[240] French judges interpreted Schneider's claim as an attempt to challenge its own liability and enforcing it meant to them that they would run counter to the finality of the Commission's decision.[241] The Tribunal de commerce de Grenoble was of the view that contribution claims are part of EU law. It expressed that even if the Commission did not decide on the internal apportionment of liability, national courts are not in power to remedy this shortage.[242]

2.2.1.3 European Union Courts Resolve the Conflict

The divergent jurisprudence of national courts did not last for long. Siemens Österreich appealed the decision on fines to the GCEU and gave it an opportunity to discuss the question of whether the internal apportionment of fines between those jointly and severally liable falls under the Commission's competence.[243] This question was difficult for EU Courts to answer, and again different conclusions were reached.[244]

[236] Commission decision of 24 January 2007 in Case COMP/F/38.899 – *Gas Insulated Switchgear*, C(2006) 6762 final.

[237] Ibid., Article 2(k).

[238] Tribunal de commerce de Grenoble, 18.12.2009, 2007J00528.

[239] Ibid.

[240] Ibid., 8.

[241] Ibid., 8.

[242] Ibid., 10.

[243] GCEU, *Siemens Österreich*, para. 113.

[244] For other analyses of this case, see Opper, *Die gesamtschuldnerische Bußgeldhaftung*, 159–170; Bieber, *Die gesamtschuldnerische Haftung*, 91–94; Körner, *Die Gesamtschuld im Kartellbußgeldrecht*, 216–219; Georges Decocq, 'D'utiles précisions sur le régime de la solidarité pour le paiement d'une amende' (2014) 7 *Contrat Concurrence Consommation*, 165 *et seq*.; Idot, 'Responsabilité des sociétés mères', 1 *etseq*.; Bodenstein, 'BGH in Sachen Calciumcarbid', 143 *et seq*.; Braun and Kellerbauer, 'Das Konzept der gesamtschuldnerischen Verantwortlichkeit – Teil 2', 215; Alexander Jüchser, 'Gesamtschuldnerausgleich zwischen Mutter- und Tochtergesellschaft im Falles Schadensersatzes' (2012) 10 *Wirtschaft und Wettbewerb*, 1049 *et seq*.; Aberle, *Sanktionsdurchgriff*, 137–138; von Laufenberg,

The GCEU stated that joint and several liability was an autonomous concept of EU law. As such, it should be interpreted by reference to the objectives of competition law and, when necessary, also to the general principles of national legal systems.[245] The consequence of this interpretation was that

> [i]t is ... exclusively for the Commission, in exercising its power to impose fines under Article 23(2) of Regulation No 1/2003, to determine the respective shares of the various companies of the fines imposed on them jointly and severally, in so far as they formed part of the same undertaking, and that task cannot be left to the national courts.[246]

For the GCEU, the question of apportioning the fine was a matter of EU law. Furthermore, it was not only the Commission's mandate but also an obligation to decide on such an apportionment. The GCEU's view was that if the Commission had not decided on the internal allocation of liability, it should be assumed that the internal shares of liability for the fine were equal.[247]

Advocate General Mengozzi took a different view. He observed that joint and several liability included an external and internal dimension. He stated that while it was true that the external dimension of joint and several liability fell within the Commission's competence, the same was not true of its internal dimension.[248] Advocate General Mengozzi concluded that the effective application of EU competition law and its deterrence were achieved upon the imposition of fines. It exceeded the objectives of effectiveness and deterrence to determine internal relationships between those jointly and severally liable for the fine. In fact, such a task might slow down the Commission's investigation.[249] Despite this, the Commission could still divide the fine between joint and several debtors as this could serve other principles of EU law, such as the principle of legal certainty or the principle of penalty specificity.[250]

The CJEU largely followed the reasoning of AG Mengozzi, especially his division between external and internal aspects of joint and several liability. The CJEU's view was that the external aspect was vested in the Commission as such a regime of liability strengthens the effectiveness of EU competition law. This is in contrast to the internal aspect of joint and several liability, which had no influence on

Kartellrechtliche Konzernhaftung, 239 *et seq.*; Braun, *Das Konzept der gesamtschuldnerischen Verantwortlichkeit*, 420 *et seq.*

[245] GCEU, *Siemens Österreich*, para. 155–156.

[246] Ibid., para. 157.

[247] Ibid., paras. 158–159.

[248] CJEU, Joined cases C-231/11 P, C-232/11 P and C-233/11 P, *Siemens Österreich and Others, Siemens Transmission and Distribution Ltd, Siemens Transmission and Distribution SA and Nuova Magrini Galileo SpA v. European Commission*, ECLI:EU:C:2013:578 ('*Siemens Österreich*'), paras. 53–54.

[249] Ibid., paras. 56–58.

[250] Ibid., para. 54–55, 59.

competition law enforcement.[251] According to the CJEU, since EU law did not provide for a legal basis, the Commission could not determine the infringers' shares of liability.[252] The CJEU stated that

> where there is no contractual agreement as to the shares to be paid by those held jointly and severally liable for payment of the fine, it is for the national courts to determine those shares, in a manner consistent with EU law, by applying the national law applicable to the dispute.[253]

In other words, the internal division of liability between those jointly and severally liable for the fine should be dealt with by national courts. The mention of EU law compliance nonetheless indicates that the CJEU recognised the right to claim contribution as a matter of EU law, but it placed its exercise at a national level. This means that the Member States have the freedom to decide how such enforcement will follow, provided that the framework for exercising contribution claims complies with EU law (see further in Section 2.5).

The same approach was followed in the context of private antitrust enforcement. Directive 2014/104/EU does not envisage any power of the Commission to determine internal shares of liability for those jointly and severally liable for the damage caused by their anticompetitive behaviour. Article 11(5) of Directive 2014/104/EU states that

> *Member States shall ensure* that an infringer may recover a contribution from any other infringer, the amount of which shall be determined in the light of their relative responsibility for the harm caused by the infringement of competition law.

National legal orders are thus responsible for establishing the framework for contribution claims that can be enforced with respect to the liabilities stemming from EU competition law. This is valid both for public and private law enforcement.

2.2.2 *Should the National Jurisdiction for Contribution Claims Be Approved?*

The *Siemens Österreich* case presents three different ways of dealing with the problem of joint and several liability.[254] First, it can be argued that joint and several

[251] CJEU, *Siemens Österreich*, para. 60
[252] Ibid., para. 61.
[253] Ibid., para. 62.
[254] For other commentaries on the problem of Commission's powers to determine internal shares of joint and several liability, see Sebastian Felix Janka, 'Parent Liability and Claims for Recovery between Joint and Several Debtors according to EU Antitrust Law' (2014) 35 *European Competition Law Review*, 12, 594 *et seq*.; Bodenstein, 'BGH in Sachen Calciumcarbid', 143–144; Alexandre Geulette, 'La solidarité pour le paiement des amendes en droit de la concurrence de l'Union' (2014) 2 *Revues des Affaires européennes*, 433 *et seq*.; Armati Leonardo, '*Siemens Österreich*, *Areva* and *Alstom*: Joint and Several Liability in the Gas-insulated Switchgear Cartel' (2015) 6 *Journal of European Competition Law and Practice*, 1, 26–28; Opper, *Die gesamtschuldnerische Bußgeldhaftung*, 159 *et seq*.; Bieber, *Die gesamtschuldnerische Haftung*, 91–106.

liability in the context of competition law is an autonomous EU concept, covering both its internal and external aspects. The Commission or the judges identifying the antitrust infringement have the power and obligation to decide on dividing the fine between those held jointly and severally liable for it. Second, the Commission and judges' power to establish competition law liability may cover only the external aspect of joint and several liability. This is because only the external aspect plays a role in competition law enforcement. Finally, a middle ground is possible, as explained by AG Mengozzi. The external dimension is definitely within the powers of an entity establishing the violation of EU competition law, but the internal aspect is not wholly excluded, as it can be justified by the principle of legal certainty and the principle of penalty specificity. Let us look into these options in more detail.

2.2.2.1 Joint and Several Liability as an Autonomous Concept of EU Law

The General Courts' view that joint and several liability is an autonomous concept of EU law was provided without much explanation. Nonetheless, it seems that the General Court perceived it as a part of the system of enforcement of EU competition law 'like the concept of "undertaking"'.[255] A similar understanding is expressed in the literature. Tobias Bieber, Julia Körner, Juliane Kokott and Daniel Dittert explain that the reason is that the Commission uses joint and several liability as a part of its fining policy.[256] The two latter authors also add that the autonomous meaning of joint and several liability is necessary to ensure a 'common level playing field' among varied interpretations of joint and several liability in the EU Member States.[257]

This approach is correct to a certain extent. Joint and several liability is imposed by the European Commission under peculiar circumstances that can be explained by the principle of effectiveness of EU competition law. Joint and several liability also improves effective antitrust enforcement in the area of private law. All this, coupled with this special function of safeguarding effective competition may be a reason to claim that this type of liability is unique in the context of EU competition law.

However, this position becomes more questionable when we focus on the idea that joint and several liability has two facets and regulates both relations between (i) the creditors and the joint and several debtors and (ii) internally among the joint and several debtors. It is undisputable that joint and several liability is inherent to competition law when it comes to the first relationship. It facilitates competition law enforcement by the European Commission and victims of antitrust

[255] GCEU, *Siemens Österreich*, para. 155.

[256] Bieber, *Die gesamtschuldnerische Haftung*, 67–69, Körner, *Die Gesamtschuld im Kartellbußgeldrecht*, 30–37; Kokott and Dittert, 'Die Verantwortlichkeit von Muttergesellschaften', 681.

[257] Kokott and Dittert, 'Die Verantwortlichkeit von Muttergesellschaften', 681.

infringements. It is however more difficult to identify the specific way in which competition law is enforced when antitrust liability is allocated among individual infringers, and the General Court at least does not specify this. One could imagine a scenario in which a peculiar allocation of liability endangers enforcement of competition law, for instance, when a violator escapes antitrust liability. But does this mean that the Commission or a judge needs to decide upon contribution at the same time as a violation of EU competition law is found? This is a matter of proportionality, as it is definitely plausible to keep contribution claims beyond the mandate of competition law enforcers but impose appropriate safeguards on their exercise (e.g. one can prohibit granting total indemnity).

Another issue is that joint and several liability is adopted in EU competition law in its very classic civil law form. Contrary to what is claimed by Juliane Kokott and Daniel Dittert, the Study Group on the European Civil Code, Acquis Group and European Group on Tort Law agree that all EU Member States share the same core of joint and several liability. Namely, there is more than one debtor (i), each of the debtors can be called upon to satisfy the debt (ii) and the creditor is entitled to receive the debt only once (iii).[258] All these features are also present in EU competition law. In public enforcement, the Commission holds jointly and severally liable at least two companies (i), it has a freedom to enforce the fine against each of them (ii)[259] and it cannot enforce a higher amount than is established in its decision (iii).[260] In private enforcement, Article 11 of Directive 2014/104/EU states that undertakings that jointly committed antitrust law violation are jointly and severally liable '[i], with the effect that each of those undertakings is bound to compensate for the harm in full, and the injured party has the right to require full compensation from any of them [ii] until he has been fully compensated [iii].' These definitions are fully in line with the traditional civil law concept of joint and several liability, and there is no need for a specific EU term for joint and several liability.

Eventually, the Court of Justice of the European Union rejected the view that joint and several liability is an autonomous concept of EU law:[261] 'the General Court erred in law by finding . . . that the concept of joint and several liability for the payment of fines is an autonomous concept'.[262] This was mainly a policy decision. The Court of Justice of the European Union probably took the GCEU's proposal as too cautious and believed that there was no need to impose the task of dividing liability for fines on European Commission officials as this would deplete

[258] See III-4:102(1) and III-4:103(2) of the DCFR, Articles 9:101(1) and (2) of the PETL. Christian von Bar and Eric Eric (eds.), *DCFR*, paras. III-4:102(1) and III-4:103(2); European Group on Tort Law, *PETL*, Article 9:101(1) and (2).

[259] Opinion of Advocate General Stix-Hackl, *Aristrain*, para. 117. See also Bieber, *Die gesamtschuldnerische Haftung*, 69–71; Körner, *Die Gesamtschuld im Kartellbußgeldrecht*, 27, 175; Kellerbauer and Weber, 'Das Urteil Siemens VA Tech', 667.

[260] Körner, *Die Gesamtschuld im Kartellbußgeldrecht*, 27.

[261] GCEU, *Siemens Österreich*, para. 155; GCEU, *Areva*, para. 213.

[262] CJEU, *Siemens Österreich*, para. 67.

procedural efficiency reached by the very reliance on joint and several liability. Competition law enforcement is similarly protected but with less burden on the part of the Commission when national courts deal with the question of contribution 'in a manner consistent with EU law'.[263] The same is true for private enforcement, where dealing with internal allocation of liability between antitrust infringers could slow down the process of granting damages to victims of violations. It is thus advisable to enforce contribution subsequently to the litigation on damages.

2.2.2.2 Remedying the Extensive Application of Joint and Several Liability

Advocate General Mengozzi proposed a very orthodox understanding of joint and several liability as composed of an external and an internal dimension. The traditional understanding of joint and several liability nonetheless did not stop AG Mengozzi from conferring the power to allocate individual liabilities between those jointly and severally liable for antitrust fines to the European Commission. For Advocate General Mengozzi, this proposal would address some of the criticism expressed by the competition law community on the extensive application of joint and several liability in EU competition law.[264]

Advocate General Mengozzi's arguments are of particular importance for public enforcement and heavily criticised the Commission's fining policy. The objections are that the Commission breaches the principles of personal liability,[265] *nulla poena sine lege*,[266] *in dubio pro reo*,[267] and runs counter to the companies' right of defence,[268] legal certainty,[269] the rule of law,[270] and the narrow prerequisites of piercing the corporate veil[271] when relying on joint and several liability. The main idea behind these claims is that law as such is addressed to strictly defined legal

[263] Ibid.

[264] In this line, AG Mengozzi, *Siemens Österreich*; Bieber, *Die gesamtschuldnerische Haftung*, 104.

[265] Opper, *Die gesamtschuldnerische Bußgeldhaftung*, 114; Bieber, *Die gesamtschuldnerische Haftung*, 62–63; Heinichen, *Unternehmensbegriff und Haftungsnachfolge*, 136–137, 224; Braun and Manuel Kellerbauer, 'Das Konzept der gesamtschuldnerischen Verantwortlichkeit – Teil 2', 212–213; Brettel and Thomas, 'Unternehmensbußgeld', 53–54, 61–62; Bosch, 'Verantwortung der Konzernobergesellschaft', 372–375, 377–378.

[266] Opper, *Die gesamtschuldnerische Bußgeldhaftung*, 115–116; Körner, *Die Gesamtschuld im Kartellbußgeldrecht*, 140–156; Bieber, *Die gesamtschuldnerische Haftung*, 59–62; Heinichen, *Unternehmensbegriff und Haftungsnachfolge*, 103–104, 146, 262; Braun and Kellerbauer, 'Das Konzept der gesamtschuldnerischen Verantwortlichkeit – Teil 2', 212; Christoph von Laufenberg, *Kartellrechtliche Konzernhaftung*, 96–103.

[267] Opper, *Die gesamtschuldnerische Bußgeldhaftung*, 119; Heinichen, *Unternehmensbegriff und Haftungsnachfolge*, 105; von Laufenberg, *Kartellrechtliche Konzernhaftung*, 90–96.

[268] Körner, *Die Gesamtschuld im Kartellbußgeldrecht*, 157–204.

[269] Bieber, *Die gesamtschuldnerische Haftung*, 62–63.

[270] Heinichen, *Unternehmensbegriff und Haftungsnachfolge*, 262; Körner, *Die Gesamtschuld im Kartellbußgeldrecht*, 86–91.

[271] Vormizeele, 'Die EG-kartellrechtliche Haftungszurechnung', 1016–1017; von Laufenberg, *Kartellrechtliche Konzernhaftung*, 103–109.

entities. This includes companies but not the EU law concept of an undertaking. Even though much ink has been spent by the competition law community to express its concerns,[272] the EU Courts firmly maintain that joint and several liability is justified by EU competition law.[273] Advocate General saw in *Siemens Österreich* an opportunity to reconcile the usual views of the EU Courts with the postulates of practitioners and scholarship. By allowing the Commission to allocate antitrust liability between individual companies, the Commission would satisfy the principle of legal certainty or penalty specificity.[274]

The Court of Justice of the European Union decided not to follow the AG's proposal, which needs to be approved.[275] The analysis made in Section 2.1 has demonstrated that the functions of external and internal aspects of joint and several liability are different. While the external aspect serves effective competition law enforcement, the internal aspect fulfils other objectives, predominantly in the sphere of fairness. The external dimension of joint and several liability is covered by the Commission's mandate because it is connected to competition law enforcement. The internal dimension of joint and several liability is, however, not specific to competition law and is thus beyond its mandate.[276]

Recourse to other principles of law is insufficient to justify the Commission's activity in this sphere. This is due to the principles of proportionality and subsidiarity.[277] While the principles regarding penalty specificity and legal certainty can be realised by the Commission by setting individual fines, fairness and equality can be perfectly fulfilled at a national level. In fact, national courts are better placed than the Commission to divide liability between joint and several debtors. The conflict is between private parties and concerns a matter known to civil courts – the payment of the debt. The CJEU's decision to deny the Commission the competence to deal with the internal aspects of joint and several liability and give this competence to national courts is thus justified.

In the private enforcement context, AG Mengozzi's arguments are of limited relevance – national courtsare only starting to apply joint and several liability and there is no need to apply corrective measures, especially given the CJEU's judgment in *Sumal*, which limited the possibility of imposing liability on subsidiaries whose activity has no connection with the antitrust infringment (see Section 3.4.2.2). Notwithstanding, from the standpoint of antirust infringers, it is favourable to

[272] See notes 265–271.

[273] See Section 2.1.2.

[274] Krüger, *Kartellregress*, 177–178.

[275] For approving opinions, see Bodenstein, 'BGH in Sachen Calciumcarbid', 143–144. For disapproving opinions, see Leonardo, '*Siemens Österreich*, *Areva* and *Alstom*', 27; Thomas, 'Die Gesamtschuld', 685.

[276] See Section 2.2.1.3.

[277] For more on the principle of subsidiarity, see Craig, EU *Administrative Law*, 367; Paul P. Craig, 'Subsidiarity: A Political and Legal Analysis' (2012) 50 *Journal of Common Market Studies*, 1, 72 *et seq*.

establish their liability once and with respect to both their creditors and their co-conspirators. The problem is that, as stated above, any efficiency gained by antitrust infringers might be made at the cost of slowing down the process of granting compensation to those who sustained antitrust damages.

2.2.2.3 Internal Dimension of Joint and Several Liability within the Competence of National Courts

The Court of Justice of the European Union's final word was to strictly adhere to the division between the external and the internal dimensions of joint and several liability and the consequences it entails. It agreed with the GCEU and AG Mengozzi that the liability of antitrust violators vis-à-vis the European Commission is pivotal for the enforcement of EU competition law. However, it admitted that this is not the case for the settlement of debts between violators of EU competition law.[278] The judgment of the CJEU deserves approval insofar as it separates the role played by the internal and external aspects of internal liability. It is also consistent with the conclusions reached in the analysis made in Section 2.1.

2.2.3 *Requirements Stemming from EU Law*

Although it was modest about the competence of the European Commission in deciding about contribution claims, the CJEU did not leave out the effectiveness of EU competition law enforcement unprotected. It held that while 'it is for the national courts to determine those shares', this needs to be done 'in a manner *consistent with EU law*'.[279] More precisely, the CJEU identified three elements that must be observed by national courts in the name of the duty to cooperate under Article 4 of the Treaty on the European Union: the Commission's identification of entities that are jointly and severally liable; the Commission's determination of the maximum amount that may be claimed from each of the entities held jointly and severally liable; and the respect to the Commission's information concerning the infringement. These three requirements are all connected to the content of Commission's decisions on fines and will be interpreted precisely in Section 2.2.5 on the impact that the Commission's decisions have on contribution litigation. It suffices to state that the conditions specified by the CJEU are the safeguards considered as essential to guarantee the effectiveness of EU competition law.

In the same vein, national jurisdictions were chosen to deal with contribution claims in the context of private enforcement. Similarly, as in public enforcement, some limitations to the exercise of the right to contribution also appear in private enforcement. Directive 2014/104/EU states in Article 11(5) that

[278] CJEU, *Siemens Österreich*, paras. 59–60.
[279] Ibid., para. 62.

[t]he determination of that share as the relative responsibility of a given infringer, and the relevant criteria such as turnover, market share, or role in the cartel, is a matter for the applicable national law, while *respecting the principles of effectiveness and equivalence.*

The EU legislator decided to set up only core principles of the right to claim contribution and let Member States regulate the details of how such a right should be exercised.[280] Requiring compliance with the principles of effectiveness and equivalence is thus not surprising as this is a usual limit to the principle of procedural autonomy.[281] The aim of these principles is to safeguard the rights determined by EU law but applied within the framework of national laws.[282]

The principle of effectiveness means that national rules cannot make it impossible or excessively difficult to rely on rights derived from EU law.[283] This implies that while EU Member States have a large amount of freedom in designing contribution claims, these rules must be capable of being effectively exercised in antitrust law. Practically, this signifies that the conditions for granting contribution must be feasible to apply in an antitrust context.

The principle of equivalence means that claims derived from EU law cannot be treated as less favourable than comparable domestic law claims.[284] The freedom of Member States to design claims for antitrust damages is thus limited to giving at least the same enforcement of contribution claims in antitrust that already exists in national laws. This is a minimum condition, as the principle of effectiveness may require a more favourable treatment of contribution claims in EU competition law than exists in domestic law to be adopted.

2.2.4 *Do Contribution Claims Endanger the Effective Enforcement of EU Competition Law?*

The national competence to deal with the internal aspect of joint and several liability carries a risk of competition law being put in a secondary position to civil

280 On this way of law making, see CJEU, Case 33/76, *Rewe-Zentralfinanz eG and Rewe-Zentral AG v. Landwirtschaftskammer für das Saarland*, ECLI:EU:C:1976:188, para. 5; Katri Havu, 'EU Law in Member State Courts: 'Adequate Judicial Protection' and Effective Application – Ambiguities and Nonsequiturs in Guidance by the Court of Justice?' (2015) 8 *Contemporary Readings in Law and Social Justice*, 1, 159–161, 166–170.

281 See CJEU, Joined cases C-89/10 and C-96/10, *Q-Beef NV v. Belgische Staat and Frans Bosschaert v. Belgische Staat, Vleesgroothandel Georges Goossens en Zonen NV and Slachthuizen Goossens NV*, ECLI:EU:C:2011:555, para. 32.

282 Katri Havu, 'EU Law in Member State Courts', 159.

283 Ibid., 162–164. For the interpretation of these terms, see, for instance, CJEU, Case 199/82, *Amministrazione delle Finanze dello Stato v. SpA San Giorgio*, ECLI:EU:C:1983:318, paras. 12–14; CJEU, Case 68/79, *Hans Just I/S v. Danish Ministry for Fiscal Affairs*, ECLI:EU:C:1980:57, para. 18

284 Havu, 'EU Law in Member State Courts', 162. For the interpretation of these terms, see, for instance, CJEU, Case C-78/98, *Shirley Preston and Others v. Wolverhampton Healthcare NHS Trust and Others and Dorothy Fletcher and Others v. Midland Bank plc*, ECLI:EU:C:2000:247, paras. 49, 55–61; CJEU, Case C-326/96, *B.S. Levez v. T.H. Jennings (Harlow Pools) Ltd*, ECLI:EU:C:1998:577, para. 42.

law, which is usually the main domain of national courts. This risk has been certainly limited by the CJEU in *Siemens Österreich* by enlisting the elements that must be respected when allocating antitrust liability between individual infringers.[285] Unfortunately, neither the CJEU nor Directive 2014/104/EU deals with the most intriguing question – that is, whether national courts can grant an antitrust violator total indemnity from competition law liability without endangering the effective enforcement of EU competition law.

This is an important practical question, especially as the effectiveness of EU law is likely to be the main defence argument for those joint and several debtors that are requested to fully indemnify their co-conspirators. The argument that the effective enforcement of EU competition law is endangered may also be put forward throughout the process of claiming contribution, for instance, while deciding about the available causes of action, the criteria to divide antitrust liability or whether to enter into a liability sharing agreement. Hence, the impact of contribution claims on the effective enforcement of EU competition law is highly relevant.

2.2.4.1 What Is the 'Effectiveness of EU Competition Law'?

EFFECTIVENESS IN PUBLIC ENFORCEMENT It is difficult to define the principle of the effectiveness of EU competition law[286] as the CJEU has used it on multiple occasions with the aim of achieving various objectives.[287] In substantive terms, the effectiveness of EU competition law means ensuring that markets are competitive.[288] The CJEU recently went into this idea in some detail in *Otis*:

[285] CJEU, *Siemens Österreich*, para. 63.

[286] *Effectivness* is referred to as a principle of EU law or even a fundamental right according to Article 47 of the Charter of Fundamental Rights of the European Union, OJ C 326, 26.10.2012, pp. 391–407. See also Leczykiewicz, 'Private Party Liability in EU Law', 277.

[287] The principle of effectiveness is sometimes used as an *elimination rule*. It allows national provisions to be disregarded where they make the enforcement of EU rights *practically impossible* or *excessively difficult*. On other occasions, the principle of effectiveness is used to provide for a minimal content of remedies that ensure the protection of EU law. Yet in other cases, the principle of effectiveness allows for the creation of *hybrid EU remedies*. Such remedies combine elements of national law with changes required to ensure the effective protection of EU rights. On direct effect of EU law and supremacy of EU law, see Wulf Henning Roth, 'Effet utile im europäischen Kartellrecht' (2013) 3 *Wettbewerb in Recht und Praxis*, 257 *et seq*. On hybrid remedies, see Norbert Reich, 'Horizontal Liability in EC Law: Hybridization of Remedies for Compensation in Case of Breaches of EC Rights' (2007) 44 *Common Market Law Review*, 705 *et seq*. On minimal remedies, see Leczykiewicz, 'Private Party Liability in EU Law', 278.

[288] Regulation 1/2003 refers to the term *effectiveness* on multiple occasions: by defining the objectives of competition law enforcement (Recitals 1, 5, 34), the actors enforcing EU competition law (Recitals 6, 8), the remedies to the infringement (Recitals 12, 30) and the procedure governing competition law investigations (Recitals 19, 25, 26, 28). In many cases, the principle of effectiveness is an administrative paradigm that relates to efficiency in using resources to

> the law of Member States must, in particular, take into account the objective pursued by Article 101 TFEU, which strives to guarantee effective and undistorted competition in the internal market, and, accordingly, prices set on the basis of free competition.[289]

This can be achieved in the most efficient way by deterring undertakings from violating rules that secure the competitive market dynamic.[290] Should the breach already have occurred, the remedies shall restore and improve the breached market equilibrium.[291] These aims are realised by the remedies adopted by the Commission as a reaction to the breach of EU competition law and by the Commission's ability to detect infringements.[292]

One of the most frequently used antitrust remedies is financial fines.[293] It was proven in Section 2.1.1.1 that Regulation 1/2003 consequently realises the objective of providing for sufficiently high fines that are deterrent. The imposition of joint and several liability also contributes to the latter aim, as established in Section 2.1.2.1.[294]

While the effectiveness of EU competition law has a wider scope, for the purpose of assessing the impact of contribution claims on antitrust enforcement, it can be thus concluded that the effectiveness of EU competition law means ensuring deterrence in public enforcement.

EFFECTIVENESS IN PRIVATE ENFORCEMENT In a broad sense, the effectiveness in private enforcement means exactly the same as in public antitrust enforcement, as claims for antitrust damages generally strengthen the working of the EU rules on

exercise a societal impact on competition policy. What seems to be important in the case of contribution is the effectiveness of EU competition law as understood in Recitals 1, 5, 12, 30, 34.

289 CJEU, Case C-435/18, *Otis Gesellschaft m.b.H. and Others v. Land Oberösterreich and Others*, ECLI:EU:C:2019:1069 ('*Otis*'), para. 26.

290 See, for instance, Paolo Buccirossi, Lorenzo Ciari, Tomaso Duso, Giancarlo Spagnolo and Cristiana Vitale, 'Deterrence in Competition Law' (2009) 285 *GESY Discussion Paper*, 2 *et seq.*; Jan Broulík, 'Two Contexts for Economics in Competition Law. Deterrence Effects and Competitive Effects' (2018) 17 *TILEC Discussion Paper*, 2; OECD, 'Competition Policy: Promoting Efficiency and Sound Markets' (2012), available at https://oecd.org/cleangovbiz/toolkit/50037123.pdf, 12; United Nations Conferenceon Trade and Development, 'Appropriate Sanctions and Remedies, Sixth United Nations Conference to Review All Aspects of the Set of Multilaterally Agreed Equitable Principles and Rules for the Control of Restrictive Business Practices' (8–12 November 2010), TD/RBP/CONF.7/5, available at https://unctad.org/en/Docs/tdrbpconf7d5_en.pdf, para. 6.

291 OECD, 'Competition Policy', 12; United Nations Conference on Trade and Development, 'Appropriate Sanctions and Remedies', para. 6; Ioannis Lianos, 'The Principle of Effectiveness, Competition Law Remedies and the Limits of Adjudication' (2014) 6 *CLES Research Paper Series*, 10. In that sense also Körner, *Die Gesamtschuld im Kartellbußgeldrecht*, 224.

292 United Nations Conferenceon Trade and Development, 'Appropriate Sanctions and Remedies', para. 6; Lianos, 'The Principle of Effectiveness', 3.

293 United Nations Conferenceon Trade and Development, 'Appropriate Sanctions and Remedies', para. 8.

294 Joint and several liability, however, does not help the Commission to deprive infringers of unlawful profits. See Section 2.1.2.1.

competition.[295] More specifically, the principle of effectiveness can be explained in private enforcement as securing a *hybrid EU remedy* that allows for enforcing the rights derived from the Treaty.[296]

A right concerned is the right to claim compensation for damage resulting from the breach of competition law provisions of the Treaty. According to *Manfredi*, claims for antitrust damages encompass compensation covering the actual loss and loss of profits expressed in nominal terms.[297] This right is established by EU law, together with its constitutive conditions of liability, such as the determination of the persons liable for antitrust infringement or causation.[298] Directive 2014/104/EU develops the content of this claim with some other elements of substantive and procedural laws: the right of full compensation, joint and several liability of infringers, the ability to claim damages as an indirect purchaser, a limited right to discovery and specific limitation periods. The traditional claim for compensation as regulated by national tort laws, together with the modifications ensured by case law and Directive 2014/104/EU, constitutes the content of the claim for antitrust damages that adequately ensures the protection of EU law. Such a remedy is seen as *sufficient* to protect the rights derived under EU law.

The rules on joint and several liability are a part of this remedy. Article 11(1) of Directive 2014/104/EU contains provisions that impose joint and several liability and guarantee its external effects. The CJEU also made it clear in *Skanska* and *Sumal* that 'the determination of entity which is required to provide compensation for damage caused by an infringement of Article 101 TFEU is directly governed by EU law'.[299] Consequently, joint and several liability in its external dimension is a part of the claim for antitrust damages. This means that it is a part of the hybrid remedy, which according to EU law meets its effectiveness standards.

Article 11(5) of Directive 2014/104/EU also provides rules on the internal aspect of joint and several liability. It provides a right to claim contribution regarding antitrust liabilities subjected to the Directive. It constitutes, however, another right whose execution needs to be confronted with the principle of effectiveness of EU law.

2.2.4.2 Analysis of Situations in Which the Effectiveness of EU Competition Law Can Be Endangered

The effectiveness in private enforcement means providing for a remedy that allows private parties to seek compensation before national courts. In public enforcement,

[295] In this line, CJEU, *Skanska*, para. 44; CJEU, *Otis*, para. 26.
[296] The analysis is made on the basis of the theory developed by Wulf Henning Roth. See Roth, 'Effet utile', 261–262.
[297] CJEU, *Manfredi*, para. 95.
[298] AG Wahl, *Skanska*, para. 66; which was confirmed by the CJEU, *Skanska*, paras. 28–35. For more on this topic, see Wamel, "Shining a Light on the Interface between EU and National Law'.
[299] CJEU, *Sumal*, para. 34; CJEU, *Skanska*, para. 28.

the effectiveness is linked with the need to ensure deterrence. The question remains whether claims for contribution are capable of impeding these aims.

PUBLIC ENFORCEMENT It intuitively seems that claims for contribution may have an effect on the way the Commission enforces competition law. Let us return to the scenario of the indemnity that was mentioned above. It may happen that judges will grant one company a full reimbursement for the sum paid as a part of the fine, which will mean that the company is entirely released from the liability initially imposed by the Commission. The judgment granting indemnity may be thus considered as impeding the Commission's understanding of how to guarantee the effective enforcement of EU competition law.[300]

To verify this hypothesis, let us take a more granular look and analyse whether the effectiveness as defined in Section 2.2.4.1 is at risk in any of the situations in which the Commission imposes joint and several liability: the notion of undertaking, the doctrine of single economic entity and the doctrine of economic continuity.

Undertaking and Single Economic Entity As established in Section 2.1.2.1, joint and several liability is used as a result of applying the concept of undertaking and the closely related concept of the single economic entity. Companies that form one undertaking in the meaning of EU law are assumed to lack individual decision-making power, while others exercise a decisive influence over them.

In such a situation, claims for contribution are unlikely to endanger the principle of effectiveness of EU competition law. If the starting point of the Commission's reasoning is the fact that some companies are not independent enough to make their own market decisions, the objectives of competition law enforcement policy cannot be effectively addressed to them. Individual deterrence is effective if it is directed towards companies that cannot decide their own business strategy.[301] As a result, the individual deterrence must be directed at the single economic entity in order to encompass companies that have the real decisional power. A subsequent apportionment of liability among companies does not endanger the effectiveness of EU fining policy as long as the payment comes from within the single economic entity.

One may try to rebut this by claiming that some companies assumed by the Commission to be part of one undertaking are in fact independent. The Commission applies the concept of undertaking widely and often following the presumption of exercising a decisive influence and not its factual exercise. When a company that is in fact independent escapes antitrust liability following its claim for contribution, the Commission's fine would fail to achieve a deterrent effect. This criticism is justified, and if the situation described above materialises, it is an example of ineffective competition law enforcement.

[300] See note 290.

[301] Similar conclusion in Bosch, 'Kartellrechtswidriges Handeln der Tochtergesellschaft', 375.

Nevertheless, from the dogmatic standpoint, it cannot be argued that it is the right to claim contribution that jeopardises the effectiveness of EU competition law. First and foremost, by imposing joint and several liability, the Commission cannot guarantee that every entity fined will pay at least some proportion of the fine. It may happen that one of the companies fined by the Commission decides to voluntarily make a payment to the Commission in the amount corresponding to the entire fine.[302] In this moment, the Commission's debt is extinguished, and it cannot address another company for the payment by claiming that if it does not contribute to the payment, individual deterrence would not be achieved. In order to achieve individual deterrence, the Commission should fine the companies individually. Second, the Commission uses joint and several liability having presumed the lack of independence of some companies. If such a presumption does not hold true, the Commission is not entitled to consider that the companies form one undertaking and should fine each of them individually. This would ensure that individual deterrence is reached and would exclude any impact that contribution claims may have on the effective enforcement of EU competition law. Consequently, the criticism must be made against the extensive application of the concept of undertaking and not against contribution claims.

With respect to general deterrence, contribution claims also have little effect. General deterrence takes place in the moment of fining companies jointly and severally since it is the moment when the Commission sends a message to society that violations of competition law are fined. Whether there is a contribution between companies or not does not change the message that has been already delivered by the Commission in the fining decision.

Economic Continuity As demonstrated in Section 2.1.2.1, joint and several liability is also used as a result of the economic continuity doctrine. It is used to hold acquirers of a business that infringed EU competition law liable for the fines together with the seller of the business. In this scenario, joint and several liability bundles different undertakings in order to ensure that the fine is paid by at least one of them.

In the case of economic continuity doctrine, it can be claimed that contribution claims have an impact on who finally bears the liability. If a company is released from the liability, this may be read as interfering with the Commission's understanding of the effectiveness of EU competition law.

This reasoning is misguided. As indicated in Section 2.1.2.1, joint and several liability is not able to guarantee individual deterrence but merely increases the chances that the Commission receives the payment for the fine from any of the companies fined as jointly and severally liable.

302 Opinion of Advocate General Stix-Hackl, *Aristrain*, para. 117.

In addition, the principle of individual deterrence is difficult to satisfy from the outset in situations in which the economic continuity doctrine applies. The company that acquired the business is liable for actions on which it had no influence. It is thus difficult to see the principle of individual deterrence directed at it, as such a principle should prevent unlawful conduct from being entered into *again*. In contrast, the company that sold the assets no longer has the power to influence the behaviour of the business that is no longer under its control and thus it also cannot prevent the infringement from being committed *again*.[303] The principle of individual deterrence can apply in this case only insofar as the company owns other businesses apart from the one it sold. This was expressed, for instance, by Mario Siragusa, representing Pirelli in the appeal from the Commission's decision in the cable cartel: 'It is not at all a dissuasive situation. Eighteen years ago Pirelli left the market – it's on Prysmian [the purchaser of cable business] you have to impose the dissuasive effect.'[304]

Regarding general deterrence, contribution claims cannot impact it as such claims are enforced after the Commission has sent a message that violations of competition law are fined. In addition, it is doubtful that the Commission sends the right message by fining companies who physically could not have any impact on the decision to engage or not in anticompetitive practices.

Overall, the case-by-case analysis of the impact that contribution claims may have on effective antitrust enforcement reveals that this influence is very limited. There is no impact on general deterrence, as contribution claims take place subsequently to the adoption of public decisions. Regarding individual deterrence, contribution claims may have an impact on it only in two cases: when the Commission wrongly assumes that companies constitute an undertaking and in the case of the economic continuity doctrine if the seller of a business infringing competition law is still commercially active.

The impact that contribution claims have on effective antitrust enforcement seems, however, irrelevant in light of the finding that the Commission cannot achieve any deterrence directed at specific companies when holding them jointly and severally liable with other companies. Most fundamentally, companies held jointly and severally liable for the fine have the freedom to decide who voluntarily pays it before the Commission starts its enforcement proceeding. The Commission thus cannot require that every company contribute to the payment of the fine. As a result, the criticism that contribution claims endanger individual deterrence shall be reformulated into the criticism on the wrongful imposition of joint and several liability.

303 Heinichen, *Unternehmensbegriff und Haftungsnachfolge*, 225.

304 Michael Acton, 'Pirelli Challenges Cable Cartel Liability at EU's Top Court' (6 November 2019) *Mlex*, available at https://mlex.com/GlobalAdvisory/DetailView.aspx?cid=1140994&siteid=244&rdir=1

PRIVATE ENFORCEMENT The impact of contribution claims on the effective enforcement of EU competition law is also limited in the context of private enforcement.

The content of the right for compensation of the antitrust damage includes the external aspect of joint and several liability. Those damaged by competition law violations have the right to choose the entity from which they will claim compensation and the right to revert to other debtors until the damage is fully compensated.[305] This supports the effective enforcement of private claims for antitrust damages.

Contribution claims do not have any impact in this regard. This is due to the simple fact that contribution claims are principally exercised after the claim for antitrust damages is already enforced.[306] As a result, they cannot deteriorate the legal position of the antitrust victim, deprive it of the right to choose the entity to address or influence the amount of compensation. The objectives sought by joint and several liability in its external aspect are satisfied the moment that compensation is paid. The antitrust victim has already enjoyed the convenience brought by joint and several liability. It has been compensated for the damage and has been restored to the position in which it was before the infringement took place. The problem of internal allocation of liability is thus of 'no further interest' from the standpoint of the need to protect the EU rights and the need to enforce competition law.[307] As a consequence, contribution claims are not capable of interfering with the effectiveness of private competition law enforcement.

Contribution claims may, however, impact the enforcement of competition law in rare cases when it is possible to claim contribution before the creditor has been satisfied. This is the case of German claims for *Mitwirkung* and *Befreiung* and English *quia timet* injunctions.[308] If debtors are allowed to claim contribution from each other in the same time as the creditor enforces its payment, this jeopardises the effects brought by joint and several liability. The criticism towards contribution claims enforced prior to the creditor's satisfaction is, however, general to tort law. In all cases in which it is allowed, such contribution is made at the expense of the creditor. As a result, *Mitwirkung* and *Befreiung* claims and *quia timet* injunctions are already very controversial in the discussed legal orders.[309] Given that such claims are a rare phenomenon, it is advised to reject a possibility to claim contribution before the creditor is satisfied in the context of EU competition law. In this way, the interference between contribution claims and effectiveness of EU competition law would be eliminated in its entirety (see further in Section 3.3.2.2).

305 See Section 2.1.3.2.
306 See Section 3.3.1.2.
307 For a similar conclusion, see Körner, *Die Gesamtschuld im Kartellbußgeldrecht*, 225.
308 See Section 3.3.1.2.
309 See Section 3.3.2.2.

2.2.4.3 Siemens Österreich Judgment

The impact of contribution claims on the effective enforcement of EU competition law can be demonstrated by referring to the external and internal aspects of joint and several liability, as suggested by the *Siemens Österreich* judgment.

Joint and several liability is granted to guarantee the better legal standing of the creditor. This improves the effective enforcement of EU competition law.

In contrast, the internal aspect of joint and several liability, which has as a subject the relationship between the debtors, has little effect on the enforcement of EU competition law. The analysis undertaken above proves that such an effect exists in cases when either the imposition of joint and several liability is incorrect or contribution claims are allowed to run in parallel to claims for antitrust damages. This interference can be fully eliminated by correcting the way joint and several liability is imposed and establishing that contribution can be claimed only after the creditor is satisfied. As put by the CJEU,

> the objective of *joint and several liability* resides in the fact that it constitutes an additional legal device available to the Commission to *strengthen the effectiveness* of the action taken by it for the recovery of fines imposed for infringement of the competition rules, since that mechanism reduces for the Commission, as creditor of the debt represented by such fines, the risk of insolvency, which is part of the objective of *deterrence* pursued generally by competition law …
>
> The determination, in the context of the *internal relationship* of those held jointly and severally liable for payment of a fine, of the shares each of them is required to pay *does not pursue that dual objective*. That is a contentious issue, to be resolved at a later stage, and, in principle, *the Commission no longer has any interest in the matter*, where the fine has been paid in full by one or more of those held liable.[310]

The analysis undertaken above proves that this statement is correct and the negative effect of contribution on competition law enforcement exists only in cases when either the imposition of joint and several liability is incorrect or contribution claims are allowed to run in parallel to claims for antitrust damages. The argument that the effectiveness of EU competition law is endangered could therefore play a role in litigation that involves such aspects, meaning *quia timet* injunctions, *Mitwirkung* claims or the instances when the Commission applies the notion of joint and several liability too extensively.

Disputes about the effective enforcement of EU competition law can be, however, entirely avoided. The interference between joint and several liability and EU competition law appears only in extraordinary circumstances when either joint and several liability or the right to contribution are already stretched to their extremes. As regards joint and several liability, this interference can be fully eliminated by

[310] CJEU, *Siemens Österreich*, paras. 59–60.

ensuring that the very imposition of joint and several liability is in line with the principle of effective competition law enforcement. For instance, by fining an acquirer and a seller of a business infringing competition law individually, one avoids the risk that any of the companies will escape liability. As regards *quia timet* injunctions and *Mitwirkung* claims, one should reconsider whether they should be available in the context of EU competition law. As will be explained in more detail in Chapter 3, these claims are already controversial in traditional tort laws. The effectiveness of EU competition law does provide one more argument against their use. As the clash between joint and several liability and EU competition law is not inherent, perhaps it is better to make a call to law makers, judges and competition law enforcers to reduce the identified interference from the outset.

Due to the limited effect that contribution claims have on competition law, it is not necessary to consider arguments related to competition law enforcement at the stage of contribution litigation. The principle of effective enforcement of EU competition law is satisfied and extinguished the moment the antitrust debt is paid. Consequently, any ideas to link the internal apportionment of antitrust liability with the aims of ensuring compensation, restitution, deterrence or prevention are misguided.[311]

2.2.4.4 The Calcium Carbide Judgment

From this standpoint, it is interesting to observe that the argument about the effectiveness of EU competition law still finds its place in contribution litigation. German regional courts in *Calcium carbide* adopted a very favourable approach to EU competition law and maintained its extensive protection even following the CJEU's judgment in *Siemens Österreich*.[312] The facts of this case have already been mentioned in Section 2.3.1.1, and the case considered Arques' contribution claim for the payment of the antitrust fine imposed on several companies constituting one undertaking in the meaning of EU law.[313]

The LG München took the role of protecting the enforcement of EU competition law and declined Arques' claim for contribution for three reasons.[314] First, it argued that contribution would counter the Commission's decision to impose joint and several liability.[315] Second, it could put the single economic entity doctrine into question as ultimately only some companies would be liable for the infringement.[316]

[311] A contrary view is represented by the BGH in the *Calcium carbide* case. See also Opper, *Die gesamtschuldnerische Bußgeldhaftung*, 193; Weinhold, *Der Gesamtschuldnerausgleich*, 172; Thomas, 'Die Gesamtschuld', 684–686; Köhler, 'EU-Kartellgeldbußen', 281–284.

[312] See Section 2.2.4.4.

[313] Ibid.

[314] LG München, BeckRS 2013, 10095, Section II(1)(a).

[315] Ibid., Section II(1)(a)(aa).

[316] Ibid.

Third, the Commission's intent to achieve repression and prevention could be disrupted by contribution claims.[317]

The OLG München also dismissed Arques' claims, however, due to different reasons.[318] The OLG München's starting point was that Arques had a right to claim contribution under § 426(1)(1) of the BGB.[319] The application of the single economic entity doctrine impeded, however, the use of regular criteria for dividing the liability, in particular fault and causation under § 254 of the BGB.[320] According to the OLG München, the relevant criteria for apportioning liability were illicit gains.[321] As the value of the mother company's shares increased due to the infringement, the mother company achieved illicit gains and could not claim contribution.[322]

The BGH took a slightly different stance but eventually also emphasised the need to protect the effectiveness of EU competition law.[323] It relied to a large extent on the *Siemens Österreich* judgment and the division between the external and internal aspects of joint and several liability.[324] This led it to consider contribution claims from a traditional standpoint and discuss the usual criteria for distributing liability, fault and causation.[325] However, the BGH eventually decided to resolve the dispute in an innovative way. When deciding about relative shares of liability, it relied on factors that are decisive for the determination of the Commission's fine, such as turnover,[326] market shares[327] and illicit gains.[328] The BGH claimed that by using these criteria it would align contribution claims with the principle of effective enforcement of EU competition law and deterrence.[329]

The *Calcium carbide* case is a good example of the confusion concerning contribution claims in EU competition law that unfortunately prevails after *Siemens Österreich*. Three German courts understood the impact of the public law nature of EU competition law differently. The LG München took a view that contribution claims could not be exercised at all as this would interfere with the Commission's imposition of joint and several liability. This view cannot be accepted following *Siemens Österreich* and the CJEU's decision to confer the power to deal with such claims to national courts. The OLG München found the allocation of liability possible, although in this particular case it dismissed the claim. The judges

[317] Ibid.
[318] OLG München, BeckRS 2012, 8896, Section II(2).
[319] Ibid., Section II(2)(a)(2).
[320] Ibid., Section II(2)(a)(1)(BBB).
[321] Ibid., Section II(2)(a)(2).
[322] Ibid., Section II(2)(a)(2)(bb).
[323] BGH, BeckRS 2015, 00033, Tenor.
[324] Ibid., paras. 15, 24.
[325] Ibid., para. 32.
[326] Ibid., para. 71.
[327] Ibid., para. 74.
[328] Ibid., para. 84.
[329] Ibid., paras. 55, 63–64.

were not confused by the public nature of EU competition law, but they were also far from consciously observing the division between the external and internal aspects of joint and several liability.

The position of BGH is a step forward. It is appreciable that the BGH recognised the CJEU's division of the internal and external aspects of joint and several liability. Nonetheless, the BGH did not apply this division further on. Principles of effectiveness and deterrence were both held to be decisive when deciding on relative liabilities of joint and several debtors. This is incoherent with the recognised division. These principles play a role in the external aspect of joint and several liability but not the internal one. As demonstrated in Section 2.2.4.2, these principles are realised the moment the fines are paid. As such, they cannot be influenced by subsequent disputes between debtors regarding how to spread the payments internally. While there is nothing wrong in relying on competition law-specific criteria when dividing antitrust liability, this is not because contribution claims need to enforce competition law, but because such criteria best reflect the context of the dispute and are capable of creating equality among co-infringers of EU competition law.

In sum, the *Calcium carbide* case demonstrates how much confusion joint and several liability causes in EU competition law. In light of this, the CJEU's judgment in *Siemens Österreich* is a welcomed development. The CJEU established clearly that the external and internal aspects of joint and several liability are separate matters which have different functions and take different places in the system of competition law enforcement. While the external aspect of joint and several liability is closely connected with such enforcement, this is not the case of the internal aspect. This leads to the conclusion that public law-related objectives apply only to the external aspect of joint and several liability and contribution claims have little impact on the enforcement of EU competition law.

2.2.5 *What Requirements Sets EU Competition Law for Contribution Claims?*

The analysis of the intersection between contribution claims and the enforcement of EU competition law is two-dimensional. So far we have analysed the impact of contribution claims on competition law enforcement and demonstrated the need to refrain from focusing on ensuring the effectiveness of competition law enforcement. This section reverses the question and asks what impact EU competition law has on contribution claims, which is necessary to understand the requirements that EU competition law sets on contribution litigation. The following paragraphs examine the impact of establishing competition law liability by means of the Commission's decision and by means of courts' judgments.

Section 2.3.4 above has indicated that national judges dealing with contribution claims in the context of public antitrust enforcement must respect the Commission's decisions. The CJEU has identified three elements that must be observed: (i) the catalogue of those held jointly and severally liable, (ii) the determination of the maximum amount of what may be claimed from each of the entities held jointly and severally liable and (iii) the information contained in the Commission's decisions.[330]

These requirements are analysed in the paragraphs below. The analysis takes a broader view and also encompasses private antitrust enforcement, as the Commission's decision may have an impact not only on contribution claims following the liability stemming from antitrust fines but also on the liability established in follow-on private actions.

2.2.5.1 Catalogue of Entities Held Jointly and Severally Liable

In *Siemens Österreich*, the CJEU held that contribution claims must be compliant with EU law. This requires them to respect the Commission's identification of those jointly and severally liable for antitrust fines, as expressed by the very same judgment:

> In that context, the duty to cooperate in good faith ... applies in actions for indemnity ... [T]he Commission's decision establishing joint and several liability for payment of a fine, in that it ... identifies the entities held so liable ... lays down the legal framework within which a ruling must be given on those actions.[331]

The consequence of this is that contribution claims with respect to the liability for fines may be brought only against those who have been previously held liable by the Commission.

This limitation does not arise with respect to the liabilities for damages established by national courts. Directive 2014/104/EU is silent about the entities from which contribution should not be requested. The recent *Skanska* judgment, which discusses the application of joint and several liability in private enforcement, also does not impose such a limitation (see Section 2.1.2.3).[332] Finally, Advocate General Pitruzzella in *Sumal* expressively allows the claimants to establish private law liability for competition law infringements with respect to entities other than those named in the Commission's decisions.[333] While AG Pitruzzella's opinion relates to claims for damages, the same should hold true in contribution litigation.

CONTRIBUTION CLAIMS IN PUBLIC ENFORCEMENT Theoretically, it would be possible to bring forward a contribution claim against companies that avoided liability in the Commission's infringement decision, but according to the claimant

330 CJEU, *Siemens Österreich*, para. 63.
331 Ibid.
332 CJEU, *Skanska*, para. 47.
333 CJEU, *Sumal*, paras 55–66; AG Pitruzzella, *Sumal*, paras. 70–77.

were also involved in the antitrust infringement. The CJEU in *Sumal* seems to endorse such a possibility. It finds that the Commission's decisions are only conclusive with respect to the entities that were held liable for competition law infringements. In particular, the judgment states that when the Commission identifies infringers of EU competition law, it does not either explicitly or implicitly find that other companies are non-liable. As a result national courts may establish that a legal person not concerned by the Commission's decision violated EU competition law – alongside those named in the Commission's decision – without violating Article 16 (1) of Regulation 1/2003. This is especially relevant for follow-on claims.[334]

However, *Siemens Österreich* definitely excludes the possibility of attributing liability of other companies than those fined by the Commission in the context of contribution claims. It clearly states that contribution claims must respect 'the entities held [jointly and severally] liable' in the Commission's decision.[335] This is because of *Siemens Österreich*'s consideration that joint and several liability and deterrence is determined in the Commission's decisions.

For *Siemens Österreich*, joint and several liability is applied constitutively by the European Commission, meaning that its application stems from the Commission's decision rather than substantive law. The Court of Justice of the European Union reserves the power to decide which entities are held jointly and severally liable to the European Commission, so as national courts must respect the Commission's decision. National courts that deal with the question of contribution cannot therefore go beyond the Commission's decision and establish that companies not named so far in an infringement decision are also liable for the infringement in question and need to pay contribution to their conspirators.

This position can be perfectly justified by the procedural framework for competition law enforcement. First and foremost, whilst Article 101 of TFEU is the legal basis for the assessment of whether there has been the infringement of competition law or not, the concrete consequences of an infringement, such as fines, are imposed on the basis of Article 23(b) of Regulation 1/2003. According to this provision, the Commission may impose fines, but it does not need to do so. It can equally well establish a violation of EU competition law without imposing fines or adopt a commitment decision. Fines are therefore not an automatic consequence of an infringement. It is the Commission's call whether to impose them or not, and it is up to the Commission to decide how they should be determined. The Commission has leeway when deciding on which specific entities to impose the decision on and whether to fine companies individually or jointly and severally.[336] As AG Pitruzzella illustrates, the Commission exercises discretion in choosing the addressees of its decision for reasons linked to procedural expediency or the evidentiary basis

[334] Ibid.
[335] CJEU, *Siemens Österreich*, para. 63.
[336] See Section 2.1.1.1. In this line, also AG Pitruzzella, *Sumal*, paras 70–76.

available.[337] Decisions also reflect the Commission's idea about deterrence and effective competition law enforcement. They cannot be revisited once contribution is decided on.[338] This is especially important for contribution claims that could potentially reduce the size and the liability for fines. By contrast, these considerations do not come into play in the context of the liability established in follow-on claims for damages. Rather than modifying the Commission's fines, they add private law liability alongside.

Consequently, the Commission's determination of those held jointly and severally liable for fines needs to be respected in contribution litigation. This means that one cannot claim contribution from companies other than those that have been designated by the Commission.

CONTRIBUTION CLAIMS IN PRIVATE ENFORCEMENT The liability for antitrust damages is established by national courts, and neither Directive 2014/104/EU nor the CJEU has expressed the need for limiting the catalogue of entities from which contribution can be claimed.

Article 11(1) of Directive 2014/104/EU stipulates that infringers of EU competition law are jointly and severally liable for the harm caused. On this basis, national judges who deal with a claim for contribution can establish that the defendant infringed EU competition law and is jointly and severally liable with the claimant. The judges' power to decide about the liability of antitrust infringers has also been confirmed in the recent *Skanska* and *Sumal* judgments. In both cases, the CJEU expressively allows national courts to establish liability for infringements of EU competition law; it allows them to apply the notion of the economic continuity and the notion of undertaking, thus presumably also joint and several liability.[339] Pitruzzella[340] These cases confirm the ability of national judges to establish the liability of antitrust infringers with the aim of deciding about contribution claims. This applies to the joint and several liability applicable between separate undertakings pursuant to Article 11(1) of Directive 2014/104/EU and to the one applicable between companies forming a single undertaking. For instance, if Deutsche Telekom AG can be called to pay compensation for anticompetitive practices undertaken by its subsidiary, Slovak Telekom s.r.o. Telekom AG can also establish the liability of Slovak Telekom s.r.o. in an action for contribution.

It is also completely natural to establish the liability of some competition law infringers in contribution litigation. Contrary to the Commission's decisions that have the ambition to holistically assess a competition law infringement, findings reached in private lawsuits are by their nature limited to the claims brought forward

337 AG Pitruzzella, *Sumal*, para. 73.

338 Similarly, Julia Körner, *Die Gesamtschuld im Kartellbußgeldrecht*, 92–104.

339 CJEU, *Skanska*, paras. 47 and 51; CJEU, *Sumal*, para. 67

340 Pitruzzella

and the parties involved in the litigation. The ideal scenario is of course when victims of antitrust infringements sue all competition law infringers, allowing judges to divide antitrust liability directly after deciding on compensation. It is, however, much more frequent that claims for antitrust damages are selectively addressed. It is therefore completely normal that there are antitrust infringers whose tort and liability has not been established. In this situation, an infringer whose liability has been established by courts may wish to call upon the entities that it thinks are co-liable for the misconduct to share the burden of liability that was established against it.

The interesting question is whether the same conclusions apply to follow-on claims for damages. In follow-on actions, the claimants do not prove the liability of the alleged competition violators but rely on the Commission's decision in this aspect.[341] As a consequence, one could consider the application of *Siemens Österreich* in order to determine whether those liable for antitrust damages can claim contribution from the co-infringers not named in the Commission's decision. This would result in imposing a limitation on the catalogue of addresses of contribution claims in this setting. This should, however, not be the case. First, as the CJEU in *Sumal* rightly pointed out that the Commission's decisions identifying competition law violations are only conclusive with respect to the entities held liable. It is possible to establish liability for competition law infringements in private lawsuits.[342] Second, the Court of Justice of the European Union's reasoning in *Siemens Österreich* is underpinned by considerations about the Commission's role in effective and deterrent enforcement of competition law.[343] The liability for damages established in follow-on actions for damages is still the liability for damages; the follow-on character of a dispute decides solely on evidence needed to establish the infringement.[344] In contrast to fines, liability for damages is not determined on the basis of deterrence but based on the damage inflicted on victims of antitrust infringements.[345] While private antitrust enforcement still has some deterrence function, this is considered mainly from the standpoint of increased detection. Directive 2014/104/EU prohibits granting any damages that exceed the damage actually sustained by those harmed by anticompetitive practices.[346] As the size of damages is not determined by deterrence considerations, there is no need to protect it in contribution litigation.

341 See Article 9 of Directive 2014/104/EU.

342 CJEU, *Sumal*, paras 55–63; see also AG Pitruzzella, *Sumal*, para. 73.

343 CJEU, *Siemens Österreich*, para. 59.

344 For more on the binding force of Commission's decisions in follow-on actions, see Miguel Sousa Ferro, 'Antitrust Private Enforcement and the Binding Effect of Public Enforcement Decisions' (2019) 2 *Market and Competition Law Review*, 3, 51.

345 See Article 3 of Directive 2014/104/EU.

346 See Article 3(3) of Directive 2014/104/EU.

Overall, European Union competition law does not pose any obstacle to grant contribution with respect to liabilities established in private actions for antitrust damages.

2.2.5.2 Determination of the Maximum Amount of What May Be Claimed from Each of Those Jointly and Severally Liable

In *Siemens Österreich*, the CJEU held that contribution claims must respect the Commission's determination of the maximum amount of what may be claimed from each infringer:

> In that context, the duty to cooperate in good faith ... applies in actions for indemnity before the national courts and tribunals ... [T]he Commission's decision establishing joint and several liability for payment of a fine ... determines the maximum amount that may be claimed from each of those entities by the Commission.[347]

There are two scenarios in which this statement may apply: when the Commission bundles joint and several liability with individual liability and when the Commission uses the 10 per cent turnover cap.

Bundling Joint and Several Liability with Individual Liability The scenario that the CJEU probably had in mind in *Siemens Österreich* was the phrase frequently used by the Commission in establishing liability. One example comes from the *International Removal Services* decision:

> For the infringement ... the following fines are imposed: ... EUR 4 500 000 on Gosselin Group NV, of which Stichting Administratiekantoor Portielje is held jointly and severally responsible for the amount of EUR 370 000.[348]

Arguably the CJEU made national courts cautious not to revisit the maximal amounts of liability for which each company is held liable.[349] Such a statement is, however, unnecessary. National judges cannot revisit the liability amounts established by the Commission in contribution litigation. By imposing liability in the same way as in *International Removal Services*, the Commission bundles two types of liability: joint and several liability imposed on several addressees and individual liability imposed on one addressee. Taking the *International Removal Services* decision as an example, it is clear that Stichting Administratiekantoor Portielje

[347] CJEU, *Siemens Österreich*, para. 63.

[348] Article I(e) of Commission decision of 11 March 2008 in Case COMP/38.543 – *International removal services*, C (2008) 926 final. For such a way of imposing liability, see also Article 2(a), (f) and (i) of the decision referred above or Article I(a), (c), (d), (e) of Commission decision of 28 January 2009 in Case COMP/39.406 – *Marine Hoses*, not published yet.

[349] CJEU, *Siemens Österreich*, para. 63.

and Gosselin Group NV are jointly and severally liable for EUR 370 000 and Gosselin Group NV is individually liable for EUR 4 130 000 (EUR 4 500 000–EUR 370 000). Per contribution claims, the courts deal only with joint and several liability (EUR 370 000) and not with individual liability (EUR 4 130 000). There is therefore no risk that the smaller amount of liability that is joint and several would be anyhow modified by referring to a higher amount including one company's individual liability. These are two different liabilities, and only one of them is subject to the contribution litigation.

Applying the 10 per cent Turnover Cap The CJEU's statement on respecting the Commission's determination of the maximum amounts parties can seek in contribution claims may also refer to the application of the 10 per cent *turnover cap*.

Article 23(2) of Regulation 1/2003 lays down the following:

> For each undertaking and association of undertakings participating in the infringement, the fine shall not exceed 10% of its total turnover in the preceding business year.

The turnover cap is applied because the Commission wishes for companies to continue to exist following the payment of antitrust fines.[350] With this in mind the CJEU stated that the 10 per cent turnover cap should principally apply to separate addressees of the Commission decision.[351] The Commission should specify the maximum amount for which companies are liable if the companies no longer belong to the infringing undertaking[352] or were held liable under the economic continuity doctrine. Such an assessment took place in *Lundbeck*.[353] The

[350] Case T-54/06, *Kendrion NV v. European Commission*, ECLI:EU:T:2011:667 ('*Kendrion*'), para. 91.

[351] Ibid., para. 92. Only if an undertaking that breaches competition law still exists in the moment of adopting the decision, the Commission may calculate the 10 per cent cap collectively with respect to all addresses that form such an undertaking, see Ibid., para. 92; GCEU, Joined cases T-71/03, T-74/03, T-87/03 and T-91/03, *Tokai Carbon Co. Ltd, Intech EDM BV, Intech EDM AG and SGL Carbon AG v. Commission of the European Communities* ECLI:EU:T:2005:220, para. 390; GCEU, Case T-377/06, *Comap SA v. European Commission* ECLI:EU:T:2011:108, para. 111; Case T-385/06, *Aalberts Industries NV and Others v. European Commission* ECLI:EU:T:2011:114, para. 125; GCEU, *Kendrion*, para. 92. However, see also Case T-191/06, *FMC Foret, SA v. European Commission*, ECLI:EU:T:2011:277, para. 324, in which the CJEU introduces another balance and states that when the undertaking exists in unchanged form in the moment of adopting the decision, the Commission *must* apply 10 per cent turnover limit collectively. See also Bieber, *Die gesamtschuldnerische Haftung*, 44; Opper, *Die gesamtschuldnerische Bußgeldhaftung*, 213–214; Martin Buntscheck, 'Die gesetzliche Kappungsgrenze für Kartellgeldbußen. Bedeutung und Auslegung im Lichte der neuen Bußgeld-Leitlinien von Kommission und Bundeskartellamt' (2007) *Europäische Zeitschrift für Wirtschaftsrecht*, 423–426; Koch, 'Sanktionsdurchgriff im Unternehmensverbund', 558–559; Lukas Aberle, Sanktionsdurchgriff, 92; Hans-Peter Roth, 'Für 10% Gesamtumsatzgrenze einer Geldbuße ist jeweilige Konzernzugehörigkeit maßgeblich' (2014) *Gesellschafts- und Wirtschaftsrecht*, 439.

[352] Ibid.

[353] Commission decision of 19 June 2013 in Case AT.39226 – *Lundbeck*, C(2013) 3803 final.

Commission analysed the 10 per cent turnover cap for separate companies individually. It implemented it by bundling joint and several liability with individual liability, similarly to the *International Removal Services* decision:

> For the infringement . . . the following fines are imposed: . . . Merck KGaA: EUR 21 411 000 of which jointly and severally with Generics [UK] Limited: EUR 7 766 843.[354]

In this example, the liabilities of Merck KGaA and Generics [UK] Limited differ, i.e. because of a separate application of the 10 per cent turnover cap.[355] The Commission clearly indicated the difference between the companies' relative liabilities. It imposed joint and several liability for the common liability (that is equal to Generics [UK] Limited's liability) and the individual liability on Merck KGaA (for the outstanding sum that would reflect their higher liability). As indicated in Section 2.1.5.2, there is no risk that national judges in contribution litigation will not respect the maximum liabilities imposed due to the 10 per cent turnover question. This is due to the imposition of two different types of liability, contribution concerning only one of them.

The question remains whether the 10 per cent turnover limit applies in contribution litigation when the Commission has not undertaken the task of applying the cap individually to the companies it held jointly and severally liable. This question is not covered by *Siemens Österreich*. It is, nonetheless, worth investigating it, as it may be used in contribution litigation to lower the relative liability of one party.

It seems that there is no simple answer to this query. On the one hand, there is no place in civil law to apply objectives pursued by the Commission's fining policy. As said above, the limitation to the height of fines has been established in order to avoid interfering with the market structure and endangering the economic existence of companies infringing competition law.[356] By contrast, civil law is in principle indifferent to economic consequences of enforcing debts.[357] As national courts deal with the post-decision reality, they should treat antitrust liability as any other liability and not engage in considerations that are relevant only from the perspective of the Commission's fining policy.

On the other hand, researched legal orders set a principle that a relative liability established in contribution litigation cannot place debtors in a worse position than they would be if they were liable for the entire debt alone.[358] For instance, if a

354 Ibid., Article 2(1).
355 Ibid., para. 1382.
356 See note 351.
357 Christian Kersting, 'Gesamtschuldnerausgleich bei Kartellgeldbußen' (2016) *Neue Zeitschrift für Kartellrecht*, 151. However, see notes 143 and 157 in Chapter 3.
358 For German law, see Opper, *Die gesamtschuldnerische Bußgeldhaftung*, 213; for Polish law, see Judgment of the Supreme Court from 17.03.1970, II PR 659/68, OSNCP 1970, nr 12, poz. 231; Lewaszkiewicz-Petrykowska, *Wyrządzenie szkody przez kilka osób*, 168; Marek, 'Roszczenia regresowe', 292; for English law, see Mitchell, *The Law of Contribution*, 244, 268.

debtor could lower damages because of its insufficient financial abilities, the same reduction applies in a dispute on contribution pursuant to Polish law.[359] Similarly, in English law, if a debtor could limit its liability to a creditor by invoking specific defences, the same is applicable in proceedings on contribution.[360] This is very relevant when we consider the 10 per cent turnover cap. If the Commission held only a given company liable for antitrust infringement, the application of the 10 per cent turnover cap would lead to a lower liability than the one factually imposed on it and other debtors with disregard to the cap. This lower liability should be the maximum amount of liability considered for the debtor in contribution litigation.[361]

As a result, if the Commission applies the 10 per cent turnover cap to individual companies, this determination is also valid for contribution claims. In addition, the 10 per cent turnover cap should be considered in contribution litigation even if it is not applied by the Commission.

INFORMATION CONTAINED IN THE COMMISSION'S DECISIONS Apart from identifying those jointly and severally liable and setting the amount of liability, the Commission's decisions usually contain extensive information on the facts that matter in contribution litigation. The decision usually describes the infringement and the details concerning the implementation of the anticompetitive practice. This includes the identity of infringers, their role, their conduct and the length of the conduct.[362] It is worth investigating what impact this information has on contribution claims.

First, the information included in the Commission's decision is a source of knowledge for those involved in a lawsuit concerning the apportionment of liability. As those claiming contribution are violators of EU competition law, they should be aware of the facts concerning the committed breach. For instance, in cartel cases, the violators participate in personal meetings and exchange information, so they will be aware of other cartelists' involvement in the infringement. Nevertheless, in certain situations, those liable for antitrust infringements have limited insight into details concerning the violation. For instance, in *Volkswagen II*,[363] Volkswagen AG

[359] See Article 440 k.c., Lewaszkiewicz-Petrykowska, *Wyrządzenie szkody przez klika osób*, 168.

[360] See, for instance, *Yuille v. B & B Fisheries (Leigh) Ltd and Bates (The Radiant)* [1958] 2 Lloyd's Rep 596; Mitchell, *The Law of Contribution*, 244.

[361] For a similar conclusion, see Opper, *Die gesamtschuldnerische Bußgeldhaftung*, 213. Jonas von Kalben and Alexander Sekunde also allow the application of the 10 per cent turnover cap to keep the fine proportionate to the size of the legal entity, see Jonas von Kalben and Alexander Sekunde, 'Relative Responsibility of Joint and Severally Liable Units in Public and Private Enforcement of EU Competition Law – What Role for Economic Criteria?' (2016) 37 *European Competition Law Review*, 1, 4. The BGH also allows considering the 10 per cent turnover cup but for the reason of aligning contribution claims with the aims of public antitrust enforcement, see BGH, BeckRS 2015, 00033, para. 53.

[362] Alan Riley, 'Beyond Leniency: Enhancing Enforcement in EC Antitrust Law' (2005) 28 *World Competition*, 3, 386–387.

[363] Commission decision of 29 June 2001 in Case COMP/F-2/36.693 – *Volkswagen*, OJ L 262, 2.10.2001, pp. 14–37.

coerced its distributors by means of circulars and letters to enforce its anticompetitive policy. All Volkswagen's distributors consequently aligned their behaviour. Nevertheless, they were only aware of the overall policy to a limited degree.[364] As a result, the evidence supporting distributors' contribution claims would come from the Commission's decision.[365]

Secondly and most fundamentally, the findings made by the Commission need to be respected by national judges dealing with contribution claims. According to *Siemens Österreich*, a duty to cooperate in good faith[366] makes judges rely on the findings established by the Commission.[367] The reliance on such findings also has strong support in Article 16 of Regulation 1/2003.[368] This provision ensures that the findings made by EU acts are binding for national courts. This encompasses the statement of fact and law[369] connected to establishing the compliance with Articles 101 and 102 of TFEU.[370] The binding power of the Commission's conclusions applies when national courts deal with the same matter as the Commission.[371] It is somewhat dubious whether the requirement of the identity of the matter is met as the contribution is a different matter to establishing infringement of EU competition law. Nonetheless, the question of liability for infringement is also a preliminary matter in contribution claims, which could lead to the application of Article 16 of Regulation 1/2003.

The principle of supremacy also protects conclusions made in EU decisions from being disregarded and re-discussed by national courts.[372] The binding effect of the Commission's decision is rooted in the separation of powers between the EU and

364 Ibid., paras. 103–104.

365 Another source of information in this situation would be the right to access the Commission's file.

366 On the duty to cooperate in good faith, see Roth, 'Effet utile', 261; Richard Wish and David Bailey, *Competition Law* (New York: Oxford University Press, 2012), 216; Wolfgang Durner, 'Die Unabhängigkeit nationaler Richter im Binnenmarkt – Zu den Loyalitätspflichten nationaler Gerichte gegenüber der EG-Kommission, insbesondere auf dem Gebiet des Kartellrechts' (2004) 4 *Zeitschrift Europarecht*, 561–572.

367 On the prohibition of running counter to the findings established in the Commission's decision, see Case C-344/98, *Masterfoods Ltd v. HB Ice Cream Ltd*, ECLI:EU:C:2000:249, paras. 49–52.

368 Contrary, Körner, *Die Gesamtschuld im Kartellbußgeldrecht*, 232–236.

369 Durner, 'Die Unabhängigkeit nationaler Richter', 549; Körner, *Die Gesamtschuld im Kartellbußgeldrecht*, 232; Daniel Dohrn, *Die Bindungswirkung kartellrechtlicher Entscheidungen der Kommission sowie deutscher und mitgliedsstaatlicher Kartellbehörden und Gerichte im deutschen Zivilprozess* (Köln: Carl Heymanns Verlag, 2010), 44.

370 Körner, *Die Gesamtschuld im Kartellbußgeldrecht*, 233; Dohrn, *Die Bindungswirkung kartellrechtlicher Entscheidungen*, 49 *et seq*.

371 Hans-Helmut Schneider, 'Art. 16 VO 1/2003' in Günter Hirsch, Frank Montag and Franz Jürgen Säcker (eds.), *Münchener Kommentar. Europäisches und Deutsches Wettbewerbsrecht. Kartellrecht, Missbrauchs- und Fusionskontrolle*, 2 vols. (München: C.H. Beck, 2007), vol. I, paras. 9, 11, 1716–1717.

372 Körner, *Die Gesamtschuld im Kartellbußgeldrecht*, 234–235; Durner, 'Die Unabhängigkeit nationaler Richter', 558.

the Members of the EU, and Commission's decisions have an *erga omnes* effect. Accordingly, the declaration of infringement by the Commission is binding on national judges regardless of the parties to the dispute.[373] As a result, national judges dealing with lawsuits relating to the same or a related factual background that was already evaluated by the Commission must respect the Commission's findings. It means in practice that judges cannot reach other conclusions than the Commission did without making an application under Article 267 of TFEU. As a consequence, the Commission's assessment is binding upon national judges.[374]

A practical question may arise regarding the parts of the Commission's decision that are binding in contribution litigation. Disputes on claims for damages prove that it is challenging to determine which parts of Commission decisions are binding in follow-on private law litigation. For instance, in the *Royal Mail* case pending before the Competition Appeal Tribunal, it was discussed whether both the operative part of the Commission's decision and the recitals are binding on national courts. The conclusion was that a recital is binding on national courts if 'the finding in the recital is an essential basis or the necessary support for a determination in the operative part, or necessary to understand the scope of the operative part'.[375] Similar discussions are likely to appear with respect to other elements of the Commission's decisions. The growing body of jurisprudence in the private enforcement context[376] can also help determine the exact scope of the binding effect of the Commission's decisions in disputes on contribution.

The impact of the Commission's decisions on contribution claims differs depending on the factual constellation of the case. In the context of private enforcement, the Commission's decisions have a significant influence on contribution claims. Companies engaged in contribution litigation are treated by the Commission as separate undertakings. As a result, the Commission assesses their roles separately. The infringement decision may, therefore, contain a lot of information relevant for contribution. On the contrary, when claims for contribution are brought forward in the context of public enforcement, the Commission's decisions may have a more limited impact. The Commission assesses the actions of undertakings and not individual companies. That being said, the Commission may still describe the infringement in detail and pay attention to particular companies and their actions. For instance, the Commission held ArcelorMittal Verderio Srl and its subsidiary ArcelorMittal Fontaine SA jointly and severally liable for the fine imposed for their participation in the prestressing steel cartel. Although the

373 Ferro, 'Antitrust Private Enforcement', 64. See also CJEU, *Otis*, para. 54.

374 The sanction-related decision parts are not binding on national courts, see Dohrn, *Die Bindungswirkung kartellrechtlicher Entscheidungen*, 46; Durner, 'Die Unabhängigkeit nationaler Richter', 558. There is also no general supremacy and no *erga omnes* binding power of Commission's decisions, see Durner, 'Die Unabhängigkeit nationaler Richter', 558–560.

375 *Royal Mail Group Limited v. DAF Trucks Ltd and Others* [2020] CAT 7, para. 68.

376 See, for instance, CJEU, *Otis*, para. 65; *Development Ltd v. ABB AB* [2018] EWHC 2616 (Ch).

companies were treated as a single undertaking, the Commission mentioned that '[ArcelorMittal Fontaine SA] participated from that date [of its foundation] in the Zurich Club ... There was also a frequent presence at the cartel meetings later on in Club Europe of Messrs (...), (...), (...), (...) all employees of [ArcelorMittal Fontaine SA] at certain points in time ...' and '[s]ince 03.04.1995 [ArcelorMittal Verderio Srl] participated directly in the cartel, in particular in Club Italia ... Moreover it was designated co-ordinator for Italy in Club Europe'.[377]

The Commission's decisions also have a different impact depending on the type of competition law infringement and the procedure used to establish it. The Commission deals differently with infringements by object and by effect. Only the latter describes the consequences of the infringements and identifies competition harm.[378] The Commission's decision also differs based on the procedure used. While infringement decisions contain a full-fledged description of the violation, decisions adopted as settlements contain only a brief description of such events.[379] It is recognised that settlement decisions are sometimes so vague that they are useless in follow-on claims on damages,[380] not to mention contribution litigation.

In conclusion, the Commission's infringement decisions have some impact on contribution litigation. The extent of this impact depends on the type of the decision, and the proceeding used to adopt the findings made by the Commission must be respected by national courts in contribution litigation.

2.2.5.3 What Is the Impact of National Judgments on Antitrust Damages for Subsequent Contribution Claims?

The courts' judgments setting compensation for those injured by competition law violations may also interfere with subsequent claims for contribution.

Judgments determining the liability for competition law violations contain information that may be useful in contribution litigation. A dispute between the antitrust violator and those damaged concerns facts connected to the infringement. Actions for damages aim at establishing infringements of competition law and damages that can compensate them.[381] For the sake of determining these elements, national judges assess given conducts and the roles that the alleged tortfeasors played. This information can also be used in subsequent lawsuits on contribution.

377 Commission decision of 30 June 2010 in Case COMP/38.344 – *Prestressing Steel*, C(2010) 4387 final, paras. 707–710.

378 See, for instance, CJEU, Case C-67/13 P, *Groupement des cartes bancaires (CB) v. European Commission*, ECLI:EU:C:2014:2204 paras. 49 and 52.

379 See, for instance, Commission decision of 27 January 2016 in Case AT.40028 – *Alternators and Starters*, C(2016) 223 final, Section 4; Commission decision of 15 July 2015 in Case AT.40098 – *Blocktrains*, C(2015) 4646 final, Section 4.

380 Ferro, 'Antitrust Private Enforcement', 61.

381 See, for instance, CJEU, *Manfredi*, paras. 61–63; CJEU, Case C-199/11, *Europese Gemeenschap v. Otis NV and Others*, ECLI:EU:C:2012:684, paras. 43–44.

The impact of judgments establishing antitrust infringement is, however, limited. Most fundamentally, claims for damages and claims for contribution involve different parties. This means that the judgments on damages have no *res judicata* effect on the lawsuits dealing with contribution. The effects of such judgments are thus only informal. For instance, judgments adopted in the actions for antitrust damages may serve as evidence in contribution litigation.[382]

Even when used informally, the judgments concerning claims for damages should be used with caution. As actions for damages deal with a relationship that exists between a given tort victim and a given tortfeasor, they only can give a partial image of the entire infringement. This information may be insufficient to demonstrate how different is the liability of each tortfeasor. This is an issue that lies at the heart of the contribution dispute.

In conclusion, when dealing with contribution claims, one must respect the catalogue of entities held jointly and severally liable by the Commission, the 10 per cent turnover cap and information included in the Commission's decision. This means that national judges dealing with contribution claims cannot counter any of the Commission's conclusions made with respect to these issues. In particular, they cannot state that an entity other than the addressee of the Commission's decision is liable for the antitrust violation at hand, they cannot counter factual and legal findings made by the Commission with respect to the antitrust infringement and they should apply the 10 per cent turnover cap individually to companies involved in contribution litigation.

2.2.6 *Are Contribution Claims Different in the Public and Private Enforcement Contexts?*

The analysis undertaken above has demonstrated that the requirements that EU competition laws impose on contribution claims are similar in the contexts of public and private enforcement. This leads us to the question of whether we can consider the issue of contribution jointly for public and private enforcement.

First, joint and several liability is used in both systems of competition law enforcement. In public enforcement, the Commission applies joint and several liability due to its definition of undertaking, single economic entity and economic continuity, which boils down to ensuring the effectiveness of EU competition law. In private enforcement, joint and several liability aims at improving the procedural position of those damaged by antitrust infringement. This in turn increases the chances that they will commence an action against competition law infringers, leading to more effective competition law enforcement. As a result, the reason for imposing joint and several liability for both types of enforcement is to ensure their effectiveness.

[382] See, for instance, Civ. I, 19.06.1973: Bull. Civ. I 208; Civ. II, 22.10.1975: Bull. Civ. II 235.

Second, the internal and external aspects of joint and several liability are distinguished in both types of enforcement. In public enforcement, such a division was confirmed by the CJEU in *Siemens Österreich*.[383] In private enforcement, these two aspects of joint and several liability are regulated separately. Article 11(1) of Directive 2014/104/EU deals with the external relationship, while Article 11(5) of the Directive concerns the internal relationship. This division applies similarly in public and private enforcement. While the liability of joint infringers towards the Commission and those damaged by the violation is intertwined with the effectiveness of EU competition law, the apportionment of such a liability in subsequent claims for contribution has no influence on it. Nonetheless, in both types of antitrust violations, national judges must respect the existing Commission decisions establishing violations of EU competition law.

Third, both public and private competition law enforcement have decided in favour of introducing the right to claim contribution. Section 2.1 has demonstrated that it is not necessary for a legal system to couple external joint and several liability with the existence of the contribution rule regarding the internal relationship. The choice of whether to introduce the right to contribution or not belongs to the legislator.[384] This choice was made in favour of contribution both in the private and public enforcement of EU competition law. In *Siemens Österreich*, the CJEU attributed the power to decide the internal allocation of fines to EU Member States. Directive 2014/104/EU made a similar choice. Under Article 11(5), it obliged EU Member States to guarantee the right to claim contribution for those held jointly and severally liable for antitrust damages.

Furthermore, the EU says relatively little about how contribution claims should be enforced in both private and public enforcement. In both systems, it is the role of national legal systems to provide for contribution claims. The freedom of Member States is limited only by general principles. In public enforcement, the only requirement is compliance with EU law. In private enforcement, contribution claims must observe the principles of effectiveness and equivalency.

These similarities establish that there is one right to contribution that applies uniformly to public and private enforcement. Consequently, one should favour a homogeneous framework for contribution claims in antitrust regardless of whether the right to claim contribution is exercised in the context of public or private antitrust enforcement. Such a solution would enhance legal coherence, lead to uniform interpretation and bring more certainty for companies. Coherence is especially important in light of the most recent *Skanska* judgment and follow-on cases, which involve joint and several liability established both in public and private enforcement. Treating a right to claim contribution in antitrust as a uniform right is

383 CJEU, *Siemens Österreich*, paras. 59–60.
384 Contrary Thomas, 'Die Gesamtschuld', 685.

also preferable in terms of achieving this study's goal of designing a simple and efficient framework for contribution claims in antitrust.

2.3 CONCLUSIONS

The analysis conducted in this chapter has attempted to clarify some misconceptions about the relationship between joint and several liability and the enforcement of EU competition law.

It has been demonstrated that contribution claims are not an automatic consequence of the fact that joint and several liability applies; to the contrary, no-contribution systems are generally possible. The right to claim contribution needs thus to be established in a given legal order. Contribution claims have been endorsed by EU competition law, and they apply both in the context of public and private enforcement.

The intersection between contribution claims and EU competition law is much more limited than it seems at first sight. Apart from general requirements set by EU law in terms of adherence to the Commission's decisions and the principles of equivalence and efficiency, there are only limited points of contact between contribution claims and antitrust. Principally, contribution claims have little impact on effective antitrust enforcement. The jurisdiction to deal with contribution claims is national, and the impact that contribution claims have on competition law enforcement is minimal. Both in public and private enforcement, contribution claims mainly take place when the antitrust debt has already been paid. The creditor is satisfied at this moment, and competition law has already been effectively enforced. The question of contribution is thus of no relevance for competition law enforcement.

The intersection is more significant when the influence of EU competition law on contribution litigation is considered. The analysis undertaken in this section has revealed that when dealing with contribution claims one must respect the catalogue of entities held jointly and severally liable by the Commission, the 10 per cent turnover cap and information included in the Commission's decision. This means that national judges dealing with contribution litigation cannot counter any of the Commission's conclusions made with respect to these issues. In particular, they cannot state that an entity other than the addressee of the Commission's decision is liable for the antitrust violation at issue, they cannot counter factual and legal findings made by the Commission with respect to the antitrust infringement and they should apply the 10 per cent turnover cap individually to companies involved in contribution litigation.

3

Enforcing Contribution Claims under National Laws

While the previous chapter asked *whether* contribution claims are allowed in EU competition law, this chapter investigates *how* contribution claims can be brought forward. As demonstrated above, the right to claim contribution in competition law is ensured by EU law, but its exercise takes place under national laws. Hence, this chapter focuses on investigating national rules on contribution and their application in the competition law context.

The paragraphs below investigate the laws of England and Wales, Germany, France and Poland. This choice of jurisdiction was made having in mind that these laws are examples of different legal traditions (common law, Germanic law, Napoleonic law and Socialist-influenced law) and therefore represent a variety of rules on joint and several liability.

The assessment is both pragmatic and critical. On the one hand, it provides the readers with the tools they need for pursuing contribution claims in the researched jurisdictions and it analyses questions that are likely to appear on this occasion. Does a right to claim contribution exist in a given legal order? On what basis and in which form can contribution be claimed? Against whom can contribution be claimed? What legal test must be met to receive contribution? What is the criterion for allocating liability between antitrust infringers? The chapter also makes legal practitioners aware of the points that can be debated. This applies in particular to the criteria for allocating antitrust liability. The chapter analyses the possible methods of dividing liability: relative fault, causation, illicit gains, values of sales, market shares and *pro capita*. It describes their advantages and disadvantages, giving those faced with contribution claims a comprehensive overview of possible solutions to resolve a dispute.

At the same time, the chapter reflects on whether the requirements and modifications stemming from EU competition law require the adoption of a competition law–specific approach to contribution. It is demonstrated that the traditional framework for contribution claims leads to many shortcomings when applied in the competition law context. First, not all tools usually available for contribution can be used in competition law. Second, the implementations of Directive 2014/104/EU influenced regular rules on contribution. Third, some traditional methods for dividing antitrust liability may damage the legal system as they lead to an incoherent adjudication in the competition law setting. Against this background, the chapter makes proposals on how rules on contribution can be improved to meet the needs of competition law.

After an introductory discussion about the preconditions for contribution claims stemming from EU competition law (Section 3.1), the investigation follows the order of questions that appear for those envisioning contribution litigation. It discusses the availability of the right to contribution (Section 3.2), the legal bases for contribution claims (Section 3.3), the addressees of such claims (Section 3.4), the applicable legal tests (Section 3.5) and the criteria for establishing relative liabilities (Section 3.6). Each section first identifies the national rules on contribution (Sub-sections 1), then discusses their application in EU competition law (Sub-sections 2) and concludes with critical remarks and recommendations (Sub-sections 3). The chapter closes with a discussion on whether traditional rules on contribution are sufficient to provide for an effective right to contribution in the context of competition law or if a specific competition law–specific approach is needed (Section 3.7).

3.1 COMPETITION LAW CONTEXT OF THE DISPUTE

The Member States enjoy significant freedom in determining the content of the right to contribution and the conditions of contribution claims. As the previous chapter established, the right to claim contribution was granted by EU law but its exercise proceeds under national laws. EU competition law provides only some general principles that the Member States need to respect when designing their national rules on contribution for antitrust liabilities.

3.1.1 *EU Law and the Principles of Equivalence and Effectiveness*

In public antitrust enforcement, the Member States' freedom is theoretically unlimited. *Siemens Österreich* essentially requested contribution claims to be compliant with EU law and to be adjudicated in line with the infringement decisions adopted by the European Commission.[1] In the context of private antitrust enforcement, the limitations are the principles of effectiveness and equivalence (see Section 2.2.3). The first principle demands that national laws use conditions that will not impede the EU right to claim contribution in competition law. In practice, they should be adequate to competition law and not make the exercise of the right for contribution practically impossible. The principle of equivalence means that EU Member States

[1] CJEU, *Siemens Österreich*, para. 63.

should not treat the contribution claims established in Directive 2014/104/EU worse than equivalent rights existing in national legal systems.[2]

Compliance with EU law and the principles of effectiveness and equivalence is not only binding for national lawmakers but also provides us with a frame of reference for identifying the national regimes for contribution in the context of competition law. Although in strict terms, EU law sets different requirements for public and private enforcement, it is advisable to apply them consistently in both areas. It is unimaginable to develop contribution rules for private enforcement that violate EU law, as the latter enjoys supremacy. Inversely, it is advisable to rely on the principles of equivalence and effectiveness in public enforcement. In this area, the CJEU's starting point when establishing the right to contribution was to rely on solutions that already exist in national legal orders, which goes in line with the principle of equivalence. It is also essential that contribution claims are able to be effectively exercised as the failure of national legal orders to provide for an effective contribution right would mean that antitrust infringers are left without the possibility to enforce their right to claim contribution.

3.1.2 *Main Features of Competition Law*

In order to satisfy the principle of effectiveness and to provide for an effective right to claim contribution, one needs to have in mind that competition law is a complex area of law, which can be difficult to fit into a traditional civil law framework. It is therefore necessary to have in mind some main characteristics of competition law that need to be accommodated by the rules on contribution.

First, competition law's intricacy stems from the infinite number of anticompetitive practices that occur in different constellations. There are both horizontal and vertical anticompetitive agreements. There are also agreements with different anticompetitive aims, for instance, price fixing, market sharing, bid-rigging, boycotts, limitations to innovation, and interference with market development. Each of these practices requires an individual economic assessment. This may cause difficulties for contribution litigation, as the assessment must be done not only for the practice as such but also for each of the companies involved in it individually.

Second, the complexity of contribution litigation results from the fact that competition law liability can be established by different means – both public and private enforcement. This not only causes problems of legal classification of actions for contribution but also requires a different assessment of relative liability. Whilst in the context of public antitrust enforcement, contribution claims are enforced between companies that are liable for the behaviour of only one of the companies, in private antitrust enforcement the dispute is between the companies who are individually liable for their own behaviour.

[2] More on the principles of effectiveness and equivalence in Section 2.2.3.

Third, complications are caused by the mass character of competition litigation.[3] With the increase in private antitrust enforcement, contribution litigation is likely to concern a big number of debts and involve many debtors. This is because competition law violations usually generate a massive amount of dispersed damages, which trigger a corresponding number of claims for damages and a corresponding amount of contribution claims.[4] This setting is unusual for the traditional framework for contribution claims, which deals only with one debt and a few joint and several debtors.

The difficulties in dealing with complex and massive contribution claims in competition law have been already observed by Carsten Krüger[5] and Antonia Hösch.[6] The multitude of such claims can be managed to some extent by procedural tools.[7] However, substantive law should account for such characteristics of contribution litigation in competition law. In this respect, a reasoned choice of the criterion for division of liability is essential. On top of this, one should keep in mind that as competition law is complex in itself, one should prefer contribution rules that are simple and effective. If contribution claims lead to a high cost of adjudication and create uncertainty, their practical use can be questioned and lead to a factual denial of the right to claim contribution.

Overall, the above-named factors are considered as a benchmark for identifying and assessing national rules on contribution and their application in the framework of competition law. The principle of equivalence encourages us to first investigate the pre-existing rules for contribution claims. The principle of effectiveness requires us to ask whether they ensure an effective right to claim contribution in competition law.

3.2 DOES A RIGHT TO CLAIM CONTRIBUTION EXIST IN NATIONAL LEGAL ORDERS?

The previous chapter has demonstrated that contribution claims are required under EU competition law. However, it has also been pointed out that there is no

[3] Krüger, *Kartellregress*, 115–148; Weinhold, *Der Gesamtschuldnerausgleich*, 199–203; Hösch, *Der schadensrechtliche Innenausgleich*, 320; Krüger, 'Der Gesamtschuldnerausgleich', 11–12.

[4] Krüger, *Kartellregress*, 115–119.

[5] Ibid., 115 *et seq.*

[6] Hösch, *Der schadensrechtliche Innenausgleich*, 316 *et seq.*

[7] This question is left open here as the book does not cover procedural issues. For a discussion on procedural aspects, see Hösch, *Der schadensrechtliche Innenausgleich*, 320–325; Williams, *Joint Torts and Contributory Negligence*, 175–194; Mitchell, *The Law of Contribution*, 103–115; Maria Jędrzejewska, *Współuczestnictwo Procesowe* (Warszawa: Wydawnictwo Prawnicze, 1975); Canin, *Les actions récursoires*, 201 *et seq.*; Rogers, 'Multiple Tortfeasors', 74; Ulrich Magnus, 'Multiple Tortfeasors under German Law' in W. V. Horton Rogers (ed.), *Unification of Tort Law: Multiple Tortfeasors* (Den Haag: Kluwer Law International, 2004), 94; Nesterowicz and Bagińska, 'Multiple Tortfeasors', 159; Rogers, 'Comparative Report', 294–295; John Anthony Jolowicz, 'Procedure and Substance – Apportionment of Damages' (1988) *The Cambridge Law Journal*, 32–34; Anthony M. Dugdale, 'The Civil Liability (Contribution) Act 1978' (1979) 42 *The Modern Law Review*, 2, 188–189; Krüger, 'Überlegungen zur Gesamtschuld', 87–89.

necessary relationship between joint and several liability and contribution claims. The question remains whether national legal orders recognise contribution claims and allow them in EU competition law.

3.2.1 *Comparative Analysis*

Nowadays, each of the researched jurisdictions provides for the right to claim contribution, and this right is available for competition law–related liabilities. However, this was not always and not everywhere the case.

In the beginning, English courts refused to allow tortfeasors who paid compensation to recover contribution from other co-tortfeasors under the *Merryweather v. Nixan* doctrine.[8] The reason for denying the right to claim contribution was the principle *ex turpi causa non oritur action*,[9] which states that it is unjust to derive benefits from one's own wrongful acts. Lord Dundin explained that this is 'because of the underlying proposition that no man can claim damages when the root of the damage which he claims is his own wrong'.[10] Because the tortfeasor's misconduct caused the damage, it was unjust to let it minimise the compensation paid by addressing others for contribution. Early German common law also disputed a general right to contribution.[11] The majority excluded it in the case of intentional misconduct in line with Roman law, specifically Justinian's Novellae 99.[12] Similarly to English law, this position was justified by tortfeasors' fraudulent behaviour.

In both jurisdictions, the no-contribution rule was gradually repealed. In England, an increasing number of exceptions to *ex turpi causa* appeared.[13] Finally, the no-contribution rule was abolished with the Tortfeasors Act 1935[14] and the Contribution Act 1978.[15] In Germany, the change was brought by first

8 See note 154 in Chapter 2.

9 Rogers, 'Multiple Tortfeasors', 71.

10 Lord Dunedin, *Weld-Blundell v. Stephens* [1920] AC 956, 976.

11 In early German law contribution rights existed exceptionally, see Meier, *Gesamtschulden*, 558–559, 571–577; Götte, *Gesamtschuldbegriff und Regressproblem*, 103–104. In the nineteenth century, it was disputed whether there is a general principle of contribution; the majority opinion was that joint and several liability was neutral with respect to contribution and contribution claims were allowed when agreed by the parties or when the statute specifically provided them, see Meier, *Gesamtschulden*, 573.

12 Some authors allowed, however, a contribution claim based on subrogation or by using *condition sine cause* or *action negotiorum gestorum* also in such cases, see Meier, *Gesamtschulden*, 571–575; Bentele, *Gesamtschuld und Erlass*, 129; Ehmann, *Die Gesamtschuld*, 46.

13 Rogers, 'Multiple Tortfeasors', 71; Williams, *Joint Torts and Contributory Negligence*, 87–94; Mitchell, *The Law of Contribution*, 69–78.

14 Law Reform (Married Women and Tortfeasors) Act 1935 [Ch. 30], Section 6.

15 Civil Liability (Contribution) Act 1978 [Ch. 47] ('Contribution Act 1978'), Section 2. Common law has also extended the right to contribution to many areas of law, including the liabilities for tax debts or the liabilities of company directors for the company debts, see Mitchell, *The Law of Contribution*, 73–74.

codifications, which introduced the right to claim contribution.[16] Currently, in both countries, it is believed that the right to contribution applies widely, even in intentional torts.[17]

A quite different development took place in France and Poland. The French Code Civil guaranteed a general right of contribution from early on in the case of *solidarité*. This was initially interpreted to also cover liability from torts and crimes.[18] The choice of such a solution is described as an import of both ancient Roman law and oriental law endorsed by Justinian, in which joint and several liability was treated as a mutual guarantee.[19] The Polish Prawo Zobowiązań also decided to introduce the general right to claim contribution in torts, which was transposed without significant changes into the current Kodeks Cywilny.[20] There has also been a strong trend to apply the provisions on contribution in a wide and general way.[21]

This favourable approach to the right to claim contribution continues in France and Poland. In France, contribution rights are regularly described as main effects (*effets principaux*) of *solidarité*,[22] and contribution is available in the case of obligations *in solidum*.[23] In Poland, it is currently believed that the right to claim

[16] Meier, *Gesamtschulden*, 577.

[17] Williams, *Joint Torts and Contributory Negligence*, xli, 87–88.

[18] It was a subsequent narrow interpretation of *solidarité* and a development of liability *in solidum*, which casted doubts on the right to claim contribution in torts. The majority agreed that such a right existed yet on a different legal base than the one applicable to *solidarité*, see Mignot, *Les obligations solidaires*, 13, 76 *et seq*.

[19] Mignot, *Les obligations solidaires*, 13, 76 *et seq*.; Canin, Les actions récursoires, 6.

[20] Article 137 of the Prawo Zobowiązań reads: 1. *Jeżeli szkodę wyrządziło kilka osób wspólnie, odpowiedzialność ich jest solidarna, chyba że udowodnione będzie, kto w jakim stopniu przyczynił się do wywołania szkody*. 2. *Kto z pomiędzy zobowiązanych solidarnie do odszkodowania zapłacił całkowitą wartość szkody, ten ma prawo żądać od każdego z pozostałych zwrotu części, którą oznaczy sąd z uwzględnieniem okoliczności, a zwłaszcza winy każdego*. The Prawo Zobowiązań has adopted the contribution rule with reference to Code Napoleon and Swiss Civil Code, see Till, *Polskie prawo zobowiązań*, 52–53. For more on this topic, see Komisja Kodyfikacyjna, Podkomisja Prawa o Zobowiązaniach, *Uzasadnienie Projektu Kodeksu Zobowiązań*. 2 vols. (Warszawa: Wydawnictwo Urzędowe Komisji Kodyfikacyjnej, 1934), vol. I(4); Komisja Kodyfikacyjna, Podsekcja III Prawa Cywilnego, *Projekt prawa o zobowiązaniach*, 2 vols. (Warszawa: Wydawnictwo Urzędowe Komisji Kodyfikacyjnej, 1932), vol. I(4); Komisja Kodyfikacyjna, *Uzasadnienie projektu kodeksu zobowiązań* (Warszawa: Komisja Kodyfikacyjna Rzeczpospolitej Polskiej, 1939); Till, *Polskie prawo zobowiązań*; Grzegorz Jędrejek, 'Polski Kodeks Zobowiązań z 1933 Roku. Powstanie, źródła, znaczenie dla Europejskiego prawa obligacyjnego' (2001) XI *Roczniki Nauk Prawnych*, 1, 47.

[21] Lewaszkiewicz-Petrykowska, *Wyrządzenie szkody przez kilka osób*, 140, 177; Stefan Buczkowski, 'Z zagadnień regresu' (1952) 1 *Przegląd Ustawodawstwa Gospodarczego*, 43, 444; Grzybowski, 'Roszczenia zwrotne', 41–42; Szpunar, 'Roszczenia regresowe', 29.

[22] See, for instance, Rémy Cabrillac, *Droit des obligations* (Paris: Dalloz, 2016), 330–331; Gaël Chantepieand and Mathias Latina, *La réforme du droit des obligations. Commentaire théorique et pratique dans l'ordre du Code civil* (Paris: Dalloz, 2016), 722–724.

[23] French law on joint and several liability has been recently subjected to a major transformation under ordonnance n° 2016-131 of 10 February 2016. After multiple projects suggesting changes to civil law – Project Catala, Project Terré, Senat proposals of 2008 and 2010 – a new law on the general part of the law on obligations has been adopted. This reform also has a significant

contribution always exists when it is commercially needed.[24] This approach emerged under socialist law that supported the principle of social and not individual responsibility.[25]

3.2.2 *Competition Law Analysis*

The historical analysis of contribution claims reveals that the right to claim contribution exists in all researched jurisdictions. There are thus no general obstacles to claim contribution by those who are jointly and severally liable for antitrust debts.

Although infringement of competition law is an intentional act, in England and in Germany intentional wrongdoing no longer prevents those who committed it from seeking contribution. France and Poland have been traditionally favourable towards contribution rights, and this trend continues. As a result, the general right to claim contribution should be available also for those infringing antitrust laws.

3.2.3 *Conclusions*

This high-level analysis has not indicated any obstacles that could jeopardise the right to contribution and its application in EU competition law. The researched jurisdictions' approach to support and widely apply contribution claims also gives sufficient room to enforce such claims in EU competition law and therefore deserves approval.

3.3 LEGAL BASIS AND TYPES OF CONTRIBUTION CLAIMS

The next step to establish if antitrust infringers have the right to claim contribution is to verify what legal actions they can take to claim contribution. Claims for contribution can be exercised in different variations and in different time periods. The traditional rules on contribution have also been influenced by the researched countries' implementations of Directive 2014/104/EU.

impact on tort law. The first chapter called *Les modalités de l'obligation* contains new provisions (Articles 1306–1319) on joint and several liability. Article 1316 of the Code Civil provides for the principle of contribution, however, without introducing material changes when compared to the former version of the Code Civil. The Article covers the text of former Articles 1213, 1214 and 1215 of the Code Civil. On the reform and its impact on joint and several liability, see Mignot, 'Principe de division'; Marc Mignot 'L'ordonnance du 10 fevrier 2016', 7; Antoine Hontebeyrie, 'Régime général des obligations : l'essentiel d'une réforme substantielle' (2015) 249 *Droit et Patrimoine. Dossier*, 33–34, 36; Antoine Hontebeyrie, 'Quelques incidences de la réforme du droit des obligations en matière de responsabilité civile' (2015) 249 *Droit et Patrimoine. Dossier*, 57; Antoine Hontebeyrie, 'Pluralité de sujets', paras. 3–4, 6–7; Pimont and Roux-Sibillon, 'Obligations plurales', paras. 3, 5–6, 15–18, 29–31; Bougerol, 'La réforme de la solidarité passive', paras. 5, 7, 14 *et seq.*; Martin, 'Article 1310', 1–2.

24 Lewaszkiewicz-Petrykowska, *Wyrządzenie szkody przez kilka osób*, 141.

25 Bieniek, 'Pojęcie regresu', 890–891; Buczkowski, 'Z zagadnień regresu', 445.

3.3.1 *Comparative Analysis*

3.3.1.1 Types of Claims and Relevant Legal Bases

THE RIGHT TO CLAIM CONTRIBUTION English law on contribution distinguishes between contribution claims sought when the co-debtors are liable for the same 'debt' and for the same 'damage'. Whereas the first situation is governed by common law and equity,[26] the second is regulated under the Contribution Act 1978.[27] The essence of the right to contribution in common law was expressed in *Whitham v. Bullock*:

> If, as between several persons or properties all equally liable at law to the same demand it would be equitable that the burden should fall in a certain way, the Court will so far as possible, having regard to the solvency of the different parties, see that, if that burden is placed inequitably by the exercise of the legal right, its incidence should be afterwards readjusted.[28]

The Contribution Act 1978 introduces the right to claim contribution in a brief way. Under Section 2(1),

> any person liable in respect of any damage suffered by another person may recover contribution from any other person liable in respect of the same damage (whether jointly with him or otherwise).

Contribution can be claimed in England in different variations: as a personal right or as subrogation. The personal right for contribution is believed to lie in unjust enrichment. The enrichment occurs because one or more, but not all, of the debtors, by fulfilling their own obligation, also discharge the others from their debts.[29] Regarding subrogation, the claimant is entitled to be treated like the creditor: as though its payment did not extinguish the debt, but the debt was transferred to it in order to secure its rights against the defendant.[30]

Polish law also distinguishes situations where co-debtors are liable for the same *damage* and for the same *debt*. Article 441(2) of the k.c., which is the source of the right to claim contribution, requires that joint and several debtors are liable for the same *damage*. Article 441(2) of the k.c. reads that

[26] Mitchell, *The Law of Contribution*, 66; The Law Commission, *Contribution*, paras. 14–15.

[27] Mitchell, *The Law of Contribution*, 65.

[28] The Law Commission, *Contribution*, para. 12.

[29] Mitchell, *The Law of Contribution*, 43–63. However, Glanville Llewelyn Williams also discusses whether it is a *quasi*-contract right and Charles Mitchell asks whether it is a right of reimbursement, see Williams, *Joint Torts and Contributory Negligence*, 84 and Mitchell, *The Law of Contribution*, 74–78.

[30] Mitchell, *The Law of Contribution*, 8, 270–282.

> if damage results from an action or omission of several persons, the one who remedies the damage may demand that the other persons reimburse a relevant part, depending on the circumstances, and especially on the fault of a given person and on the extent to which he contributed to the damage arising.[31]

As a result, it is believed that *regres sensu stricto* applies only in cases of joint and several liability for the same damage. However, in the case of liability for the same debt, it is believed that Article 441(2) of the k.c. can be applied by analogy.[32] This is called *regres sensu largo*.[33] The division between *regres sensu stricto* and *largo* has no significant impact on the content of the claim for contribution. Its introduction in fact allows for applying the provisions on contribution to a larger variety of situations than those stipulated in the Polish civil code.[34]

Polish law is also simpler than English law regarding the different variations in which claims for contribution can be asserted. Polish law provides for only one type of contribution claim, which is a personal right. It is generally believed that Article 441 of the k.c. sets out the legal framework for contribution claims in a comprehensive way[35] and is *lex specialis* to other provisions of the civil code.[36] This excludes other rules (for instance, subrogation) from being used in contribution litigation.[37]

German and French laws do not follow the English and Polish distinction between the liability for the same *damage* and for the same *debt*. Their rules on contribution relate to the fact that joint and several liability applies rather than what this liability refers to. Both legal orders provide for different types of contribution claims.

[31] See note 140 in Chapter 2.

[32] The examples of contribution claims *sensu largo* can be found in Articles 356 and 471 of the k. c., social security law or insurance law.

[33] Marek Safjan, 'Art. 441' in Krzysztof Pietrzykowski (ed.), *Kodeks cywilny. Komentarz*, 2 vols. (Warszawa: C.H. Beck, 2011), vol. I, para. 5; Lewaszkiewicz-Petrykowska, *Wyrządzenie szkody przez kilka osób*, 140 *et seq*.; Bieniek Gerard, 'Solidarność; Regres' in Jacek Gudowski (ed.), *Komentarz do art. 441 Kodeksu cywilnego* (2013) *LEX*, para. 18; Buczkowski, 'Z zagadnień regresu', 444.

[34] Safjan, 'Art. 441', para. 5.

[35] Tadeusz Kasiński, 'Roszczenia regresowe z art. 441 para 3 kodeksu cywilnego' (1972) 9 *Nowe Prawo*, 387; Safjan, 'Art. 441', para. 6; Tomasz Antoszek, 'Art. 441' in Maciej Gutowski (ed.), *Duże Komentarze Becka. Kodeks cywilny. Komentarz*, 2 vols. (Warszawa: C.H. Beck, 2016), vol. I, paras. 3–5; Lewaszkiewicz-Petrykowska, *Wyrządzenie szkody przez kilka osób*, 143; Marek, 'Roszczenia regresowe', 288; Adam Szpunar, 'The Law of Tort in the Polish Civil Code' (1967) 16 *The International and Comparative Law Quarterly*, 1, 95.

[36] See, for instance, Kasiński, 'Roszczenia regresowe', 388; Bieniek, 'Pojęcie regresu', 895–897; Piotr Tereszkiewicz, 'Solidarność dłużników w świetle europeizacji prawa obligacyjnego' in Joanna Haberko, Adam Olejniczak, Agnieszka Pyrzyńska and Dorota Sokołowska (eds.), *Współczesne problemy prawa zobowiązań* (Poznań: Wolters Kluwer Polska, 2014), para. 3.4.

[37] Ibid.; Grzybowski, 'Roszczenia zwrotne', 41 *et seq*.; Buczkowski, 'Z zagadnień regresu', 444; Longchamps de Bérier Roman, *Polskie Prawo Cywilne. Zobowiązania*, 5 vols. (Lviv: Księgarnia Wydawnictwa Gybrynowicz i Syn, 1938), vol. II, 57; Till, *Polskie prawo zobowiązań*, 52–53.

In Germany, there are two principal types of contribution claims – the personal claim (*Ausgleichspflicht*) under § 426(1) of the BGB and subrogation (*Legalzession*) under § 426(2) of the BGB.[38] Paragraph 426(1) of the BGB provides that

> [t]he joint and several debtors are obliged in equal proportions in relation to one another unless otherwise determined.[39]

Paragraph 426(1) of the BGB is a source of the right for contribution for those who paid more than their own shares of liability. This rule is also considered the most general and most comprehensive rule on contribution.[40] Paragraph 426(2) of the BGB[41] relies on the previous paragraph and stipulates that subrogation is possible when one of the joint and several debtors paid more than its own share of liability.[42]

[38] For the use of these legal bases for competition law contribution claims, see Weinhold, *Der Gesamtschuldnerausgleich*, 104; Körner, *Die Gesamtschuld im Kartellbußgeldrecht*, 228; Hösch, *Der schadensrechtliche Innenausgleich*, 161, 191; Jüchser, 'Gesamtschuldnerausgleich', 1048; Jens Kuhlmann, *Rückgriffsgrundlagen bei Gesamtschuld, Bürgschaft und Schadensversicherung in Deutschland, England und Schweden* (Berlin: BMV Berliner Wissenschafts-Verlag, 2005), 64; von Kalben and Sekunde, 'Relative Responsibility', 2; Kersting, 'Gesamtschuldnerausgleich bei Kartellgeldbußen', 149, 153; von Laufenberg, *Kartellrechtliche Konzernhaftung*, 244–252; Köhler, 'EU-Kartellgeldbußen', 280–281.

[39] See note 139 in Chapter 2.

[40] Kerstin Thoma, *Der internationale Regress. Formen und Gerichtszuständigkeit – unter Berücksichtigung des deutschen, österreichischen, schweizerischen und französischen materiellen Regressrechts* (Hamburg: Verlag Dr. Kovač, 2007), 37; Schmidt, *Gesamtschuld und Gesamtschuldregress*, 168–171.

[41] Paragraph 426(2) of the BGB reads: '*Soweit ein Gesamtschuldner den Gläubiger befriedigt und von den übrigen Schuldnern Ausgleichung verlangen kann, geht die Forderung des Gläubigers gegen die übrigen Schuldner auf ihn über. Der Übergang kann nicht zum Nachteil des Gläubigers geltend gemacht werden*' ('To the extent that a joint and several debtor satisfies the obligee and may demand adjustment from the other obligors, the claim of the obligee against the other obligors passes to him. The passing of title may not be asserted to the disadvantage of the creditor').

[42] Kuhlmann, *Rückgriffsgrundlagen bei Gesamtschuld*, 62–63. A number of authors have advocated for the use of other legal bases for contribution claims. In particular paras. 254, 255, 677–687, 812(1)(1)(2), 817(2), 826, 831, 840(2) of the BGB, paras. 33(1)(1) and (33)(3)(1) of the GWB have been considered. These legal bases are, however, not commonly considered as sources of the right to claim contribution. They are also of limited use due to their narrow scopes, specific sphere of application and primary standing of § 426 of the BGB for contribution litigation. With respect to § 255 of the BGB, see Jürgen Stamm, *Regreßfiguren im Zivilrecht. Eine Rückbesinnung auf die Gesamtschuld unter Neubewertung des Zessionsregresses gemäß § 255 BGB und der Drittschadensliquidation* (Berlin: Duncker & Humblot, 2000), 31 *et seq*., 95–109; Meier, *Gesamtschulden*, 872–873. With respect to paras. 677–687 of the BGB see Thoma, *Der internationale Regress*, 61–65; Kuhlmann, *Rückgriffsgrundlagen bei Gesamtschuld*, 64, 117; Selb, *Schadensbegriff und Regreßmethoden*, note 75; Meier, *Gesamtschulden*, 892–896. With respect to § 812(1)(1)(2) of the BGB, see Kuhlmann, *Rückgriffsgrundlagen bei Gesamtschuld*, 178–179; Stamm, *Regreßfiguren im Zivilrecht*, 109–114; Meier, *Gesamtschulden*, 887–891; Dieter Medicus *Bürgerliches Recht* (Köln, Berlin, Bonn, München: Vahlen, 2002), para. 915. With respect to other legal bases, see Krüger, *Kartellregress*, 52; von Laufenberg, *Kartellrechtliche Konzernhaftung*, 255–262.

French law also guarantees both a personal claim (*action personelle*) and subrogation (*subrogation légale*) to claim contribution.[43] Subrogation is the most popular way of securing contribution claims in France.[44] The basis is Article 1346 of the Code Civil:[45]

> Subrogation takes place by the sole operation of law in favour of a person with a legitimate interest in it who satisfies a debt provided that their satisfaction discharges as against the creditor another person who is subject to the final burden in respect of all or part of a debt.

As in other jurisdictions, subrogation is based on the fiction that the payment of the debtor did not extinguish the creditor's claim but put the debtor in the position of the creditor vis-à-vis the remaining debtors.[46] The claimant can request up to the entire sum paid personally from other debtors as if it were the original creditor,[47] provided that it paid in excess of its own liability share.[48]

The personal claim for contribution is another frequently asserted type of contribution in French law.[49] The existence of such a right was clearly confirmed by the judgment of the Cour de Cassation (1st Civil Chamber) of 7 June 1977.[50] However, a relevant legal basis for such a claim is still disputed.[51] It is argued that the personal

43 Apart from these three general legal bases, there is a specific contribution claim in the field of trade (*recours cambiaire*), which considers '*du signataire de la lettre de change solvens, du souscripteur ou de l'endossataire solvens du billet à ordre ou, encore du donneur d'aval ayant d'effectuer le paiement*' on the basis of Articles L.511-44(3), L.512-3, L.511-21(9) of the Code de Commerce. Taking into account this very specific application, this type of contribution claim is not available to antitrust infringers and will not be considered further on. For more details on this type of contribution claim, see Ranouil, *Les recours entre coobligés*, 101–103.

44 Mignot, *Les obligations solidaires*, 612; Canin, *Les actions récursoires*, 107. See also Carbonnier Jean, *Droit civil. Les obligations*, 4 vols. (Paris: Presses Universitaires de France, 1992), vol. IV, 540–542; Patrice Jourdain, 'Pour un réexamen du droit de recours en contribution' (2009) 3 *Responsabilité civile et assurances*, 3, para. 6; Chantepie and Latina, *La réforme du droit des obligations*, 843–844; Philippe Le Tourneau, *Droit de la responsabilité et des contrats* (Paris: Dalloz, 2012), 670–671; François Chénedé, *Le nouveau droit des contrats et des obligations* (Paris: Dalloz, 2016), 269; Jacques Boré 'Le recours', para. A.

45 See note 136 in Chapter 2.

46 Ranouil, *Les recours entre coobligés*, 99–101, 149; Canin, *Les actions récursoires*, 115.

47 Ranouil, *Les recours entre coobligés*, 146–147; Canin, *Les actions récursoires*, 115.

48 Mignot, *Les obligations solidaires*, 615; Canin, *Les actions récursoires*, 121–122. On other limitations, see Canin, *Les actions récursoires*, 122–124.

49 Jourdain, 'Pour un réexamen', para. 6; Le Tourneau, *Droit de la responsabilité*, 670–671; Cabrillac, *Droit des obligations*, 330–331; Chénedé, *Le nouveau droit*, 269; Boré, 'Le recours', para. A.

50 Civ. I, 7.06.1977: JCP 1978 II 19003.

51 Personal action is considered a natural and historically first type of contribution claim that arouse already in *droit commun*. However, there are no specific provisions of the Code Civil that would regulate it, see Ranouil, *Les recours entre coobligés*, 96–97; Jacques Mestre, 'La pluralité d'obligés accessoires' (1981) *Revue trimestrielle de droit civil*, 125 *et seq.*; Lionel Andreu, *La réforme du régime général des obligations* (Paris: Dalloz, 2011), 106.

claim for contribution can be exercised on the basis of the *action mandati*,[52] the *action negotiorum gestorum*,[53] under Article 1317 of the Code Civil[54] or according to general principles of law such as equity,[55] prevention of unjust enrichment[56] or under rules used to establish a given liability.[57]

French law differs from the other legal orders insofar as it provides for an additional legal basis that is specific to contribution claims in EU competition law.[58] Decree of 9 March 2017 (no. 2017-305), which implemented Directive 2014/104/EU into the French legal order, added a new provision to the Code de Commerce. Article L.481-9 of the Code de Commerce reads that

52 See, for instance, Ranouil, *Les recours entre coobligés*, 96; Chantepie and Latina, *La réforme du droit des obligations*, 724; Cabrillac, *Droit des obligations*, 330–331; Chénedé, *Le nouveau droit*, 269.

53 See, for instance, Philippe Le Tourneau and Jérôme Julien, 'Solidarité' (2013) *Répertoire de droit civil Dalloz*, para. 154; François Terré, *Pour une réforme du droit de la responsabilité civile* (Paris: Dalloz, 2011), para. 1256; Philippe Malaurie, Laurent Aynes and Philippe Stoffel-Munck, *Droit civil. Les obligations* (Paris: Defrénois, 2004), para. 1381; Chantepie and Latina, *La réforme du droit des obligations*, 724; Cabrillac, *Droit des obligations*, 330–331; Chénedé, *Le nouveau droit*, 269.

54 Ranouil, *Les recours entre coobligés*, 179 *et seq*. Article 1317 of the Code Civil reads: '*Entre eux, les codébiteurs solidaires ne contribuent à la dette que chacun pour sa part. Celui qui a payé au-delàde sa part dispose d'un recours contre les autres à proportion de leur propre part. Si l'un d'eux est insolvable, sa part se répartit, par contribution, entre les codébiteurs solvables, y compris celui qui a fait le paiement et celui qui a bénéficié d'une remise de solidarité*' ('As between themselves, the contribution of each joint and several debtor is limited to his own share. A debtor who has satisfied the obligation beyond his own share has a right of recourse against the others in proportion to their own shares. If one of the debtors is insolvent, his share is divided amongst the other solvent debtor, including the one who has satisfied the obligation and the one who has benefited from a release of his joint and several obligation').

55 Canin, *Les actions récursoires*, 139 *et seq*.; Pierre Raynaud, 'La nature de l'obligation des coauteurs d'un dommage : obligation "in solidum" ou solidarité ?' in *Mélanges dédiés à Jean Vincent* 'L'extension en jurisprudence de la notion de solidarité passive' (1939) *Revue trimestrielle de droit civil* (Paris: Dalloz, 1981), 320.

56 See, for instance, Civ. I, 04.04.2001: JCP 2002 I 134; Cour de cassation (1st Ch. Civ.), 7.06.1977: JCP 1978 II 19003.

57 See, for instance, Civ. I, 07.07.1965: JCP G 1965 II 14376; Civ. III, 08.07.1971: Bull. Civ. III 448. Academics note that the multiplicity of legal bases for the personal contribution claim is, however, merely a theoretic discussion. The reason is that the rules named above are *quasi*-identical and differ only with respect to the question of what payments are recoverable. See, for instance, Marine Ranouil, *Les recours entre coobligés*, 164 *et seq*.; François Chabas 'Remarque sur l'obligation in solidum', 310; Jean Vincent, 'L'extension en jurisprudence de la notion de solidarité passive' (1939) *Revue trimestrielle de droit civil*, 601.

58 Other implementations of Directive 2014/104/EU into national legal orders refer to the right to claim contribution that already existed in traditional civil laws of the researched jurisdictions. See Ustawa z dnia 21 kwietnia 2017 r. o roszczeniach o naprawienie szkody wyrządzonej przez naruszenie prawa konkurencji, Dz.U. 2017 poz. 1132 ('Polish Act'); Neuntes Gesetz zur Änderung des Gesetzes gegen Wettbewerbsbeschränkungen of 1 July 2017, Bundesgesetzblatt Jahrgang 2017 Teil I Nr. 33, Bonn, 8. July 2017 ('9. GWB-Novelle'); The Claims in respect of Loss or Damage Arising from Competition Infringements (Competition Act 1998 and Other Enactments (Amendment)) Regulations 2017, [2017 No. 385] ('UK Act').

if several entities concurrently undertook an anticompetitive practice, they are jointly and severally (*solidairement*) liable for resulting damages; among themselves they contribute to the debt according to the gravity of their faults and causal role in generation of damage.[59]

THE RIGHT TO CLAIM INDEMNITY English law also distinguishes between claims for contribution and indemnity. Indemnity claims are essentially regular contribution claims. The difference is that they cover the entire payment and not its part.[60] Common law and equity allow for such claims under certain circumstances.[61] According to Lord Selborne LC in *Duncan, Fox and Co v. North and South Wales Bank*, an indemnity claim can be brought forward when

> [t]here is a primary and a secondary liability of two persons for one and the same debt and the debt being, as between the two, that of one of those persons only, and not equally of both, so that the other, if he should be compelled to pay he would be entitled to reimbursement from the person by whom (as between the two) he ought to have been paid.[62]

Section 2(2) of the Contribution Act of 1978 provides for the right to claim indemnity under the following terms:

> the court shall have power in any such proceedings to exempt any person from liability to make contribution, or to direct that the contribution to be recovered from any person shall amount to a complete indemnity.

Polish law also provides to some extent for a special claim for indemnity. Under Article 441(3) of the k.c.,

> anyone who remedies damage for which he is liable despite lack of fault has a recourse claim against the perpetrator if the damage was caused due to a fault on the perpetrator's part.

The wording of this provision suggests that this rule has a narrow scope of application. According to the majority of scholars, this claim applies when one of the debtors is liable on the basis of fault and the other is not.[63] The narrow scope of

59 Article L. 481-9 of the Code de Commerce reads: '*Lorsque plusieurs personnes physiques ou morales ont concouru à la réalisation d'une pratique anticoncurrentielle mentionnée à l'article L. 481-1, elles sont solidairement tenues de réparer le préjudice en résultant. Elles contribuent entre elles à la dette de réparation à proportion de la gravité de leurs fautes respectives et de leur rôle causal dans la réalisation du dommage*'.

60 See, for instance, *Whitham v. Bullock* [1939] 2 KB 81, 87.

61 The Law Commission, *Contribution*, paras. 9–11.

62 *Duncan, Fox and Co v. North and South Wales Bank* [1880] 6 AC 1, 110, HL.

63 See Ohanowicz, 'Glosa', 142; Szpunar, 'Glosa', 21, 23; Marek, 'Roszczenia regresowe', 294. See also Judgment of the Supreme Court from 16.10.1958, III CR 81/58, OSPiKA 1960, nr 1, poz. 6 and Ruling of the Supreme Court from 25.04.1962, I CR 469/61, OSNC 1963. nr 3, poz. 75.

Article 441(3) of the k.c. does not have, however, in practice a lot of meaning. It is believed that the judges can always grant indemnity under Article 441(2) of the k.c. and do not need to rely on Article 441(3) of the k.c.[64]

The distinction between different legal bases for indemnity claims and contribution claims is characteristic to English law. German,[65] French[66] and most of Polish laws[67] allow for indemnity claims without distinguishing them from contribution claims. In these legal orders, indemnity is just a claim for 100 per cent contribution. It is the judges' discretion whether to award a partial contribution or a total one.

3.3.1.2 The Right to Claim Contribution Before the Creditor Has Satisfied Its Rights

The claim for contribution arises in principle only *after* the creditor has satisfied its rights against joint and several debtors. This is because contribution claims are a reaction to the creditor's freedom to choose from whom to claim the debt. They are only needed when a given debtor has paid in excess of its own liability share.

German and English laws allow, however, exceptional claims for contribution in parallel or before the creditor has satisfied its rights. In Germany, the right of contribution under § 426(1) of the BGB can be exercised as a claim for participation (*Mitwirkunganspruch*). Such a claim can be made before the claimant has paid the creditor its debt in order to make other debtors participate in the fulfilment of the debt up to their respective shares of liability.[68] In this way, a joint and several debtor can pay its part of debt upfront to its co-debtors and be released from its liability (this is a so-called *Befreiung*).[69]

64 See Safjan, 'Art. 441', paras. 10, 12; Bieniek, 'Solidarność; Regres' paras. 19, 41–38; Grzegorz Karaszewski, '*Komentarz do art. 441 Kodeksu cywilnego*' (2014) *LEX*, paras. 8–9; Marek, 'Roszczenia regresowe', 91–297; Nesterowicz and Bagińska, 'Multiple Tortfeasors', 156; Wojciech Dubis, *Komentarze Kodeksowe. Kodeks Cywilny. Komentarz* (Warszawa: C.H. Beck, 2014), 789; Agnieszka Rzetecka-Gil, 'Warunki odpowiedzialności solidarnej za szkodę. Komentarz do art. 441 Kodeksu cywilnego' (2011) *LEX*, para. 16; Antoszek, 'Art. 441', paras. 16–17; Śmieja Andrzej, 'Art. 441' in Adam Olejniczak (ed.), *Prawo zobowiązań – część ogólna. System Prawa Prywatnego*, 21 vols. (Warszawa: C.H. Beck, 2014), vol. VI, 682; Lewaszkiewicz-Petrykowska, *Wyrządzenie szkody przez kilka osób*, 161–162; Adam Olejniczak, 'Art. 441' in Andrzej Kidyba (ed.), *Kodeks cywilny. Komentarz. Zobowiązania. Część ogólna*, 4 vols. (Warszawa: Wolters Kluwer Polska, 2014), vol. III, para. 3.

65 See, for instance, BGH, NJW 1971, 752, 753–754.

66 See, for instance, de la Bâtie, 'Responsabilité délictuelle', 165–166.

67 See Section 3.3.1.1.

68 Thoma, *Der internationale Regress*, 46; Kuhlmann, *Rückgriffsgrundlagen bei Gesamtschuld*, 127–128; Schmidt, *Gesamtschuld und Gesamtschuldregress*, 121; Meier, *Gesamtschulden*, 601–626; Bernhard Prediger, *Zur Auslegung und Anwendung der Regelungen im BGB über die Gesamtschuld* (Frankfurt am Main: Peter Lang, Europäische Hochschulschriften, 1988), 84.

69 The claims for participation (*Mitwirkungs-* and *Befreiunganspruch*) are justified by the fact that in German doctrine it is assumed that the co-debtors together constitute a community –

English law also provides for the possibility to claim contribution before the creditor has satisfied its rights against joint and several debtors. Such a claim is exercised as a specific remedy, *quia timet* injunction. It allows the claimant to ask the court to make the defendant perform its obligation to the creditor before the claimant is called by it. This remedy is granted when it would be inappropriate for the claimant to cover the entire liability owed to the creditor alone.[70] Judges can adopt three types of orders. First, a declaratory one: the court declares that the claimant is entitled to contribution should it be requested to pay the creditor.[71] Second, an order exonerating the claimant from future payment and requesting the defendant to pay the creditor.[72] Third, an order requesting the defendant to establish a fund, which would reimburse the claimant upon its payment to the creditor.[73]

French and Polish laws do not provide for any special type of contribution claim that could be brought forward before the creditor has exercised its rights against the debtors.

3.3.1.3 Modifications to the Right to Claim Contribution Brought by Implementations of Directive 2014/104/EU

Directive 2014/104/EU requires EU Member States to ensure the right to claim contribution in private antitrust enforcement. The Directive calls for the introduction of a general rule that[74]

> an infringer may recover a contribution from any other infringer, the amount of which shall be determined in the light of their relative responsibility for the harm caused by the infringement of competition law.[75]

The obligation to introduce this rule could have inspired EU Member States to modify the already existing frameworks for the right to claim contribution. This is the approach taken by the French legislator, who adopted a new rule on contribution under Article L.481-9 of the Code de Commerce (see Section 3.3.1.1).

Other researched jurisdictions were not so far-going in their law making. The Polish act implementing Directive 2014/104/EU merely refers to Article 441(2) of the

Schuldgemeinschaft. See Meier, *Gesamtschulden*, 602, 627–639, 684–691; Prediger, *Gesamtschuld*, 152–163.

70 Mitchell, *The Law of Contribution*, 8, 285–288; Williams, *Joint Torts and Contributory Negligence*, 148–150.

71 Mitchell, *The Law of Contribution*, 265–266, 282–285.

72 Ibid., 266, 285–288.

73 Ibid., 266.

74 Directive 2014/104/EU requires also establishing special rules on contribution with respect to those engaged in consensual dispute resolution, immunity recipients and small and medium undertakings. These special rules are the subject of Chapter 4.

75 Article 11(5) of Directive 2014/104/EU.

k.c. as a relevant provision for dealing with contribution claims in the context of private antitrust enforcement.[76]

A similar approach was adopted by the UK and German bills implementing the Directive. The UK law refers to the Contribution Act 1978 as a relevant instrument for claiming contribution.[77] The German 9. GWB-Novelle[78] also establishes in its § 33d that traditional rules on joint and several liability apply.[79] Both of these bills nevertheless modify the way in which the contribution should be assessed. The UK bill requires that

> [t]he amount of contribution that one person liable in respect of the loss or damage may recover from another must be determined in the light of their relative responsibility for the whole of the loss or damage caused by the infringement.[80]

German law sets a specific criterion for the internal division of liability, which is 'a proportion of the harm caused by each of the antitrust infringers'.[81] Such a criterion is not present in § 426(1) and § 426(2) of the BGB, which require an equal division of liability if no other apportionment is established.

This demonstrates that although there is no sector-specific legal basis for contribution claims dealing with antitrust issues in England and Germany, general provisions are modified to serve competition law aims.

3.3.1.4 Conclusions

This comparison demonstrates that similarities in contribution regimes among the researched jurisdictions are limited. Their likeness concerns the fact that in most researched countries contribution claims can be exercised either as a personal right or as subrogation (with the exception of Poland).

76 See Articles 5(3) and 6(1) of the Polish Act.

77 See Section 16(1) of the UK Act.

78 See note 58.

79 Paragraph 33d GWB reads: *(1) Begehen mehrere gemeinschaftlich einen Verstoß im Sinne des § 33a Absatz 1, sind sie als Gesamtschuldner zum Ersatz des daraus entstehenden Schadens verpflichtet. Im Übrigen finden die paras. 830 und 840 Absatz 1 des Bürgerlichen Gesetzbuchs Anwendung. (2) Das Verhältnis, in dem die Gesamtschuldner untereinander für die Verpflichtung zum Ersatz und den Umfang des zu lesitenden Ersatzes haften, hängt von den Umständen ab, insbesondere davon, in welchem Maß sie den Schaden verursacht haben. Im Übrigen finden die paras. 421 bis 425 sowie 426 Absatz 1 Satz 2 und Absatz 2 des Bürgerlichen Gesetzbuchs Anwendung. ((1) Where several infringers jointly commit an infringement pursuant to § 33a(1), they shall be jointly and severally liable for the harm caused by the infringement. Furthermore, paras. 830 and 840(1) of the German Civil Code shall apply. (2) The proportion to which the joint and several debtors shall be liable, in relation to one another, to pay damages and the amount that has to be compensated shall depend on the circumstances of the case, in particular, on the extent to which they have caused the harm. Furthermore, paras. 421 to 425 as well as § 426(1) sentence 2 and (2) of the German Civil Code shall apply.)*

80 See note 58, Section 38(2).

81 See § 33d(2) of the GWB.

At this point, the similarities end. England and Wales divide contribution claims based on whether liability for a *debt* or for a *damage* is in question and distinguish contribution and indemnity claims. Such divisions of the right to claim for contribution are generally not present in other researched legal orders.

English and German laws also differ from the other legal orders researched in that they make it possible to claim contribution *before* the creditor has satisfied its rights against the joint and several debtors. In England *quia timet* injunctions and in Germany *Mitwirkung* and *Befreiung* claims allow the claimant to enforce contribution before or in the moment when the creditor starts to enforce its claims.

Finally, the researched jurisdictions implemented Directive 2014/104/EU in a different way. The French legislator decided to introduce a special provision on the right to claim contribution in the context of private antitrust enforcement. Other researched legal orders generally referred to the existing rules on contribution.

3.3.2 *Competition Law Analysis*

The issues arising if the above rules are applied in the competition law context are multitudinous. In particular, it is worth verifying which types of contribution claims can be used in competition law, whether contribution claims enforced prior to the satisfaction of the creditor's debt are available in competition law and whether contribution claims are enforced under different rules in the context of public and private antitrust enforcement.

3.3.2.1 Types of Claims Available in the Context of EU Competition Law

THE PERSONAL RIGHT TO CLAIM CONTRIBUTION In all researched EU legal orders, the personal right to claim contribution is available in competition law.

Contribution claims resulting from joint and several liability imposed in private antitrust enforcement clearly fall within the scope of the English Contribution Act of 1978.[82] The conditions for its application are met in the case of actions for antitrust damages. Infringers of competition law cause damage to third parties and are liable for this damage as joint and several debtors. The UK's implementation of Directive 2014/104/EU also clearly states that Section 1 of the Contribution Act of 1978 applies in the case of contribution claims sought in the context of private competition law enforcement. Regarding the liability for the Commission's fine, contribution claims should be available in English common law and equity. Although the review of case law has not revealed any contribution litigation specific to competition law, the current catalogue of claimants includes co-debtors of

[82] Similarly Nathy Dunleavy, 'Contribution among Antitrust Defendants in English Law' (2009) 30 *European Competition Law Review*, 1, 23.

statutory liabilities or liabilities against public authorities, such as tax debts.[83] As a result, contribution claims in antitrust should be allowed as well.

German *Ausgleichsklage* is also applicable to antitrust law liabilities. Although § 426 of the BGB is controversial as sometimes joint and several liability is not easy to establish,[84] in competition law such liability is established by virtue of law.[85] The application of § 426(1) of the BGB in antitrust is also confirmed by the BGH in the *Calcium carbide* judgment[86] and § 33d as introduced by the 9. GWB-Novelle.

France and Poland have traditionally given a wide scope to the right to contribution. In France, the personal claim for contribution has a multitude of possible legal bases. These range from general notions such as equity to Article L.481-9 of the Code de Commerce, which is specifically tailored to competition law. In Poland, Article 441(2) of the k.c. applies in the context of private antitrust enforcement. In other situations, Article 441(2) of the k.c is applied by analogy in the form of *regres sensu largo*. In light of such wide interpretations of the personal claim for

[83] See note 87.

[84] For a review of positions, see, for instance, Kuhlmann, *Rückgriffsgrundlagen bei Gesamtschuld*, 69–70; Meier, *Gesamtschulden*, 30*et seq*.; Schmidt, *Gesamtschuld und Gesamtschuldregress*, 24 *et seq*.; Helmut Rüßmann, '§ 421 BGB' in Markus Junker (ed.), *Juris Praxis Kommentar – BGB. Schuldrecht*, 6 vols. (Saarbrücken: juris, 2010), vol. II(1), paras. 9–20; Markus Gehrlein, '§ 421 BGB' in Heinz Georg Bamberger and Herbert Roth (eds.), *Kommentar zum Bürgerlichen Gesetzbuch*, 3 vols. (München: C.H. Beck, 2012), vol. I, paras. 5–8; Peter Bydlinski, '§ 426 BGB' in Wolfgang Krüger (ed.), *Münchener Kommentar zum Bürgerlichen Gesetzbuch. Schuldrecht. Allgemeiner Teil*, 14 vols. (München: C.H. Beck, 2012), vol. II, paras. 9–43; Lars Böttcher, '§ 421 BGB' in Harm-Peter Westermann, Barbara Grunewald and Georg Maier-Reimer (eds.), *Erman Bürgerliches Gesetzbuch* (Köln: OVS Verlag Dr. Otto Walter Schmidt, 2011), paras. 8–14. Paragraph 426 of the BGB is sometimes claimed to apply only to the *echte Gesamtschuld*; however, it is not excluded that it would apply also to *unechte Gesamtschuld* if other provisions are unable to provide for a contribution right. For more on *unechte Gesamtschuld*, see Schmidt, *Gesamtschuld und Gesamtschuldregress*, 86–98; Barbara Völzmann-Stickelbrock, '§ 421 BGB' in Barbara Dauner-Lieb, Thomas Heidel and Gerhard Ring (eds.), *Nomos Kommentar. BGB Schuldrecht*, 8 vols. (Baden-Baden: Nomos, 2014), vol. II(1), paras. 18–21; Gehrlein, '§ 421 BGB', paras. 14–18; Peter Bydlinski, '§ 421 BGB' in WolfgangKrüger (ed.), *Münchener Kommentar zum Bürgerlichen Gesetzbuch. Schuldrecht. Allgemeiner Teil*, 14 vols. (München: C.H. Beck, 2012), vol. II, paras. 60–71; Böttcher, '§ 421 BGB', para. 25. For more on particular theories of establishing *echte Gesamtschuld*, see Ludwig Enneccerus and Heinrich Lehmann, *Recht der Schuldverhältnisse* (Tübingen: Mohr, 1958), para. 313 II; Schmidt, *Gesamtschuld und Gesamtschuldregress*6*et seq*.; Selb, *Schadensbegriff und Regreßmethoden*, 14; Thomas Thiede, 'Private Enforcement of Anti-trust Damages in Europe. A Germanic Perspective on Directive 2014/104/EU' (2016) *ELTE Law Journal*, 151; Ehmann, *Die Gesamtschuld*, 30 *et seq*.; Helmut Rüßmann, 'Die Abgrenzung der Gesamtschuld von anderen Schuldnermehrheiten - BGHZ 59, 97' (1974) *Juristische Schulung*, 292.

[85] LG München, BeckRS 2013, 10095, para. II(1)(aa); Thoma, *Der internationale Regress*, 40–42; Weinhold, *Der Gesamtschuldnerausgleich*, 104; Christian Kersting and NicolaPreuß, *Umsetzung der Kartellschadensersatzrichtlinie (2014/104/EU). Ein Gesetzgebungsvorschlag aus der Wissenschaft* (Baden-Baden: Nomos, 2015), para. 112. However, Julia Körner claims that joint and several liability cannot be binding upon national judges under Article 16 of Regulation 1/2003 and the principle of supremacy of EU law, see Körner, *Die Gesamtschuld im Kartellbußgeldrecht*, 232–236.

[86] BGH, BeckRS 2015, 00033, paras. 53 *et seq*.

contribution in France and Poland, such claims seem to also be available in the competition law context.

SUBROGATION In England, Germany, and France, contribution can be claimed by means of subrogation. The existence of such a claim may be disputed in the context of public competition law enforcement. The problem is that, in the case of subrogation, the entity claiming contribution enters into the legal situation of the creditor. In public enforcement, the creditor is not a private party whose rights can be easily transferred. It is the role of the European Commission – a public body with administrative powers – to enforce the debt. It is difficult to imagine how a debt with rights typical to the Commission could be transferred to private parties.

This is not a novel problem as it boils down to the question of whether subrogation can be used when the subrogated entity is a public authority. This question was answered positively in the researched legal orders. Subrogation has already appeared and was accepted in England, Germany and France in the context of public-law liabilities, such as those regarding tax, custom and crimes.[87] The German BGH also did not express any concerns when faced with a request to claim contribution through subrogation in *Calcium Carbide*.[88] As a result, it is very likely that subrogation-based claims for contribution would be allowed in the context of public competition law enforcement.

A specific concern regarding subrogation exists in France. Following the introduction of a specific competition law claim under Article L.481-9 of the Code de Commerce, the question arises as to whether antitrust infringers could still enjoy the claim based on subrogation under Article 1346 of the Code Civil. It seems that the risk of derogating Article 1346 of the Code Civil is not high. In public enforcement, Article 1346 of the Code Civil applies directly, while Article L.481-9 of the Code de Commerce could apply only *per analogy*. The latter provision is thus unlikely to become the exclusive basis for the right to claim contribution. Even in private enforcement, it is unlikely that French judges would refrain from the traditional use of subrogation only because of Article L.481-9 of the Code de Commerce.[89] This is because there are no provisions on the priority or exclusive application of this rule. Coupled with a long tradition of using subrogation, this makes derogation from the

87 See, for instance, BGH, NJW 1973, 1077, 1078; BGH, NJW 1963, 1873, 1874; Cass. Crim., 21.05.1959: JCP 1959 IV. 85; Crim., 12.01.1966 and 22.02.1966: Gaz. Pal. 1966 I 425; *Brook's Wharf and Bull Wharf Ltd v. Goodman Bros A* [1937] 1 KB 534, 544–545.

88 The claim under § 426(2) of the BGB was rejected because the claim based on § 426(1) of the BGB was also rejected, see LG München, BeckRS 2013, 10095, para. II(1)(b), OLG München, BeckRS 2012, 8896, para. II(2)(a)(cc). The application of § 426(2) of the BGB was left open by the BGH, see BGH, BeckRS 2015, 00033, para. 116.

89 According to Marine Ranouil, the multiplicity of legal actions for contribution is not accidental, but a response to an increased exposure of some entities to liability, see Ranouil, *Les recours entre coobligés*, 127–128, 135–136. French courts may be thus hesitant to refrain from one of the options for contribution.

latter unlikely. As a result, it is expected that contribution claims based on subrogation would apply in competition law cases adjudicated under French law.

INDEMNITY As described in Section 3.3.1.1, indemnity claims are mostly adjudicated under the same rules as contribution claims. England and, to a limited extent, Poland are the exceptions. It is interesting to ask whether separate indemnity claims are available in the context of liabilities stemming from EU competition law.

In England, *Duncan, Fox and Co v. North and South Wales Bank* sets two conditions for indemnity claims: the liabilities must concern the same debt and one liability must be primary to another one. In Poland, the condition to claim indemnity is that the claimant not be at fault, while the defendant be clearly at fault.[90]

These conditions are difficult to satisfy in the context of private antitrust infringement. Both the claimant and the defendant participate in a concerted action, and their behaviour is principally similarly blameful. As a result, the discussed indemnity claim seems to be excluded.

The rules on indemnity may, however, apply in the case of competition law liability established by the decisions of the European Commission. In fact, two interpretations are possible.

On the one hand, it may be argued that those jointly and severally liable for the fine are placed on an equal footing and indemnity claims are excluded. The reason is that the Commission found them all liable in the same way when ensuring the effective enforcement of EU competition law. Such reasoning is supported by *Kendrion*, in which the GCEU claims:

> as regards the payment of the fine, the joint and several liability between two companies constituting such an economic entity cannot be reduced to a type of security provided by the parent company in order to guarantee payment of the fine imposed on the subsidiary.[91]

On the other hand, there is often one company directly involved in the anticompetitive strategy and other companies fined by the Commission to ensure the effectiveness of the fine. On this basis, it could be claimed that the addressees' liability differs and not all of them are equally blameful for antitrust infringement. The CJEU stated in *Siemens Österreich* that

> where, in a relationship entailing vertical capital links of that kind, the parent company in question is itself deemed to have infringed EU competition rules, *its liability for the infringement is wholly derived from that of its subsidiary.*[92]

90 See note 63.
91 GCEU, *Kendrion*, para. 56.
92 CJEU, *Siemens Österreich*, para. 47

The way to reconcile these two interpretations is to rely upon the division between the external and internal dimensions of joint and several liability.[93] In the external dimension, the liability of those fined jointly and severally is equal for all undertakings concerned as it is established for the purposes of EU competition law enforcement. The internal dimension has no special functions with respect to competition law, and liability should be interpreted according to traditional civil laws as the Commission lacks any jurisdiction. Consequently, the liability of individual companies may be considered unequal: one company is liable for its personal acts and another company acts as a guarantor of the payment. Following this reasoning, one should be able to claim indemnity for liabilities stemming from the Commission's decisions.

3.3.2.2 Claiming Contribution Before the Creditor Has Been Satisfied

English and German laws on contribution make it possible to claim contribution before the creditor has received the debt owed by joint and several debtors. English *quia timet* injunctions and German *Mitwirkung* and *Befreiung* claims are, however, controversial and should be rejected in the competition law context.

A first argument against the use of such claims is general to tort law. Contrary to contractual claims with respect to which liability can be assessed upfront,[94] in tort the amount of liability is unknown until the wrongdoer is called to pay the debt. In cases of joint and several liability, it is difficult to require one of the several debtors to contribute its share to the payment of the debt if the overall amount of compensation is not established yet.[95]

A second and decisive argument for rejecting *quia timet* injunctions and *Mitwirkung* and *Befreiung* claims is that their exercise would breach the principle of effectiveness of EU competition law. By allowing them, one would allow contribution litigation to take place in parallel to the moment when the creditor is seeking compensation. This results in a disadvantage for the creditor. It limits the solvency of some debtors and the creditor's choice as to from whom to claim the debt. Since joint and several liability's objective is to increase the chances of enforcing the creditor's debt, *quia timet* injunctions and *Mitwirkung* and *Befreiung* claims are contradictory to the principle of effectiveness of EU competition law.[96] As a

[93] See Section 2.1.2.4.

[94] Mitchell, *The Law of Contribution*, 267, 269; Kuhlmann, *Rückgriffsgrundlagen bei Gesamtschuld*, 126; Schmidt, *Gesamtschuld und Gesamtschuldregress*, 195; Meier, *Gesamtschulden*, 603, 639; Götte, *Gesamtschuldbegriff und Regressproblem*, 29*et seq.*; Prediger, *Gesamtschuld*, 81*et seq.*

[95] Ibid.

[96] Contrary, Inderst and Thomas, *Schadensersatz bei Kartellverstößen*, 400 and Hösch, *Der schadensrechtliche Innenausgleich*, 186. Due to the rejection of *Mitwirkung* and *Befreiung* claims in competition law, such claims will not be analysed further on.

consequence, they should be prohibited in the case of liability stemming from EU competition law.

3.3.2.3 Uniform Regime or Separate Regimes for Claiming Contribution in the Context of Private and Public Enforcement

Jurisdictions range from having one distinct singular regime to multiple separate regimes to deal with contribution claims in antitrust. An application of the traditional framework of contribution claims to competition law requires an assessment of the regimes in the researched jurisdictions.

English law is an example of a jurisdiction that clearly provides for two different regimes for the liabilities established in public and private antitrust enforcement. The key reason for this is a distinction between contribution for debt and for damage, which is dealt with either under common law and equity or under the Contribution Act. These different bodies of law apply to contribution claims sought respectively in the context of public and private enforcement.

Although a distinction between contribution claims sought in the case of liability for damage and for debt also exists in Polish law, Poland provides for a singular regime for contribution claims in antitrust law. Formally, Polish law applies Article 441(2) of the k.c. directly only in case of the liability for the damage (*regres sensu stricto*). However, the same provision is applied by analogy when the liability is for debt (*regres sensu largo*). The difference between these contribution claims is believed to be only nominal.[97] As a result, although competition law liabilities may be put into different categories depending on the type of enforcement, Polish law provides for substantially the same claim for contribution. This state has not been changed by the Polish implementation of Directive 2014/104/EU.[98]

German and French laws tend to follow the Polish model. In principle, both in Germany and in France it does not matter whether the claim for contribution is enforced in the context of public or private enforcement of EU competition law. German § 426(1) and (2) of the BGB use the term *Gesamtschuld*, and French law uses the terms *solidarité* and *obligation in solidum* to determine the application of the right to claim contribution. Joint and several liability is imposed both for the payment of fines to the European Commission and for the payment of damages, so the distinction between public and private enforcement is of limited relevance. The BGH also expressly confirmed that the liability stemming from the Commission's fines is comparable with the liability for torts based on fault.[99] This indicates that in

[97] See note 64.

[98] Ibid., Article 5(3). See also Dominik Wolski, 'Solidarna odpowiedzialność naruszycieli' in Tadeusz Skoczny (ed.), *Prawo konkurencji. 25 lat* (Warszawa: Wolter Kluwers Polska, 2015), para. 2.2.2. This statement does not refer to modifications to the special regimes of joint and several liability, which are discussed in Chapter 4.

[99] BGH, BeckRS 2015, 00033, para. 43.

Germany and France there should be one regime for contribution claims in all kinds of antitrust liability.

One interesting question is whether the modifications introduced by French and German implementations of Directive 2014/104/EU only apply to private antitrust enforcement. This would create a split between contribution claims sought in this context and in public antitrust enforcement. As mentioned above, the French implementation of the Directive introduced a new legal basis for contribution claims; the German one added a new criterion for determining the debtors' relative liabilities.[100] Such modifications apply directly only to contribution claims sought in the context of private antitrust enforcement, as the wording of the relevant provisions suggests.[101] This leads to a different treatment of contribution claims sought in private and public antitrust enforcement.

As such a split is not traditional to France and Germany, it appears to be doubtful whether it is desirable to complicate the existing contribution system. At any rate, it should be asked whether it is possible and recommended to apply the modifications included in French and German implementations of Directive 2014/104/EU by analogy to contribution claims sought in the context of public antitrust enforcement. This seems to be a possible and reasonable option. The French bill introduced a new legal basis for contribution claims that are specific to competition law, but general enough that it can be applied in the case of liabilities stemming from both public and private enforcement.[102] The 9. GWB-Novelle's modification was to name a criterion (*Verursachung*) to determine debtors' relative liability.[103] As this term is already in line with the current adjudication under § 426 of the BGB (see Section 3.6.1.2), it is recommended that it be used generally in public and private enforcement.

3.3.2.4 Conclusions

There are multiple legal bases available in the researched jurisdictions for antitrust infringers envisioning contribution litigation. In England and Wales, these are the claims based on Section 2(1) of the Contribution Act, claims in common law and

[100] This statement does not refer to modifications to the special regimes of joint and several liability, which are discussed in Chapter 4.

[101] Article L. 481-9 of the Code de Commerce reads: '*Lorsque plusieurs personnes physiques ou morales ont concouru à la réalisation d'une pratique anticoncurrentielle, elles sont solidairement tenues de réparer le préjudice en résultant*' ('If several entities concurrently undertook an anticompetitive practice, they are jointly and severally liable for *resulting damages*'). § 33d(1) of the GWB reads: '*Begehen mehrere gemeinschaftlich einen Verstoß im Sinne des § 33a Absatz 1, sind sie als Gesamtschuldner zum Ersatz des daraus entstehenden Schadens verpflichtet*' ('Where several infringers jointly commit an infringement pursuant to § 33a(1), they shall be jointly and severally liable *for the harm caused by the infringement*').

[102] See Section 3.3.1.1.

[103] Ibid.

equity, both as a personal right and subrogation, as well as specific indemnity claims. In Germany, these are personal and subrogation claims pursuant to § 426(1) of the BGB and § 426(2) of the BGB. In France, both subrogation and personal claims are available pursuant to a number of legal bases, including Article 134 of the Code Civil, Article 1317 of the Code Civil and Article L. 481-9 of the Code de Commerce. In Poland, there is only one legal basis available, Article 441(2) of the k.c.; however, it has a wide and universal scope of application. This variety of legal bases and their ability to accommodate the competition law context of the dispute is satisfying from the standpoint of the principle of effectiveness. A choice of various legal tools allows the claimant to match the instrument to its needs.

On the other hand, from the very early stage of choosing a relevant legal basis, claiming contribution may be a challenge. The claimant and the defendant face a lot of legal uncertainty over which of the instruments they should use in a dispute on contribution.

Additionally, most legal orders researched do not have a legal basis tailored towards competition law. Even those that do fail to establish the relationship that this legal basis has with other ways of securing contribution. This leads to additional uncertainty over which of the legal bases applies.

Finally, competition law mandates that not all of the available types of contribution can be applicable in a competition law context. This concerns contribution claims that are enforced before the creditor has satisfied its debt.

The relationship between contribution claims exercised in the context of public and private enforcement is not clear either. France and Germany have introduced a partial regulation of contribution claims in the area of private antitrust enforcement, which raises some doubts. It is uncertain whether the traditionally unitary system for contribution claims has been split between the legal bases applicable to public and private antitrust enforcement. It is also unknown whether a unitary system will be maintained by the application of the rules tailored to competition law coherently in the public and private enforcement contexts.

In order to simplify the framework for contribution claims, a major recommendation would be to establish one claim tailored to competition law that would apply both in the context of public and private antitrust enforcement. The French Article L. 481-9 of the Code de Commerce is a good example. This is a personal claim for a contribution that covers indemnity. It can be exercised after the satisfaction of the debt owed to the creditor. A single legal basis that is specifically dedicated to EU competition law will guarantee the effective right to contribution while allowing contribution to be claimed in a simple and predictable way.

3.4 ADDRESSEES OF CONTRIBUTION CLAIMS

Another question arising for those considering claiming contribution is against whom such claims can be brought forward. The crucial issue is whether it is possible to claim contribution from entities other than the addressees of already adopted judgments and decisions establishing antitrust liability.

3.4.1 *Comparative Analysis*

The researched jurisdictions are unanimous in stating that it is possible to claim contribution from entities whose liability has not been established beforehand. What matters is the ability of the claimant to prove in the proceeding on contribution that the defendant is also jointly and severally liable for the liability in question.[104]

3.4.2 *Competition Law Analysis*

While traditional civil laws take a wide and inclusive approach towards the entities that can be brought into contribution proceedings, this position is more uncertain when we consider EU competition law. It has been established in Section 2.2.5.1 of Chapter 2 that competition law limits the catalogue of entities from which contribution can be claimed in the public enforcement context.

3.4.2.1 Liability Established in the Commission's Decisions

The feeling that not all companies that participated in the infringement have been fined is perfectly plausible given the Commission's wide discretion in choosing addressees of its decisions. For instance, it is possible that a subsidiary was encouraged to engage in an anticompetitive practice by its former parent company, which before the adoption of the Commission's decision sold the subsidiary and its role in the infringement was not accounted for by the European Commission. Such a company may be interested in requesting its former parent to contribute to the payment of fines that are imposed on it.

Based on national civil laws, it would be possible to bring forward a contribution claim against the companies that avoided liability in the Commission's infringement decision. However, EU competition law excludes this possibility. First, liability is imposed in the Commission's decisions in a constitutive way. Second, the Commission determines the fines having specific companies in mind and with the aim to deter them from engaging in anticompetitive practices again. Third, the Commission's decisions enjoy supremacy over national laws. In this light, it is

[104] With regard to England and Wales, see, for instance, Williams, *Joint Torts and Contributory Negligence*xli. With regard to Germany, see, for instance, Magnus, 'Multiple Tortfeasors under German Law', 102. With regard to Poland, see Judgment of the Supreme Court from 07.03.1978, III CZP 14/178, not published. With regard to France, see Canin, *Les actions récursoires*, 44, 48; Ranouil, *Les recours entre coobligés*, 249; Henri Mazeaud et al., *Traité théorique et pratique*, vol. II, 955.

impossible to establish joint and several liability independently from the Commission in contribution litigation. The Commission's decision to impose joint and several liability on chosen companies needs to be respected pursuant to the principle of cooperation as concluded in *Siemens Österreich* (see Section 2.2.3).

Consequently, the Commission's determination of those held jointly and severally liable for the Commission's fines needs to be respected. This means that one cannot claim contribution from other companies than those who have been designated by the Commission.

3.4.2.2 Liability Established in the Courts' Judgments

It is even more likely for the need for contribution to arise in the context of private enforcement. Victims of antitrust infringements can claim compensation for the sustained damage only from chosen infringers of EU competition law, even though more entities were involved in it. For instance, if a company is a victim of bid rigging, it is likely to sue the company that won the contract and not all other co-conspirators. As a result, antitrust infringers need to commence contribution proceedings to share the burden of liability with the other co-infringers.

The need for contribution can also arise among companies that share corporate links. In *Skanska* and *Sumal*, the CJEU established that national courts can apply the doctrines of economic continuity and undertaking in the same way as the European Commission, further extending the catalogue of companies that can be held jointly and severally liable for infringements of EU competition law.[105] However, single economic units may break up in the moment when the Commission adopts a decision and the companies that once shared corporate links are unlikely to pay for third-party liabilities. This dynamics is even more visible when the courts would apply the notion of economic continuity and impose joint and several liability on companies who split and followed different corporate paths much earlier. In reaction to the claims brought forward by private claimants against specific infringers, the latter may request a contribution from anybody they think are co-liable for the misconduct. This includes also the cases when the infringer's contribution claim is based on the notion of the undertaking, single economic unit and economic continuity. Although such concepts are most frequently used in the context of public enforcement, the Skanska and Sumal cases confirm they can be deployed in private litigation. If contribution claims follow subsequently, also the infringer can establish that its co-conspirator is liable for the damage, because it belonged to the same undertaking in the moment of violation.

As discussed in Section 2.2.5.1 of Chapter 2, EU competition law does not set any limitations as to from whom and how contribution can be claimed in this situation, because the liability concerns private damages. . In this context, The liability is

[105] CJEU, *Skanska*, para. 51.

established by a private court, and there is no Commission decision that specifies the measure of deterrence and punishment. The liability established in proceedings on damages reflects the harm sustained by victims of antitrust infringements, and there is no room to attach to the damages an additional element of deterrence that would need to be later on protected in contribution litigation (see Section 2.1.1.2).

The practical question is whether claims for contribution can be made in all configurations when the notion of a single economic unit is applied. For instance, one may wonder whether contribution can be claimed or not by a subsidiary from its parent company, inversely by a parent company ('bottom-up'), from its subsidiary or by a subsidiary ('top-down'), from another subsidiary. This of course depends on the extent to which national courts can apply joint and several liability. Contribution claims are a flip side of the joint and several liability coin, and contribution can be claimed in all constellations joint and several liability is applied. Based on *Skanska* and *Sumal*, joint and several liability can apply both 'bottom-up' and 'top-down', and there is no reason why not to apply it to sister companies, as the Commission also holds such companies liable for antitrust infringements. The bottom line of the CJEU's reasoning is that the notion of undertaking needs to be applied in the same way in private enforcement as it is applied now in the public one.[106] This means that contribution claims can be enforced in all constellations, because competition law attributes obligations relating to compliance and liabilibity to entire undertakings, that is all companies following a united conduct on the market. As put by AG Pitruzzella, 'there is no logical reason why liability cannot be attributed not only in the 'bottom-up' sense (from the subsidiary to the parent company), but also in the 'top-down' sense (from the parent company to the subsidiary).'[107]

That said, the claimant has to prove contributionliability of the co-infringers differently, depending on whether itthe claimant is a subsidiary suing its former parent company or a parent company suing its former subsidiary. In the first scenario, the claimant has to show a single condition - that its parent excercised decisive control over its commercial policy. In the second scenario, the claimant needs to also prove:

> the existence of a specific link between the economic activity of that[the] subsidiary and the subject matter of the infringement for which the parent company was held to be responsible, that subsidiary.[108]

This additional requirement for establishing 'top-down' liability has been introduced for a pragmatic reason, as many corporate groups are 'conglomerates' active across a range of industries. For example, a corporate group can be active in various sectors, from traditional manufacturing to banking to restuaration and hospitality. If one subsidiary participates in a cartel between hotels, this has no connection with

[106] CJEU, *Skanska*, para. 47.
[107] AG Pitruzzella, *Sumal*, para. 52.
[108] CJEU, *Sumal*, para. 51

the activity of its another subsidiary, say a petrochemical producer, and the latter should no bear any liability. The proof of 'specific link' between the subdisiary's and parent's economic activity remedies the risk of imposing liability on companies that had nothing to do with the antitrust infringement.

This is a welcome step. Although one may ask whether this condition is actually necessary in the context of contribution litigation, which is fully dedicated to approportionment of antitrust liability. As will be shown in Section 3.6, below, there exist many criteria for division of antitrust liability that can be perfectly used to attribute liability to those who were actually involved in the infringement (e.g., relative fault or causation) and that can show with more granularity the contribution of each company to the infringement and occurance of harm.

On a more general note, it is also interesting to observe that the CJEU decided to require a proof of 'specific link' between the parent's and subsidiary's economic activity' only for the 'top-down' attribution of liability. Of course, in strict terms, parent company is always active in the same area as its subsidiary, so there is no need to prove this element in the 'bottom-up' scenario. However, in practice parent companies engagement in its subsidiaries' activities can be sometimes illusionary. Consider pure holding companies, investment funds, foundations that can exercise decisive influence over their subsidiaries and be liable for antitrust infringements. The Commission has so far not hesitated to impose fines on such companies even though it is highly unlikely that they actually follow the activities by their subsidiaries, let alone have any impact on their commercial conduct.

This practice has been for decenials of holding various entities jointly and severally liable only because they belong to the same corporate group is, however, often considered excessive,[109] and it is surprising to see that the CJEU did not impose any limitation on imposing 'bottom up' liability when it took the decision to restrict the downwards attribution of liability.

3.4.2.3 Conclusions

Both private and competition laws take a favourable position and they do not limit the catalogue of potential addresees of contribution claims in a significant way.

Private laws are especially claimant-frinedly. Under researched national laws, competition law infringers can freely establish the liability of their co-infringers in proceedings on contributionand, as a result, effectively realise their right to claim contribution.

This inclusive approach of national laws with respect to the catalogue of addressees of contribution claims is appreciated from the standpoint of the mass character of claims for antitrust damages. As explained above, private antitrust enforcement is dependent on the activity of victims of anticompetitive practices. They, in turn,

[109] See notes 265–271 in Chapter 2.

typically bring forward their claims for damages against only some antitrust infringers. The ability of antitrust infringers to commence a new proceeding and establish the antitrust liability of their co-conspirators that were off the radar of those sustaining damage not only provides for equality between antitrust infringers but also increases the enforcement of EU competition law. This is definitely beneficial for the entire system of competition law enforcement.

While national laws do not impose any limitations with respect to addresses of contribution claims, such limitations do stem from EU competition law and apply to public antitrust enforcement. The constitutive and supranational character of the Commission's decisions establishing liability prevents national judges from establishing the liability of other entities than those named in the Commission's decisions in the context of contribution litigation. In such a situation, contribution claims may only be brought forward against those held jointly and severally liable for the infringement by the Commission. This, of course, means that the catalogue of addressees of contribution claims is different in public and private antitrust enforcement. This discrepancy is, however, unavoidable due to a strong deterrent role of fines in contrast to compensation paid in private lawsuits.

The national rules on from whom contribution can be claimed are simple, inclusive and predictable. This is appreciated, and it is recommended that this tendency be maintained in future developments in EU competition law.

3.5 LEGAL TESTS

Another question to consider by those bringing forward contribution claims is what legal test they must meet in order to receive contribution.

3.5.1 *Comparative Analysis*

3.5.1.1 Contribution Claims

There are multiple legal tests for contribution claims as there are many causes of actions currently available in the researched jurisdictions. The conditions for claiming contribution thus slightly differ depending on the type of claim.

In England, the tests vary depending on the law applicable in the dispute and the type of claim. In contribution claims in common law, it must be proven that both debtors were liable for the payment of the same debt (i) and the claimant's payment discharged the defendant from its own obligation (ii). As judges need to proportionally divide the burden of liability between the debtors, the claimant should demonstrate that it has paid more than its 'fair share' of the debt (iii). For an indemnity claim in common law, English authors frequently refer to the case *Brook's Wharf and Bull Wharf Ltd v. Goodman Bros A*, which requires the claimant to demonstrate that the defendant and it are liable for the same debt (i), the defendant's debt is discharged when the claimant has been legally compelled to pay (ii) and defendant's liability is primary while the claimant's one is secondary (iii). Under the Contribution Act, the claimant must essentially only demonstrate that the defendant and itself are liable in respect of the same damage. It is up to judges to decide on the amount of contribution and whether it amounts to indemnity.[110]

In Germany, there are close but different tests for the claims for contribution and subrogation. For the claim for contribution, § 426(1) of the BGB sets three requirements: the defendant and the claimant must be joint and several debtors (i), the payment must have been made to the creditor (ii) and the payment must exceed the proportion in which the claimant is internally liable for the debt (iii). The test for subrogation under § 426(2) of the BGB relies on the previous provision. It is also required that the claimant and the defendant be jointly and severally liable (i). The claimant must satisfy the obligation to the benefit of the creditor, which means that the payment to the creditor must have been already made in the moment of submitting the claim (ii). Finally, the claimant must be entitled to claim contribution (iii). The third condition refers to § 426 (1) of the BGB and means that the payment made to the creditor exceeds the proportion in which the claimant is to bear the burden of liability internally.[111]

In France, the legal test for the personal claim for contribution varies depending on the legal basis used to ascertain it. By way of example, Article 1317 of the Code Civil requires three elements: the claimant and the defendant must be jointly and severally liable for the debt (i), the claimant must satisfy the debt (ii) and it must do it in excess of its own portion of liability (iii). For the subrogation claim, Article 1346 of the Code Civil requires that the claimant pay the creditor (i) an amount exceeding its own share of liability (ii).[112]

In Poland, the conditions for making a claim under Article 441(2) of the k.c. are the payment of the debt (i) by one of the joint and several debtors (ii) at least in an excess of the part for which the debtor is individually liable (iii). A stricter legal test is required under Article 441(3) of the k.c. The claimant should have paid the debt (i), it should not have caused the damage nor be blameful for it (ii) and the damage must have been caused solely at the fault of somebody else (iii).[113]

[110] See The Law Commission, *Contribution*, para. 11; Mitchell, *The Law of Contribution*, 82–83, 119–120, 128–133, 141–149, 175–182; Williams, *Joint Torts and Contributory Negligence*, 96 *et seq.*

[111] See Markus Gehrlein, '§ 426 BGB' in Heinz Georg Bamberger and Herbert Roth (eds.), *Kommentar zum Bürgerlichen Gesetzbuch*, 3 vols. (München: C.H. Beck, 2012), vol. I, paras. 12–13, 44; Helmut Rüßmann, '§ 426 BGB' in Markus Junker (ed.), *Juris Praxis Kommentar – BGB. Schuldrecht*, 6 vols. (Saarbrücken: juris, 2010), vol. II(1), paras. 22–23, 26; Böttcher '§ 426 BGB', paras. 13, 49; Thoma, *Der internationale Regress*, 27, 45–47; Völzmann-Stickelbrock, '§ 421 BGB', para. 2.

[112] See Ranouil, *Les recours entre coobligés*, 164, 216–222, para. 233; Boré, 'Le recours'; de la Bâtie, 'Responsabilité délictuelle', 165–166; Canin, *Les actions récursoires*, 112; François Chabas , *L'influence de la pluralité de causes sur le droit à réparation* (Paris: Librairie générale de droit et de jurisprudence, 1967), 75.

[113] Marek Sychowicz, 'Art. 441' in Gerard Bieniek, Helena Ciepła, Stanisław Dmowski, Jacek Gudowski, Krzysztof Kołakowski, Marek Sychowicz, Tadeusz Wiśniewski and Czesława Żuławska (eds.), *Komentarz do kodeksu cywilnego. Zobowiązania*, 6 vols. (Warszawa:

Contribution claims generally follow a similar logic. It seems that all researched jurisdictions require the claimant and the defendant to be jointly and severally liable. This condition appears with slight modifications. In some cases, no specific joint and several liability is required, but merely liability for the same debt.[114] In other cases, no common liability is required, but the liability must be with respect to the same creditor.[115] In certain cases, the relevant liability is narrowed to the liability for the damage.[116] Second, all researched jurisdictions require the claimant to make a payment to the creditor that discharges the debt of the defendant. This condition applies unanimously in all researched jurisdictions. Third, all investigated legal orders request the payment to the creditor to be in excess of the claimant's own share of liability.[117] In almost all jurisdictions, the relevant burden of proof lies on the claimant. The only exception is English law insofar as it is the judges' role to decide on the amount of contribution.

3.5.1.2 Indemnity Claims

The regulation of indemnity claims varies in the researched jurisdictions. Whilst German and French laws do not specify such claims and apply the same tests as in the case of contribution,[118] England and Poland provide for some special rules.

In both England and Poland, the first two conditions of claiming indemnity are identical with contribution claims. There must be a liability for the same debt[119] and the claimant must make a payment that discharges the debt of the defendant. The third condition differs. In England, it is required that the liabilities are of different ranks.[120] In Poland, the claimant must demonstrate either that it did not cause and

LexisNexis, 2010), vol. III, 120; Gerard Bieniek, 'Art. 441' in Gerard Bieniek, Helena Ciepła, Stanisław Dmowski, Jacek Gudowski, Krzysztof Kołakowski, Marek Sychowicz, Tadeusz Wiśniewski and Czesława Żuławska (eds.), *Komentarz do kodeksu cywilnego. Zobowiązania*, 4 vols. (Warszawa: LexisNexis, 2011), vol. III, para. 26; Tomasz Antoszek, 'Art. 441', para. 16.

114 English common law, see the literature referred to Ibid.

115 French subrogation, see Section 3.3.2.1.

116 Poland and English Contribution Act, see Section 3.3.2.1.

117 The researched jurisdictions use different terms for this condition. In English common law, the phrase 'fair share of debt' is used, while the Contribution Act uses the phrase 'extent of responsibility'. In Germany, it is '*Anteile*', which can be translated as liability 'shares'. In France, the personal right to contribution requires the payment exceeding the own '*part et portion de dette*', which can be translated as 'part and proportion' of the debt. In Poland, the term is '*odpowiednia część*', which means an 'appropriate part' of damage. These terms are similar. They are also all vague, as none of them allows for determining the exact share of liability. These criteria are defined subsequently in law or in case law and are discussed in Section 3.6.3.

118 With regard to France, see, for instance, Civ. I, 06.02.1979: Bull. Civ. I 45; Civ. III, 22.06.1977: D. 1977 IR 472. With regard to Germany, see, for instance, BGH, 1988, 133, 133; Peter Bydlinski'§ 426 BGB', para. 14; Sonja Meier, *Gesamtschulden*, 595.

119 There is a slight difference between these two legal orders. In Poland, joint and several liability is required.

120 See note 62.

cannot be blamed for the damages or that it is not liable at all.[121] The English wording is wider than the Polish one. It seems that the claimant may try to prove any difference between the levels of relative liability that exist between itself and the defendant. In Poland, the claimant must establish that it is not guilty of the tort.

3.5.2 *Competition Law Analysis*

In this context, the legal tests for contribution claims seem to be applicable in the EU competition law context. No competition law–specific obstacles have been identified. In the case of contribution claims, the three usual conditions required by national laws can be easily met in EU competition law. Joint and several liability of co-infringers of EU competition law is clearly established in law as demonstrated in Section 2.1.2. The conditions regarding the payment of liability in excess of one' own relative liability depend on the facts of the case and the behaviour of the claimant. However, competition law does not set any *per se* obstacles from meeting them. The crucial part of the contribution claim is for the claimant to prove that its payment exceeds its own share of liability.

On the other hand, indemnity claims in England and Poland seem to be available only in the context of public enforcement, as demonstrated in Section 3.3.2.1. In both legal systems, liabilities of co-debtors must be of a different nature, which is difficult to establish in the context of private antitrust infringements. However, it is still possible to argue that indemnity claims are available in the case of fines established by the Commission. It may be argued that the liability of those directly engaged in competition law breaches is different. While some companies are held liable for their own acts, the liability of other companies is *derived* because of the principle of effectiveness of EU competition law (see Section 3.2.2).[122]

3.5.3 *Conclusions*

This comparative analysis has indicated that contribution claims are largely aligned in the EU. By contrast, separate indemnity claims are only available in England and Poland. For this to be triggered, it must be respectively established that the liabilities in question are of different ranks or have a different relation with respect to fault.

The essential element of the claim for contribution is to prove that the payment exceeds one's own share of liability. The legal tests deployed by national laws for contribution claims do not create any obstacles when such claims are exercised in competition law context. Hence, the principle of effectiveness is respected. The most challenging element of the usual tests, which is the applicability of joint and several liability, is not problematic in EU competition law.

[121] See Section 3.3.1.1.
[122] CJEU, *Siemens Österreich*, para. 47.

Some criticisms can be made with respect to the division between contribution and indemnity claims. The latter are likely to apply only in the context of public antitrust enforcement. While this divergent treatment of public and private enforcement is not a problem as it is regular for the Commission to hold companies liable based on formal reasons rather than their involvement in anticompetitive practices, it is doubtful whether this justifies a separate indemnity claim with an individual legal test. As French and German national rules show, it is perfectly feasible to grant indemnity based on regular rules on contribution by simply treating indemnity as 100 per cent contribution. There is also no need for special legal tests, as 100 per cent contribution can be awarded just by deploying regular criteria for assessing relative liability (e.g. fault, causation).

Furthermore, while legal tests are similar in the researched jurisdictions in broad terms, they vary in detail. Differences occur not only on a per-country basis but also within the researched legal orders. This is the result of the multiplicity of legal bases for contribution claims and the fact that each of them triggers a slightly different legal test. The claimants must be aware of these differences and take them into account when deciding which cause of action to deploy to seek contribution. From a policy standpoint, it is superfluous and damaging for legal certainty to operate with a great number of tests to decide contribution.

De lege ferenda, legal tests for contribution claims can be simplified. It has been expressed above that contribution claims should be exercised on the basis of a single legal basis. This section adds that they should also be subject to a single legal test. The current legal tests provide for a good benchmark for developing it. For instance and in line with the current state, the test can include the requirement that (i) the claimant and the defendant be held jointly and severally liable for an antitrust debt, and (ii) the claimant has paid this debt (iii) in excess of its own share of liability. National judges should also be able to grant both a partial contribution and indemnity based on this test. The question of whether indemnity is possible or not would depend on the establishment of relative liability, which can be in a specific case non-existent.

3.6 CRITERIA FOR ESTABLISHING RELATIVE SHARES OF LIABILITY

The investigated legal tests reveal that the key condition to successfully claim contribution is to prove that one has paid in excess of its own relative liability. Relative liabilities are in turn determined by various criteria, such as fault, causation or illicit gains. The choice of criteria that are used to decide relative liabilities is the paramount of contribution litigation as they determine the ultimate liability of antitrust infringers. They are also the key litigation point – each party is interested in relying on a criterion that minimalises its own relative liability.

The allocation of relative liabilities can indeed significantly vary depending on the criterion used to divide antitrust liability. Let us imagine a cartel that is organised by a small undertaking. The company is very active in enforcing anticompetitive agreements, it makes threats to disobedient co-conspirators and it organises the entire infrastructure for the exchange of information. This company is likely to bear a relatively high share of liability if relative blamefulness is considered. However, if a market share or illicit gains are the criteria to divide liability, the company can bear a minimal share given its small presence on the market and insignificant volumes of sales. Depending on a situation, each antitrust infringer is prone to lean towards certain criteria for the division of liability. This is likely to be a source of conflict between antitrust infringers.

In theory, there are a lot of criteria that can be used to divide antitrust debts. Intuitively, we can think of relative fault, causation or illicit gains. EU competition law provides some additional suggestions. For instance, in the context of public enforcement, the *Siemens Österreich* judgment names relative responsibility, culpability or an equal division of liability.[123] In private enforcement, rec. 37 of the Directive 2014/104/EU suggests turnover, market share, or role in the cartel as the criteria to establish relative responsibility for the harm caused by an anticompetitive practice. These criteria are nonetheless not named by EU law in a binding way. Both *Siemens Österreich* and Directive 2014/104/EU refer to national laws to decide on the criteria used to divide antitrust liability.[124]

The sections below therefore investigate the criteria applicable under national laws and verify whether it is also possible to consider the competition law–specific criteria named in *Siemens Österreich* and Directive 2014/104/EU in claims for contribution relating to antitrust liabilities.

3.6.1 *Comparative Analysis*

3.6.1.1 Open-Ended Rules

The majority of the legal orders researched provide for a broad, open-ended rule to determine relative liabilities.

In France, the criteria for the internal apportioning of liability are not named in positive law. French case law also uses a vague expression that suggests co-debtors should be ultimately liable for their 'share and proportion of the debt'.[125] The exception in this respect is Article L.481-9 of the Code de Commerce. This Article establishes that 'fault' and 'causation' matter for the relative liabilities of those infringing competition law.

[123] Ibid., para. 71.

[124] Ibid., para. 71 and Rec. 37 of the Directive 2014/104/EU.

[125] See case law referred to in Section 3.3.1.1.

English law is similarly vague. In common law, it has been stated that 'it would be equitable that the burden should fall in a certain way'.[126] Section 2(1) of the Contribution Act reads that contribution should be 'just and equitable having regard to the extent of that person's responsibility for the damage in question'. The criteria of 'just and equitable' has been only to a limited extent concretised by the UK's implementation of Directive 2014/104/EU. Section 38(2) of the UK Act adds that relative liabilities are determined 'in the light of [the tortfeasors'] relative responsibility for the whole of the loss or damage caused by the infringement'. Specific criterion for dividing liability among joint and several debtors is only present in equity. It is claimed that 'equity is equality'. In equity, pro capita apportionment is preferred unless it is unjust.[127]

In Germany, the central rule for establishing the method for determining relative liability is § 426 of the BGB. It provides that if it is not otherwise established, the debtors are 'equally' liable.[128] This is, however, only a last resort rule, and a contractual determination between the codebtors is first considered, followed by the criteria established by law and other criteria stemming from the circumstances of the case.[129] Paragraph 254(1)of the BGB is used as a common reference for legal criteria.[130] This provision refers to the 'circumstances of the case' being considered

[126] *Craythorne v. Swinburne* [1807] , 14. Ves. Jun. 160, 165, 33 ER 482.

[127] Kuhlmann, *Rückgriffsgrundlagen bei Gesamtschuld*, 200–201; The Law Commission, *Contribution*, para. 8; Mitchell, *The Law of Contribution*, 79–80.

[128] See note 137 in Chapter 2.

[129] Peter Bydlinski, '§ 426 BGB', para. 14; Martin Gebauer, '§ 426 BGB' in Thomas Pfeiffer (ed.), *Soergel Bürgerliches Gesetzbuch Schuldrecht*, 3 vols. (Stuttgart: Kohlhammer, 2009), vol. III, para. 17; Völzmann-Stickelbrock, '§ 426 BGB', para. 7; Thoma, *Der internationale Regress*, 44; Hösch, *Der schadensrechtliche Innenausgleich*, 196; Weinhold, *Der Gesamtschuldnerausgleich*, 106–107; Krüger, *Kartellregress*, 53–56; Rust, 'Kartellverstoß und Gesamtschuld', 508; Meinrad Dreher, 'Die Haftungsverteilung bei der gesamtschuldnerischen kartellrechtlichen Schadenersatzhaftung' in Stefan Bechtold, Joachim Jickeli and Mathias Rohe (eds.), *Recht, Ordnung Und Wettbewerb: Festschrift Zum 70. Geburtstag Von Wernhard Möschel* (Baden-Baden: Nomos, 2011), 151; Ehmann, *Die Gesamtschuld*, 104, 116.

[130] This provision refers principally to contributory negligence and is applied by analogy to contribution claims. See BGH, NJW, 1972, 1802. See also Bydlinski, '§ 426 BGB', paras. 4, 21; Gebauer, '§ 426 BGB', para. 30; Völzmann-Stickelbrock, '§ 426 BGB', para. 13; Rüßmann, '§ 426 BGB', para. 7; Thoma, *Der internationale Regress*, 45; Dreher, 'Die Haftungsverteilung', 160; Ehmann, *Die Gesamtschuld*, 117; Weinhold, *Der Gesamtschuldnerausgleich*, 107; Körner, *Die Gesamtschuld im Kartellbußgeldrecht*, 251; Krüger, *Kartellregress*, 54, 63; Hösch, *Der schadensrechtliche Innenausgleich*, 196; Magnus, 'Multiple Tortfeasors under German Law', 92; Rust, 'Kartellverstoß und Gesamtschuld', 502; Uwe Hüffer, *Der Rückgriff gegen den deliktisch handelnden Schädiger bei Entschädigungsleistungen Dritter* (Heidelberg: Carl Winter Universitätsverlag, 1970), 13. The analogy is not necessary for Wulf Götte, who believes that the criteria of *Verursachung* and *Verschulden* can be directly applied within § 426 of BGB, see Götte, *Gesamtschuldbegriff und Regressproblem*, 154. It is also generally claimed that § 840 (2) of the BGB is a source of criteria for contribution; however, its application is disputed in competition law, see Bydlinski, '§ 426 BGB', para. 21; Gebauer, '§ 426 BGB', para. 23; Völzmann-Stickelbrock, '§ 426 BGB', para. 12; Rüßmann, '§ 426 BGB', para. 7; Selb, *Schadensbegriff und Regreßmethoden*, 38; Thoma, *Der internationale Regress*, 44; Schmidt,

to establish the relative liability.[131] The German implementation of Directive 2014/104/EU also refers to a broad term of 'causing the harm' ('*Verursachung*') as a criterion of dividing liability.

Polish Article 441(2) of the k.c. also takes a broad approach to criteria forth apportionment of liability by referring to the 'circumstances of the case' ('*okoliczności*'). It, however, explains that such circumstances mean in particular 'fault' ('*wina*') and 'causation' ('*przyczynić się*').[132] Article 441(3) of the k.c. relies only on the criterion of 'fault' ('*wina*') to divide liability.[133]

3.6.1.2 Fault, Causation and Other Criteria

With the exception of French Article L.481-9 of the Code de Commerce, English equity and Polish Article 441(3) of the k.c., the rules on determining relative liability are vague. This opens the door for judges' interpretations. Blamefulness[134] and causation became the principle criteria for determining relative liabilities in all the researched jurisdictions. This, however, did not prevent judges from also applying other criteria for dividing liability between joint and several debtors.

Gesamtschuld und Gesamtschuldregress, 159; Ehmann, *Die Gesamtschuld*, 104; Hösch, *Der schadensrechtliche Innenausgleich*, 196; Rust, 'Kartellverstoß und Gesamtschuld', 508; Köhler, 'Kartellverbot und Schadensersatz', 101; Krüger, *Kartellregress*, 57; Krüger, 'Der Gesamtschuldnerausgleich', 10; Olivier Gänswein, 'Gesamtschuldnerausgleich unter Kartellbeteiligten: Bestimmung des Haftungsanteils und Verjährung der Ausgleichsansprüche' (2016) *Neue Zeitschrift für Kartellrecht*, 5051. The BGH has expressively confirmed that this rule applies to competition law cases both in private and public enforcement. See BGH, BeckRS 2015, 00033, paras. 43 *et seq.* This is approved by the literature, see Hanno Schaper and Peter Stauber, 'Ausgewählte Themen des neuen Kartellschadensersatzrechts – Schadensersatz, Abwälzung, Gesamtschuld und Innenausgleich' (2017) *Neue Zeitschrift für Kartellrecht*, 283; Krüger, *Kartellregress*, 63–67; Krüger, 'Der Gesamtschuldnerausgleich', 9–10; Hendrik Schwenke, 'Die Richtlinie für private Kartellschadensersatzklagen und der Gesamtschuldnerausgleich: Wie kann Art. 11 V. ins deutsche Recht umgesetzt werden?' (2015) *Neue Zeitschrift für Kartellrecht*, 385; Mäsch, 'Innenausgleich', 268–269; Gänswein, 'Gesamtschuldnerausgleich unter Kartellbeteiligten', 51.

[131] Paragraph 254(1) of the BGB reads: '*Hat bei der Entstehung des Schadens ein Verschulden des Beschädigten mitgewirkt, so hängt die Verpflichtung zum Ersatz sowie der Umfang des zu leistenden Ersatzes von den Umständen, insbesondere davon ab, inwieweit der Schaden vorwiegend von dem einen oder dem anderen Teil verursacht worden ist*' ('Where fault on the part of the injured person contributes to the occurrence of the damage, liability in damages as well as the extent of compensation to be paid depend on the circumstances, in particular to what extent the damage is caused mainly by one or the other party').

[132] See the text of the rule, note 138 in Chapter 2.

[133] See Section 3.3.1.1.

[134] For the needs of this book, the term culpability is used interchangeably with related terms of fault and blamefulness.

In England and Wales, liability has traditionally been divided into blamefulness[135] and causation.[136] These criteria are still in use, although there is some confusion on what culpability and causation actually mean.[137] In addition, a number of other criteria are accepted. Charles Mitchell claims that one is illicit gains.[138] Nathy Dunleavy adds that the relative size of companies or the companies' behaviour after the misconduct may play a role in apportioning liability.[139] The way that Directive 2014/104/EU was implemented also opens a way for the criteria named in the Directive, such as the companies' turnover or market shares. Finally, *pro capita* apportionment has been observed in situations when judges had insufficient information to apply other rules.[140]

In Germany, § 254(1) of the BGB[141] first refers to the broadly named circumstances of the case ('*Umstände*') and then specifies that these circumstances should relate to what has caused the damage ('*inwieweit der Schaden . . . verursacht worden ist*'). The term *verursacht* requires for German scholars the assessment of two criteria – causation and fault.[142] The term '*Umstände*', however, allows other factors

135 Williams, *Joint Torts and Contributory Negligence*, 157; Mitchell, *The Law of Contribution*, 196–199; Dunleavy, 'Contribution among Antitrust Defendants', 23. See, for instance, *Weaver v. Commercial Process Co.* [1947] 63 TLR 466; *J (a child) v. Wilkins* [2001] Personal Injury and Quantum Reports 179; *Dubai Aluminium Co Ltd v. Salaam* [1999] 1 Lloyd's Rep. 415, varied on appeal [2001] 1 QB 113, CA.

136 Williams, *Joint Torts and Contributory Negligence*, 157; Mitchell, *The Law of Contribution*, 93, 195; Dunleavy, 'Contribution among Antitrust Defendants', 23; Graham Virgo, 'Contribution Revisited' (2008) 67 *The Cambridge Law Journal*, 2, 256. See, for instance, *Smith v. Bray* [1939] 56 TLR 200, 200; *Schott Kern Ltd v. Bentley* [1991] 1 QB 61, 75–79 CA; *Gray* [2006] EWCA Civ. 1496, 251.

137 Blamefulness and causation are often confused, see Mitchell, *The Law of Contribution*, 192–193, 196; Dunleavy, 'Contribution among Antitrust Defendants', 24 and cases referred.

138 Mitchell, *The Law of Contribution*, 183–184. See, for instance, *Dubai Aluminium* [2002] UKHL 48, 149, 151.

139 Dunleavy, 'Contribution among Antitrust Defendants', 27.

140 Mitchell, *The Law of Contribution*, 190–192. Nathy Dunleavy claims that it yet happens rarely, see Dunleavy, 'Contribution among Antitrust Defendants', 27. See, for instance, *Downs v. Chappel* [1997] 1 WLR 426, 445, CA.

141 See note 131.

142 The majority opinion is that causation is assessed in the first line and then follows fault, see BGH, NJW 1969, 789, 790; BGH, NJW 2006, 896, 897. See also Dreher, 'Die Haftungsverteilung', 156; Opper, *Die gesamtschuldnerische Bußgeldhaftung*, 208; Krüger, *Kartellregress*, 64; Weinhold, *Der Gesamtschuldnerausgleich*, 107; Hösch, *Der schadensrechtliche Innenausgleich*, 199; Inderst and Thomas, *Schadensersatz bei Kartellverstößen*, 403; Walter Dunz, 'Abwägungskriterien bei der Schadensausgleichung' (1964) 46 *Neue Juristische Wochenschrift*, 2133. The reversed order is suggested by Peter Bydlinski'§ 426 BGB', para. 21. An exclusive application of fault is suggested by Werner Rother, 'Die "vorwiegende Verursachung"' (1983) 33 *Versicherungsrecht*, 793 and Heinrich Glaßer, *Der Gesamtschuldnerausgleich zwischen deliktisch haftenden Schuldnern* (München: VVF, 1995), 39.

to be taken into account.[143] The case law shows that very varied criteria are used in contribution litigation, starting from illicit gains[144] to very specific factors such as insurance protection of the debtors, economic consequences of bearing the liability or relations of kinship.[145] As evidenced by the *Calcium carbide* litigation,[146] within § 254 (1) of the BGB there is also a place for competition law–specific criteria such as financial capacity, turnover[147] and market shares.[148] Since there is a multitude of criteria available, the use of *pro capita* apportionment is the last resort method in Germany.[149]

In Poland, it is also believed that fault and causation are prime criteria for dividing liability.[150] Similarly as in Germany, the reference of Article 441(2) of the k.c. to the 'circumstances' of the case allows for using other criteria.[151] In Poland, the following criteria have been considered: illicit gains,[152] factors derived from a relationship that exists between the debtors,[153] fairness,[154] financial means[155] or relative bargaining powers.[156] Interestingly, in Poland, there is little discussion about the application of the *pro capita* rule. The reason is that this criterion is used in Article 376 of the k.c., which establishes the criteria for the division of liability in contractual relationships. The Supreme Court excluded using Article 376 of the k.c. in tort law.[157] As a result, *pro capita* apportionment is taken with hesitance, although its use is still advocated for by some commentators as the last resort rule.[158]

143 See, for instance, Dunz, 'Abwägungskriterien bei der Schadensausgleichung', 2133; Krüger, *Kartellregress*, 73–74 referring to the exceptional consideration of fairness, personal, social and economic relationships between those involved in the dispute.

144 See, for instance, OLG Stuttgart, ZIP 94, 201; OLG Hamm, NJW 2002, 1054, 1055. See also Krüger, *Kartellregress*, 67–60; Gebauer, '§ 426 BGB', paras. 30, 530; Hösch, *Der schadensrechtliche Innenausgleich*, 205; Körner, *Die Gesamtschuld im Kartellbußgeldrecht*, 262.

145 See, for instance, Hösch, *Der schadensrechtliche Innenausgleich*, 205; Körner, *Die Gesamtschuld im Kartellbußgeldrecht*, 262; Krüger, *Kartellregress*, 67–69.

146 See LG München, BeckRS 2013, 10095, para. II(1)(a)(aa); OLG München, BeckRS 2012, 8896, para.II(2); BGH, BeckRS 2015, 00033, paras. 58–63.

147 Ibid., para. 66.

148 Ibid., para. 74.

149 Ibid., para. 53–58. For the use of *pro-rata* only when it is impossible to use other criteria, see also Krüger, 'Der Gesamtschuldnerausgleich', 8; Kersting, 'Gesamtschuldnerausgleich bei Kartellgeldbußen', 150.

150 They are also claimed to be on the same footing. See, for instance, Safjan, 'Art. 441', para. 11; Antoszek, 'Art. 441', para. 23. Contrary, claiming the primary role of fault, Olejniczak, 'Art. 441', 534. See also Ruling of the Supreme Court from 25.04.1962, I CR 469/61, OSNC 1963. nr 3, poz. 75.

151 The catalogue is open-ended, see Antoszek, 'Art. 441', para. 23; Ohanowicz, 'Glosa', 143.

152 Safjan, 'Art. 441', para. 12; Rzetecka-Gil, 'Warunki odpowiedzialności solidarnej', para. 20.

153 Rzetecka-Gil, 'Warunki odpowiedzialności solidarnej', para. 20; Lewaszkiewicz-Petrykowska, *Wyrządzenie szkody przez kilka osób*, 175.

154 Rzetecka-Gil, 'Warunki odpowiedzialności solidarnej', para. 20.

155 Judgment of the Supreme Court from 15.10.2010, v. CSK 78/10, LEX nr 677911; Marek, 'Roszczenia regresowe', 291–292.

156 Lewaszkiewicz-Petrykowska, *Wyrządzenie szkody przez kilka osób*, 175.

157 Judgment of the Supreme Court from 27.02.2009, II CNP 117/08, LEX nr 599749.

158 See, for instance, Lewaszkiewicz-Petrykowska, *Wyrządzenie szkody przez kilka osób*, 175.

In France, fault has been the principal criterion to divide liability between joint and several debtors.[159] Recently, the Cour de Cassation even claimed that this is the only criterion applicable in the case of liability based on fault.[160] Nevertheless, French jurisprudence demonstrates that the causation test is usually exercised after the assessment of fault in contribution disputes.[161] *Pro capita* apportionment of liability between co-debtors has also been applied in France.[162] This criterion has been, however, adopted with reluctance[163] and subsidiarily.[164] Furthermore, French judges occasionally use criteria specific to the area in which joint and several liability is applied. For instance, liability for marriage expenses is apportioned according to the respective capacity of co-debtors.[165] Finally, French judges are open to using innovative criteria. In the *DES* litigation,[166] market shares replaced the traditional way of distributing internal liability according to the causal impacts.[167]

3.6.1.3 Discretionary Power of Judges

In all the jurisdictions researched, the judge's discretion is an essential part of the proceeding on contribution.[168] It is widely acknowledged that it is the judge's role to

[159] This criterion was already adopted in Cass. Req., 24.02.1886: S. 1886 I 460. See Canin, Les actions récursoires, 157; Mignot, *Les obligations solidaires*, 585; Ranouil, *Les recours entre coobligés*, 255; Jourdain, 'Pour un réexamen', para. 5; Corgas-Bernard, 'La pluralité de responsables', paras. 9–10; Le Tourneau, *Droit de la responsabilité*, 671; Maistre du Chambon, 'Régime de la réparation', para. 143.

[160] Civ. II, 13.01.2011: Bull. Civ. II 8. The criterion of fault has also appeared in the projects of Pierre Catala and François Terré. See Catala, *Avant-projet de réforme du droit des obligations*, 183; Terré, *Droit de la responsabilité civile*, Article 11, 3.

[161] See, for instance, Civ. II, 08.05.1978: Gaz. Pal. 1978 II 262; Civ. II, 18.01.1984: Gaz. Pal. 1984 I 125. See also Ranouil, *Les recours entre coobligés*, 266. Similarly as in England, French courts are sometimes confused whether they apply the criterion of fault or causation, see Cochet, 'La contribution', para. 4.

[162] See, for instance, Civ. II, 16.02.1962: Bull civ. II 208; Civ. II, 17.11.1976: D. 1977 IR 29. See also Canin, *Les actions récursoires*, 171–176; Ranouil, *Les recours entre coobligés*, 262; Corgas-Bernard, 'La pluralité de responsables', para. 46; Le Tourneau, *Droit de la responsabilité*, 672; Maistre du Chambon, 'Régime de la réparation', para. 143.

[163] Canin, *Les actions récursoires*, 176; Ranouil, *Les recours entre coobligés*, 263.

[164] Ranouil, *Les recours entre coobligés*, 262; Jourdain Patrice, 'Droit à réparation. Responsabilité fondée sur la faute. Notion de faute: fautes qualifiées' (2017) *JurisClasseur Civil Code*, 120–20, para. 52; Jourdain, 'Pour un réexamen', para. 13.

[165] See Article 515-4 of the Code Civil. See also Ranouil, *Les recours entre coobligés*, 250–251.

[166] Civ. II, 25.01.2007: JurisData no. 2007-037038; Civ. I, 24.09.2009: JurisData no. 2009-049535; Civ. I, 24.09.2009: JurisData no. 2009-049537; Civ. I, 28.01.2010: JurisData no. 2010-051305.

[167] Sophie Hocquet-Berg, 'Affaire du « Distilbène » : une importante avancée en matière d'indemnisation des victimes' (2009) 44 *La Semaine Juridique Edition Generale*, 381, para. 2 (b); Ranouil, *Les recours entre coobligés*, 267–268; Corgas-Bernard, 'La pluralité de responsables', paras. 14–18.

[168] The judges' discretion in awarding contribution is emphasised in all jurisdictions. With regard to England and Wales, see Williams, *Joint Torts and Contributory Negligence*, 86; Dugdale,

determine what part of liability falls on individual debtors.[169] Judges decide which of the criteria apply, which to prioritise and whether they ought to be balanced with others.[170]

The distribution of liability uses percentages[171] or vulgar fractions.[172] The apportionment does not, however, need to be done with mathematical precision. A qualitative rather than quantitative assessment takes place.[173]

3.6.1.4 Conclusions

The review of criteria used in contribution disputes in the jurisdictions researched presents a varied but overall aligned picture. There is a vast range of criteria for determining relative liabilities used in different jurisdictions. However, the common characteristics in the systems researched are that they all operate with multiple criteria for determining contribution and judges retain flexibility regarding their choice.

3.6.2 *Competition Law Analysis*

From the competition law standpoint, this state of law warrants few remarks. First, the principle of equivalence required by Directive 2014/104/EU does not set any specific requirements in this context. As the criteria for determining relative shares of liability are unsettled, there is no predetermined choice for contribution claims enforced in the context of competition law.

'The Civil Liability Act 1978', 186. With regard to France, see Canin, *Les actions récursoires*, 165; Jourdain, 'Pour un réexamen', para. 2; Le Tourneau, *Droit de la responsabilité*, 671; Corgas-Bernard, 'La pluralité de responsables', para. 43; Jourdain, 'Les recours en contribution', para. 9; Ranouil, *Les recours entre coobligés*, 257; Canin, *Les actions récursoires*, 165–166. With regard to Poland, see Lewaszkiewicz-Petrykowska, *Wyrządzenie szkody przez kilka osób*, 170.

169 See Mitchell, *The Law of Contribution*, 186; Dunleavy, 'Contribution among Antitrust Defendants', 23.

170 A review of English case law reveals that in some cases more value was given to blamefulness, in other situations the judges preferred to use causative impact or illicit gains. It has also happened that judges assessed multiple factors in parallel. See, for instance, *Downs v. Chappell* [1997] 1 WLR 426, 445, CA, *Dubai Aluminium Co Ltd v. Salaam* [1999] 1 Lloyd's Rep. 415, 476. On the choice of criteria in Germany, see Hösch, *Der schadensrechtliche Innenausgleich*, 226; Dreher, 'Die Haftungsverteilung', 161.

171 With regard to England and Wales, see The Law Commission, *Contribution*, paras. 24–25. With regard to Germany, see Böttcher, '§ 421 BGB', para. 15; Bydlinski, '§ 426 BGB', para. 14; Meier, *Gesamtschulden*, 595.

172 With regard to France, see Canin, *Les actions récursoires*, 161.

173 With regard to England and Wales, see *The Koningin Juliana* [1974] 2 Lloyd's Rep. 353, 364, CA. With regard to Germany, see Hösch, *Der schadensrechtliche Innenausgleich*, 223–226; Krüger, *Kartellregress*, 108, note 482. With regard to Poland, see Lewaszkiewicz-Petrykowska, *Wyrządzenie szkody przez kilka osób*, 170.

A second factor to note is that, given such a variety of criteria, it is uncertain which criterion for apportioning liability will be used in competition cases. The *Calcium carbide* litigation demonstrated that it is not easy to choose an appropriate criterion. This opens the door to argumentation and increases the importance of advocacy when it comes to determining the way to appropriation antitrust liability. On the other hand, this state of law causes uncertainty, which makes antitrust infringers virtually unable to assess their relative shares of liability before the judge actually decides on contribution claims.

A third factor worth considering is the wide margin of choice between criteria used in contribution litigation. This may cause the division of liability to fail where contribution litigation is massive in character. Since there are no clear guidelines about the choice of the criteria applicable in competition law, virtually every court can make a different decision in this respect. Traditionally this has not been considered a problem because contribution claims have been used as a corrective mechanism in a three-person constellation (the creditor, the claimant and the defendant)with only one claim considered for contribution. However, competition law infringements tend to have more parties involved, with multiple interlinked claims for a contribution at stake. The individual choice of criteria for each and every contribution dispute makes the contribution litigation miss its basic aim, which is the apportionment of liability.

To illustrate this, three undertakings (A, B, C) can be considered. They were involved in the infringement, in which there was only one victim, which was reimbursed by A at 100 per cent. Now A has a right to claim contribution from B and C. In the litigation between A and B, the court grants A contribution in the amount of 10 per cent from B, as it assumed that A can be apportioned 80 per cent of the blame, whilst both B and C are apportioned 10 per cent. Later, A sues C, yet the court assumes that causation was the most important criterion and apportions A with 0 per cent of the blame and C with 100 per cent. A thus receives 100 per cent contribution from C. In this way, A recovered 110 per cent of the damages paid. This result is unacceptable considering that the task was a division of the sum of 100 per cent.

Lastly, it is important to acknowledge that the choice of criteria for determining relative liability brings difficulties in all legal systems. This is in part due to the fact that judges have tried to achieve many inherently opposing objectives. They attempt to act according to the guidelines set by previous case law, but at the same time they want an apportionment that fits best the facts of the case. This sometimes means that many criteria are used as a conglomerate. Such an assessment leads to arbitrariness and lack of transparency and creates incoherence, as shown in the paragraph above.

In conclusion, the determination of relative liability is unsettled in the researched jurisdictions. On the one hand, this does not pre-determine one method used to establish liability shares in the private enforcement of EU competition law under the principle of equivalence. On the other hand, the case-by-case assessment of contribution claims is undesirable in EU competition law.

3.6.3 *Choosing a Criterion That Is Tailored to Dividing Antitrust Liability*

The following paragraphs will zoom in on the criteria that can potentially be applied in disputes on contribution in the antitrust context. In order to help those engaged in them, being litigating parties or judges, each criterion will be analysed in detail. How each criterion applies in the competition law context will be expounded, as well as its limitations, advantages and disadvantages. This is believed to help legal practitioners to make a reasoned choice on which criterion to rely on when discussing the question of contribution.

Besides explaining the practicalities of relying on various criteria for dividing antitrust liability, this section explores possible avenues for improving the traditional framework for contribution litigation. The previous paragraphs presented some of the drawbacks of using a traditional approach in establishing the criteria to divide liability in antitrust law. To provide for an effective right to claim contribution in competition law, revisiting the existing framework is recommended. Instead of relying on many broad criteria for determining the relative liabilities, it would be better to choose one criterion that would be best tailored to competition law. Contribution claims that are capable of accommodating the contribution context of the dispute would ensure an effective right to claim contribution in antitrust. Such a right is required by the principle of effectiveness laid down in Directive 2014/104/EU.

The following paragraphs take the challenge of choosing a criterion that best fits EU competition law and can be used as the single measure to divide antitrust liability. In order to make such a choice in a systematic way, it is necessary to point out the notable aspects of antitrust law, which would serve as the benchmark. The needs of EU competition law have been partly identified in the section above, and they encompass the complexity of competition law as an area of law (i), the potentially massive character of contribution litigation (ii) and the fact that liability can be established both in the context of public and private antitrust enforcement (iii).

Given these characteristics, a few principles are used to assess which criteria fit well into the context of competition law. It is assumed that the criteria for dividing liability should be feasibly applicable to various competition law infringements (principle no. i), should consider a multitude of contribution claims relating to the same infringement (principle no. ii) and should apply in both private and public competition law enforcement (principle no. iii). In light of the book's objectives, a final criterion is that the rules for dividing liability should be simple to apply (principle no. iv).

3.6.3.1 Fault

Fault is generally considered a reprehensible decision (or reprehensible failure to act) regarding illegal conduct, classified as either intention or negligence.[174] Fault is also already present in national rules on contribution. As demonstrated in Section 3.6.1.2, fault is commonly used as one of the criteria for dividing liability in civil law.[175]

The notion of fault is also present in EU competition law. Liability for violations of competition law is based on fault. Fault is required in public enforcement under

[174] For the definition of fault in English law, see, for instance, W. V. Horton Rogers, 'Fault under English Law' in Pierre Widmer (ed.), *Unification of Tort Law: Fault* (Den Haag: Kluwer Law International, 2005), 67, 69. For the definition of fault in German law, see § 276(1) BGB; see also, for instance, Grundmann Stefan, '§ 276 BGB' in Wolfgang Krüger (ed.), *Münchener Kommentar zum Bürgerlichen Gesetzbuch. Schuldrecht. Allgemeiner Teil I*, 14 vols. (München: C.H. Beck, 2019), vol. II, paras. 6 *et seq.*; Gerhard Wagner, '§ 823 BGB' in Mathias Habersack (ed.), *Münchener Kommentar zum Bürgerlichen Gesetzbuch. Schuldrecht. Besonderer Teil III*, 14 vols. (München: C.H. Beck, 2013), vol. V, paras. 28 *et seq.*; Ulrich Magnus and Gerhard Seher, 'Fault under German Law' in Pierre Widmer (ed.), *Unification of Tort Law: Fault* (Den Haag: Kluwer Law International, 2005), 104–105. For the definition of fault in French law, see, for instance, F. Vetu, 'Application de la responsabilité civile pour faute à la violation du droit des pratiques anticoncurrentielles' (2003) 48(II) *La Semaine Juridique Edition Génerale*, 10183; Hadi Slim, 'Approche comparative de la faute dans la responsabilité civile extra-contractuelle' (2003) 6 *Responsabilité civile et assurance*, 18 *et seq.*; Patrice Jourdain, 'Droit à réparation. Responsabilité fondée sur la faute. Applications de la notion de faute: imprudences et négligences; fautes commises à l'occasion d'un contrat' (2017) *JurisClasseur Civil Code*, 130-10; Suzanne Galand-Carval, 'Fault under French Law' in Pierre Widmer (ed.), *Unification of Tort Law: Fault* (Den Haag: Kluwer Law International, 2005), 92. For the definition of fault in Polish law, see Mariusz Zelek, 'Art. 415' in Maciej Gutowski (ed.), *Duże Komentarze Becka. Kodeks cywilny. Komentarz. Art. 1-449* (Warszawa: C.H. Beck, 2016), vol. I, paras. 25–30; Zbigniew Radwański and Adam Olejniczak, *Zobowiązania – część ogólna* (Warszawa, C.H. Beck, 2016), paras. 508–517; Gerard Bieniek, 'Art. 415' in Gerard Bieniek, Helena Ciepła, Stanisław Dmowski, Jacek Gudowski, Krzysztof Kołakowski, Marek Sychowicz, Tadeusz Wiśniewski and Czesława Żuławska (eds.), *Komentarz do kodeksu cywilnego. Zobowiązania*, 4 vols. (Warszawa: LexisNexis, 2011), vol. III, paras. 8–9; Maciej Kaliński, *Szkoda na mieniu i jej naprawienie* (Warszawa: C.H. Beck, 2011), 95–103; Janina Dąbrowa, *Wina jako przesłanka odpowiedzialności cywilnej* (Wrocław: Wrocławskie Towarzystwo Naukowe, 1968), 31 *et seq.*; Witold Czachórski, 'Uwagi o rażącym niedbalstwie' in Jan Błeszyński (ed.), *Witold Czachórski. Wybór prac* (Warszawa: C.H. Beck, 2015), 577–579; Lech Dzikiewicz, 'O pojęciu winy i jej trzech odmianach' (1977) IV *Państwo i Prawo*, 87 *et seq.*; Biruta Lewaszkiewicz-Petrykowska 'Wina jako podstawa odpowiedzialności z tytułu czynów niedozwolonych' (1969) *Studia Prawno-Ekonomiczne*, 87 *et seq.*; Małgorzata Sośniak, 'Elementy winy nieumyślnej w prawie cywilnym' (1975) 68 *Prace Naukowe Uniwersytetu Śląskiego*, 152 *et seq.* For a comparative study, see Pierre Widmer, 'Comparative Report on Fault as a Basis of Liability and Criterion of Imputation' in Pierre Widmer (ed.), *Unification of Tort Law: Fault* (Den Haag: Kluwer Law International, 2005), 339 *et seq.*

[175] See also Anthony Maurice Honoré, *International Encyclopedia of Comparative Law: Torts. Causation and Remoteness of Damage*, 17 vols. (Tübingen: Mohr, 1971), vol. XI, Ch. 7; PETL adopts fault as a criterion for apportioning damages, see European Group on Tort Law, *PETL*, Article 9:101(2).

Article 23(2)(a) of Regulation 1/2003.[176] Fault has also been required by the majority of EU Member States in the system of private antitrust enforcement.[177]

Given the fact that the criterion of fault is so clearly anchored both in the system of liability stemming from infringements of EU competition law and in rules on contribution, it is not surprising that it has already been considered in contribution litigation in antitrust by the BGH[178] and the CJEU.[179]

APPLICATION IN EU COMPETITION LAW The criterion of fault can be easily applied in EU competition law. This is because any antitrust violation is underpinned by a blameful decision to enter into an unlawful agreement. A starting point to assess fault is its classification according to its gradation. This can be supplemented by taking into account other factors establishing the intensity of intent.

Gradation of Fault as a Starting Point Different antitrust behaviours fit well into the traditional scale of fault gravity. This scale can be used to differentiate relative faults.[180] The most blatant type of fault is intentional wrongdoing (*dolus directus, Vorsatz/Absicht, faute intentionelle, zamiar bezpośredni*).[181] This means an intention to engage in a particular conduct with full awareness and acceptance of its consequences. This is the type of fault that appears in infringements by object. In these

[176] Article 23(2)(a) of Regulation 1/2003 reads: 'The Commission may by decision impose fines on undertakings and associations of undertakings where, either *intentionally or negligently* … infringe Article 81 or Article 82 of the Treaty'.

[177] All researched jurisdiction require fault except from England. See Ashurst, 'Study on the conditions of claims for damages in case of infringement of EC competition rules' (2004) available at https://ec.europa.eu/competition/antitrust/actionsdamages/comparative_report_clean_en.pdf,Table 5, 51.

[178] BGH, BeckRS 2015, 00033, para. 57 *et seq.*

[179] CJEU, *Siemens Österreich*, para. 71.

[180] For the gravity of faults in England, see Rogers, 'Fault under English Law' (2005), 76–77; in France, see Galand-Carval, 'Fault under French Law', 94–96; Le Tourneau, *Droit de la responsabilité*, 672; in Germany, see Magnus and Seher, 'Fault under German Law', 112; in Poland, see Lewaszkiewicz-Petrykowska 'Wina jako podstawa odpowiedzialności', 87 *et seq.*; for a comparative analysis, see Widmer, 'Comparative Report', 353–354; Christian von Bar and Eric M. Clive (eds.), *Principles, Definitions and Model Rules of European Private Law: Draft Common Frame of Reference (DCFR). Full Edition*, 6 vols. (München: Sellier European law publishers, 2009), vol. IV, 3389 *et seq.*

[181] For Germany, see Schmidt, *Gesamtschuld und Gesamtschuldregress*, 129; Hösch, *Der schadensrechtliche Innenausgleich*, 222; Krüger, *Kartellregress*, 97–98; von Bar and Clive, *DCFR*, vol. IV, 3397. For France, see Ranouil, *Les recours entre coobligé s*, 260; Corgas-Bernard, 'La pluralité de responsables', para. 45, note 66; Canin, *Les actions récursoires*, 83–86, 15 7–165; Jourdain, 'Fautes qualifiées', paras. 2 *et seq.*; von Bar and Clive, *DCFR*, vol. IV, 3394. For Poland, see Radwański and Olejniczak, *Zobowiązania – część ogólna*, 205–206; Zelek, 'Art. 415', para. 27; Kaliński, *Szkoda na mieniu*, 102; Czachórski, 'Uwagi o rażącym niedbalstwie', 577–579; Dzikiewicz, 'O pojęciu winy', 95–98; Lewaszkiewicz-Petrykowska, 'Wina jako podstawa odpowiedzialności', 87 *et seq.*; von Bar and Clive, *DCFR*, vol. IV, 3397. For England, see von Bar and Clive, *DCFR*, vol. IV, 3400–3401.

cases, undertakings decide to adopt a strategy that is commonly known to be anticompetitive and damage other market players.

Another type of fault is recklessness (*dolus eventualis, bedingter Vorsatz, faute inexcusable, zamiar ewentualny*).[182] This means that an entity intends to undertake a certain unlawful activity and accepts its consequences, which are yet uncertain. In antitrust, this is when companies engage in an activity that leads to an infringement by effect. As a result, although a strategy does not have an anticompetitive aim, the company decides to undertake it regardless of the risk that it may restrict competition.

Finally, there is negligence (*Fahrlässigkeit, faute d'imprudence ou de negligence, niedbałość*),[183] which means that misconduct is a result of a failure to act according to an objective measure required in given situations. Negligence can be further divided into the grave and light forms (*gross negligence, grobe Fahhrlässigkeit, faute lourde, rażące niedbalstwo, slight negligence, leichte Fahrlässigkeit, faute légère, lekkomyślność*), which are dependent on the extent of negligence and awareness of the risks.[184] Infringements of EU competition law appear less likely in this form, as anticompetitive behaviour is usually realised as an intended strategy.

Beyond Legal Classification of Fault The application of the criterion of fault has its own specific problems. It could be asked if there are any cases in which antitrust infringers are equally blameful.[185] The answer seems positive, at least for cartels. In principle, all cartel members are characterised by *dolus directus* as they intend to form the cartel, consciously implement it and are aware of its harmful consequences.

[182] For Germany, see Schmidt, *Gesamtschuld und Gesamtschuldregress*, 129; Hösch, *Der schadensrechtliche Innenausgleich*, 222; Krüger, *Kartellregress*, 97–98; von Bar and Clive, *DCFR*, vol. IV, 3397; Magnus and Seher, 'Fault under German Law', 101 *et seq*. For France, see Ranouil, *Les recours entre co obligés*, 251; Corgas-Bernard, 'La pluralité de responsables', para. 45, note 67; von Bar and Clive, *DCFR*, vol. IV, 3394. For Poland, see Radwański and Olejniczak, *Zobowiązania – część ogólna*, 205–206; Zelek, 'Art. 415', 1589; Kaliński, *Szkoda na mieniu*, 102; Czachórski, 'Uwagi o rażącym niedbalstwie', 577–579; Dzikiewicz, 'O pojęciu winy', 95–98; Lewaszkiewicz-Petrykowska, 'Wina jako podstawa odpowiedzialności', 87 *et seq*.; von Bar and Clive, *DCFR*, vol. IV, 3397. For England, see von Bar and Clive, *DCFR*, vol. IV, 3400–3401.

[183] For Germany, see Schmidt, *Gesamtschuld und Gesamtschuldregress*, 129; Hösch, *Der schadensrechtliche Innenausgleich*, 222; Krüger, *Kartellregress*, 97–98; von Bar and Clive, *DCFR*, vol. IV, 3410–3411. For France, see Ranouil, *Les recours entre co obligés*, 251; Jourdain, 'Fautes qualifiées', paras . 38 *et seq*.; Jourdain, 'Imprudences et négligences', para s. 1 *et seq*.; von Bar and Clive, *DCFR*, vol. IV, 3408. For Poland, see Radwański and Olejniczak, *Zobowiązania – część ogólna*, 206–207; Zelek, 'Art. 415', para. 28; Kaliński, *Szkoda na mieniu*, 102; Czachórski, 'Uwagi o rażącym niedbalstwie', 577–579; Dzikiewicz, 'O pojęciu winy', 95–98; Lewaszkiewicz-Petrykowska, 'Wina jako podstawa odpowiedzialności', 87 *et seq*.; von Bar and Clive, *DCFR*, vol. IV, 3410. For England, see von Bar and Clive, *DCFR*, vol. IV, 3413.

[184] See, for instance, Hösch, *Der schadensrechtliche Innenausgleich*, 221.

[185] For such an opinion, see Krüger, *Kartellregress*, 97–98; Weinhold, *Der Gesamtschuldnerausgleich*, 162; Hösch, *Der schadensrechtliche Innenausgleich*, 222.

The fact that the cartelists' blame is classified in the same legal category does not, however, mean that their faults are exactly the same. The intent of each cartelist differs as companies may be more or less determined to become involved in the anticompetitive strategy. In order to establish their relative faults precisely, one must go beyond legal categories of fault and refer to the factors demonstrating the intensity of the cartelists' intentions. Such factors are partly included in the Commission's Guidelines on Fines as aggravating and mitigating circumstances. An active role in the infringement (its initiation, ring leading, organisation, enforcement and maintenance) can be used as circumstances aggravating fault. A passive role –a mere presence in the meetings, deviations from the cartel policy, application for leniency – will help mitigate it.[186]

Role of Leniency Application An interesting question is whether leniency applications have any impact on establishing the relative blamefulness of antitrust infringers.[187] On the one hand, it can be claimed that the fact that an infringer of EU competition law applied for leniency does not matter for establishing how guilty it was in engaging in antitrust conduct. A decision to terminate the infringement and apply for leniency is forward-looking and does not refer to the intention to engage in illegal activity. On the other hand, other areas of law sometimes consider the termination of a violation and voluntarily remedying its consequences as active repentance that makes up for the initial guilt and reduces the sanction.[188] Following this second interpretation, leniency applications can be considered

[186] Some of these criteria are discussed in the literature, see Bieber, *Die gesamtschuldnerische Haftung*, 137–140; Cavanagh, 'Contribution, Claim Reduction', 1318; Reasoner, 'Prepared Statement', 18; Dunleavy, 'Contribution among Antitrust Defendants', 24; Weinhold, *Der Gesamtschuldnerausgleich*, 159–161; Hösch, *Der schadensrechtliche Innenausgleich*, 280–284; Krüger, 'Überlegungen zur Gesamtschuld', 82–89; Inderst and Thomas, *Schadensersatz bei Kartellverstößen*, 404–405. The two latter authors use the discussed criteria as examples of causation. The reason is that infringers' different behaviours decide about the probability of cartel's success and causation of damages. These behaviours, however, reflect also different decisions that undertakings take to enforce their anticompetitive conduct and reflect the intensity of their intention to violate laws, which allows to discuss them with connection to fault.

[187] For a discussion on this question, see also Dunleavy, 'Contribution among Antitrust Defendants', 27.

[188] In Poland, active repentance (*czynny żal*) is a general principle of penal law and applies to particular crimes, see Articles 15, 17(1), 23(1), 259 of the Kodeks Karny; see also Olga Sitarz, 'Active Repentance as an Instrument of Criminal and Penal Policy' (2009) 31 *Archiwum Kryminologii*, 159*et seq*. In Germany, *tätige Reue* is considered in a number of crimes, see paras. 24, 83a, 87(3), 98(2), 149(3), 158, 320, 298(3) of the Strafgesetzbuch, see also Morten Blöcker, *Die tätige Reue* (Baden-Baden: Nomos, 2000). In France, the principle is that *le repenteur actif* operates only when the violation has not been consumed. However, there are multiple examples in which the events that followed the infringement are considered under active repentance exemption, see Articles 1810, 138, 144, 285 of the Code Pénal; see also Paul Savey-Casard, 'Le repentir actif en droit pénal français' (1972) 3 *Revue de science criminelle et de droit pénal comparé*, 515.

mitigating circumstances for establishing the degree of blame in contribution litigation.[189]

Negligence in the Context of Public Enforcement Another matter to consider is the notion of negligence in the context of public antitrust enforcement. It has been claimed that a parent company can be held jointly and severally liable for the infringement of its subsidiary.[190] Some claim that this is because of a failure on the part of the parent company to prevent its subsidiary from entering into illegal conduct.[191]

This is a controversial finding as such behaviour cannot be considered negligence.[192] The failure to act is an omission and not an active act. In order for the omission to be blameful, there must be an obligation to act that has not been fulfilled.[193] The problem is that EU law does not set an obligation for the parent company to supervise its subsidiaries in terms of antitrust compliance.[194] The furthest EU law went was to occasionally treat antitrust-compliance programmes as a mitigating circumstance for reducing fines.[195] This is in no way an imposition of a rule requiring supervision of antitrust compliance in corporate groups.

Fault in the Context of Public Enforcement and Follow-On Actions This brings us to another issue linked with assessing fault in the context of public antitrust enforcement and follow-on actions. It has been argued that the Commission's determination of blame should be accepted as a matter of superiority of EU law in contribution litigation.[196] In order to not interfere with the Commission's fining policy, national judges are advised not to use the criterion of fault in contribution litigation.[197]

This is a misguided view as it ignores the division between the external and internal aspects of joint and several liability. As demonstrated in Chapter 2, the Commission's competency is restricted to the external dimension, with the internal

[189] For leniency as a factor in the internal liability apportionment, see Christian Kersting, 'Perspektiven der privaten Rechtsdurchsetzung im Kartellrecht' (2008) 3 *Zeitschrift für Wettbewerbsrecht*, 267; Krüger, *Kartellregress*, 484. Contrary, Florian Bien, 'Überlegungen zu einer haftungsrechtlichen Privilegierung des Kartellkronzeugen' (2011) *Europäische Zeitschrift für Wirtschaftsrecht*, 889 *et seq.*

[190] Opper, *Die gesamtschuldnerische Bußgeldhaftung*, 113, 127–130.

[191] Bieber, *Die gesamtschuldnerische Haftung*, 132–133.

[192] Also rejecting BGH, BeckRS 2015, 00033, paras. 57 *et seq.*; Körner, *Die Gesamtschuld im Kartellbußgeldrecht*, 252, 259.

[193] Körner, *Die Gesamtschuld im Kartellbußgeldrecht*, 258; Antonia Hösch, *Der schadensrechtliche Innenausgleich*, 154; Morice Honoré, *Causation and Remoteness of Damage*, vol. XI, 42, 47.

[194] See Aberle, *Sanktionsdurchgriff*, 77.

[195] See, for instance, Commission decision of 7 October 2009 in Case COMP/39.129 – *Power Transformers*, C(2009) 7601 final.

[196] Jüchser, 'Gesamtschuldnerausgleich', 1055. See also Köhler, 'EU-Kartellgeldbußen', 281*et seq.*

[197] Ibid. See also BGH, BeckRS 2015, 00033, para. 47.

one left to national judges. This division also applies to the assessment of fault, which is differently analysed by the Commission and national judges. The Commission assesses fault with respect to the collective entity, the undertaking in the meaning of EU competition law.[198] This was recently confirmed by AG Pitruzzella, who concluded that the existence of a single economic unit 'is entirely independent of any fault on the part of the parent company' and it is liable because a member of its economic unit was to blame for the violation of competition law.[199] By contrast, national judges assess the fault of individual companies in order to decide on their relative shares of liability. Consequently, there is nothing preventing national judges from concluding that some companies are not blameful of an infringement, although they have been held liable for it by the Commission.

This solution is in line with the perception that joint and several liability imposes ultimate liability on those directly involved and blameful.[200] It happens regularly in researched jurisdictions that those strictly liable receive indemnity from those causing damage because of their action, those vicariously liable from those causing damage or the guarantors from guarantees.[201] Indemnifying an entity in internal relations due to the application of the fault criterion is thus nothing new.

Following this understanding of joint and several liability, indemnity can be granted in several situations. For instance, some companies are held liable only because they belong to the same corporate group as an infringer or because they acquired the business that infringed competition law in the past.

Indemnity obviously does not apply if the companies that were held jointly and severally liable for the infringement materially contributed to it and are also guilty of it. In order to identify whether this is the case, special attention needs to be paid to the activity of the companies' corporate bodies[202] and internal documents[203] that reveal who has initiated, supervised or encouraged the infringement.[204]

ADVANTAGES The main advantage of using fault as a criterion for dividing antitrust liability is its ability to apply to all areas of EU competition law regardless of how it is

[198] The assessment here only refers to the concept of undertaking and the single economic entity doctrine. The place of guilt is not assessed for the doctrine of economic continuity. This is because the assessment of guilt is actually lacking in this case and it is doubtful whether the Commission meets the thresholds of guilt established in Article 23(2)(a) of Regulation 1/2003.

[199] AG Pitruzzella, *Sumal*, para. 46.

[200] von Kalben and Sekunde, 'Relative Responsibility', 2; Ranouil, *Les recours entre coobligés*, 113.

[201] See, for instance, *Whitby v. Burt Boulton and Hayward Ltd.* [1947] KB 918; *Dubai Aluminium Co Ltd v. Salaam* [2002] UKHL 48, 149; Civ. II, 14.01.1998: JCP 1998 II 10045; Civ. I, 16.05.1960: D 1960, 737 note Tunc; BGH, NJW 1971, 752, 753–754; BGH, NJW 1966, 1262, 1263. See also Jacques Boré, 'La causalité partielle en noir et blanc ou les deux visages de l'obligation "in solidum"' (1971)1.2369 *La Semaine Juridique*, para. D.

[202] Bieber, *Die gesamtschuldnerische Haftung*, 131.

[203] Körner, *Die Gesamtschuld im Kartellbußgeldrecht*, 256.

[204] Mansdörfer, 'Verbandshaftung', 216.

enforced. Fault is assessed based on the decision-making process and not the consequences that blameful decisions incur.

Even if in some instances relative faults seem to be similar, the degrees of fault vary and they are able to demonstrate the relative liability of antitrust infringers. At the same time, the fault gradation is settled[205] and interpreted consistently across different EU legal orders.[206] This allows for transparency and legal certainty.

In addition, the application of this criterion is manageable. Judges assess fault regularly.[207] The issue of access to evidence is also not problematic. Although anticompetitive practices are held as secret, the relevant information is likely to be provided by the claimant as it was also a part of the anticompetitive strategy.[208] Furthermore, some information about the relative fault of antitrust infringers can be retrieved from the Commission's decision. This information may be present in the Commission's assessment of aggravating and mitigating circumstances, the gravity of the infringement and the deterrence bonus.[209]

Finally, the criterion of fault can remedy criticism about the Commission's extensive application of joint and several liability. The fault criterion gives an opportunity to ultimately indemnify non-blameful companies that were fined by the Commission whilst keeping them externally liable as guarantors of payment. Although this is not the objective of contribution claims, using fault in contribution litigation benefits the general fining policy.[210]

DISADVANTAGES The fundamental disadvantage of using fault as a criterion for determining relative antitrust liability relates to problems with its quantification.[211] Fault can be assessed only qualitatively by comparing which fault is larger or smaller to other faults. It is virtually impossible to determine concrete numbers that would reflect relative faults.[212]

The problems with quantification turn into problems with incoherence in adjudicating contribution claims. Even if expressed numerically, each judge can give their personal weight to the gradation scale, for instance, 70 per cent:30 per cent or 85 per

205 Similarly Canin, *Les actions récursoires*, 83.

206 See, for instance, von Bar and Clive, *DCFR*, vol. IV, 3390 *et seq.*; Maurice Honoré, *Causation and Remoteness of Damage*, vol. XI, Ch. 7.

207 Angland, 'Joint and Several Liability', 2395–2396; John Baker, 'The Use of Assumpsit for Restitutionary Money Claims 1600–1800' in Eltjo J. H. Schrage (ed.), *Unjust Enrichment: The Comparative Legal History of the Law of Restitution* (Berlin: Duncker and Humblot, 1999), 64.

208 Contrary, Opper, *Die gesamtschuldnerische Bußgeldhaftung*, 89.

209 Similarly Dunleavy, 'Contribution among Antitrust Defendants', 25; Weinhold, *Der Gesamtschuldnerausgleich*, 162.

210 The use of this criterion is advocated for by Tobias Bieber, see Bieber, *Die gesamtschuldnerische Haftung*, 149.

211 Dunleavy, 'Contribution among Antitrust Defendants', 25; Cavanagh, 'Contribution, Claim Reduction', 1318; Canin, *Les actions récursoires*, 169.

212 Cavanagh, 'Contribution, Claim Reduction', 1318; Baker, 'The Use of Assumpsit', 63.

cent:15 per cent or *dolus directus* when compared to negligence. If there are many contribution claims and they are dealt with in separate proceedings, judges of different courts may arrive at varying percentages, which will not sum to 100 per cent. This may turn contribution litigation into failure, counter the objective of fairness[213] and lead to a lack of transparency and legal certainty.[214]

The solution to this problem has been suggested by Stéphane Bréna. She advocates for fixing concrete percentages for a given type of fault when compared to another type of fault, for instance, *dolus directus* + *dolus directus* = 50 per cent:50 per cent, *dolus directus* + negligence = 100 per cent:0 per cent, etc.[215] This, however, does not solve the entire problem. Each type of fault can be further divided according to additional factors discussed above. It is obviously possible to follow Stéphane Bréna's reasoning and fix percentages for different aggravating and mitigating circumstances, for instance, +10 per cent for ringleaders, −20 per cent for leniency applicants. This exercise is, however, difficult. There are an infinite number of factors that may be used to assess fault.

CONCLUSIONS It is possible to develop a fault-based test for apportioning antitrust liability based on two steps. The first step is to determine the grade of fault. The second step is to consider other factors specific to the infringer's intent.

The main advantage of using the criterion of fault in contribution claims is its ability to be universally applied in EU competition law regardless of the competition practice (principle no. i) and type of enforcement (principle no. iii). This method also seems to be relatively easy to apply because of the qualitative character of the assessment and judges' experience in dealing with fault (principle no. iv). The – at least in part – discretionary quantification of fault has, however, a very significant negative impact on the coherence of the contribution system (principle no. ii), which leads to the disqualification of this method in cases involving a large number of parties.

3.6.3.2 Causation

Causation is a term that defines a link between misconduct and harm.[216] This link is broken down in some jurisdictions into the link between the defendant's conduct and the infringement of the creditor's right and the link between infringement and

[213] Kirgis, 'Apportioning Tort Damages in New York: A Method to the Madness' (2001) 75 *St. John's Law Review*, 429.

[214] Dunleavy, 'Contribution among Antitrust Defendants', 25.

[215] Stéphane Bréna, *Les recours en contribution* (Montpellier: Université Montpellier 1, 2005), 230 *et seq*.

[216] Marta Infantino and Eleni Zervogianni, *Causation in European Tort Law* (Cambridge: Cambridge University Press, 2017), 282; von Bar and Clive, *DCFR*, vol. IV, 3547 *et seq*.

the harm suffered by the creditor that needs to be compensated.[217] As demonstrated in Section 3.6.1.2, causation is widely present in EU legal orders as a criterion for apportioning liability.

Causation is also applicable in competition law. It is particularly present when assessing the relationship between anticompetitive behaviour and its effects. It is also central in claims for antitrust damages as it must be established that the damage is caused by the anticompetitive agreement and not by other factors.[218]

APPLICATION IN EU COMPETITION LAW The standards of causation vary from one country to another.[219] In general, England utilises a 'but for' test.[220] According to this test, causative factors encompass only the conditions that the harm would not have occurred. In Poland, the causation standard is similar to the English one, utilising a '*sine qua non*' causation test. This test is a tool to select only the most closely related factors to the occurrence of the damage. The Polish law uses the yardstick of 'normal consequences' of an act or an omission to determine the scope of recoverable damage.[221] In Germany, the 'sine qua non' concept is also part of causation test. German law requires the damaging event to be adequate ('*Adäquanz*'), such that it is causative only under ordinary circumstances and that the damages are within the preventive sphere of the infringed norm ('*Schutzzweck der Norm*').[222] In France, the

[217] Sandy Steel, *Proof of Causation in Tort Law* (Cambridge: Cambridge University Press, 2015), 39; von Bar and Clive, *DCFR*, vol. IV, 3582 *et seq*. In English law, this is the causation of the *gist* of the tort and the causation of consequential losses. In Germany, these two types of causation are called '*haftungsbegründende Kausalität*' and '*haftungsausfülende Kausalität*', see Wagner, '§ 823 BGB', para. 56. In Poland, the causation is also understood as a prerequisite of liability and a limitation to the extent of recoverable damage, see Katarzyna Ludwichowska-Redo, 'Basic Questions of Tort Law from a Polish Perspective' in Helmut Koziol (ed.), *Basic Questions of Tort Law from a Comparative Perspective* (Wien: Jan Sramek Verlag, 2015), 203. This distinction is the least prominent in French law and appears rarely; it is between the '*lien entre le fait du défendeur et le dommage initial*' and the '*lien entre le dommage initial et ses conséquences ultérieures*', see Marta Infantino and EleniZervogianni, *Causation in European Tort Law*, 18.

[218] Ashurst, 'Study', 72–75.

[219] Marta Infantinoand Eleni Zervogianni, *Causation in European Tort Law*, 282.

[220] Mitchell, *The Law of Contribution*, 184; W. V. Horton Rogers 'Causation under English Law' in Jaap Spier (ed.), *Unification of Tort Law: Causation* (Den Haag: Kluwer Law International, 2000), 39. This test is completed by the possibility of the defendant to prove that the harm would have occurred without its involvement *on the balance of probabilities*. See, for instance, *South Australia Asset Management Corpn v. York Montague Ltd and Banque Bruxelles Lambert SA v. Eagle Star Insurance Co Ltd* [1996] U.K.H.L. 10.

[221] von Bar and Clive, *DCFR*, vol. IV, 3577; Dybowski Tomasz in Zbigniew Radwański (ed.), *System Prawa Prywatnego. Prawo zobowiązań – część ogólna*, 21 vols. (Warszawa: C.H. Beck and Instytut Nauk Prawnych Polskiej Akademii Nauk, 2002), vol. II, 247 *et seq*.; Radwański and Olejniczak, *Zobowiązania – część ogólna*, 87–88.

[222] As stressed in note 217, causation relates in Germany to both '*haftungsbegründende Kausalität*' and '*haftungsausfüllende Kausalität*'. Besides, German tort law requires a breach of duty with respect to '*haftungsbegründende Kausalität*' ('*Kausalität der Pflichtwidrigkeit*). It is also possible

doctrine is split whether to use the '*sine qua non*' theory or the theory of equivalence of conditions.[223] The latter allows a consideration of all factors that influenced the creation of the damage, as well as those that, although not strictly necessary, were instrumental for its occurrence.[224]

The application of these tests in disputes on contribution has proven troublesome. Where the '*sine qua non*' test applies, the question arises over how to attribute relative importance where different actions were all necessary conditions for harm.[225] In the system of equivalence of conditions, the impossibility of determining the causal impact of individual factors is considered a reason for adopting joint and several liability.[226] Using causation as a criterion for dividing liability could therefore prove challenging.[227] The solution to these problems in the jurisdictions researched was to interpret causation differently in contribution litigation. It is treated as an assessment of 'probative potency' or 'generation risk'.[228] The essential question is to ask whether the actions of one party have been more influential in causing harm than those of another party.[229]

This question can be easy or difficult to answer in EU competition law depending on the context in which joint and several liability was imposed. An easy scenario is when only one of those liable for antitrust harm has caused it, for instance, if a parent company's behaviour is irrelevant and liability only arises for its shareholdership of a subsidiary. However, most competition law cases involve complex causal relationships. Article 101 of TFEU requires the existence of an agreement or at least a tacit understanding between undertakings for a competition law violation to occur. This means that antitrust infringements are likely to involve multiple actors whose actions are concurrent and all have an influence on misconduct. This makes it difficult to separate the probative force of the parties involved in the infringement

to take into account security obligations ('*Verkehrssicherungspflichten*') and policy ('*wertende Überlegungen*'). See Wagner, '§ 823 BGB', paras. 70–74; Helmut Heinrichs, '§ 249 BGB' in Peter Bassenge, Gerd Brudermüller, Uwe Diederichsen, Wolfgang Edenhofer, Helmut Heinrichs, Andreas Heldrich, Hans Putzo, Hartwig Sprau and Heinz Thomas Walter Weidenkaff, *Palandt. Bürgerliches Gesetzbuch* (München: C.H. Beck, 2004), paras. 59 *et seq.*; Magnus, 'Multiple Tortfeasors under German Law', 64–66.

[223] Ludwichowska-Redo, 'Basic Questions of Tort Law', 203; von Bar andClive, *DCFR*, vol. IV, 3574–3575.

[224] Mignot, *Les obligations solidaires*, 406; von Bar and Clive, *DCFR*, vol. IV, 3574.

[225] Dunz, 'Abwägungskriterien bei der Schadensausgleichung', 2134; Meier, *Gesamtschulden*, 591.

[226] See, for instance, Patrice Jourdain, 'Droit à réparation. Lien de causalité. Détermination des causes du dommage' (2013) *JurisClasseur Civil Code*, 160, para. 13; Maryse Deguergue, 'Causalité et imputabilité' (2013) 370–460 *JurisClasseur Responsabilité civile et Assurances*, para. 5 *et seq.*; Mignot, *Les obligations solidaires*, 206, 229–235; Geneviève Viney, 'Apres la réforme du contrat, la nécessaire réforme des textes du Code civil relatifs à la responsabilité' (2016) 4 *La Semaine Juridique EditionGenerale*, 99, para. 12.

[227] Ibid.

[228] See, for instance, Jourdain, 'Détermination des causes du dommage', 160, para. 12.

[229] See, for instance, Mitchell, *The Law of Contribution*, 193; Jourdain, 'Pour un réexamen', para. 23.

and to decide whose involvement was decisive for the occurrence of anticompetitive harm.

In order to see the probative force of those involved in antitrust infringements clearly, one should ask what factors led the anticompetitive harm to occur. It may be a type of infringers' activity that would have an impact on the probability of causing harm.[230] Take cartel initiators an example. It is possible that without the existence of the company that took initial steps to set it up, the cartel would have never occurred. It may also be a type of relationship between various actors that was decisive for the occurrence of a harmful practice.[231] It is possible that an anticompetitive vertical agreement has been concluded only as a result of the bargaining power of one undertaking. Finally, characteristics of an undertaking (for instance, its market power) or even external factors (for example, drop in demand) can contribute to misconduct and generated damage. In sum, causation seems to be a very broad criterion covering various factors.

Economic Models Assessing Causation Two models for the application of causation have been developed for contribution disputes in antitrust. They both relate to cartels, probably because the theory on the creation and operation of cartels is the most developed one.

Carsten Krüger assumes that the specific activities of those involved in the cartel decide its creation and the extent to which it causes harm. He anchors its model in the prisoner's dilemma.[232] Through this prism, he assesses what impact cartelists' individual actions have on the creation and maintenance of the cartel. In particular, he refers to the behaviours supporting the cartel – ringleading, applying coercive measures, sanctioning unagreed behaviours, recruiting new cartel members –and behaviours weakening it: deviating from the cartel policy adopted, disclosing the cartel and applying for leniency.[233]

Stefan Napel and Gunnar Oldehaver take as a measure of causation the impact of the companies' participation in anticompetitive conduct on the creation of damage. Their starting point is a question of how much overcharge increases with a given undertaking joining the anticompetitive agreement. According to Stefan Napel and Gunnar Oldehaver, such impact is dependent on the factors shaping supply and demand. They take as an example two factors – price and location – and design a model that can explain the relative causation of each undertaking's causative potential. They use a merger simulation model to simulate the behaviour of

[230] This can also be assessed as decisive for fault, see Section 3.6.3.1. See also Mitchell, *The Law of Contribution*, 193, 196; Körner, *Die Gesamtschuld im Kartellbußgeldrecht*, 248.

[231] Mitchell, *The Law of Contribution*, 193.

[232] Krüger, *Kartellregress*, 76.

[233] Ibid., 77. The factors named by Carsten Krügercan also be assessed in terms of fault, as indicated in Section 3.6.3.1.

cartelists and the Shapley model to determine the attribution of damages to individual companies.[234]

As a non-economist, the author's assessment of these methods is limited. Nonetheless, the existence of these two models proves that there are multiple ways of proving causation and there may be as many models as are types of antitrust infringements and factors that come into play in their realisation. The factors named by Carsten Krüger, Stefan Napel and Gunnar Oldehaver seem to be only examples of what can be relevant for anticompetitive harm. Other circumstances may also be decisive for restricting competition, for instance, the undertakings' relative bargaining power or durations of individual involvements in the misconduct.

ADVANTAGES Causation is a general criterion that can apply to the entire body of competition law.[235] It is a matter of fact and is neither dependent on the type of competition law enforcement nor on the type of competition law violation. The types of anticompetitive conducts are relevant only when it comes to choosing the factors related to causation. As causation is a broad category that covers different factors, it fits well into various factual setups.

The main reason for adopting causation as a criterion for determining relative shares of liability is its ability to give concrete quantifiable results that are sound with economic theory. As proven by Carsten Krüger, Stefan Napel, and Gunnar Oldehaver, it is possible to create models that would give numbers to the probative value of the impact of the companies' participation in the infringement on harm created. Because of the use of economic theories, the arbitrariness of results is limited.

DISADVANTAGES Anticompetitive conduct is a complex phenomenon and differs greatly from the cases classically invoked to illustrate the importance of causation. For example, the probability of harming others by using a knife or a stick in a street fight or driving at 150 km/h rather than at 100 km/h when causing an accident does not help with respect to competition law infringements. Competition law infringements are caused by a combination of circumstances. Although the choice of factors relevant for causation can be backed by economic theory, economics may not always give definitive answers to who caused the breach. This means that it is impossible to completely exclude arbitrariness when applying causation as a criterion for dividing antitrust liability. This is especially true considering that in causation analysis it is possible to construct multiple models using different factors. As a

[234] Stefan Napel and Gunnar Oldehaver, 'Kartellschadensersatz und Gesamtschuldnerausgleich – Ökonomisch faire Schadensaufteilung mit dem Shapley-Wert' (2015) *Neue Zeitschrift für Kartellrecht*, 135 *et seq*.

[235] In favour of this criterion, Marine Ranouil, *Les recours entre coobligés*, 264.

result, it seems that the criterion of causation does not promote the coherence of the contribution system and legal certainty.

Furthermore, causation is more difficult[236] and more expensive to use than the criterion of fault to determine relative shares of liability. Economic models allow a qualitative assessment to be turned into a quantitative one. However, this would prove time consuming and likely necessitate hiring an economic consultancy. While costs increase, it is uncertain whether the full-fledged assessment of causation brings proportional benefits when compared with a qualitative analysis based on fault. In the end, arbitrary adjudication is a concern that also plagues causation.

CONCLUSIONS The existing literature proves that it is feasible to develop a test based on causation to determine relative shares of liability in antitrust contribution litigation. Such a test should be first based on selecting a factor or a basket of factors contributing to the realisation of the misconduct and damage and second on quantifying the relative value of these factors for each antitrust violator.[237]

The advantage of using causation is that it can apply in EU competition law regardless of the type of infringement (principle no. i) and competition law enforcement (principle no. iii). The arbitrariness of the choice of factors that are weighted in the contribution dispute can also be limited by using economic theories on the nature of different antitrust infringements. However, this increases the complexity of the dispute and its costs (principle no. iv). Additionally, the choice of relevant factors and methods for assessing causation leaves a margin for arbitral decisions and thus impedes the aim of providing coherence in contribution adjudication (principle no. ii). These disadvantages lead us to reject causation as the criterion for dividing liability between antitrust infringers.

3.6.3.3 Illicit Gains

Illicit gains are the benefits achieved by those engaged in illegal activities, particularly financial torts and financial crimes. The principle of deterrence and the sense of basic justice demand to prevent those who breached the law from enjoying the benefits of such behaviour.

These objectives are realised in civil law via the rules on unjust enrichment. The main principle is that those enriched at the expense of others in circumstances that the law sees as unjust should return illicit gains. Illicit gains appear as a criterion of dividing liability between joint and several debtors as demonstrated in Section 3.6.1.2.

[236] On complexity in general, see Hösch, *Der schadensrechtliche Innenausgleich*, 201; Jourdain, 'Pour un réexamen', para. 21; Dreher, 'Die Haftungsverteilung', 156. On limitations of quantitative assessment, see Mignot, *Les obligations solidaires*, 410. On asymmetry of information, see Dreher, 'Die Haftungsverteilung', 156.

[237] In line with the theory of de Birkmeyer referred to by Mignot, *Les obligations solidaires*, 406.

The aim of depriving antitrust infringers of illicit gains is also observed in competition law. According to paragraph 31 of the Guidelines on Fines, the Commission may apply a special deterrence bonus to the basic amount of the fine in order to make the fine exceed the illegal gains.

Consequently, the concept of depriving the wrongdoer of illicit gains is well anchored both in civil law and competition law. This criterion has been in fact already considered in antitrust contribution litigation.[238]

APPLICATION IN EU COMPETITION LAW The most common objective of antitrust infringements is to achieve financial gains. These profits should be in principle quantifiable and could serve as a clear benchmark for dividing liability between antitrust infringers.

The most straightforward way to determine the companies' illicit gains is to analyse their financial records, identify the sales related to the market influenced by the competition law infringement and establish which part of the gain was made thanks to the anticompetitive strategy. The last part of this exercise is challenging. The gain that is made due to misconduct is the difference between the gain that would have been achieved in competitive conditions ('counterfactual scenario') and the anticompetitive gain ('factual scenario').[239] The problem is that the former value can only be estimated as the counterfactual gain has never been factually realised.

The counterfactual gain can be inferred by using a number of methods.[240] For instance, margins of profit may be compared across different periods of time to demonstrate the most probable counterfactual margin. It is also possible to run a full-fledged market simulation based on the models developed by industrial organisations to establish a probable margin of profit that was achievable under competitive conditions.

Limitations of Using the Criterion of Illicit Gains The use of illicit gains to determine relative shares of antitrust liability is limited in several ways. First, infringers are not only liable for the harm that translated into their own gains but also for

[238] OLG München, BeckRS 2012, 8896, para. II(2)(A)(bb); BGH, BeckRS 2015, 00033, para. 92.

[239] This consideration addresses Kai-Uwe Opper's concern that the gain used to apportion damages might not have been solely achieved due to anticompetitive behaviour, see Opper, *Die gesamtschuldnerische Bußgeldhaftung*, 166. Carsten Krüger believes that it is possible to simply use the factual gain achieved by the infringer and deduct the costs of its achieving in order to establish an illicit gain; however, this calculation disregards that some part of profits is regular and only some part results from the anticompetitive strategy, see Krüger, *Kartellregress*, 92.

[240] See Communication from the Commission on quantifying harm in actions for damages based on breaches of Article 101 or 102 of the Treaty on the Functioning of the European Union, 2013/C 167/07.

other harm – for example, the so-called umbrella damages.[241] Liability for such damage is imposed on the infringers although they were not those who extracted the gains from it. The calculation of liability based on gains enjoyed by the infringer is not going to cover this part of liability.[242]

Second, it is difficult to establish antitrust gains if infringements are not price-based. The anticompetitive strategy may consist of securing long-term purchase options or impeding product innovation.[243] The gains from such practices are not monetary in a short run. They may be undertaken to exclude competitors or to develop markets in a favoured direction. The quantification of the gains that are likely to materialise in the very distant future is difficult, if not impossible.

Third, illicit gains cannot differentiate the liabilities of companies that are vertically connected. Where there is a cartel, one can determine companies' individual gains and compare them.[244] This is not the same in vertical agreements where undertakings are part of the same supply chain. In order to decide which of the undertakings enjoyed the gain, the pass-on rate needs to be analysed. This is a feasible but difficult task.[245]

Finally, similar problems appear when the criterion of illicit gains is applied in the context of public antitrust enforcement. When dealing with companies belonging to the same corporate group, the principal difficulty is that only one of them achieved the profits stemming from the infringement in a direct way. The question of who has in the end enjoyed the profit can be answered by observing the structure of the corporate group or profit transfer agreements.[246] However, gains may be easily transferred within the corporate group, and it may be difficult to establish whether they were used to pay shareholders of the mother company, were spent by the subsidiary or transferred to another company in a corporate group. Even more fundamentally, it seems implausible to distribute gains between a parent company and its subsidiary as the value of the subsidiary is always a part of the value of the mother company.[247] Some have tried to compare the gains of parent companies and subsidiaries, but the result tends to be biased and systematically leads to a greater liability for the parent company.[248]

[241] Alleviated prices allow some companies not participating in the infringement to also inflate their prices. On the problem of umbrella damage, see for instance, Roger D. Blair and Christine Piette Durrance, 'Umbrella Damages: Towards a Coherent Antitrust Policy' (2018) 36 *Contemporary Economic Policy*, 2, 241 *et seq.*; Till Schreiber and Vasil Savov, 'Kone v. Commission: Umbrella Damages Claims' (2014) 5 *Journal of European Competition Law and Practice*, 8, 548*et seq.*

[242] Inderst and Thomas, *Schadensersatz bei Kartellverstößen*, 406–407.

[243] See, for instance, Commission decision of 24 July 1991 in Case IV/31043 –*Tetra Pak II*, OJ L 72, 18.3.1992, p. 1–68.

[244] In analogy to the methods described in the Guidelines on Fines.

[245] For difficulties in applying this criterion in the case of vertical agreements, see also Hösch, *Der schadensrechtliche Innenausgleich*, 294; Körner, *Die Gesamtschuld im Kartellbußgeldrecht*, 261.

[246] Inderst and Thomas, *Schadensersatz bei Kartellverstößen*, 415.

[247] Similar observation von Kalben and Sekunde, 'Relative Responsibility', 3.

[248] Bieber, *Die gesamtschuldnerische Haftung*, 129.

ADVANTAGES The authors advocating for utilising illicit gains to apportion liability[249] appreciate that this approach delivers precise results based on a quantitative rather than a qualitative methodology. They also claim that illicit gains are easy to show and quantify.

Illicit gains also have clear basis in civil law and law on contribution claims. The vast majority of jurisdictions have laws on unjust enrichment and try to deprive infringers of illicit gains.[250] The use of this criterion also corresponds to the nature of financial misconduct, which includes competition law.[251]

Finally, the use of illicit gains emphasises modern civil law's focus on redistribution rather than punitive justice. At the same time, the idea of depriving infringers of illicit gains corresponds to the desire of providing for fairness and justice.[252]

DISADVANTAGES The claim that by using the illicit gain criterion one can obtain a mathematically precise division of liabilities[253] does not hold true in competition law. Even in the easiest case of calculating cartelists' illicit gains, results are based on assumptions used to describe the potential gains in the counterfactual scenario. The range of methods to establish the illicit gains is wide, and there is no single number that would reflect illicit gains. The models used to approximate illicit gains are complex, expensive and data consuming and, even if applied, are not at all immune from doubts.

In addition, the further away we are from a price-fixing cartel, the more difficult it is to use the criterion of illicit gains to determine relative antitrust liability. This can still be possible in the case of vertical agreements, but additional elements (for instance, pass-on) need to be taken into account. In the case of non-price infringements, only a rough assessment of gains is possible. Finally, illicit gains cannot be used when the Commission applies the concept of the single economic entity.

CONCLUSIONS The distribution of antitrust liability according to illicit gains relies on sophisticated economic models.

Although these models lead to quantifiable results, they do not ensure coherence in contribution adjudication (principle no. ii). Illicit gains are best used with respect to price-based horizontal infringements; their application beyond this matter comes with serious obstacles (principle no. i). Apportioning antitrust liability on the basis of illicit gains is not possible in all contexts in which joint and several liability applies.

[249] See Opper, *Die gesamtschuldnerische Bußgeldhaftung*, 213. This criterion is also used by Krüger, *Kartellregress*, 90–95; von Kalben and Sekunde, 'Relative Responsibility', 5.

[250] von Kalben and Sekunde, 'Relative Responsibility', 5; Schwenke, 'Die Kartellschadensersatzklagen und der Gesamtschuldnerausgleich', 385.

[251] Dunleavy, 'Contribution among Antitrust Defendants', 23; Dreher, 'Die Haftungsverteilung', 157.

[252] von Kalben and Sekunde, 'Relative Responsibility', 5.

[253] Dunleavy, 'Contribution among Antitrust Defendants', 24.

It is also inapplicable in the case of the Commission's application of its concept of undertaking (principle no. iii). Finally, dividing antitrust liability according to infringers' illicit gains is complex and expensive (principle no. 4). Due to these disadvantages, this method of dividing liability in contribution litigation should be rejected.

3.6.3.4 Values of Sales

In competition law, the term *value of sales* is used for the company's turnover that covers infringement-related sales.[254] This criterion is usually used as a proxy for illicit gains, which also gives a feeling for the size of the business involved. Although the value of sales is a notion that is close to illicit gains, it requires separate treatment as it applies differently in EU competition law and has a different potential in contribution litigation.

The idea of using the value of sales to divide liability between antitrust infringers has been principally developed in the literature. The inspiration is the Commission's use of the value of sales for the estimation of its fines.[255] The value of sales is not a criterion present in national rules on contribution.

The idea of using the value of sales in order to apportion the liability for antitrust infringements has already been considered by courts dealing with contribution litigation.[256]

APPLICATION IN EU COMPETITION LAW Liability can be divided between antitrust infringers in a simple way on the basis of their infringement-related sales.[257] Turnover data is generally available in the companies' records and accounting. In addition, if the Commission's fining decision is available, approximate values of sales can be simply retrieved from it.[258] The availability of such data depends, however, on the specificity of this data to given companies and their confidentiality.[259]

[254] Guidelines on Fines, paras. 13 *et seq*.

[255] von Kalben and Sekunde, 'Relative Responsibility', 3; Körner, *Die Gesamtschuld im Kartellbußgeldrecht*, 261; Opper, *Die gesamtschuldnerische Bußgeldhaftung*, 211; Bieber, *Die gesamtschuldnerische Haftung*, 127.

[256] BGH, BeckRS 2015, 00033, paras. 71, 74 *et seq*.

[257] Cavanagh, 'Contribution, Claim Reduction', 1317; Weinhold, *Der Gesamtschuldnerausgleich*, 151; Bieber, *Die gesamtschuldnerische Haftung*, 126.

[258] See, for instance, Commission decision of 22 November 2017 in Case AT.39881 – *Occupant Safety Systems supplied to Japanese Car Manufacturers*, C(2017) 7670 final, para. 113; Commission decision of 21 February 2018 in Case AT.39920 – *Braking Systems*, C(2018) 925 final, paras. 94, 96.

[259] See, for instance, Commission decision of 8 February 2017 in Case AT.40018 – *Car battery recycling*, C(2017) 900 final, in particular paras. 289 *et seq*. and 348, where there is no information on value of sales; Commission decision of 21 February 2018 in Case AT.40113 –*Spark Plugs*, C(2018) 929 final, para. 93.

Contrary to complicated calculations needed to establish illicit gains, values of sales are readily available and can simply be compared to establish relative shares of infringers' liability.

Limitations of Using the Criterion of Values of Sales The application of the values of sales criterion in antitrust contribution litigation raises similar concerns to the application of the criterion of illicit gains. The assumption is that the values of sales reflect illicit gains. This, however, holds true only for price-based infringements.[260] The connection between values of sales and anticompetitive conduct is not maintained in the case of non-pricing abuses[261] or damage made outside of own sales, for instance, umbrella damages.[262]

Similarly to illicit gains, the criterion of values of sales does not work for vertical agreements. In vertical agreements, the parties are part of the same supply chain. The same infringement-related sales apply to both of them, and the difference in values reflects the companies' position in the supply chain and their need to add their own profit margin to the sales. The value of sales is, in principle, higher for those placed down the supply chain. The difference in values of sales has thus nothing to do with the infringement. The criterion based on values of sales is incapable of reflecting differences in relative liabilities in vertical constellations.[263]

As in the cases of illicit gains, the value of infringement-related sales cannot apply to contribution claims between the companies belonging to one undertaking in the meaning of EU competition law. Since there is only one value of sales involved, the company that gained it would always be the only one liable.

ADVANTAGES The supporters of this criterion invoke the ease of using values of sales.[264] They are right that values of sales are easily available and no further operation on the data is required to use them for dividing liability.

[260] Similarly von Kalben and Sekunde, 'Relative Responsibility', 3–5.

[261] In the case of boycott, see Cavanagh, 'Contribution, Claim Reduction', 1317; Section of Antitrust Law of the American Bar Association, *Contribution and Claim Reduction*, 42.

[262] Cavanagh, 'Contribution, Claim Reduction', 1317; Weinhold, *Der Gesamtschuldnerausgleich*, 85.

[263] Weinhold, *Der Gesamtschuldnerausgleich*, 152; Opper, *Die gesamtschuldnerische Bußgeldhaftung*, 211; Bieber, *Die gesamtschuldnerische Haftung*, 126–127; Section of Antitrust Law of the American Bar Association, 'Report on Contribution and Claim Reduction' (14 December 2005) available at https://americanbar.org/content/dam/aba/administrative/antitrust_law/at-comments/2005/12-05/contribution_claim_comm.pdf, 21.

[264] Rust, 'Kartellverstoß und Gesamtschuld', 509; Kersting and Preuß, *Umsetzung der Kartellschadensersatzrichtlinie*, paras. 9(2), 20. See also Dreher, 'Die Haftungsverteilung', 158; Weinhold, *Der Gesamtschuldnerausgleich*, 151; Bieber, *Die gesamtschuldnerische Haftung*, 126, Cavanagh, 'Contribution, Claim Reduction', 1316; Schwenke, 'Die Kartellschadensersatzklagen und der Gesamtschuldnerausgleich', 385; Gänswein, 'Gesamtschuldnerausgleich unter Kartellbeteiligten', 52; Köhler, 'Kartellverbot und Schadensersatz', 103.

They are also right that the criterion of values of sales is an objective measure to divide liability.[265] Values of sales are rough company data that do not leave much room for judges' interpretations and do not change depending on their use in one or another litigation. Consequently, values of sales are capable of introducing coherence to the contribution system.

The criterion based on values of sales also increases legal certainty.[266] Companies can calculate their values of sales and assess their competitors' values of sales before contribution litigation starts.

DISADVANTAGES Values of sales are only a rough and imprecise approximation of companies' relative liability. They are only a proxy for illicit gains as they do not isolate the factors non-related to the infringement (for instance, different cost structures, companies' efficiency).[267] They also do not cover all types of illicit gains derived from antitrust infringements.

In addition, the values of sales criterion share all criticism addressed to illicit gains as it applies well only to horizontal price-based anticompetitive practices. In particular, it is difficult to apply to vertical agreements and contribution claims sought in the context of the Commission's notion of undertaking.

CONCLUSIONS Liability can be easily divided between individual infringers by using their values of sales as such data can be easily retrieved from companies' accounting records (principle no. iv).

The main advantage of using values of sales is their availability and their straightforward application. This allows for reaching objective results that can coherently apply in several judicial proceedings (principle no. ii).

On the other hand, values of sales are difficult to apply across varied constellations in which infringements of competition law occur. Values of sales are of limited use in non-price-based anticompetitive practices, vertical agreements (principle no. i) and in the context of public antitrust enforcement (principle no. iii). For the latter reason, the criterion of values of sales should be rejected.

3.6.3.5 Market Shares

Market shares are a tool commonly used in EU competition law. Market shares indicate which proportion of the relevant market is served by the undertaking in question. This indicates the companies' market power and competitive constraints

265 Similar view, Weinhold, *Der Gesamtschuldnerausgleich*, 151.
266 Similar view, Bieber, *Die gesamtschuldnerische Haftung*, 126.
267 Dreher, 'Die Haftungsverteilung', 158; Schwenke, 'Die Kartellschadensersatzklagen und der Gesamtschuldnerausgleich', 385.

they face.[268] A usual competition law analysis starts with defining the companies' positions in the relevant markets in order to verify whether the market has been affected by the anticompetitive practice to an appreciable extent.[269]

Although market shares have not been traditionally used in civil law, they have appeared as a response to new developments. Environmental catastrophes or damage caused by dangerous goods have proven to be problematic as their victims cannot identify the specific entity that harmed them.[270] As a response to such situations, US law proposed to use the companies' market shares to delimit the companies' proportional liabilities.[271] Market shares were believed to reflect the likelihood that one company or another produced a good that was harmful in a given case.

This type of assessment has also been applied in the European Union. In the French case *Distilbène (DES)*,[272] women whose mothers took diethylstilboestrol or DES during pregnancy suffered vaginal cancer and claimed damages from two companies that produced and marketed the substance in France at that time, UCB Pharma and Novartis. The problem was that it was impossible to determine which company's substances the claimants' mothers took. The courts held the two companies jointly and severally liable in line with the French treatment of impossibility to determine who within a group of entities caused damage. The novelty occurred when deciding on contribution as the judges determined the companies' relative liabilities according to their shares in the diethylstilboestrol/DES market.[273]

Given that market shares are central to competition law and have also appeared in the framework of civil law, it is not surprising that there have been preliminary attempts to apply this criterion to antitrust contribution litigation.[274]

268 Commission Notice on the definition of relevant market for the purposes of Community competition law, OJ C 372, 9.12.1997, p. 5–13, para. 2.

269 Communication from the Commission, Notice on agreements of minor importance that do not appreciably restrict competition under Article 101(1) of the Treaty on the Functioning of the European Union (De Minimis Notice). OJ C 291, 30.8.2014, p. 1–4, para. 1.

270 Allen Rostron, 'Beyond Market Share Liability: A Theory of Proportional Share Liability for Nonfungible Products' (2003) 52 *UCLA Law Review*, 161.

271 Market shares where applied for the first time in DES litigation; see also other cases involving market share liability, for instance *In re "Agent Orange" Prod. Liab. Litig.*, 597 F. Supp. 740, 816–842 (E.D.N.Y. 1984), aff'd, 818 F.2d 145 (2d Cir. 1987); *Mahar v. Hanover House Indus., Inc.*, No. CA 880156, 1995 WL 1146188 (Mass. Super. Ct. Dec. 12, 1995), *Russo v. Material Handling Specialties Co.*, No. 9101209, 1995 WL 1146853 (Mass. Super. Ct. Aug. 29, 1995); *Sindell v. Abbott Labs.*, 607 P.2d 924, 925, 927 (Cal. 1980) first to adopt the theory. See Rostron, 'Beyond Market Share Liability', 153; Harvey Teff, '"Market Share" Liability: A Novel Approach to Causation' (1982) (31) *The International and Comparative Law Quarterly*, 4, 840.

272 Civ. II, 02.04.1997: Bull. Civ. II 112; Civ. II, 05.02.1960: D 1960, 365.

273 Hocquet-Berg, 'Affaire du « Distilbène »', para. 6.

274 BGH, BeckRS 2015, 00033; Antitrust Modernization Commission, 'Report and Recommendations', 256. See also United States Supreme Court, *Texas Industries*.

APPLICATION IN EU COMPETITION LAW Defining relevant markets is a complex exercise as they can only encompass products and areas that belong to the same category. In the language of EU competition law, this is defined by the supply-side and demand-side substitutability. It is believed that products A and B belong to the same market if consumers/producers switch from product A to product B if there is a small but permanent increase (5–10 per cent) in the price of one product.[275] Market definitions can become a centre of dispute as the behaviour of customers and suppliers is difficult to estimate.[276]

Conflicts about the relevant market definition are yet mostly avoided in contribution litigation. This is because contribution adjudication follows the Commission's and a judicial finding that competition law was violated. The market definition must then be necessarily already established in the case. Hence, the court's task is to only request the companies' values of sales and volumes.

In addition, sometimes concrete market shares are already available in Commission decisions and judgments on antitrust damages. Sometimes information on market shares is part of confidential information; however, the Commission can still provide a range of market shares (0–10 per cent, 10–20 per cent).[277] Such approximation should already be sufficient for the needs of contribution litigation.

Limitations of Using the Criterion of Market Shares Market shares, like illicit gains and values of sales, can be perfectly applied in the case of horizontal price-fixing agreements. In cartels, each infringer has a certain share of the market concerned by the anticompetitive practice. These shares can be easily compared.

In contrast to the criteria of illicit gains and values of sales, the criterion of market shares can also apply to horizontal non-pricing abuses. For instance, if companies agree to restrict their investment in the technological advancement of products, the consumers' damage consists of deprivation of innovation, which is made proportionally to the companies' market shares.

A difficult question is whether we can apply the market shares criterion in the context of anticompetitive vertical agreements. This seems impossible. Market shares are incomparable as they reflect the companies' position on two distinct markets.[278] To put it in practical terms, imagine an anticompetitive agreement between an automotive manufacturer and its supplier. The automotive

[275] The same test applies to assess the geographic area; it is asked whether, the same product would be sourced from different areas in the case of price increase.

[276] Frank H. Easterbrookin, 'The Antitrust Equal Enforcement Act. Hearings before the Committee on the Judiciary' (1982 House of Representatives J-97-15), 201; John E. Lopatka, 'Missed Opportunity: The Enforcement Recommendations of the Antitrust Modernization Commission' (2008) 53 *Antitrust Bulletin*, 698.

[277] See, for instance, Commission decision, *Lundbeck*, para. 215; Commission decision of 27 November 2013 in Case AT.39633 – *Shrimps*, C(2013) 8286 final, para. 8 and note 11.

[278] In favour of this view, Weinhold, *Der Gesamtschuldnerausgleich*, 156; Schwenke, 'Die Kartellschadensersatzklagen und der Gesamtschuldnerausgleich', 385.

manufacturer has 20 per cent shares on the market for family cars. The supplier has 30 per cent on the market for automotive fasteners. The difference in the companies' market shares is incomparable as they operate on different markets.

Finally, there is a question of contribution claims between those held jointly and severally liable because of the Commission's notions of undertaking and the doctrine of economic continuity. In this context, a comparison of market shares is of no use either. There is only one entity that directly committed an antitrust infringement, and only its market shares matter from a competition law perspective. For example, assume that a company engaged in a cartel is a steel company, which has 60 per cent of shares in the EU market for steel. The Commission imposed a fine on it, but it also held its holding company jointly and severally liable for the fine. The holding company is a global investment bank with a 15 per cent market share on the market for global investing. The difference in market shares of these companies is in no connection with the antitrust infringement. Only the steel company's market share matters from the standpoint of violation of EU competition law.

ADVANTAGES The market shares criterion has a broader scope of application in competition law than the previously discussed illicit gains and values of sales criteria. It applies generally to all types of competition law infringements. This is due to the double nature of market shares. They can be interpreted as a proxy of both illicit gains[279] and causation.[280]

The criterion of market shares serves as a proxy for illicit gains given that market shares are proportional to the ability to gain profits. Given that the antitrust infringement took place, said profits would be in part illicit.

Market shares also indicate causation related to both the generation of damage and the realisation of misconduct.[281] Regarding the first type of causation, companies generate damage in proportion to their relative presence on the market. This shows how causal the participation of one company was to generating damages. Regarding the second type, market shares are a proxy of market power.[282] The more market power the company has, the easier it is to enforce an anticompetitive strategy. This is because cartelists aim to cover the entire market with their

[279] For such an understanding, Timothy James Stanley, 'An Analysis of the Rules of Contribution and No Contribution for Joint and Several Liability in Conspiracy Cases' (1994) 35 *Santa Clara Law Review*, 1, 94; Weinhold, *Der Gesamtschuldnerausgleich*, 154. Contrary, Inderst and Thomas, *Schadensersatz bei Kartellverstößen*, 406.

[280] In favour, Kersting, 'Rechtsdurchsetzung im Kartellrecht', 266; Dreher, 'Die Haftungsverteilung', 157; Weinhold, *Der Gesamtschuldnerausgleich*, 153; Krüger, *Kartellregress*, 78 *et seq.*; Schwenke, 'Die Kartellschadensersatzklagen und der Gesamtschuldnerausgleich', 385. Contrary, Inderst and Thomas, *Schadensersatz bei Kartellverstößen*, 405–406; Gänswein, 'Gesamtschuldnerausgleich unter Kartellbeteiligten', 52.

[281] Rostron, 'Beyond Market Share Liability', 162.

[282] For market shares as a proxy of market power, see Krüger, *Kartellregress*, 79; Schwenke, 'Die Kartellschadensersatzklagen und der Gesamtschuldnerausgleich', 385.

agreement and try to persuade companies outside of the cartel to join it. If a company with significant market shares (for instance, 40 per cent) decides to join the cartel, this gives the promise of success and can persuade other companies to join it as well. Consequently, market shares indicate the impact of individual companies in the realisation of misconduct.

Another advantage of dividing liability according to market shares is their objectivity and ability to provide coherent results.[283] Market shares are in principle available in the judgment or decision that establishes the violation of antitrust law. Market shares can be retrieved by all judges dealing with contribution claims with the same result even if they handle the case in separate proceedings and in different moments. The fact that market shares are already available in the case gives those engaged in contribution litigation an objective reference for their relative liabilities. As market shares are already established, they do not change depending on the way judges exercise their discretionary powers. If the European Commission states that a given company had 20 per cent of market shares, this percentage will be coherently used in all contribution disputes.

DISADVANTAGES The most frequently named disadvantage of using the market share criterion in contribution litigation is the complexity of its use.[284] Some authors claim that it is not easy to define the relevant market. Market definition is often heatedly argued in competition law cases. This may cause inefficiencies in contribution litigation, in which market definition becomes a central problem.[285] In addition, market shares change over time,[286] and they must sometimes be calculated for different markets,[287] which leads to complex assessments.

It is notable that market shares are an imperfect measure for dividing liability between antitrust infringers. They are merely a proxy and not an exact reflection of other factors.[288] This means that market shares will never reveal the full picture of the causation and the illicit gains. Regarding causation, market shares show only the market power and disregard every other factor that may matter for causation (for instance, companies' actions, market conditions). Market power is also only partially determined by market shares, and other factors may be decisive (for example, access

[283] Antitrust Modernization Commission, 'Report and Recommendations', 254. Roman Inderst, Stefan Thomas and Olivier Gänswein also claim their reliability, see Inderst and Thomas *Schadensersatz bei Kartellverstößen*, 405; Gänswein, 'Gesamtschuldnerausgleich unter Kartellbeteiligten', 52.

[284] Weinhold, *Der Gesamtschuldnerausgleich*, 155–156; Polden and Sullivan, 'Contribution and Claim Reduction', 418–419; Hösch, *Der schadensrechtliche Innenausgleich*, 288; Schaper and Stauber, 'Gesamtschuld und Innenausgleich', 283; Gänswein, 'Gesamtschuldnerausgleich unter Kartellbeteiligten', 52.

[285] Ibid.

[286] Weinhold, *Der Gesamtschuldnerausgleich*, 153.

[287] Polden and Sullivan, 'Contribution and Claim Reduction', 418–419.

[288] Similarly Dreher, 'Die Haftungsverteilung', 157; Krüger, *Kartellregress*, 79 *et seq.*

to specific technologies).[289] Regarding illicit gains, market shares are typically based on values of sales, and as indicated above, they do not take into account several factors (for instance, companies' differences in costs and efficiency).

Finally, market shares cannot be applied generally in EU competition law. As described above, they cannot be a basis for dividing liability when vertical anticompetitive agreements are in question or when the Commission finds multiple companies jointly and severally liable for the fine.

CONCLUSIONS The criterion of market shares can be feasibly applied to antitrust contribution disputes. After defining the markets where the infringement occurred and after calculating the market shares, judges can accordingly determine the relative liability for antitrust infringement.

The primary advantage of using market shares is that they can be simply applied by referring to the information included in the judgments or decisions establishing the violation of EU competition law (principle no. iv). They can also provide for objective results, leading to a coherent contribution adjudication (principle no. ii). Since market shares or at least market definitions are already determined in the case, judges can uniformly rely on them even if they take part in different proceedings.

Market shares are not a perfect criterion. They cannot be applied in the context of vertical agreements (principle no. i) or in the context of public antitrust enforcement (principle no. iii). Market shares are also only an imperfect proxy of other criteria, such as illicit gains and causation.

3.6.3.6 Pro Capita *Division*

Pro capita apportionment is the equal division of liability according to the number of entities involved in an infringement. For instance, if the total liability for an infringement was EUR 1 million and there were four companies liable, a *pro capita* division leads to individual liabilities of EUR 0.25 million each.

The *pro capita* division of joint and several liability is present in every researched national tort law as a *last resort* rule in contribution litigation.

The idea of relying on *pro capita* apportionment in contribution cases concerning competition law has also been expressed by the CJEU in *Siemens Österreich* and in legal literature.[290]

[289] See, for instance, Barry E. Hawk, *Common Market and International Antitrust: A Comparative Guide* (New York and Washington: Aspen Law & Business, 1990), 788–789; Kellie Curry Raper, H. Alan Love and C. Richard Shumway, 'Distinguishing the Source of Market Power' (2007) 89 *American Journal of Agricultural Economics*, 1, 78.

[290] CJEU, *Siemens Österreich*, para. 71. See also Weinhold, *Der Gesamtschuldnerausgleich*, 158; Körner, *Die Gesamtschuld im Kartellbußgeldrecht*, 263; Bieber, *Die gesamtschuldnerische Haftung*, 107–109.

APPLICATION IN EU COMPETITION LAW *Pro capita* apportionment of liability operates in the same way in competition law as in other fields of law. The amount of liability is simply divided by the number of entities involved. The use of this criterion is not dependent on the type of abuse or the type of antitrust enforcement that was used to establish the infringement of EU competition law.

ADVANTAGES The main advantage of this criterion is its simplicity[291] and low cost.[292] As the calculation is enclosed in one simple formula, no specific data or economic experts are needed.

Another reason for applying this criterion is its general use. *Pro capita* apportionment can be used in a uniform way in the entire body of competition law.

The *pro capita* division of liability is also expressed in numerical terms and does not provide room for any arbitrary judgment.[293] It guarantees clear and coherent results, which can be uniformly applied in many separate contribution lawsuits. This criterion also provides for legal certainty.[294]

According to some authors, *pro capita* division fits well into the nature of contribution claims understood as a mechanism to provide for fairness.[295] Fairness is often described in terms of equal treatment.[296] *Pro capita* apportionment is the essence of equal treatment since every antitrust infringer is ultimately liable for exactly the same amount.

DISADVANTAGES The central drawback of *pro capita* apportionment concerns its ability to provide for fairness and equal treatment. Ostensibly, *pro capita* sharing is in line with the principle of equality. All companies are in the same situation – they committed an antitrust infringement. They are thus treated the same way – they are ultimately liable for the same amount. However, upon closer inspection of the use of *pro capita* apportionment, each infringer will have a different attitude and impact upon the infringement. For instance, some were more blameful than others,[297] they

[291] William Bruce Davis, 'Multiple Defendant Settlement in 10b-5: Good Faith Contribution Bar' (1989) 40 *Hastings Law Journal*, 1253–1270; Cavanagh, 'Contribution, Claim Reduction', 1318; Dreher, 'Die Haftungsverteilung', 159; Weinhold, *Der Gesamtschuldnerausgleich*, 57; Opper, *Die gesamtschuldnerische Bußgeldhaftung*, 200.

[292] Polden and Sullivan, 'Contribution and Claim Reduction', 420; Easterbrook, Landes and Posner, 'Contribution among Antitrust Defendants', 365–366; Dreher, 'Die Haftungsverteilung', 159; Weinhold, *Der Gesamtschuldnerausgleich*, 157.

[293] Canin, *Les actions récursoires*, 169.

[294] Weinhold, *Der Gesamtschuldnerausgleich*, 157.

[295] Canin, *Les actions récursoires*, 169; Cochet, 'La contribution', para. 21; Mignot, *Les obligations solidaires*, 411.

[296] See, for instance, Mitchell, *The Law of Contribution*, 191–192.

[297] Bruce Davis, 'Multiple Defendant Settlement', 1270; Polden and Sullivan, 'Contribution and Claim Reduction', 420; Cavanagh, 'Contribution, Claim Reduction', 1319; Canin, *Les actions récursoires*, 176–177. See also the historical development of case law on the basis of § 426 of the BGB that limited *pro capita* determination to the benefit of other criteria, Meier,

contributed to the infringement differently,[298] and they profited from the infringement in diverse amounts.[299] The *pro capita* rule does not account for such differences.

In fact, *pro capita* division can be particularly unfair for small and medium undertakings.[300] They are likely to have a minimal effect on the restriction of competition, but the *pro capita* liability could exceed their financial capacity to cover it. As a result, the *pro capita* apportionment is called only rough justice[301] or even substantial injustice.[302]

Due to all of these reasons, *pro capita* division is considered only as a last resort rule.[303]

CONCLUSIONS The *pro capita* criterion consists in dividing the total amount of liability by the number of antitrust infringers.

Its advantage is that it can be generally (principles no. i and iii) and coherently (principle no. ii) applied in competition law. It is also easy to administer (principle no. iv).

However, *pro capita* apportionment is simplistic and does not take into account any factors related to the infringement. It brings us only a little further than the no-contribution rule: from no fairness to rough fairness. As a consequence, this rule should be considered only if none of the other criteria can apply in the context of competition law.

3.6.3.7 Other Criteria

Competition law scholars have named a number of other criteria that could apply to the apportionment of antitrust liability. These criteria are considered collectively as they all suffer from significant drawbacks.

SIZE OF THE UNDERTAKING The size of the undertaking in terms of its overall turnover or number of employees is another possible criterion for establishing

Gesamtschulden, 594; Dreher, 'Die Haftungsverteilung', 160; Weinhold, *Der Gesamtschuldnerausgleich*, 158.

[298] Cavanagh, 'Contribution, Claim Reduction', 1319; Canin, Les actions récursoires, 176–177; Weinhold, *Der Gesamtschuldnerausgleich*, 158.

[299] Weinhold, *Der Gesamtschuldnerausgleich*, 158.

[300] Ibid., 157.

[301] William F. Baxterin 'The Antitrust Equal Enforcement Act. Hearings before the Committee on the Judiciary' (1982 House of Representatives J-97-15), 25; William F. Baxter in 'Antitrust Damage Allocation. Hearings before the Subcommittee on Monopolies and Commercial Law of the Committee on the Judiciary' (1983 House of Representatives 118), 62.

[302] Cavanagh, 'Contribution, Claim Reduction', 1320; Krüger, *Kartellregress*, 53; Dreher, 'Die Haftungsverteilung', 160.

[303] The BGH also rejected the pro capita criterion in *Calcium Carbide*. See BGH, BeckRS 2015, 00033.

relative antitrust liabilities.[304] This is sometimes applied in English and Polish contribution cases[305] and allegedly has a basis in the Commission's decisions. The undertaking's size has also been considered by the BGH as one of the criteria for internal distribution of liability in the public enforcement context[306] in order to protect the deterrence of the Commission's fines.[307]

This reasoning is flawed, and the criterion of the undertaking's size should be excluded from contribution analysis. As demonstrated in Chapter 2, the idea that contribution claims should provide for deterrence is misguided as it disregards the division between the internal and external aspects of joint and several liability.

The *size* of an undertaking is also a blurred term. It is not clear whether this refers to the company's turnover or if its size should be counted by the number of employees.

Regardless of this, the size of the undertaking is neither a basis of liability in tort law nor it is linked with competition law infringement.

In addition, the idea of reflecting the impact of an undertaking on misconduct may be expressed better by some other criteria described above –an infringement-related value of sales and market shares.

FINANCIAL CAPACITY Another criterion that is substantially close to the undertaking's size is its financial capacity. It is claimed by some that utilising this criterion would provide a strong deterrence factor.[308] Additional benefits include the fact that financial capacity is utilised by the Commission to set fines, so this would align apportionment of liability with the Commission's fining policy.[309]

Nevertheless, the use of this criterion would be misguided. The logic used to justify the use of financial capacity by the Commission cannot be mapped onto contribution litigation. As proven in Chapter 2, the deterrence factor of EU competition law is not at stake in contribution litigation. As a civil law matter, there is no need to be mindful of keeping market structures unchanged. The use of the criterion of financial ability in contribution litigation is thus mistaken.

CRITERIA BASED ON THE COMMISSION'S GUIDELINES ON FINES A group of criteria proposed for dealing with contribution are retrieved from the

304 Dunleavy, 'Contribution among Antitrust Defendants', 27; Bieber, *Die gesamtschuldnerische Haftung*, 143–144; Inderst and Thomas, *Schadensersatz bei Kartellverstößen*, 407–408; von Laufenberg, *Kartellrechtliche Konzernhaftung*, 272–275.

305 See Section 3.6.1.2.

306 BGH, BeckRS 2015, 00033, para. 71.

307 Ibid.

308 von Kalben and Sekunde, 'Relative Responsibility', 4, 6; Opper, *Die gesamtschuldnerische Bußgeldhaftung*, 202.

309 Ibid. See Guidelines on Fines, para. 35. See also von Laufenberg, *Kartellrechtliche Konzernhaftung*, 270–272.

Commission's Guidelines on Fines. They include the gravity of the infringement,[310] its geographic scope and implementation, the combined market shares of the parties,[311] duration of the infringement,[312] needs of deterrence,[313] termination of the infringement upon the intervention of the Commission, negligence, limited participation in the infringement, cooperation with the Commission, encouragement to undertake the anticompetitive agreement on the part of public authorities or legislation,[314] recidivism, ringleading or using coercive measures to enforce an anticompetitive agreement, refusal to cooperate or obstructing the Commission's investigation,[315] illicit gains,[316] and inability to pay the fine.[317] The idea to refer to some of these criteria appeared in the *Calcium carbide* judgment.[318] The proposal to consider them was also made multiple times in the literature.[319]

The idea underpinning the use of the Commission's criteria for fine setting in contribution cases is based on the understanding that contribution claims need to guarantee the effectiveness of sanctions imposed by the Commission.[320] This reasoning is unacceptable and based on the misguided idea that contribution claims are meant to support the aims pursued by the Commission (see Chapter 2). A general reference to the Commission's Guidelines on Fines is thus improper.

The criteria present in the Commission's Guidelines on Fines may still be considered selectively applicable. Attempt to use the Commission's Guidelines on Fines in this way, however, also fails. Some of the criteria used by the Commission to set the fine apply to all infringers equally and thus cannot differentiate relative shares of liability.[321] A group of factors relate to the circumstances that are not connected with the infringement. They take place before or after the infringement.[322] As a result, there are only a few potential criteria left to consider: the value of sales, duration of the infringement, role in the infringement and degree of fault. These have all been covered in paragraphs above, either as separate criteria or as a

310 Guidelines on Fines, para. 19.
311 Ibid., para. 22.
312 Ibid., para. 24.
313 Ibid., para. 30.
314 Ibid., para. 29.
315 Ibid., para. 28.
316 Ibid., para. 31.
317 Ibid., para. 36.
318 BGH, BeckRS 2015, 00033, para. 71.
319 See, for instance, Opper, *Die gesamtschuldnerische Bußgeldhaftung*, 193–216; Dreher, 'Die Haftungsverteilung', 158; Inderst and Thomas, *Schadensersatz bei Kartellverstößen*, 407; von Laufenberg, *Kartellrechtliche Konzernhaftung*, 277–281.
320 Opper, *Die gesamtschuldnerische Bußgeldhaftung*, 193.
321 These are the nature of infringement, its geographic scope, implementation, and combined market shares of the parties.
322 This is the case of deterrence, the termination of the infringement upon the Commission's intervention, cooperation with the Commission, recidivism and inability to pay.

part of the causation test. In light of this, the reference to the Guidelines on Fines is unnecessary.

AMOUNTS OF FINES Finally, some have advocated linking relative liability with the amounts of antitrust fines.[323] The idea is to simply compare the fines granted by the Commission and on this basis determine the internal attribution of liability between those jointly and severally liable for antitrust harm.

This approach is oversimplified. The value of fines is determined by the Guidelines on Fines. As demonstrated above, many of the criteria in the Guidelines have no connection with the infringement or cannot be applied in contribution litigation.

3.6.3.8 Choosing the Criteria Applicable to Contribution Claims

It is claimed by some that there is no criterion that can effectively determine relative liabilities in competition law.[324] A thorough review of possible benchmarks still leaves hope that some criteria can be effectively applied in competition law and satisfy the principle of effectiveness set by Directive 2014/104/EU.

IS THERE A CASE FOR *PRO CAPITA* APPORTIONMENT? It has been said at the outset that from the competition law standpoint, four principles are of particular importance when choosing the criterion to apportion antitrust liability: the ability to apply to different types of competition law infringements (i), the ability to provide for coherent results given the multiplicity of contribution claims (ii), the ability to apply to both public and private enforcement (iii) and the ease of the criterion's application (iv).

Pro capita division meets all four criteria and could be considered the best for distributing liability. The downside is that it completely disregards the individual engagement of companies in the infringement. This is why most of the researched jurisdictions treat this type of apportionment only as a last resort rule. Before adopting it in competition law, other solutions must be explored.

Apart from *pro capita*, none of the other criteria meets all four traits identified as necessary for contribution in the antitrust context. The criterion of fault has universal application in competition law; it is applicable in both private and public enforcement and can be applied with reasonable ease. Nonetheless, it raises serious concerns about guaranteeing coherence. The criterion of causation can also be universally applied to different types of competition law infringements and enforcement. However, its use is very complicated and likely to lead to incoherence. The criterion of market shares can apply across different competition law restrictions, it

[323] Dreher, 'Die Haftungsverteilung', 159.

[324] Krüger, *Kartellregress*, 110.

TABLE 3.1. *Choice of criteria for dividing competition law liabilities*

Criteria	Variety (i)	Coherence (ii)	Generality (iii)	Simplicity (iv)
Fault	✓	×	✓	✓
Causation	✓	×	✓	×
Illicit gains	×	✓	×	×
Values of sales	×	✓	×	✓
Market shares	✓	✓	×	✓
Pro capita	✓	✓	✓	✓

Source: own work

ensures coherence, and its application can proceed relatively easily. However, market shares cannot determine the relative liability of companies in vertical relations and of those subject to public competition law enforcement. Illicit gains and value of shares cannot be universally applied to various antitrust practices, and they cannot be applied in the context of public enforcement (Table 3.1).

In light of this, *pro capita* apportionment seems to be the most advantageous solution to resolve the issue of how to divide liability between antitrust infringers.

THE TWO-PILLAR FORMULA Another solution is to establish a formula that includes two complementary criteria for dividing liability so that they can jointly satisfy the principles identified as crucial for contribution litigation in antitrust.

Market Shares The criterion of market shares enjoys some unique features that make it a good tool to divide antitrust liability.

Firstly and most fundamentally, market shares have a close, multidimensional connection to antitrust infringement. This is because market shares are a proxy of causation as well as a proxy of illicit gains. Thus, market shares are a single criterion, but at the same time a proxy of multiple criteria.

Secondly, the shortcomings of the market share criterion seem to be easier to remedy than those of other criteria. The drawback of market shares is that they cannot apply to joint and several liability established by the Commission and to vertical agreements. This deficiency can be resolved by simply applying another criterion for these two cases. By contrast, the shortcomings of other criteria are much more difficult to remedy. Fault and causation lack the ability to provide for coherent results for which no solution seems to exist in substantive law terms. Values of sales share the same shortcomings as market shares but have a more limited scope of application. The same concerns illicit gains, which are difficult to administer. This leads to market shares being adopted as a principal criterion for dividing antitrust liability.

Fault Two options can be considered for cases in which market shares cannot determine relative antitrust liability: fault and causation. Value of sales and illicit gains are not complementary to the criterion of market shares. They are difficult to apply to vertical agreements and in the context of public enforcement.

Between fault and causation, fault is preferable. Causation has two serious disadvantages. It is much more difficult to apply as it encompasses a conglomerate of various factors. Additionally, it might be challenging to use this criterion in the context of joint and several liability imposed in public antitrust enforcement. The reason is that companies may be closely related because they belong to the same corporate entity. It can thus be difficult to establish the contribution factors that relate separately to them.

In contrast, the criterion of fault is much easier to administer in the context of public antitrust enforcement. First, it is easy to determine the individual companies' grades of fault and further characteristics of their intent in the case of vertical agreements and arrangements characteristic to public antitrust enforcement. Second, the criterion of fault can remedy the shortcomings of the Commission's fining policy. The Commission's extensive interpretation of the term undertaking and the Commission's approach to the sale of assets have been criticised as in breach of the principle *nulla crimen sine culpa*. The application of the criterion of fault in contribution disputes can bring justice to those who are fined without being individually blameful. The criterion of fault is thus not only preferable from the perspective of contribution law claims, but it should also be encouraged from the standpoint of general fining policy.

The Complementary Role of Market Shares and Fault The bundling of market shares with fault as the criteria for dividing antitrust liability creates synergies. The market shares criterion is used in the majority of cases as it can be applied to different competition law practices. Its main value is that it is able to be applied coherently and easily in multiple proceedings on contribution. The criterion of fault is used in vertical agreements and public antitrust enforcement. In this area, there are only a few joint and several debtors, and the risk of incoherence is much lower. In such situations, the assessment of fault seems to be particularly important. This is because the element of blamefulness is disregarded when the liability is imposed. The Commission does not take it into account in an individual way. It is also common to vertical agreements that some companies are forced by a party with a stronger bargaining position to undertake anticompetitive strategies.

The combination of market shares and fault thus is an optimal formula to decide relative antitrust liability. This formula consists of two pillars that complement each other. It uses the market shares criterion to provide for a simple and coherent method for contribution litigation that is used in the majority of cases, and it takes into account the criterion of fault in situations requiring such consideration without posing a risk to the coherence of contribution adjudication.

CONCLUSIONS National civil laws take a flexible approach towards the choice of criteria to decide contribution claims, and the judges welcome various methods for the division of liability. This allows for applying a criterion that is specific to competition law, on the one hand, but opens the door to incoherent and incorrect adjudication, on the other hand. Establishing a fixed formula to divide antitrust liability is therefore advised.

The review of various possible options demonstrates that there are two options for choosing the criteria for contribution claims in competition law: the application of *pro capita* apportionment (i) and the use of market shares for most cases of private antitrust enforcement and fault in the context of vertical agreements and public enforcement (ii).

As the main function of contribution claims is to provide for fairness (see Section 2.2.3) and *pro capita* division is deficient in this respect, the second option is preferred.

3.7 COMPETITION LAW–SPECIFIC APPROACH TO CONTRIBUTION CLAIMS

When establishing the right to contribution for liabilities stemming from competition law, EU Courts and lawmakers decided to rely on national laws. In line with this proposal, the paragraphs above analysed how traditional civil rules on contribution apply in competition law. This assessment has demonstrated a range of considerations and changes that need to be taken into account when relying on traditional rules on contribution in the context of EU competition law.

3.7.1 *Necessary Modifications to Traditional Rules on Contribution*

The compliance with EU law, its effective enforcement and the principle of effectiveness require modifications of several currently existing rules for contribution. If we follow a contribution proceeding step by step, the following modifications are necessary.

First, the legal bases that allow contribution to be sought before the antitrust debt has been paid are excluded. This is the case of English *quia timet* injunctions and German *Mitwirkung* and *Befreiung* claims. Their application runs against the principle of effective competition law enforcement.

Second, competition law requires the catalogue of entities from which contribution can be requested to be limited. Traditionally, contribution claims can be brought forward against anybody whose joint and several liability for the debt in question can be established. In the case of liabilities for antitrust fines, the adherence to the Commission's decision nonetheless demands such claims to be limited only to the addressees that are already named in the Commission's decision.

Third, it is difficult to maintain the current approach to the allocation of debt among those jointly and severally liable for it. The existing rules on contribution give judges great flexibility in determining relative liabilities. They can mix and match various criteria to divide liability according to the peculiarities of each case. This approach is unacceptable in the context of competition law, where there is a multitude of intertwined contribution proceedings. The right to contribution in the context of competition law can be ensured effectively only by setting a criterion/criteria that would determine relative liabilities for antitrust debts upfront.

3.7.2 *Shortcomings of the Civil Law and Competition Law Blend*

The number of modifications to traditional rules on contribution required to make them applicable in the competition law context makes it doubtful whether we are still dealing with a traditional civil law framework for contribution. It is already rather a blend of civil law and competition law rules. While this mixture can provide for a right to claim contribution that is enforceable in the competition law context, this does not mean that this is an optimal solution.

First, it is doubtful whether all types of contribution claims and their various legal bases are needed. The great number of provisions and doctrines that can be relied on to claim contribution is an effect of a historic development of law. However, this state now shreds the right to contribution into many pieces. To claim indemnity, the claimant must follow a specific cause of action. To divide antitrust liability equally, the claimant must bring a claim in equity. To rely on a specific competition law–focused approach, the claimant should rely on Article L. 481-9 of the Code de Commerce. The multitude of available tools and their applications bundled with the lack of settled judicial practice on how to apply them in competition law causes uncertainty for those envisioning contribution litigation.

Second, it is unsure whether contribution claims in private and public enforcement would be dealt with under the same rules or not. The picture is complicated by rules introduced with Directive 2014/104/EU. The laws implementing the Directive either introduce new legal bases or modify the existing legal order. This raises questions of what impact such legislation has on the exercise of contribution claims and whether it would apply only to the area of private enforcement or by analogy, also to public enforcement. On top of that, legal tests that are deployed in contribution litigation differ depending on private and public enforcement if indemnity is claimed.

Third, while it is recommended to rely on upfront selected criteria to divide antitrust liability between several debtors, this is not yet the letter of the law. Currently, national judges enjoy a great margin of choice when deciding on the criteria used to determine relative liabilities. The paragraphs below call for coherence and adjudication according to an upfront established set of rules. However, each judge is now free to decide whether to follow this recommendation. Until legislative action is taken, there is a great risk of incoherence in contribution litigation. It is therefore possible that even a single liability would be divided incorrectly as it would be adjudicated by different judges in separate proceedings based on different criteria. The criteria themselves are likely to be heatedly disputed as they can tip the dispute on contribution into one direction or another. The lack of coherence and transparency in this crucial moment of a dispute results in a lack of legal certainty and the infringers' inability to assess their relative liabilities before judges announce their verdict. This is an appreciable effect that can put the right to contribution into question, increase litigation costs and have a negative effect on competition law enforcement.

These complexities and uncertainties put the entire system of enforcement of contribution claims at risk. This may in practice lead to low enforceability of contribution claims in antitrust or even to their lack of enforcement. Such a state of affairs is inacceptable in the European Union as the no-contribution rule would be in breach of EU law and commonly recognised principles, such as proportionality and equality.

3.7.3 *Competition Law–Specific Rules on Contribution*

Against this background, it is proposed to take a competition law–specific approach to the right to contribution in EU competition law and to introduce a simple and efficient set of rules for contribution.

Contribution should be based on a single type of claim in the form of a personal right to contribution that is available in the context of public and private enforcement. Such a rule can follow the wording proposed by Article L. 481-9 of the Code de Commerce reads that

> if several entities concurrently undertook an anticompetitive practice, they are jointly and severally (*solidairement*) liable for resulting damages; among themselves they contribute to the debt according to the gravity of their faults and causal role in generation of damage.[325]

This claim should be available as a partial contribution or indemnity, without introducing any separation between these two types of claims. This right should become available at the moment when the debtor pays a part of a debt exceeding its own share of liability. Any earlier exercise of this right should be prohibited as interfering with the principle of effectiveness of EU competition law.

[325] Article L. 481-9 of the Code de Commerce reads: '*Lorsque plusieurs personnes physiques ou morales ont concourru à la réalisation d'une pratique anticoncurrentielle mentionnée à l'article L. 481-1, elles sont solidairement tenues de réparer le préjudice en résultant. Elles contribuent entre elles à la dette de réparation à proportion de la gravité de leurs fautes respectives et de leur rôle causal dans la réalisation du dommage*'.

The claim for contribution should respect the decision of the European Commission in terms of the catalogue of entities from which joint and several liability can be claimed.

There should be a single legal test to assess contribution claims. This test should require that the claimant and the defendant be jointly and severally liable for the antirust debt (i), the claimant has paid the debt (ii), and it has done so in excess of its relative liability (iii).

It is necessary to introduce a clear criterion for dividing liability when deciding about contribution between infringers of EU competition law. This should be a two-pillar rule consisting of the assessment of market shares (applicable in the case of horizontal agreements) and fault (applicable in the case of vertical agreements and in the context of public enforcement). This rule ensures that the division of liability is adapted to different kinds of antitrust infringements and enforcements and the contribution adjudication is simple and coherent.

To sum up, the following rule for contribution is suggested:

> If several entities are jointly and severally liable for fines or damages stemming from a violation of EU competition law, they should contribute to the debt among themselves according to their shares on the market affected by the violation; in case it is impossible to determine relative liabilities based on market shares, contribution takes place according to relative faults.

Contribution can be claimed when the debtor has paid the antitrust debt in excess of its own share of liability from the entities jointly and severally liable for the same debt with respect to the decisions of the existing European Commission.

4

Modifications of Joint and Several Liability with Respect to Certain Groups of Entities

The previous chapter demonstrated that the legal framework for enforcing contribution claims is complicated and marked with legal uncertainty. This is, however, only a partial assessment of joint and several liability in competition law. Apart from the general rules on joint and several liability that have been described in Chapters 2 and 3 ('general regime'), Directive 2014/104/EU introduced special rules on joint and several liability ('special regime'). The special liability regime of joint and several liability concerns three groups: those engaged in consensual dispute resolution (Section 4.1), immunity recipients (Section 4.2) and small and medium enterprises (Section 4.3). These rules add another level of complexity to contribution claims in antitrust.

The aim of this chapter is to outline the modifications to the general rules on joint and several liability (Sub-sections 1). The assessment starts with the analysis of policy arguments and the search for the logic behind the special rules on joint and several liability. It is asked whether the special treatment of privileged groups is justified (Sub-sections 2) and whether the rules provided by Directive 2014/104/EU meet the envisioned aims (Sub-sections 3). Subsequently, the assessment takes a pragmatic angle, and it is asked how the special regimes of joint and several liability operate in practice (Sub-sections 4). Finally, each section concludes and gives recommendations based on both policy and pragmatic considerations (Sub-sections 5). This chapter closes with conclusions (Section 4.4).

4.1 ENTITIES ENGAGED IN CONSENSUAL DISPUTE RESOLUTION

Directive 2014/104/EU provides for special rules on joint and several liability for those engaged in consensual dispute resolution. The Directive recognises that antitrust damage can be compensated in a consensual way, and this should be accounted for in contribution adjudication.

4.1.1 *Special Regime of Joint and Several Liability for Those Engaged in Consensual Dispute Resolution*

Directive 2014/104/EU introduces a special regime of joint and several liability for those engaged in consensual dispute resolution, meaning out-of-court settlements, arbitration, mediation and conciliation.[1]

According to the Directive, when the creditor and one of the joint and several debtors settle, two effects arise. First, the creditor's overall debt is reduced with the amount corresponding to the settling debtor's relative liability.[2] Second, the non-settling debtors do not have a right to claim contribution from the settling debtor.[3] This mechanism is known as 'proportionate claim reduction' in the US literature and is used to separate the effects that settlement has on non-settling debtors when joint and several liability is applied (see more in Section 4.1.3.1).

The Directive also ensures coherence between consensual and non-consensual dispute resolution. It requires national courts dealing with contribution claims to also consider damages paid in settlements.[4]

4.1.2 *Justification of the Special Regime*

A liability system without the modifications introduced by Directive 2014/104/EU would be perfectly feasible. According to the general rules, the creditor could settle

1 Recital 48 of Directive 2014/104/EU. These methods are discussed together as they are all based on the idea that the parties settle their rights or allow an arbitrator to resolve the issue, which should have no impact on the debtors that are not part of this dispute resolution.

2 See Article 19(1) of Directive 2014/104/EU: 'Member States shall ensure that, following a consensual settlement, the claim of the settling injured party is reduced by the settling co-infringer's share of the harm that the infringement of competition law inflicted upon the injured party.' This is implemented by Section 39 of the UK Act using the expression 'share of loss or damage'; the UK Act adds that the reduction is made 'regardless of the terms of the consensual settlement'; by § 33f(1) of the GWB referring to '*Höhe seines Anteils an dem Schaden*'; by Article L. 481-13(1) of the Code de Commerce by referring to '*la part du préjudice imputable au codébiteur*'; by Article 6(1) of the Polish Act using the expression '*część odpowiadającą kwocie, do której zwrotu byłby zobowiązany sprawca naruszenia, który zawarł ugodę*'.

3 See Article 19(2) of Directive 2014/104/EU: 'Any remaining claim of the settling injured party shall be exercised only against non-settling co-infringers. Non-settling co-infringers shall not be permitted to recover contribution for the remaining claim from the settling co-infringer.' This is implemented by Section 41 of the UK Act; the UK Act adds that the reduction is made 'regardless of the terms of the consensual settlement'; by § 33f(1) of the GWB; by Article L. 481-13(1) of the Code de Commerce; by Article 6(1) of the Polish Act.

4 See Article 19(3) of Directive 204/104/EU: 'When determining the amount of contribution that a co-infringer may recover from any other co-infringer in accordance with their relative responsibility for the harm caused by the infringement of competition law, national courts shall take due account of any damages paid pursuant to a prior consensual settlement involving the relevant co-infringer.' This is implemented by Section 38(3) of the UK Act; by Article L.481-14 of the Code de Commerce; there is no provisions on this in German and Polish Acts implementing the Directive.

for a part of the debt with a chosen debtor and claim the remaining amount of the debt from others. The settling debtor could claim contribution if payment exceeded its own proportion of liability. Non-settling debtors could claim contribution from the settling defendant if they paid more than their own share of liability. This raises the question of what reasons there could be for adopting a different treatment to the one described here.

4.1.2.1 Interference between Joint and Several Liability and Settlements

The general rules on joint and several liability have some undesirable effects on settlements. Most fundamentally, the right to claim contribution after the debt has been settled runs counter to the assumption that settlement resolves a dispute in a *final* way. The main reason to conclude settlements is to settle liabilities by making concessions.[5] If the settling debtor can claim contribution from other parties or other parties can claim contribution from it, the liability is not finally settled and is subsequently modified. The lack of finality may discourage companies from concluding settlements.

Economists indicate that there is a further interference between rules on joint and several liability and settlements.[6] If outcomes of disputes between the creditor and different debtors are not correlated,[7] joint and several liability leads to litigation.[8] This is because joint and several liability increases the creditor's chances of receiving the entire debt payment from any joint and several debtor. As a result, its minimal settling amount is likely to be too high for the debtor to make a corresponding offer. Although some antitrust actions may be generally correlated,[9] the connection is

5 See, for instance, Lynn A. Baker, 'Mass Torts and the Pursuit of Ethical Finality' (2017) 85(5) *Fordham Law Review*, 2, 1943 *et seq.*; Charles Silver and Lynn Anne Baker, 'Mass Lawsuits and the Aggregate Settlement Rule' (1997) 32 *Wake Forest Law Review*, 760 *et seq.*

6 The impact of joint and several liability on settlements is controversial in economic literature, see Lewis A. Kornhauserand Keith T. Takeda, 'N-Defendant Litigation and Settlement: The Impact of Joint and Several Liability' (2008) 109 *New York University Law and Economics Working Papers*, 1, 15; Nicholas Dopuch, Daniel E. Ingberman and Ronald R. King, 'An Experimental Investigation of Multi-defendant Bargaining in "Joint and Several" and Proportionate Liability Regimes' (1997) 23 *Journal of Accounting and Economics*, 219; Lewis A. Kornhauserand Richard L. Revesz, 'Multidefendant Settlements: The Impact of Joint and Several Liability' (1994) 23 *The Journal of Legal Studies*, 1, 41 *et seq.*; Lewis A. Kornhauser and Richard L. Revesz, 'Settlements under Joint and Several Liability' (1993) 68 *New York University Law Review*, 447 *et seq.*; Howard F. Chang and Hilary A. Sigman, 'Incentives to Settle under Joint and Several Liability: An Empirical Analysis of Superfund Litigation' (2000) 29 *The Journal of Legal Studies*, 1, 206 *et seq.*; Cavanagh, 'Contribution, Claim Reduction', 1302.

7 Meaning that the result of one litigation depends on the result of another litigation.

8 Kornhauser and Revesz, 'Settlements under Joint and Several Liability', 449–453; Kornhauser and Revesz, 'Multidefendant Settlements', 50–57, 65–67; Dopuch, Ingberman and King, 'Multi-defendant Bargaining', 192.

9 Meaning that the results of one litigation depend on the result of another litigation. For instance, Lewis A. Kornhauser and Keith T. Takeda state that civil antitrust conspiracy cases

loosened when there is strong evidence only against one infringer or some personal defences exist.[10] In such cases, settlements would be discouraged merely because joint and several liability applies.

The impact of joint and several liability on the settlement rate has been even more pronounced in US antitrust law. According to many, joint and several liability with its no-contribution rule encourages settlements.[11] This is for two main reasons. First, US antitrust infringements are mainly established through private lawsuits. These are both expensive and challenging in terms of providing evidence. Settlement with one of the alleged infringers is thus attractive to the creditor. It can obtain financing and access to information on the functioning of the cartel that can be used in lawsuits against other infringers (the so-called 'Mary-Carter settlements').[12] Second, treble damages are available in the United States. Settling the claim allows the alleged infringer to pay only for singular damages and to avoid their tripling in court.[13] This incentive to settle only increases with time. The more co-infringers settle, the higher the probability that the infringer in question will be sued in trial and need to pay treble damages. This causes a so-called race to settle.[14] An essential element of this system is the no-contribution rule, which makes the settlement amounts final.[15] According to some, allowing contribution claims would decrease the incentive to settle since the settling parties would still need to contribute to high amounts paid by other debtors in trials.[16]

4.1.2.2 Desirability of Settlements

Protecting and fostering settlements is seen positively from the standpoint of competition law enforcement.[17] The main advantage of settlements is that they grant compensation to those harmed by an antitrust infringement without the need to run full-fledged lawsuits. This ensures cost savings for the creditor, the debtor and the

such as price fixing are likely to be nearly perfectly correlated, see Kornhauser and Takeda, 'N-Defendant Litigation and Settlement', 1, 15.

10 Peyer, 'Compensation and the Damages Directive', 21.

11 See, for instance, Polinsky and Shavell, 'Contribution and Claim Reduction', 449–450, 461.

12 See, for instance, Easterbrook, Posner and Landes, 'Contribution among Antitrust Defendants', 366, note 75; Cavanagh, 'Contribution, Claim Reduction', 1297.

13 Polinsky and Shavell, 'Contribution and Claim Reduction', 458.

14 See, for instance, Cannon, 'Antitrust Remedies Reform Proposal', 117; Polinsky and Shavell, 'Contribution and Claim Reduction', 458; Hviid and Medvedev, 'The Role of Contribution', 11; Easterbrook, Landes and Posner, 'Contribution among Antitrust Defendants', 354.

15 Polinsky and Shavell, 'Contribution and Claim Reduction', 458.

16 Cannon, 'Antitrust Remedies Reform Proposal', 118; Cavanagh, 'Contribution, Claim Reduction', 1297–1302; Leslie, 'Judgment-Sharing Agreements', 747 *et seq.* Contrary, Kornhauser and Revesz, 'Settlements under Joint and Several Liability', 474–475, 480.

17 See, for instance, Davis, 'Multiple Defendant Settlement', 1259; Wanli Zhou, 'The Effects of Joint and Several Liability Rule on Collusion and Antitrust Settlement' (2015) 4 *The Bonn Journal of Economics*, 1, 77; Bovis and Clarke, 'Private Enforcement', 68.

judicial system.[18] The creditor gets compensation in a quicker, cheaper and more secure way.[19] The debtor saves the costs of litigation and pays lower damages than it would otherwise pay following a lawsuit in a public court. Public resources are saved as the parties reach a mutually acceptable solution without relying on public courts.[20]

These savings are made without damage to the system of competition law enforcement. Actually, settlements can increase the enforcement of competition law. Since legal tests and evidence requirements can be more relaxed in consensual dispute resolution, more victims of antitrust infringements can receive compensation.[21]

Settlements are also positively perceived by businesses. Among multiple benefits of settlements, the parties can enjoy the confidentiality of a dispute, the maintenance of their usual commercial relationships, the adjudication or mediation by experts, good faith in bringing a dispute to an end, and swift resolution of the dispute.[22] Due to these advantages, consensual dispute resolution is often preferred to litigation. For instance, such preference was expressed by Lufthansa after concluding a settlement with Deutsche Bahn for damages stemming from the air cargo cartel: '[i]nstead of continuing costly legal proceedings for years to come, it would be in the interests of all sides if we were able to reach an agreement with the remaining cartelists'.[23]

4.1.2.3 Considerations Made in Directive 2014/104/EU

Directive 2014/104/EU encourages settlements. First, Recital 5 of the Directive expresses that lawsuits are only one method of seeking compensation. Other ways of claiming compensation are expressively encouraged in Recital 48:

> infringers and injured parties should be encouraged to agree on compensating for the harm caused by a competition law infringement through consensual dispute resolution mechanisms, such as out-of-court settlements (including those where a judge can declare a settlement binding), arbitration, mediation or conciliation. Such consensual dispute resolution should cover as many injured parties and infringers as legally possible. The provisions in this Directive on consensual dispute resolution are therefore meant to facilitate the use of such mechanisms and increase their effectiveness.

[18] Zhou, 'Joint and Several Liability Rule', 77; on advantages and disadvantages of consensual dispute resolution, see Kern, 'Law Enforcement', 353–356.

[19] Weinhold, *Der Gesamtschuldnerausgleich*, 228; Davis, 'Multiple Defendant Settlement', 1259.

[20] Cavanagh, 'Contribution, Claim Reduction', 1312.

[21] Krüger, 'Überlegungen zur Gesamtschuld', 91.

[22] Modzelewska de Raad, 'Consensual Dispute Resolution', 55–57.

[23] Deutsche Bahn, 'Deutsche Bahn Settles Damages Litigation with Lufthansa' (26 August 2019), *Mlex*, available at https://mlex.com/GlobalAdvisory/DetailView.aspx?cid=1123288&siteid=244&rdir=1.

The Directive also protects settlements from negative interferences with other rules. For instance, the design of limitation periods takes into account the option that the parties may be engaged in a consensual dispute resolution.[24] If a settlement is reached before the Commission has adopted its decision on fines, the settlement can also be considered as a mitigating factor and lead to a decrease in the fine.[25] In this light, it is not surprising that there are also special rules on settlements in the context of joint and several liability.

4.1.2.4 'Once-and-for-All' Settlement?

Recital 48 is also interesting in terms of identifying the reasons for encouraging consensual dispute resolution mechanisms. It reads:

> Achieving a "once-and-for-all" settlement for defendants is desirable in order to reduce uncertainty for infringers and injured parties. Therefore, infringers and injured parties should be encouraged to agree on compensating for the harm caused by a competition law infringement through consensual dispute resolution mechanisms.

This is a bizarre objective for consensual dispute resolutions, as they are generally not capable of settling disputes 'once-and-for-all'. First and most fundamentally, the main characteristic of consensual dispute resolution mechanisms is that they are only applicable for the parties expressly agreeing to use them. If one joint and several debtor does not give its consent to join the proceeding, such a proceeding cannot in principle encompass it.[26]

Second, consensual dispute resolution is used rather exceptionally to resolve multiparty disputes. It is definitely more difficult to consensually negotiate a settlement acceptable to many parties than to give a judgment that would determine their legal situation. The Commission's choice to utilise a 'once-and-for-all' settlement is

[24] See Articles 18(1) and 18(2) of Directive 2014/104/EU. See also Recitals 49 and 50 of Directive 2014/104/EU.

[25] See Article 18(3) of Directive 2014/104/EU.

[26] See, for instance, in the context of arbitration, Article 22.1(viii) of London Court of International Arbitration (LCIA) Rules 2014 (1 October 2014), available at https://lcia.org/Dispute_Resolution_Services/lcia-arbitration-rules-2014.aspx; Article 24(b) Singapore International Arbitration Centre (SIAC) Rules 2013 (1 April 2013), available at https://siac.org.sg/images/stories/articles/rules/SIAC%202013%20Rules_5th%20Edition.pdf; Article 17.5 of the United Nations Commission on International Trade Law (UNCITRAL) Ad Hoc Rules 2013 (16 December 2013) 68/109, available at https://uncitral.un.org/sites/uncitral.un.org/files/media-documents/uncitral/en/uncitral-arbitration-rules-2013-e.pdf. See also Martin Domke, *Domke on Commercial Arbitration* (Eagan: West Group, 1984), 1–2; Klas Laitinen, *Multi-party and multi-contract arbitration mechanisms in international commercial litigation. A study on institutional rules of consolidation, joinder, and intervention from a Finnish perspective* (2013) available at https://helda.helsinki.fi/bitstream/handle/10138/44922/klaslaitinenprogradu.pdf?sequence=2.

thus surprising. Ultimately, this could probably be better achieved in court litigation by, for example, introducing a compulsory joinder.

4.1.3 *Realisation of the Objectives*

Directive 2014/104/EU introduces a special regime for joint and several liability, which is called in the US legal writing 'proportionate claim reduction' (Section 4.1.3.1). The benefits of the proportionate claim reduction rule can be best explained by a comparison of the possible regimes for contribution and settlements (Section 4.1.3.2).

4.1.3.1 Definitions

The 'proportionate claim reduction' rule is a variation of a so-called *pro tanto* claim reduction and can be best explained by reference to it.

Under the '*pro tanto*' rule, the overall amount of damages owed by debtors to the creditor is reduced by the amount for which one of the debtors settled with the creditor.[27] Imagine that there are two internally equally liable debtors (A, B) that owe the creditor (X) a sum of 100. Under the '*pro tanto*' rule, if A settles for 30, X's claim is reduced to 70 and X can still claim 70 from B.

Proportionate claim reduction is a modification of this rule. Its basis is also claim reduction, but the reduction takes place on the basis of the relative shares of liability and not the settlement amount.[28] In the example above, if A settles for 30 and the relative liability shares are established *pro capita*, X's claim is reduced to 50 ($100 - {}^{1}/_{2} \times 100 = 50$). X can claim 50 from B.

4.1.3.2 Comparison

Proportionate claim reduction is believed to be the best rule to protect incentives to settle from the negative effects of joint and several liability.[29] In order to prove its benefits, the influence of joint and several liability on settlements under three possible regimes will be compared: the regular contribution rule, '*pro tanto*' and proportionate claim reduction.

27 Kornhauser and Revesz, 'Settlements under Joint and Several Liability', 438; Marcel Kahan, 'The Incentive Effects of Settlements under Joint and Several Liability' (1996) 16 *International Review of Law and Economics*, 389.

28 Kornhauser and Revesz, 'Settlements under Joint and Several Liability', 438.

29 Zhou, 'Joint and Several Liability Rule', 87; Daniel Klerman, 'Settling Multidefendant Lawsuits: The Advantage of Conditional Setoff Rules' (1996) 25 *The Journal of Legal Studies*, 1, 445 *et seq*. On the superiority of proportionate claim reduction to *pro tanto* reduction, see also Kahan, 'Settlements under Joint and Several Liability', 395.

Under joint and several liability with a right to claim contribution, there are few incentives to settle as each debtor is liable in the amount determined by their relative shares of liability, regardless of how much they settle for.[30] The debtors have no incentive to negotiate their best deal with the creditor, knowing that the discount they receive will be redistributed between all debtors in contribution litigation.

Under the '*pro tanto*' claim reduction rule, both the settling party and the creditor are protected. The creditor always recovers the entire debt as it receives the settlement amount from the settling party and the rest of the debt from non-settling parties.[31] As there is no right to claim contribution, the settling party keeps the negotiated bargain. This encourages settlements. Nonetheless, settlement has a negative impact on the position of non-settling debtors.[32] The overall claim is reduced by the amount negotiated by the settling debtor, which means that if the settling defendant settles for an amount lower to its own share of liability, other debtors would need to pay in excess of their own relative liability.[33] The risks involved with settlement are thus placed on non-settling parties.

The proportionate claim reduction rule encourages settlements.[34] Similarly to the '*pro tanto*' rule, it eliminates contribution litigation and the re-discussion of the settling party's relative liability.[35] This rule isolates the effects of settlements on non-settling debtors better than the '*pro tanto*' rule. By reducing the debt by the share of the settling debtor's liability, the settlement sum has no impact on non-settling debtors.[36] If the sum is lower than the settling debtor's share of liability, the result works to the loss of the creditor. The overall claim is reduced by the higher amount of the settling debtor's share of liability.[37] If the sum is higher than the settling debtor's share of liability, this has a negative effect on the settling debtor as he pays more than he ought to pay according to his relative liability.[38] In both scenarios, the liability of other joint and several debtors remains the same and corresponds to their own relative liability.

Against this background, it seems that Directive 2014/104/EU made a reasoned choice of selecting the proportionate claim reduction rule in order to balance its objective to encourage settlements with the application of joint and several liability.

30 Polinsky and Shavell, 'Contribution and Claim Reduction', 459 in the case of risk aversion.
31 Kornhauser and Revesz, 'Settlements under Joint and Several Liability', 439.
32 Ibid., 485–486.
33 Ibid.
34 Ibid., 487–488.
35 Ibid.
36 Polden and Sullivan, 'Contribution and Claim Reduction', 421; Sarah Ford, 'Claims for Contribution in Competition Damages Actions: The Impact of the EU Damages Directive' (2015) 36 *European Competition Law Review*, 8, 328–329.
37 Kornhauser and Revesz, 'Settlements under Joint and Several Liability', 439; Ford, 'Contribution in Competition Damages Actions', 328–329.
38 Kornhauser and Revesz, 'Settlements under Joint and Several Liability', 483.

4.1.4 *Practical Application*

4.1.4.1 The Settling Debtor's Position

On the high-level of analysis, the modified rules on joint and several liability incentivise debtors to settle. The no-contribution rule guarantees the ultimacy of settlement and thus maintains the debtors' will to bargain. This picture, however, is less clear when one looks into the practical application of the rules provided in Article 19(1) of Directive 2014/104/EU.[39] According to these rules, the settling debtor is likely to have difficulty calculating its own liability share and needs to wait for a long time until its settlement becomes final.

CALCULATION OF THE PARTIES' OWN LIABILITY SHARES The central point of every settlement is the determination of one's minimal and maximal settlement offer.[40] When a partial settlement is considered, this assessment must be made with respect to the debtor's own share of liability. It is then essential for the debtor to actually know its relative share of liability. This seems impossible under the current legal framework. Directive 2014/104/EU clarifies in recital 51 that the same benchmark for determining relative liability applies in settlements as in judicial disputes on contribution. This benchmark is, however, not concretely established. It is the role of national laws to decide on a relevant criterion (see Section 3.1.1).

The lack of a clear benchmark for assessing relative liability can impede the debtors' willingness to settle. First, it is unclear under which law its claims would be dealt with and which law would decide on the relevant benchmark. Infringements of EU antitrust law imply that there is an effect on EU trade, and claims for damages may be enforced in a cross-border setting.[41] Second, there is great legal uncertainty about which criterion for establishing liability would be applied even if a national law were to be established. Currently, none of the researched legal systems take a clear stance on the criteria used to determine relative antitrust liability (see Section 3.6.1.1). The uncertainty about the criterion to determine relative liability shares makes it difficult for the debtor to determine its own liability and hence its

[39] On the practical application of the rules on joint and several liability for the settling infringers, see also Carsten Koenig, 'Making Contribution Work: The Liability of Privileged and Non-privileged Injurers in EU Competition Law' (2018) 14 *European Competition Journal*, 126.

[40] Settlement lies somewhere between the minimum amount for the plaintiff to settle and the maximum amount for the defendant to settle, see Easterbrook, Landes and Posner, 'Contribution among Antitrust Defendants', 355.

[41] On the issue of cross-border enforcement of claims for antitrust damages, see, for instance, Mihail Danov and Florian Becker, 'Governance Aspects of Cross-Border EU Competition Actions: Theoretical and Practical Challenges' (2014) 10 *Journal of Private International Law*, 3, 359; Mihail Danov, Florian Becker and Paul Beaumont, *Cross-border EU Competition Law Actions* (Oxford: Portland, Hart Publishing, 2013).

settlement offer.[42] The margin of error is enormous. For instance, relative liability based on fault can be very different from the one based on market shares.

Uncertainties about the settling of debtor's relative liability were recognised in a dispute between Cartel Damages Claims (CDC), a company consolidating various claims for damages, and Shell, Esso and Total, the cartelists on the paraffin wax market. Cartel Damages Claims concluded a settlement with another cartelist, Sasol, and continued the lawsuit against Shell, Esso and Total. In order to grant CDC full compensation for the sustained damage, the Hague District Court reduced the CDC's claim by the value corresponding to Sasol's liability. In line with the proportionate claim reduction rule, the Hague District Court calculated Sasol's relative liability and decreased CDC's claim against Shell, Esso and Total accordingly. It was only at that moment that Sasol could observe whether it had concluded an advantageous settlement agreement. The other cartelists, as well as the Hague District Court, did not exclude the possibility that Sasol could have in fact overcompensated CDC, which was the issue that the Hague District Court intended to keep in mind when adjudicating at the next stages of the proceeding.[43]

LONG-TIME PERIOD UNTIL THE CLAIM IS ULTIMATELY SETTLED One of the main advantages of settlements as compared to litigation is a quick and final dispute resolution.[44] The proportionate claim reduction rule usually ensures this advantage as settlement is treated as final. This advantage is nonetheless contradicted by Article 19(3) of Directive 2014/104/EU:

Member States shall ensure that where the non-settling co-infringers cannot pay the damages that correspond to the remaining claim of the settling injured party, the settling injured party may exercise the remaining claim against the settling co-infringer.[45]

This rule provides that, for the sake of the principle of full compensation,[46] the settlements be treated as final only under the condition that the creditor successfully claims the remaining part of damages from other debtors. This provision attempts to

[42] On difficulties of determining the settlement amount *ex ante*, see also Martin Seegers, 'Interaction of the Rules on Joint and Several Liability and Settlements under the EU Directive on Damage Actions' (2014) 7 *Global Competition Litigation Review*, 3, 146–147; Inderst and Thomas, *Schadensersatz bei Kartellverstößen*, 418; Rust, 'Kartellverstoß und Gesamtschuld', 511; Carsten Krüger 'Die haftungsrechtliche Privilegierung des Kronzeugen im Außen- und Innenverhältnis gemäß dem Richtlinienvorschlag der Kommission' (2013) *Neue Zeitschrift für Kartellrecht*, 487.

[43] The Hague District Court, judgment of 21 September 2016 in Case C/09/414499/HA ZA 12-293, *CDC Project 14 SA v. Shell Petroleum N.V. and Others*, paras. 2.21 and 2.22.

[44] See Section 4.1.2.2.

[45] This is implemented by Part 4 Section 40 of the UK Act using the term *unable to pay*; by § 33f (1) of the GWB referring to the term *keinen vollständigen Ersatz erlangen konnte*; by Article L.481-13(2) of the Code de Commerce using the term *après les avoir préalablement et vainement poursuivis*; by Article 6(2) of the Polish Act using the term *nie może zapłacić*.

[46] See Recital 61 of Directive 2014/104/EU.

strike a balance between settlements, joint and several liability and the right to receive full compensation. This raises the question of whether the balance provided in Article 19(3) of Directive 2014/104/EU is right.

The suspension of a settlement's finality is a forceful intrusion into rules on settlement. It is the main idea of settlement to resolve a dispute in a final way.[47] The exceptions to it may effectively limit the use of settlements. No one would decide to invest their resources in a settlement if an additional dispute resolution may come into play. In this light, exceptions to the principle of finality should be made only in extraordinary situations.

The principle of full compensation does not seem to require suspending the finality of settlements. By entering into a settlement, the creditor agrees to make concessions to the debtor, and by that, it agrees that it will not receive the full amount of damages to which it is entitled. It makes a choice between full compensation received after a long court litigation or a secure settlement in a smaller amount but sooner.[48] As a result, it seems that protection of the principle of full compensation in settlements is inappropriate, especially if concurring with the settlements' finality.[49]

The practical application of Article 19(3) of Directive 2014/104/EU also gives rise to concern. The issue is the moment in time when the creditor can get back to the settling infringer. It is the moment when 'the non-settling co-infringers cannot pay the damages that correspond to the remaining claim'. The term 'cannot pay' does not refer to any legal concept.[50] It is unclear whether this moment means the poor financial capacity of non-settling debtors, their insolvency, an unsuccessful legal proceeding between them and the creditor or unsuccessful enforcement of a judgment granting damages. If one chooses unsuccessful legal proceedings as the relevant benchmark, this raises further questions. It may be asked what type of judgment allows for the conclusion that the debtor could not pay. It seems unjustified to say that the debtor could not pay because the creditor's claim failed on the merits or was time barred. Therefore, it seems that the most reasonable benchmark is unsuccessful enforcement of a judgment granting damages. Such a judgment

[47] Davis, 'Multiple Defendant Settlement', 1254; Dunleavy, 'Contribution among Antitrust Defendants', 28–29; Robert F. Dobbin, 'Settlement of Private Antitrust Litigation Including Class Type Actions and Multiple Defendant Lawsuits' (1973) 34 *Ohio State Law Journal*, 525. Critically also Kersting and Preuß, *Umsetzung der Kartellschadensersatzrichtlinie*, para. 154; Krüger, 'Die Privilegierung des Kronzeugen', 487.

[48] See Charles Chatterjee and Anna Lefcovitch, *Alternative Dispute Resolution: A Practical Guide* (London and New York: Routledge, 2008), 29–31; Linda R. Singer, *Settling Disputes: Conflict Resolution in Business, Families, and the Legal System* (Boulder, San Francisco, Oxford: Westview Press, 1994), 13.

[49] Contrary, Seegers, 'Joint and Several Liability and Settlements', 145–146.

[50] The implementations of Directive 2014/104/EU have not brought more clarity as this term was simply translated into national languages.

confirms that the creditor had the right to the payment, which it cannot realise due to the debtor's inability to pay.

Another pitfall of applying Article 19(3) of Directive 2014/104/EU is that the settling debtor must wait a long time to find out whether its claim is finally settled. Under Article 10(3) of the Directive, the limitation period for claiming damages is at least five years. It starts to run only when the infringement has ceased and the creditor can identify the infringement, the harm and the identity of the infringer.[51] The limitation period also runs separately for every infringer. This means that until all limitation periods relating to all non-settling infringers have passed, the debtor cannot know whether its settlement is final. This excessive time for awaiting the settlement's finality is unacceptable.

It seems that the legislator was unconvinced by the solution chosen in Article 19 (3) of Directive 2014/104/EU. The last sentence of Article 19(3) provides that

> [t]he derogation referred to in the first subparagraph may be expressly excluded under the terms of the consensual settlement.

From the standpoint of the settling debtor's interests, it is unimaginable to settle without such a clause. It is hoped that this clause would become a standard term in settlement agreements and the subsidiary liability of those settling will become only a theoretical possibility. However, it remains to be seen how frequently this clause will be used.[52]

4.1.4.2 The Creditor's Position

Creditors decide to settle in order to save the time and money needed in court litigation. The fact that some settlements took place shows that settlements were seen as an attractive option by creditors before Directive 2014/104/EU entered into force.[53] In 2020 and 2019, there was indeed a wave of settlements with respect to actions for damages initiated around 2015. For instance, in 2019, Deutsche Bahn settled with Lufthansa with respect to damages resulting from the air cargo cartel that had been litigated before the Regional Court of Cologne since 2013. Lufthansa was also the fifth defendant that Deutsche Bahn had settled with following the

[51] Articles 10(2) and (3) of Directive 2014/104/EU.

[52] Hanno Schaper and Peter Stauber believe that such a clause would indeed become a standard term of settlements, see Schaper and Stauber, 'Gesamtschuld und Innenausgleich', 284. See also Seegers, 'Joint and Several Liability and Settlements', 148; Krüger, 'Die Privilegierung des Kronzeugen', 487.

[53] See *WH Newson Holdings Ltd v. IMI Plc* [2016] EWCA Civ. 773 and *Wolseley UK Limited and Others v. Fiat Chrysler Automobiles* N.V. *and Others* [2019] CAT 12. Antonia Hösch also mentions a settlement concluded between Deutsche Bahn and Thyssen Krupp relating to the rail cartel and a settlement concluded between CDC and Evonik in a Hydrogen peroxide cartel. See Hösch, *Der schadensrechtliche Innenausgleich*, 363.

settlements with Singapore Airlines, Air France-KLM, Qantas and SAS.[54] On 4 July 2019, WH Smith settled damages stemming from the anticompetitive setting of interchange fees (that had been pending before the High Court in London since 2015) with Visa and FunkyPigeon.com.[55] Also, in 2019, HeidelbergCement concluded a settlement with CDC for cement cartel damages disputed before the Mannheim Regional Court since 2015.[56] In late 2019 and in 2020, we have witnessed further settlements relating to sugar, sodium chlorate, cable, LCD and car carrier cartels.[57]

This is a great wave of settlements, which is generally expected to grow. Quoting the words of Michael O'Higgins, a class representative in the FOREX cartel: 'Once [private enforcement] regime gets established. I think we will reach settlements much easier, much faster and with much less expense.'[58] The question is whether Directive 2014/104/EU brings about obstacles that could change this trend. The main factors that can potentially disincentivize creditors from settling are the lack of rules on full settlements and problems connected with the calculation of damages.

SETTLEMENT ONLY WITH RESPECT TO INDIVIDUAL PART OF DEBT OR ENTIRE DEBT The general rules on joint and several liability allow the creditor to claim the entire debt from only one debtor. This is a great advantage as the creditor avoids addressing each debtor individually for its relative part of the compensation and receives the entire compensation in one proceeding. The creditor may thus ask whether it can also achieve the same effect in a settlement ('full settlements').[59] The question arises of whether full settlements are possible and how they should be exercised.

54 Mario Hilgenfeld and Nicholas Hirst, 'Lufthansa, Deutsche Bahn settle air-cargo damages litigation' (26 Autust 2019), *Mlex*, available at https://mlex.com/GlobalAdvisory/DetailView.aspx?cid=1123289&siteid=244&rdir=1.

55 Simon Zekaria, 'Visa, WH Smith Settle Antitrust Claim over Card Fees' (9 July 2019), *Mlex*, available at https://mlex.com/GlobalAdvisory/DetailView.aspx?cid=1110490&siteid=244&rdir=1.

56 Mario Hilgenfeld, 'HeidelbergCement Settles German Cement-Cartel Damages Claims with CDC' (13 August 2019), *Mlex*, available at https://mlex.com/GlobalAdvisory/DetailView.aspx?cid=1120911&siteid=244&rdir=1.

57 Vecchio Karoline Del, 'German Sugar Cartelists Fail to Settle with Food Makers, Will Face Court Ruling' (12 July 2019), *Mlex*, available at https://mlex.com/GlobalAdvisory/DetailView.aspx?cid=1111634&siteid=244&rdir=1; Cartel Damages Claims, 'CDC's Claims against Kemira Aren't Time-Barred, Dutch Court Rules' (4 February 2020), *Mlex*, available at https://mlex.com/GlobalAdvisory/DetailView.aspx?cid=1160399&siteid=244&rdir=1; Competition Appeal Tribunal, 'Prysmian Settles with Scottish Power, Other Suppliers in UK Cable-Cartel Lawsuit' (30 July 2020), *Mlex*, available at https://mlex.com/GlobalAdvisory/DetailView.aspx?cid=1213902&siteid=244&rdir=1; US Securities and Exchange Commission, 'LG Display Settles with Iiyana'; Simon Zekaria, 'Wallenius Wilhelmsen Data Provides "Smoking Gun" in Car-Shipper Operations, Daimler Tells UK Judge' (5 May 2020), *Mlex*, available at https://mlex.com/GlobalAdvisory/DetailView.aspx?cid=1184384&siteid=244&rdir=1.

58 Competition Appeal Tribunal, 'JPMorgan, UBS, Barclays, Others Face Fresh Forex-Rigging Lawsuit in UK, Court Filing Confirms' (20 December 2019), *Mlex*, available at https://mlex.com/GlobalAdvisory/DetailView.aspx?cid=1152433&siteid=244&rdir=1.

59 Similarly, Rust, 'Kartellverstoß und Gesamtschuld', 507; Bentele, *Gesamtschuld und Erlass*, 37.

Directive 2014/104/EU does not envisage full settlements and does not provide any rules on them. This is surprising given the Directive's objective to improve the standing of the creditor and its objective to promote 'once-and-for-all' settlements.[60] Settlement of the entire liability is usually allowed by national laws as long as it is agreed that the creditor will not pursue any other debtor with respect to the debt.[61]

As the Directive does not prohibit full settlements, it seems that they should be possible subject to existing national laws. This opens the door to a great variety of solutions. By way of example, it seems that national legal orders interpret the impact of full settlements on non-settling parties differently. This consequently influences the availability of contribution claims. English law assumes that the accord and satisfaction with one co-debtor discharges other debtors unless stated otherwise[62] or unless the settlement was made in bad faith.[63] In Germany, settlement of the entire debt affects co-debtors ('*Gesamtwirkung*') only if it works to the benefit of other co-debtors.[64] A similar position, with some modifications, is adopted in France[65] and in Poland.[66]

60 See Section 4.1.2.4.

61 In Germany, this is a settlement with *Gesamtwirkung*, which is allowed under § 423 of the BGB. This settlement is distinguished from a settlement with *Einzelwirkung* (which concerns a part of the debt) and a settlement with *beschränkte Gesamtwirkung* (which corresponds to a partial settlement with a reduction rule). See Weinhold, *Der Gesamtschuldnerausgleich*, 229–231; see also Bydlinski, '§ 423 BGB', paras. 2 and 5; Martin Gebauer, '§ 423 BGB' in Thomas Pfeiffer (ed.), *Soergel Bürgerliches Gesetzbuch Schuldrecht*, 3 vols. (Stuttgart: Kohlhammer, 2009), vol. III, para. 1; Bentele, *Gesamtschuld und Erlass*, 35; Inderst and Thomas, *Schadensersatz bei Kartellverstößen*, 412. For full and partial settlements in England, see Glanville Llewelyn Williams, *Joint Torts and Contributory Negligence* (London: Stevens and Sons Limited, 1951), xl, 45 *et seq.*; The Law Commission, *Contribution*, paras. 26–30. For full and partial settlements in France, see Bentele, *Gesamtschuld und Erlass*, 90; Mignot, *Les obligations solidaires*, 134–197; Mignot 'Obligation solidaire', para. 123; Tereszkiewicz, 'Solidarność dłużników', 79; Pimont and Roux-Sibillon, 'Obligations plurales', para. 30. For full and partial settlements in Poland, see Lewaszkiewicz-Petrykowska, *Wyrządzenie szkody przez kilka osób*, 93, 151–152, 168; Tereszkiewicz, 'Solidarność dłużników', 78–79; Nesterowicz and Bagińska, 'Multiple Tortfeasors', 154–155, 160.

62 See Williams, *Joint Torts and Contributory Negligence*, xl, 45 *et seq.* and case law summarised in footnote 4. See also von Bar and Clives, *DCFR*, vol. I, 993.

63 See Section 1(4) of the Contribution Act 1978. See also the Law Commission, *Contribution*, paras. 26–30; *WH Newson Holdings Ltd v. IMI Plc* [2016] EWCA Civ. 773 and *Wolseley UK Limited and Others v. Fiat Chrysler Automobiles N.V. and Others* [2019] CAT 12.

64 See Bentele, *Gesamtschuld und Erlass*, 16; Völzmann-Stickelbrock, '§ 423 BGB', paras. 2–4; Gebauer, '§ 423 BGB', para. 1; Bydlinski'§ 423 BGB', para. 6; Krüger, 'Die Privilegierung des Kronzeugen', 93; Ulrich Heidel, *Die Auswirkungen von Haftungsbeschränkungen auf die Entstehung von Gesamtschuldverhältnissen unter besonderer Berücksichtigung versicherungsrechtlicher Probleme* (Heidelberg: Dissertation, 1975), 40.

65 See, for instance, Bentele, *Gesamtschuld und Erlass*, 90; Mignot, *Les obligations solidaires*, 134–197; Mignot, 'Obligation solidaire', para. 123; Tereszkiewicz, 'Solidarność dłużników', 79; Pimont and Roux-Sibillon, 'Obligations plurales', para. 30; von Bar and Clives, *DCFR*, vol. I, 993.

66 See, for instance, Lewaszkiewicz-Petrykowska, *Wyrządzenie szkody przez kilka osób*, 93, 151–152, 168; Nesterowicz and Bagińska, 'Multiple Tortfeasors', 154–155, 160; von Bar and Clives, *DCFR*, vol. I, 993.

This varied legislation introduces uncertainty for the debtor regarding the crucial question of whether it would have a right to claim contribution from non-settling debtors or not. This ambiguity together with a high payment of the entire debt might make it unlikely to conclude a full settlement. Based on the current rules and risks, full settlements are a rare phenomenon, which is a pity for victims of antitrust infringers. They are doomed to follow in Deutsche Bahn's footsteps, which has concluded five different settlements with various cartelists and still has six to conclude if it wants to avoid litigation.

CALCULATION OF THE SETTLING DEBTOR'S SHARE OF LIABILITY Uncertainty surrounding the benchmark used to determine the settling party's relative liability also concerns the creditor. The latter negotiates the settlement with respect to the debtor's relative liability and has a great interest in assessing this liability correctly. If it is underestimated, the creditor may end up being undercompensated.[67]

Additionally, it is likely that settling parties would disagree about the amount of relative liability in question. If the creditor's strategy is to reach the highest settlement possible, it might argue for benchmarks showing the high relative liability of the settling party. The settling party is likely to minimise its relative liability share. This would lead to a dispute with the debtor trying to lower its own involvement in the infringement in order to lower the settlement amount. Conflict over the applicable benchmark is thus likely to arise.

4.1.4.3 Incentives to Settle

The analysis above proves that both the debtors and the creditor face serious challenges when trying to settle. Most fundamentally, both parties are virtually unable to determine which settlement offer to make. There are two unknown quantities: the amount of overall liability and the amount of the settling debtor's individual liability share.[68]

This uncertainty might weaken the parties' incentive to settle. In light of this, settlements are likely to occur mostly because of the great impact of other factors encouraging settlements. This could be the case, for instance, if the creditor has little chance to win in the court or if it is crucial for the creditor to stay in good commercial relations with the infringer. The settlement between HeidelbergCement and CDC is an example of such a motivation. The settlement was concluded following CDC's difficulty to convince the Manheim Regional Court that limitation periods had still not passed and following the Appellate

[67] Krüger, 'Überlegungen zur Gesamtschuld', 292.

[68] On negative effects of uncertainties concerning the quantum of liability and contribution on incentives to settle, see Polden and Sullivan, 'Contribution and Claim Reduction', 412.

Court in Düsseldorf's challenge to the way cartel claims were assembled.[69] Given that Directive 2014/104/EU has left EU Member States a lot of freedom to design their rules on antitrust damages, the enforcement of competition law claims in court may not always be easy for victims of antitrust infringements, which will, similarly to CDC in the cement cartel, rely on settlements. Settlements are therefore still likely to play a role in private antitrust enforcement.

On the other hand, it is likely that settlements in the European Union would be a much less frequent phenomenon than they are in the United States.[70] First, in the European Union, there are no treble damages. The discount thus cannot be as significant as it would be in the United States. In the European Union, both litigation and settlement negotiations take place in reference to single damages. Second, in the European Union, settlements are likely to play a less significant role than in the United States in terms of access to evidence. In the United States, settlements are used to access the evidence needed to establish antitrust infringements. The reliance on settlements in this respect is not necessary in the European Union. In the European Union, private litigation often follows an establishment of antitrust liability by a public agency.[71]

For the foregoing reasons, it seems that the Commission's objective to encourage settlements is likely to have limited effects. Settlements can still be reached. However, this would be due to the difficulty encountered by the creditor in claiming compensation in court rather than the reform introduced with Directive 2014/104/EU.

4.1.5 *Conclusions and Recommendations*

Settlements are appreciable in competition law enforcement, and they definitely deserve to be promoted. This section identifies a number of shortcomings that bring another layer of complexity to the rules on contribution and have a negative impact on settlements. It is possible to remedy some of the shortcomings identified so that concluding settlements becomes easier and more attractive. This can be achieved by simplifying the calculation of liability shares and providing rules on full settlement.

69 See note 56.

70 On the frequency of settlements in US law generally, see Kathryn E. Spier, 'A Note on Joint and Several Liability: Insolvency, Settlement, and Incentives' (1994) 23 *Journal of Legal Studies*, 55 560–561; Ginsburg, 'Comparing Antitrust Enforcement', 436. Sebastian Peyer claims that 75 per cent of cases in the United States are settled, see Sebastian Peyer, 'Myths and Untold Stories – Private Antitrust Enforcement in Germany' (2010) *Centre for Competition Policy Working Paper*, 10–12, 53. John P. Gould claims that 95 per cent of cases in the United States are settled out of court, see John P. Gould, 'The Economics of Legal Conflicts' (1973) 2 *The Journal of Legal Studies*, 2, 281.

71 See note 215 in Chapter 2.

4.1.5.1 Calculation of Liability Shares

Most of the uncertainties indicated above result from the fact that there is no clear benchmark to apportion relative shares of liability. This makes it difficult for the creditor and the settling debtor to determine their settlement offers.

This problem can be resolved by making a firm decision on the criterion applicable for the apportionment of liability between joint and several debtors. The review of possible criteria in Section 3.6.3 above gives an overview of possible options. As shown above, the criterion of market shares is preferable, supplemented with the criterion of fault in the case of vertical agreements.

Market shares are also advantageous in the context of settlements. They can be established with relative ease subsequently to follow-on claims. Market shares are already available in the Commission's decision. If a settlement concerns a stand-alone claim, market shares can be established based on the company's financial information. The key is to determine the market in which the infringement has been made. This is not an easy task; however, there is a sufficient amount of information in the Commission's and EU law's case law, literature and databases, allowing for the relevant market to be established. Companies also more and more often register their market shares (for instance, due to their distribution models, when concluding licensing agreements or undertaking mergers).

4.1.5.2 Allowing for Full Settlement

As argued above, full settlements give the creditor a strong incentive to settle. The right to claim contribution supports the use of full settlements as it ensures that the settling debtor will have a right to recover the part of the payment made in excess of its own liability share. In light of this, the possibility of concluding full settlements should be expressly recognised. Such settlements should be made under regular joint and several liability rules, and contribution should be allowed.

Having allowed for full settlement, one needs to consider what effects it could have on non-settling debtors. In general, settlement can have both negative and positive effects on non-settling debtors. If the settling debtor strikes a bad deal and overcompensates the creditor, such a settlement also leads to a higher liability of non-settling debtors by way of increasing their contribution. If the settling debtor gets a good deal and manages to lower the amount of damages, this privileges non-settling debtors as their contribution is lower. The question is what contribution the settling debtor should be allowed to claim from non-settling debtors in these cases.

The effect of overcompensation can be resolved by allowing non-settling debtors to argue the amount of liability owed to the creditor in contribution claims. In order to prove that a settling debtor has overcompensated the creditor, the non-settling debtor would need to demonstrate that the liability is in fact lower than established in the settlement. The settling party's role would be to defend its view that the settlement amount corresponds to the actual liability. The court's task would be to resolve this conflict and decide whether to allow for a regular contribution or to reduce it due to a negative effect of settlement on non-settling parties. Thanks to this solution, full settlements would be possible, and non-settling parties would have a right to defend their position on the relative liability.

Another question is how to deal with settlements that have a positive effect on non-settling parties. There are two potential solutions in this respect. The first is to allow for contribution in an amount reflecting the actual settlement. Another is to allow for a contribution that accounts for the discount reached in the settlement and allow the settling party to keep it. The second solution seems unrealistic. First, it is difficult to say what liability would have been established in the trial and what the discount gained thanks to the settlement was. Second, non-settling parties can always argue that if given a chance to settle with the creditor on their own, they could have reached a similar settlement. The fact that it was the settling party who established the creditor–debtor relationship should not have deprived them of the possible benefits of an individual dispute resolution. As a consequence, it seems fair that the discount achieved by one of the debtors is shared with other debtors. This means that the discount for the settling debtor is lower than was initially achieved. However, the settling debtor still keeps some part of it and maintains an incentive to settle.

4.2 IMMUNITY RECIPIENTS

The idea of protecting immunity recipients appeared in the course of private enforcement reform.[72] The drafters of Directive 2014/104/EU realised that those considering participating in leniency programmes may be discouraged to reveal antitrust infringements when facing a potential liability for antitrust damages.[73] In order to reconcile the interests of public and private law enforcements, joint and several liability was modified for immunity recipients.

4.2.1 *Special Regime of Joint and Several Liability for Immunity Recipients*

Directive 2014/104/EU introduces a special regime of joint and several liability for immunity recipients, which encompasses four elements.

[72] Green Paper, Section 2.7; Commission Staff Working Paper Annex to the Green Paper Damages actions for breach of the EC antitrust rules, SEC(2005) 1732, 63 *et seq.*; White Paper, Section 2.9; Commission Staff Working Paper accompanying the White Paper on Damages actions for breach of the EC antitrust rules, SEC(2008) 404, 81 *et seq.*

[73] Ibid.

Primarily, the immunity recipient is jointly and severally liable with other debtors only with respect to its direct and indirect contractors[74] under Article 11(4)(a) of Directive 2014/104/EU:

> Member States shall ensure that an immunity recipient is jointly and severally liable . . . to its direct or indirect purchasers or providers.[75]

Subsidiarily, the immunity recipient is jointly and severally liable to all other victims of the antitrust infringement. This liability is triggered when a victim cannot obtain compensation from other joint and several debtors. Article 11(4)(b) of Directive 2014/104/EU reads:

> Member States shall ensure that an immunity recipient is jointly and severally liable . . . to other injured parties only where full compensation cannot be obtained from the other undertakings that were involved in the same infringement of competition law.[76]

In the internal dimension of joint and several liability, the liability of immunity recipients is limited to the harm they caused to their direct and indirect contractors under Article 11(5) of Directive 2014/104/EU:

> The amount of contribution of an infringer which has been granted immunity from fines under a leniency programme shall not exceed the amount of the harm it caused to its own direct or indirect purchasers or providers.[77]

[74] The term 'contractors' is used for the reasons of brevity and means the purchasers and providers of immunity recipients.

[75] This is implemented by Part 4, Section 15(a) and (b) of the UK Act. English law widens the scope of this provision by treating in the same way also 'containing or derived products and services', see Section 15(b) and (d) of the UK Act. In Germany, a relevant implementation is made under § 33e(1) of the GWB; in France by Article L. 481-11 of the Code de Commerce; and in Poland by Article 5(2) of the Polish Act.

[76] This is implemented by Part 4 Section 15 of the UK Act referring to 'unable to obtain full compensation'; by § 33e(1) of the GWB referring to the term '*keinen vollständigen Ersatz erlangen konnte*'; by Article L.481-11 of the Code de commerce referring to '*n'ont pas pu obtenir la réparation intégrale de leur préjudice . . . après les avoir préalablement et vainement poursuivis*'; by Article 5(2) of the Polish Act referring to '*uzyskanie pełnego odszkodowania od innych sprawców naruszenia nie jest możliwe*'.

[77] This is implemented by para. 4 Section 16 of the UK Act referring to 'the amount of the loss or damage the immunity recipient caused to [a catalogue of entities referred in Section 15(a) to (d)]' and premising that this assessment is a derogation from a general assessment made under Section 2(1) of the Contribution Act; by § 33e(3) of the GWB referring to '*bis zur Höhe des Schadens . . . den dieser seinen unmittelbaren und mittelbaren Abnehmern oder Lieferanten verursacht hat*'; by Article L. 481-12 of the Code de Commerce using precise terms that indicate that the contribution is assessed in a regular way, however, the rule introduces a cap on it, which prohibits '*pouvoir excéder le montant dupréjudice subi par ses contractants directs ou indirects*'; by Article 5(3) of the Polish Act referring to'*wysokość szkody wyrządzonej przez podmiot zwolniony z kary jego nabywcom bezpośrednim lub nabywcom pośrednim lub dostawcom bezpośrednim lub dostawcom pośrednim*'.

Finally, Directive 2014/104/EU maintains a regular rule of contribution with respect to damage inflicted upon entities other than direct and indirect contractors under Article 11(6):

> Member States shall ensure that, to the extent the infringement of competition law caused harm to injured parties other than the direct or indirect purchasers or providers of the infringers, the amount of any contribution from an immunity recipient to other infringers shall be determined in the light of its relative responsibility for that harm.[78]

These rules provide for the privileged treatment of immunity recipients on two levels. First, the application of joint and several liability in the external aspect is limited for immunity recipients. They can be primarily addressed only by their own direct and indirect contractors. This makes other victims of antitrust infringements claim compensation from other debtors. Actions for antitrust damages initiated by other victims can be directed to immunity recipients only when other co-debtors cannot pay compensation.

Second, joint and several liability is limited in the internal aspect. The ultimate liability of immunity recipients is principally[79] capped to the amount of harm caused to direct and indirect contractors. This privilege is granted at the expense of other infringers of EU competition law, who will bear a higher share of liability than is determined by their relative liability.

4.2.2 *Justification of the Special Regime*

The special regime of joint and several liability favours immunity recipients at the expense of other antitrust infringers. It is thus justified to inquire about the rationale of treating immunity recipients specially.

4.2.2.1 Role of Leniency Programmes

Leniency programmes encompass rules that reward those who report legal violations. In antitrust, they are important for at least two reasons. First, they help competition authorities discover and condemn cartels.[80] This in turn increases the probability of cartel detection, which enhances deterrence and prevents cartels from

[78] This is not included in the UK Act implementing the Directive. The rule is implemented by § 33e(3) of the GWB referring to general rules on contribution without the limitation about the harm made to direct and indirect providers and purchasers. The rule is not included in the French Act implementing the Directive; however, it can be established e contrario from Article L.481-12 of the Code de Commerce. The relevant implementation finds place in Article 5(3) of the Polish Act and was done in the same way as in the GWB.

[79] The rule established above does not refer to umbrella damages, see Section 4.2.4.2.

[80] Kersting, 'Rechtsdurchsetzung im Kartellrecht', 267; Wouter P. J. Wils, 'Leniency in Antitrust Enforcement: Theory and Practice' (2007) 30 *World Competition*, 1, 38–41. Critically Andreas

being formed. Second, leniency programmes have a destabilising effect on cartels.[81] They create a situation similar to that present in the prisoner's dilemma. Cartel participants are better off when none of them reveal the existence of the cartel. However, as none of them are aware of the other cartelists' decision to reveal or not to reveal the cartel, each of them is tempted to apply for leniency and avoid liability. As a consequence, leniency programmes create an equilibrium in which cartelists are encouraged to break off from the cartel.[82]

Due to these advantages, the Commission makes a great use of leniency in cartel cases.[83] Since the adoption of the 2002 Leniency Note, leniency applicants were granted full immunity in 71 per cent of cartels.[84] This means that they provided

Stephan, 'An Empirical Assessment of the European Leniency Notice' (2008) 5 *Journal of Competition Law and Economics*, 3, 537 *et seq*.; Schwalbe Ulrich and Höft Jan, 'Ausgestaltung von Kronzeugenprogrammen und private Kartellrechtsdurchsetzung' in Stefan Bechtold, Joachim Jickeli, Mathias Rohe (eds.), *Recht, Ordnung und Wettbewerb – Festschrift zum 70. Geburtstag von Wernhard Möschel* (Baden-Baden: Nomos, 2012), 610–611; Florian Wagner-von Papp, 'Der Richtlinienentwurf zu kartellrechtlichen Schadensersatzklagen' (2009) 11 *Europäisches Wirtschafts- und Steuerrecht*, 452; Mareen Katt, *Die Gesamtschuldnerische Haftung des Kronzeugen* (Tübingen: Mohr Siebeck, 2019), 27 *et seq*.

81 Nicolo Zingales, 'European and American Leniency Programmes: Two Models towards Convergence?' (2008) 5 *The Competition Law Review*, 1, 8–11; Wils, 'Leniency in Antitrust Enforcement', 42–43; Philipp Kirst and Roger Van den Bergh, 'The European Directive on Damages Actions: A Missed Opportunity to Reconcile Compensation of Victims and Leniency Incentives' (2016) 12 *Journal of Competition Law and Economics*, 13–14.

82 Ibid.; Schwalbe and Höft, 'Kronzeugenprogrammen und private Kartellrechtsdurchsetzung', 602; Hviid and Medvedev, 'The Role of Contribution', 14.

83 On the success of leniency in the European Union, see Kirst and Van den Bergh, 'The European Directive on Damages Actions', 3; Frederik Silbye, 'A Note on Antitrust Damages and Leniency Programs' (2012) 33 *European Journal of Law and Economics*, 692; Cornelis Canenbley and Till Steinvorth, 'Effective Enforcement of Competition Law: Is There a Solution to the Conflict between Leniency Programmes and Private Damages Actions?' (2011) 2 *Journal of European Competition Law and Practice*, 4, 315–317; Riley, 'Enhancing Enforcement in EC Antitrust Law', 381. On its success in the United States, see Department of Justice (1993); Jeroen Hinloopen, 'An Economic Analysis of Leniency Programs in Antitrust Law' (2003) 4 *De Economist*, 416; Chen and Rey, 'On the Design of Leniency Programs', 917–918; Riley, 'Enhancing Enforcement in EC Antitrust Law', 389–391; Leslie M. Marx, Claudio Mezzetti and Robert C. Marshall, 'Antitrust Leniency with Mutliproduct Colluders' (2015) 7 *American Economic Journal: Microeconomics*, 3, 205. On the history of leniency programmes, see Ulrich Blum, Nicole Steinat and Michael Veltins, 'On the Rationale of Leniency Programs: A Game-Theoretical Analysis' (2008) 25 *European Journal of Law and Economics*, 212; Joel Davidow, 'Recent Developments in US Antitrust' (2005) 28 *World Competition*, 3, 300; Riley, 'Enhancing Enforcement in EC Antitrust Law', 377–381; Wils, 'Leniency in Antitrust Enforcement', 34–35; Schwalbe and Höft, 'Kronzeugenprogrammen und private Kartellrechtsdurchsetzung', 597.

84 The statistics encompass all publicly available cartel decisions until 8 March 2017, see Damien Geradin and Katarzyna Sadrak, 'The EU Competition Law Fining System: A Quantitative Review of the Commission Decisions between 2000 and 2017' in Nicolas Charbit, Carolina Malhado and Ellie Yang (eds.), *Douglas H. Ginsburg. An Antitrust Professor on the Bench. Liber Amicorum*, 2 vols. (New York: Concurrences, 2018), vol. I, 34–44. See also Wouter P. J. Wils, 'The Use of Leniency in EU Cartel Enforcement: An Assessment After Twenty Years' (2016) 39 *World Competition*, 327; Riley, 'Enhancing Enforcement in EC Antitrust Law', 381.

proof that allowed the infringement to be established or targeted inspections to be conducted.[85] It might be thus assumed that without the leniency programme, 71 per cent of cartels established by the Commission would not have been discovered or this would have come at a bigger expense. In addition, thanks to leniency, more information has been received by the European Commission, resulting in fines amounting to EUR 31 billion higher.[86] Leniency is thus an important element of the Commission's enforcement policy.

4.2.2.2 Interference between Joint and Several Liability and Leniency Programmes

An important piece of background information is that a leniency programme must be generous enough to be effective.[87] It must offer a reward that is high enough to offset the costs associated with a decision to whistle blow.[88] In antitrust, these costs are principally the loss of expected profits from further participation in a cartel, as well as the sanctions from being condemned as a cartelist. Before the promotion of private antitrust enforcement, the reward for immunity recipients was that they could get full indemnity for the Commission's fines.[89] With private antitrust enforcement, the calculation has changed. The reward is the same while the costs have increased because of the higher probability of being liable for private law damages.[90] Private law liability can be high. For instance, in the *Cement* cartel,

[85] See Commission Notice on Immunity from fines and reduction of fines in cartel cases, OJ C 298, 8.12.2006, pp. 17–22 ('2006 Leniency Note'), Section II, para. 8; Commission notice on immunity from fines and reduction of fines in cartel cases, OJ C 45, 19.2.2002, pp. 3–5 ('2002 Leniency Note'), Section A, para. 8.

[86] Steffen Brenner, 'An Empirical Study of the European Corporate Leniency Program' (2009) 27 *International Journal of Industrial Organization*, 6, 639. More on the effects of leniency, Caroline Buts and Lynn Vanhaverbeke, 'A Quantitative Analysis of the Efficiency of the EU's Leniency Policy' (2020) 1 *European Competition and Regulatory Law Review (CoRe)*, 12.

[87] Schwalbe and Höft, 'Kronzeugenprogrammen und private Kartellrechtsdurchsetzung', 599. See also Section 4.2.3.1.

[88] Ibid.

[89] A possible additional cost is the risk of being held liable for the infringement in other jurisdictions and the costs of cooperating with the Commission, see Hösch, *Der schadensrechtliche Innenausgleich*, 366.

[90] On the private damages' risk to undermine the public leniency programme, see, for instance, Andrei Medvedev, 'The Role of Contribution', 19; Thomas Eilmansberger, 'The Green Paper on Damages Actions for Breach of the EC Antitrust Rules and Beyond: Reflections on the Utility and Feasibility of Stimulating Private Enforcement through Legislative Action' (2007) 44 *Common Market Law Review*, 436; Jochen Glöckner, 'Individualschutz und Funktionenschutz in der privaten Durchsetzung des Kartellrechts – Der Zweck heiligt die Mittel nicht; er bestimmt sie!' (2007) 5 *Wettbewerb in Recht und Praxis*, 494–495; Wagner-von Papp, 'Der Richtlinienentwurf', 452; Jan-Stephan Ritter, 'Private Durchsetzung des Kartellrechts – Vorschläge des Weißbuchs der Europäischen Kommission' (2008) 7 *Wirtschaft und Wettbewerb*, 773; Kersting, 'Rechtsdurchsetzung im Kartellrecht', 264; Kern, 'Law Enforcement', 367.

Cemex was fined EUR 24 million, which was reduced to 12 EUR million thanks to leniency.[91] The reduction of EUR 12 million looks modest when compared to the approximately EUR 115 million for which Cemex was sued.[92] The discount offered on public fines may be thus insufficient to make leniency programmes efficient in the private enforcement era.

Joint and several liability has an impact on the calculation presented above. This is because joint and several liability increases the probability that immunity recipients will be sued for significant amounts of antitrust damages.

One interference between joint and several liability and leniency programmes is that the creditor can request compensation for the *entire damage* from any antitrust infringer. As a result, antitrust infringers are liable not only for the damage that they individually caused but also for damage caused by other joint and several debtors. Although claims for contribution are available, the initial burden for paying very high damages is significant. The wave of claims for antitrust damages that hits only one of joint and several debtors may even endanger its economic existence.[93]

Another interference is that immunity recipients are likely to become *first targets* of claims for antitrust damages.[94] This is because the Commission's decisions establishing the infringement become final with respect to immunity recipients sooner than for other debtors. In order to receive immunity, leniency applicants admit that a violation of antitrust law took place and that they participated in it.[95] This makes them uninterested in appealing the Commission's decision to EU Courts. If other infringers appeal, the Commission's decision becomes final first with respect to immunity recipients.[96] This encourages victims of antitrust violations to target immunity recipients when claiming damages.

[91] Blum, Steinat and Veltins, 'On the Rationale of Leniency Programs', 214, note 22. See also Norman Hölzel, *Kronzeugenregelungen im Europäischen Wettbewerbsrecht* (Halle: Universitätsverlag Halle-Wittenberg, 2011), 243; Bundeskartellamt, 'Bericht über die Tätigkeit in den Jahren 2003/2004', BT-Drs. 15/5790, 110.

[92] Ibid.

[93] Weinhold, *Der Gesamtschuldnerausgleich*, 10–11.

[94] Ibid., 209; Hösch, *Der schadensrechtliche Innenausgleich*, 366; Dreher, 'Die Haftungsverteilung', 162; Canenbley and Steinvorth, 'Effective Enforcement', 321; Thomas Thiede, 'Fine to Follow-On? Private Anti-trust Actions in European Law' (2017) 5 *China-EU Law Journal*, 250; Hölzel, *Kronzeugenregelungen*, 331–332; Schwalbe and Höft, 'Kronzeugenprogrammen und private Kartellrechtsdurchsetzung', 627–628; Wagner-von Papp, 'Der Richtlinienentwurf', 453; Inderst and Thomas, *Schadensersatz bei Kartellverstößen*, 409. Contrary, Krüger, 'Die Privilegierung des Kronzeugen', 485; Paolo Buccirossi, Catarina M. P. Marvão and Giancarlo Spagnolo, 'Leniency and Damages' (2015) 32 *Stockholm Institute of Transition Economics Working Paper*, 2; Kirst and Van den Bergh, 'The European Directive on Damages Actions', 12; Katt, *Haftung des Kronzeugen*, 30.

[95] Paragraph 8 of 2006 Leniency Note.

[96] Weinhold, *Der Gesamtschuldnerausgleich*, 209; Hösch, *Der schadensrechtliche Innenausgleich*, 36; Guttso, 'I'm an Immunity Applicant', 98; Hölzel, *Kronzeugenregelungen*, 333; Wagner-von Papp, 'Der Richtlinienentwurf', 453; Ritter, 'Private Durchsetzung des Kartellrechts', 773; Katt, *Haftung des Kronzeugen*, 36.

The risk that private law liability would lie principally on immunity recipients is real. In the cement cartel, CDC made a follow-on claim against six companies involved in the cartel: HeidelbergCement, Schwenk, Lafarge, Dyckerhoff, Cemex and Holcim. The decision in this case was appealed by five of the companies, and the only entity to which it became binding was Cemex, who was the leniency applicant. Cemex could have been held liable for the entire amount of damages but for the fact that the claim failed for other reasons.[97]

Given the effects that joint and several liability has on leniency applicants, the latter deserve protection.

4.2.2.3 Considerations Made in Directive 2014/104/EU

Accounting for the effects described above, Directive 2014/104/EU sets as an objective the protection of leniency programmes:

> Undertakings which cooperate with competition authorities under a leniency programme play a key role in exposing secret cartel infringements and in bringing them to an end, thereby often mitigating the harm which could have been caused had the infringement continued. It is therefore appropriate to make provision for undertakings which have received immunity from fines from a competition authority under a leniency programme to be protected from undue exposure to damages claims, bearing in mind that the decision of the competition authority finding the infringement may become final for the immunity recipient before it becomes final for other undertakings which have not received immunity, thus potentially making the immunity recipient the preferential target of litigation.[98]

This aim is coherently realised by the Directive, which, apart from special rules on joint and several liability, also introduces a limitation for antitrust victims to access the documents shared in the leniency procedure.[99]

4.2.3 *Fulfilment of the Objectives*

The protection of leniency programmes is a legitimate objective and deserves support. The next question is whether the rules adopted in Directive 2014/104/EU are an appropriate means to meet this aim.

The main issue is that Directive 2014/104/EU does not grant immunity recipients the immunity from *both* public and private liability. It maintains the reward mainly in terms of public law liability. Regarding private law liability, the Directive allows

97 See LG Düsseldorf, WuW 2007, 520 and LG Düsseldorf, BeckRS 2013, 22380.

98 Recital 38 of Directive 2014/104/EU.

99 See Recitals 26–27 and Article 6(a) of Directive 2014/104/EU; see also Robert Jürgens and Daniela Seelinger, 'Die geplante Neufassung der Kronzeugenregelung der Europäischen Kommission' (2006) 8 *Europäisches Wirtschafts- und Steuerrecht*, 339.

immunity recipients to be sued only by their direct and indirect contractors and limits the immunity recipients' liability principally to the harm suffered by them.[100]

4.2.3.1 Economic Standpoint

Economists are cautious about leniency programmes that grant immunity only for some part of liability.

Jeroen Hinloopen claims that the effectiveness of leniency depends on the difference (*net effect*) between two opposing forces – the size of the fine and the reward in the form of a fine reduction.[101] The increase in fine increases deterrence, which in turn strengthens the incentive to whistle blow.[102] However, the increase in fine may also mean that the reward is proportionally lower, which may impede the willingness to report. Leniency remains effective only if the fraction of the fine paid after applying for leniency is *low enough*.[103] This condition is always met in the case of full amnesty; however, it is uncertain whether it is met in the case of partial amnesty.[104]

Frederik Silbye demonstrates that high damages may jeopardise leniency programmes. On the one hand, higher damages lead to a higher overall sanction and thus improve deterrence. On the other hand, the equilibrium leading to reporting is no longer sustained if damages are sufficiently large to deny the pay-off for cooperation.[105] This effect might outweigh the positive effect of deterrence and may make the rewards offered by leniency programmes pro-collusive.[106] Frederik Silbye advises

[100] The limitation does not cover umbrella damages, see Section 4.2.4.2.

[101] Hinloopen, 'Leniency Programs', 428, equation n°. 12. See also Feltovich Nick and Hamaguchi Yasuyo, 'The Effect of Whistle-Blowing Incentives on Collusion: An Experimental Study of Leniency Programs' (2018) 84 *Southern Economic Journal*, 4, 1025.

[102] Hinloopen, 'Leniency Programs', 428.

[103] Ibid., 418–419, Schwalbe and Höft, 'Kronzeugenprogrammen und private Kartellrechtsdurchsetzung', 606.

[104] Hinloopen, 'Leniency Programs', 429. It is claimed that an optimal leniency programme requires full immunity, see also Blum, Steinat and Veltins, 'On the Rationale of Leniency Programs', 216; Massimo Motta and Michele Polo, 'Leniency Programs and Cartel Prosecution' (2003) 21 *International Journal of Industrial Organization*, 347; Joseph E. Harrington Jr, 'Optimal Corporate Leniency Programs' (2008) 56 *The Journal of Industrial Economics*, 2, 218. With a preference to full indemnity also Schwalbe and Höft, 'Kronzeugenprogrammen und private Kartellrechtsdurchsetzung', 606. However, it is sometimes argued that the leniency programme cannot be too generous as the leniency application may become a part of a collusive strategy, see Zhijun Chenand Patrick Rey, 'On the Design of Leniency Programs' (2013) 56 *The Journal of Law and Economics*, 4, 918; Wils, 'Leniency in Antitrust Enforcement', 48; Schwalbe and Höft, 'Kronzeugenprogrammen und private Kartellrechtsdurchsetzung', 608–609. This effect has been, however, empirically proven as non-existent by Nick and Yasuyo, 'The Effect of Whistle-Blowing Incentives on Collusion', 1025; doubtful also Schwalbe and Höft, 'Kronzeugenprogrammen und private Kartellrechtsdurchsetzung', 609.

[105] Silbye, 'Antitrust Damages and Leniency Programs', 696.

[106] Ibid., 698.

to either entirely exempt whistle-blowers from private law liability or to introduce another form of reward that would balance the increased sanction.[107]

4.2.3.2 Empirical Standpoint

The economic findings seem to be inconsistent with the way the US leniency programme operates. According to the leniency policy of 1993, immunity recipients were only exempted from criminal liability and not private liability.[108] Although there was a significant liability risk, the leniency programme was a success and contributed to a significant detection of cartels.[109]

In 2004, the ACPERA was adopted.[110] It granted immunity from criminal liability, reduced private law liability to single damages and removed joint and several liability for immunity recipients.[111] The data suggests that regardless of these bonuses, the level of leniency applications remained unchanged.[112] This is in conflict with economic theory, which suggests that by increasing the reward, leniency programmes should become more attractive to potential applicants.

This incoherence disappears when we look closer into the developments that the ACPERA brought. Although the number of leniency applications remained stable following the ACPERA, there was a substantial change in the type of leniency applications. Before, the majority of applications were only for cooperation. Following the ACPERA, there has been tremendous growth in applications leading

[107] Ibid., 699. Spagnolo also agrees that whistleblowing programmes that exempt from public-law sanctions but not from damages are inefficient. See Giancarlo Spagnolo, 'Divide et impera: Opimal Leniency Programs' (2004) 4840 *CEPR discussion paper*, 1 *et seq*. See also Buccirossi, Marvão and Spagnolo, 'Leniency and Damages', 5.

[108] United States Department of Justice, Corporate Leniency Policy of 10 August 1993, available at https://justice.gov/sites/default/files/atr/legacy/2007/08/14/0091.pdf, 1.

[109] United States Department of Justice, 'The Modern Leniency Program After Ten Years – A Summary Overview of the Antitrust Division's Criminal Enforcement' (12 August 2003), *Justice News*, available at https://justice.gov/atr/speech/modern-leniency-program-after-ten-years-summary-overview-antitrust-divisions-criminal.

[110] Antitrust Criminal Penalty Enhancement and Reform Act of 2004, 15 U.S.C. 1, Public Law 108-237, 22 June 2004, 118 Stat. 661.

[111] Ibid., Section 213(a). See also Caroline Cauffman, 'The Interaction of Leniency Programmes and Actions for Damages' (2011) 34 *Maastricht European Private Law Institute Working Paper*, 203–204; Canenbley and Steinvorth, 'Effective Enforcement', 322–323, Patrick Rey, 'Design of Leniency Programs', 917; Davidow, 'Recent Developments in US Antitrust', 300; Riley, 'Enhancing Enforcement in EC Antitrust Law', 380–381; United States Government Accountability Office, 12 *et seq*.; Zingales, 'European and American Leniency Programmes', 5 *et seq*.; Wils, 'Leniency in Antitrust Enforcement', 26–29; Guttso, 'I'm an Immunity Applicant', 101–102; Schwalbe and Höft, 'Kronzeugenprogrammen und private Kartellrechtsdurchsetzung', 597–598; Hviid and Medvedev, 'The Role of Contribution', 20–21; Riley, 'Enhancing Enforcement in EC Antitrust Law', 377.

[112] United States Government Accountability Office, 12. The empirical analysis reveals that in the six years prior to ACPERA there were fifty-four applications, while within six years after the adoption of ACPERA there were fifty-six leniency applications.

to discovery of new cartels.[113] It can thus be argued that the ACPERA led to discovery of cartels, which otherwise would have continued and remained secret. This suggests that the increase in reward has encouraged some antitrust infringers to reveal cartels.

4.2.3.3 Critical Considerations

Against this background, it is necessary to verify whether the modification of the joint and several liability regime adopted in Directive 2014/104/EU provides for a sufficient reward for immunity recipients.

The limitation of primary liability to direct and indirect contractors under Article 11(4)(1) of the Directive addresses the problem of immunity recipients becoming the primary target of claims for damages.[114] By limiting the catalogue of potential claimants, Directive 2014/104/EU prevents the use of joint and several liability as a means to massively address immunity recipients with claims for damages.

The limitation of primary liability to direct and indirect contractors is also a proportional means to mitigate the problem of imposing the main burden of antitrust liability on immunity recipients.[115] While extensive litigation involving immunity recipients is excluded, victims in their proximity can still address them with claims for damages.

The concern remains whether the cap on the immunity recipients' liability at the level of the harm caused by them to their direct and indirect contractors is sufficient.[116] Economic theory suggests that the reward must be *high enough* to encourage revealing cartels.

The effect brought by Directive 2014/104/EU can be demonstrated by comparing three scenarios: the reality without private enforcement (i), the reality with both private enforcement and Commission's fines (ii) and the reality with private enforcement but including the modifications introduced by Directive 2014/104/EU(iii) (see Figure 4.1).

[113] United States Government Accountability Office, 14–15. The amount of the latter's type of leniency application nearly doubled.

[114] For a critical view, see Tilman Makatsch and Arif Sascha Mir, 'Die neue EU-Richtlinie zu Kartellschadensersatzklagen – Angst vor der eigenen "Courage"?' (2015) *Europäische Zeitschrift für Wirtschaftsrecht*, 22; Thiede, 'Fine to Follow-On?', 250; Kersting, 'Die neue Richtlinie', 569; Inderst and Thomas, *Schadensersatz bei Kartellverstößen*, 409; Krüger 'Der Gesamtschuldnerausgleich', 13; Krüger, 'Die Privilegierung des Kronzeugen', 486; Kersting, 'Rechtsdurchsetzung im Kartellrecht', 266–268; Christian Kersting, 'Removing the Tension between Public and Private Enforcement: Disclosure and Privileges for Successful Leniency Applicants' (2014) 5 *Journal of European Competition Law and Practice*, 1, 4; Hölzel, *Kronzeugenregelungen*, 333.

[115] In contrast to the views expressed, Ibid.

[116] Similar concern has been expressed by Buccirossi, Marvão and Spagnolo, 'Leniency and Damages', 1 *et seq.*; Kersting, 'Removing the Tension', 2 *et seq.*; Guttso, 'I'm an Immunity Applicant', 103; Wagner-von Papp, 'Der Richtlinienentwurf', 453.

$$(i)\ leniency\ consideration = \frac{sanction: Commission's\ fine}{reward: Commission's\ fine}$$

$$(ii)\ leniency\ consideration$$
$$= \frac{sanction: Commission's\ fine + primarily\ liable\ for\ entire\ damages\ caused\ by\ cartel}{reward: Commission's\ fine}$$

$$(iii)\ leniency\ consideration$$
$$= \frac{sanction: Commission's\ fine + damages\ for\ the\ harm\ caused\ to\ direct\ and\ indirect\ contractors}{reward: Commission's\ fine}$$

FIGURE 4.1 *Scenarios for leniency consideration*
Source: own formula

We can observe that Directive 2014/104/EU improves the outcome of leniency consideration (iii) compared to the situation when joint and several liability is applied without modifications (ii). Directive 2014/104/EU limits the amount of primary damages from all damages caused by the cartel to only those caused to direct and indirect contractors. It is, however, not certain whether the proportion between the reward and the sanction established by Directive 2014/104/EU (iii) guarantees the same effectiveness of leniency programmes that existed before the EU's reform of private antitrust enforcement (i). Directive 2014/104/EU increased a potential sanction without proportionally increasing the reward. The question arises whether the currently existing reward is *high enough* to maintain the incentive to report.

This question is difficult to answer without empirical data. If one considers the proportion between the sanction and the reward in the abstract, it seems doubtful that the reward would be sufficient in the case of high private law liability for antitrust infringements. Take, for instance, the recent truck cartel, in which the Commission fined MAN, Daimler, Volvo Group, Iveco and DAF with fines of approximately EUR 3 billion.[117] This is followed by private lawsuits amounting to much more extensive liability than the Commission's fine. In the UK alone, it is reported that the value of total compensation for truck owners is GBP 14 billion.[118] This is more than four times the Commission's fines. Similarly, claims for damages stemming from the FOREX cartel amount to GBP 6 billion,[119] while the banks paid only EUR 1.1 billion in fines to the European Commission. The exemption from

[117] See note 1 in Chapter 1.
[118] Tristan Feunten, 'Industry-wide Trucks Cartel Face Massive Legal Claim in UK Tribunal' (30 July 2018), *Weightmans*, available at https://weightmans.com/media-centre/news/industry-wide-trucks-cartel-facing-massive-legal-claim-in-uk-tribunal/.
[119] Zekaria, 'Visa, WH Smith Settle'.

only public liability seems insufficient to encourage companies to report the cartel. Wouter P. J. Wils argues that negative effects of private enforcement on leniency may be simply remedied by increasing public penalties, so as the discount given on the fine is sufficiently high.[120] However, if private liability can be four or six times larger, an enormous increase in fines would be required. This seems unacceptable given the already very high level of public fines.

Empirical research is needed to assess the success of the Commission's limitation of liability in preserving the efficiency of the EU leniency programme. Currently, the leniency data following the adoption of Directive 2014/104/EU is not yet publicly available, as most proceedings initiated after the Directive's entry into force are still pending.[121] Nonetheless, Cecilio Madero Villarejo, Deputy Director-General in DG Competition, revealed that leniency applications 'significantly diminished' and the European Commission has recently opened 'at least' three investigations on its own initiative and lays its hopes in a new whistle-blower tool that allows for anonymous notifications of cartels.[122] A recent survey among in-house lawyers does not give a good forecast. When asked about their leniency strategies, 83 per cent of counsels expressed that their clients have less interest in applying for leniency in recent years due to the adoption of the Directive.[123]

4.2.3.4 What Is the Best Possible Option?

The problem of how to resolve the tension between joint and several liability and leniency programmes has been intensively discussed before adopting Directive 2014/104/EU. In light of this, it is worth considering whether there are better solutions for protecting leniency programmes from the effects of joint and several liability.

One of the options proposed in the Green Paper was to grant a rebate on damages for leniency applicants while making other infringers liable for the entire damage.[124] The disadvantage of this approach is that it does not provide for corrective justice. The rebate granted to leniency applicants does not take into account private law principles such as restitution or unjust enrichment. It is thus possible that leniency applicants would keep the benefits gained from the antitrust violation, while their

[120] Wils, 'Private Enforcement', 25.

[121] Johan Ysewyn and Siobhan Kahmann provide the statistics for leniency in cartel decisions adopted after Directive 2014/104/EU has been published; however, these statistics do not reflect the incentives for leniency applicants to apply for leniency as the leniency applications were lodged in these cases at the latest in 2012, so still long before the Directive was adopted, see Johan Ysewyn and Siobhan Kahmann, 'The Decline and Fall of the Leniency Programme in Europe' (2018) 1 *Concurrences,* 44 Table 3.

[122] Matthew Newman, 'EU Cartel Busters Start at Least Three Own-Initiative Probes as Leniency Candidates Dry Up, Madero Says' (12 July 2019), *Mlex*, available at https://mlex.com/GlobalAdvisory/DetailView.aspx?cid=1111720&siteid=244&rdir=1.

[123] Wils, 'Private Enforcement', 42 referring to a survey of Brussels Matters entitled 'The European Antitrust Leniency Calculus c.2016: Still Worth It?'.

[124] Green Paper, Option 29.

co-infringers would bear their share of liability.[125] The solution adopted in the Directive is thus preferable. It determines the final liability for antitrust infringement according to the harm individually caused and thus is in line with corrective justice.

Another proposal was to make leniency applicants only proportionally liable to their direct and indirect contractors.[126] This proposition would give leniency applicants the advantage of having their liability established without the need to engage in contribution litigation.[127] This approach gives more incentives to apply for leniency than the one taken in Directive 2014/104/EU. On the other hand, this solution would have a negative impact on victims of antitrust violations. The insolvency risk is shifted on them, together with the obligation to prove infringers' relative responsibility for the infringement.[128] It seems unjustified to put this burden on victims of antitrust infringements.

The Office of Fair Trade's proposal was to maintain the regular rules on joint and several liability but to give leniency applicants a right to obtain indemnity from their co-debtors.[129] This proposal is different from the others in so far as it does not give any privilege to immunity recipients with respect to liability towards antitrust victims, but only towards other infringers. This solution brings significant incentives to reveal the cartel as the reward entirely covers the liability for private law damages. On the other hand, this solution does not protect immunity recipients from becoming the target of massive amounts of claims for antitrust damages. Without protection from this effect, leniency applicants can face large costs of paying compensation and engaging in contribution litigation.[130] These costs may be so high that leniency applicants will have no financial capacity to continue their operations until they receive contribution.

Another proposal was made in Hungary.[131] It was established that the proceedings against leniency applicants can be stayed until all appeals against the decision of the

[125] Cauffman, 'Leniency Programmes and Actions for Damages', 208–210; Commission staff working paper accompanying the White Paper, para. 286; Guttso, 'I'm an Immunity Applicant', 100.

[126] Green Paper, Option 30; OFT, 'Private Actions in Competition Law: Effective Redress for Consumers and Business'(April 2007), OFT 916, paras. 7.18–7.19; Article 81(3) of the Maltese Police Act as changed by Act IV. of 2014: The Various Law (Criminal Matters) (Amendment) Act 2014 (An Act Further to Amend Various Laws Related to Criminal Matters).

[127] Cauffman, 'Leniency Programmes and Actions for Damages', 211; Commission staff working paper accompanying the White Paper, para. 291.

[128] Cauffman, 'Leniency Programmes and Actions for Damages', 201–213; Centre for European Policy Studies (CEPS), 'Making Antitrust Damages Actions More Effective in the EU: Welfare Impact and Potential Scenarios' (2007) available at https://ec.europa.eu/competition/antitrust/actionsdamages/files_white_paper/impact_study.pdf, 517–529; European Parliament resolution of 26 March 2009 on the White Paper on damages actions for breach of the EC antitrust rules (2008/2154(INI)), para. 21.

[129] OFT, 'Private Actions in Competition Law', para. 7.18.

[130] Ibid., para. 9.7, CEPS, 'Making Antitrust Damages Actions More Effective', 504.

[131] Article 88/D of Act LVII of 1996 on the Prohibition of Unfair and Restrictive Market Practices (Hungarian Competition Act). See Csongor István Nagy, 'The New Hungarian Rules on

competition authority are resolved. Leniency applicants could also refuse to pay damages provided that compensation can be received from other debtors. A right to claim contribution was provided under regular rules.[132] This option's main advantage is that it prevents leniency applicants from becoming the first targets of claims for antitrust damages without ultimately disadvantaging victims of antitrust violations. On the other hand, there is no reward in the size of liability if contribution can be claimed under usual rules. Because of the latter, this approach is inferior to the one adopted in Directive 2014/104/EU.

The review of possible options on how to shape the relationship between joint and several liability and leniency programmes reveals that there is no option that could remedy all the problems identified in this section. The balance stricken by Directive 2014/104/EU actually seems to be better than other proposals.[133] On the one hand, leniency applicants are protected from being the first targets of claims for antitrust damages, and their ultimate liability is capped. On the other hand, the leniency applicants' subsidiary liability protects victims of antitrust infringements from the risk of reduced compensation. The only criticism that applies is a concern that the ultimate liability may be too high to encourage cooperation.

4.2.3.5 Proposals for the Future

Two modifications can be considered to ensure that leniency programmes are truly effective.

One idea is to totally exempt immunity recipients from private law liability in the internal dimension.[134] This cannot be done without reducing antitrust victims' chances of receiving compensation. To respond to this concern, it may be argued that leniency drives public antitrust enforcement.[135] Leniency programmes work to the ultimate benefit of private enforcement as they reveal the existence of cartels. Most private actions are follow-on actions, so they are dependent both on the Commission's decisions and on leniency applications.[136] Providing for smaller

Damages Caused by Horizontal Hardcore Cartels: Presumed Price Increase and Limited Protection for Whistleblowers – An Analytical Introduction' (2011) 32 *European Competition Law Review*, 2, 63 *et seq*.

[132] Cauffman, 'Leniency Programmes and Actions for Damages', 216.

[133] Favourably to Hungarian conclusions, Cauffman, 'Leniency Programmes and Actions for Damages', 217, 220; Buccirossi, Marvão and Spagnolo, 'Leniency and Damages', 5–6.

[134] In favour of this idea, Kersting, 'Removing the Tension', 2 *et seq*.

[135] See, for instance, Commission staff working paper accompanying the White Paper, para. 277; European Competition Network (ECN), Resolution of the Meeting of Heads of the European Competition Authorities, Protection of Leniency Material in the Context of Civil Damages Actions, 23 May 2012, available at https://ec.europa.eu/competition/ecn/leniency_material_protection_en.pdf.

[136] Wils, 'Leniency in Antitrust Enforcement', 43–44; Wils, 'Private Enforcement', 22–23. Similarly also Canenbley and Steinvorth, 'Effective Enforcement', 320; Wagner-von Papp, 'Der Richtlinienentwurf', 453.

compensation more frequently may be considered better for competition law enforcement.

Although convincing, this interpretation may be challenged on the basis that the right to receive full compensation is more important than the protection of leniency applications.[137] The principle of full compensation has a strong legal basis both in primary EU law and in the tort law systems of EU Member States, whereas the EU leniency programme has been merely introduced as a Commission Communication, which is only a soft law instrument.[138]

As a result, a second solution is preferred. It involves giving immunity recipients a right to claim indemnity from their co-infringers while being externally liable to direct and indirect contractors, as well as subsidiarily to other antitrust victims.[139] This solution limits the first exposure of immunity recipients to claims for antitrust damages and reduces the sanction resulting from damages almost to zero. It achieves this whilst protecting the right to full compensation of antitrust victims through subsidiary liability. When analysing this solution through the prism of leniency considerations, the only costs that the immunity recipient would bear are the costs of an eventual subsidiary liability and the costs of contribution litigation. These costs are much lower than the ones that exist under current rules.

This solution is, of course, not immune from criticism either. According to some, privileging leniency applicants is already too far-going and cannot be extended any further.[140] As leniency programmes are a tool of public enforcement of EU competition law, any privileges granted to leniency applicants must be limited to public enforcement.[141] In addition, treating leniency applicants in a privileged way runs against a number of principles.[142] In particular, it reduces deterrence of EU competition law as it lowers the probability of being held liable in private law.[143] It is also unfair from the standpoint of retributive justice since it allows immunity recipients

137 For such an approach, Meinrad Dreher, 'Die Haftungsverteilung', 165 *et seq.*; Cauffman, 'Leniency Programmes and Actions for Damages', 208–209; Kersting, 'Removing the Tension', 4; Kersting, 'Die neue Richtlinie', 568. However, see also CJEU, Case C-536/11, *Bundeswettbewerbsbehörde v. Donau Chemie AG and Others Donau Chemie*, ECLI:EU:C:2013:366, paras. 29–41, in which the CJEU balanced the need to provide for effective leniency programmes and the right to access leniency documents.

138 CJEU, Case C-557/12, *Kone AG and Others v. ÖBB-Infrastruktur* AG, ECLI:EU:C:2014:1317, para. 36.

139 For a view in favour of total indemnity for immunity recipients, see, for instance, Jens Koch, 'Rechtsdurchsetzung im Kartellrecht: Public vs. private enforcement: Auf dem Weg zu einem level playing field?' (2013) 68 *Juristen Zeitung*, 393–394.

140 Kersting, 'Die neue Richtlinie', 568–569; Kersting and Nicola Preuß, *Umsetzung der Kartellschadensersatzrichtlinie*, para. 137.

141 Inderst and Thomas, *Schadensersatz bei Kartellverstößen*, 410.

142 For instance, legal certainty, proportionality, equal treatment, see Kurt Stockmann, *Recht und Wettbewerb. Festschrift für Rainer Bechtold zum 65. Geburtstag* (München: C. H. Beck, 2006), 564 *et seq.*; Inderst and Thomas, *Schadensersatz bei Kartellverstößen*, 410.

143 See, for instance, Wils, 'Private Enforcement', 43; Cauffman, 'Leniency Programmes and Actions for Damages', 205; Canenbley and Steinvorth, 'Effective Enforcement', 320.

to entirely escape liability. Finally, this solution allows immunity recipients to keep benefits from the antitrust violation.[144]

It seems that leniency programmes cannot be protected without interfering with other principles of law. The answer to how to protect leniency is dependent on the priority we give either to leniency or to other objectives. Although the criticism on the basis of deterrence and retributive justice is justified, these principles are not decisive for civil law. Deterrence is not the principal function of private antitrust enforcement. The priority of tort law is also to compensate those damaged and not to deprive infringers of their illicit gains. As leniency programmes are the engine for discovering and establishing anticompetitive agreements, protecting leniency should be the priority.

4.2.4 *Practical Application*

The special regime of joint and several liability for immunity recipients needs to be appreciated for clearly determining the scope of its application. Pursuant to Article 2 (15) of Directive 2014/104/EU, the special rules on joint and several liability apply only to the recipients of full immunity. This solution is proportional as it protects those who uncover cartels and not merely cooperate with the Commission. Directive 2014/104/EU has, however, not avoided several ambiguities concerning the way the subsidiary liability and the liability to direct and indirect contractors is determined.[145]

4.2.4.1 Subsidiary Liability

The first issue is that the term 'cannot be obtained', which is used to determine subsidiary liability, is not specific enough.[146] As already discussed in Section 4.1, it is not clear whether the inability to obtain compensation refers to difficulties in obtaining it, encompassing that the creditor lost the case on merits or is limited to unsuccessful enforcement of a judgment granting damages or insolvency.[147] For the reasons discussed in Section 4.1.4.1, it is advisable to interpret this term as unsuccessful enforcement of a judgment awarding compensation.

[144] Wils, 'Private Enforcement', 43; Wils, 'Leniency in Antitrust Enforcement', 50; Canenbley and Steinvorth, 'Effective Enforcement', 320; Hölzel, *Kronzeugenregelungen*, 318.

[145] On the practical application of the rules on joint and several liability for immunity recipients, see also Katt, *Haftung des Kronzeugen*, 54 *et seq*. and 125 *et seq*; Koenig, 'Making Contribution Work', 118 *et seq*.

[146] This is not remedied by the way the researched Member States interpreted the Directive, see note 77.

[147] Weinhold, *Der Gesamtschuldnerausgleich*, 222–223; Hösch, *Der schadensrechtliche Innenausgleich*, 377; Seegers, 'Joint and Several Liability and Settlements', 141; Krüger 'Die Privilegierung des Kronzeugen', 484. See also criticism in Section 4.1.4.1.

The second issue is the question of who should prove that the creditor could not have obtained compensation. Neither Directive 2014/104/EU nor national implementation laws contain a provision on the burden of proof.[148] From the de lege ferenda standpoint, the burden of proof should be placed on the creditor. The reason is that it is the creditor that claims that it could not have obtained compensation from other debtors. The burden of proof lies on the creditor on the basis of the principle *ei incumbit probatio qui dicit, non qui negat*. Additionally, information on the creditor's attempts to receive compensation is known principally to the creditor. The principle of protecting the creditor should not be treated as a reason to reverse the regular burden of proof, as otherwise the immunity recipient would have difficulty obtaining the relevant evidence.[149]

4.2.4.2 Liability to Direct and Indirect Purchasers and Providers

Another concern comes from the Directive's use of the terms 'liable to its direct and indirect purchasers and providers',[150] 'harm it caused to its own direct or indirect purchasers or providers'[151] and 'caused harm to injured parties other than the direct or indirect purchasers or providers'.[152] These expressions demonstrate the EU legislator's lack of understanding of how anticompetitive agreements cause the damage and make the interpretation of these terms difficult.[153]

It is not the immunity recipient that causes harm to victims of antitrust infringement, but the anticompetitive agreement. By way of comparison, imagine a collision of two vessels that caused environmental damage after an oil spill. It is wrong to say that one of the vessels caused harm to land A and a second one to land B according to their respective distance to these lands. It was their coordinated action that caused damage to both of the lands. Without the existence of any of the vessels, the crash would not have happened. The same reasoning applies to antitrust infringements. They are committed by a coordinated action, and this is the source of the damage. Following this interpretation, the immunity recipient always harms not only its own direct and indirect contractors but also other victims of the misconduct. The terms used in Article 11(5) and Article 11(6) of Directive 2014/104/EU are thus based on a mistaken understanding of interrelationship between the behaviour and its effects.

148 See the text of the Directive and national implementations in note 77.

149 For such an operation, Martin Seegers, 'Joint and Several Liability and Settlements', 144; Kersting, 'Die neue Richtlinie', 568, Kersting and Preuß, *Umsetzung der Kartellschadensersatzrichtlinie*, paras. 126–128. In favour of introducing a refutable presumption, Peter-Christian Müller-Graff, 'Kartellrechtlicher Schadensersatz in neuer Versuchsanordnung' (2015) 179 *Zeitschrift für das gesamte Handels- und Wirtschaftsrecht*, 702.

150 Article 11(4)(a) of Directive 2014/104/EU.

151 Ibid., Article 11(5).

152 Ibid., Article 11(6).

153 Critically also Schwenke, 'Die Kartellschadensersatzklagen und der Gesamtschuldnerausgleich', 383–384.

The question is how to interpret these terms. As the wording is misguided, the focus should be on what the EU legislator wanted to achieve. The White Paper indicates that the aim of these rules is to divide liability on the basis of whose sales caused the harm. So if an antitrust victim suffered damages of 100 and it acquired 30 per cent of the products affected by the infringement from the immunity recipient, the latter is liable for 30.[154] The limitation of liability in the external dimension provided in Article 11(4)(a) of Directive 2014/104/EU would thus need to be read in this sense.

Another question is how to understand the rules on contribution. Article 11(5) of Directive 2014/104/EU says that the immunity recipient pays contribution equal to its liability to its direct and indirect contractors. Article 11(6) of the Directive provides that if the immunity recipient harmed other entities, its contribution is to be assessed in light of its relative liability for this harm.

These rules seem to regulate two types of contribution claims. Article 11(5) of the Directive stipulates a contribution claim for the liability that stems from the harm antitrust infringers caused to their direct and indirect contractors. Article 11(6) of the Directive relates to another contribution claim that concerns the liability for the harm that antitrust infringers have caused to other market players, for instance, those suffering umbrella damages.[155] As a result, the cap consisting of the 'harm caused to direct or indirect purchasers or providers' would apply only to the first situation. Contribution for the liability to other entities would follow the regular rules.

The result is a three-fold system of contribution. First, regular rules on contribution are applied. Second, contribution is capped to the damage sustained by the immunity recipients' direct and indirect contractors.[156] Third, the contribution regarding damages paid to antitrust victims other than infringers' direct and indirect contractors remains uncapped. If applied in practice, this system requires a multistep proceeding.

It seems that the burden of proof for a regular contribution rests on the claimant. Then, the immunity recipient may raise that the contribution claimed actually exceeds the cap established under Article 11(5) of Directive 2014/104/EU. Finally, the claimant may argue that a part of the contribution claimed reflects damages made to entities other than the immunity recipients' direct and indirect contractors.[157] This system is extremely complicated and proof-consuming. It is doubtful

[154] See White Paper, note 128. For such an interpretation, Krüger 'Die Privilegierung des Kronzeugen', 485.

[155] Weinhold, *Der Gesamtschuldnerausgleich*, 224; Hösch, *Der schadensrechtliche Innenausgleich*, 377; Seegers, 'Joint and Several Liability and Settlements', 142–143. Contrary, Krüger, 'Die Privilegierung des Kronzeugen', 484.

[156] Similar interpretation in Schwenke, 'Die Kartellschadensersatzklagen und der Gesamtschuldnerausgleich', 388; Kersting and Preuß, *Umsetzung der Kartellschadensersatzrichtlinie*, para. 11(2).

[157] On the burden of proof, see also Weinhold, *Der Gesamtschuldnerausgleich*, 225–227.

whether such complexity is actually justified by the objective of protecting leniency programmes.

One could have thought of establishing a much simpler system of contribution. It could be concluded that the division of liability between direct and indirect contractors and other victims of antitrust infringements applies only in the external dimension of joint and several liability, with the aim of protecting immunity recipients from being massively sued as first targets. In internal relations, immunity recipients could claim indemnity.

4.2.5 *Conclusions and Recommendations*

Directive 2014/104/EU's main advantage is that it protects leniency applicants from being massively sued by all victims of antitrust infringements. The Directive also partly limits their private law liability.

Practice is yet to show whether this privileged treatment is sufficient to keep leniency programmes effective. If the number of leniency applicants drops in the coming years, immunity recipients should be exempted from private law liability. Based on the above analysis, it already seems visible that the privilege in terms of reduction of private law liability can be insufficient to ensure that leniency programmes remain effective. A suggestion is to completely exempt immunity recipients from the internal dimension of joint and several liability.

4.3 SMALL AND MEDIUM ENTERPRISES

Another group of entities that were granted a modified treatment in terms of joint and several liability are small and medium enterprises (SMEs), which means enterprises with less than 250 employees and an annual turnover not exceeding EUR 50 million and/or EUR 43 million annual balance sheet total.[158] The privilege to SMEs appeared to many as a complete surprise, given it was not considered in the preparatory works of Directive 2014/104/EU.[159]

4.3.1 *Special Regime of Joint and Several Liability for Small and Medium Enterprises*

Directive 2014/104/EU introduces a privileged treatment to small and medium enterprises that is similar to the one given to immunity recipients. Article 11(2) of the Directive provides that

> Member States shall ensure that, without prejudice to the right of full compensation as laid down in Article 3, where the infringer is a small or medium-sized

[158] See Article 11(2) of Directive 2014/104/EU.
[159] Wouter P. J. Wils, 'Private Enforcement', 28.

enterprise (SME) …, the infringer is liable only to its own direct and indirect purchasers.[160]

In order to qualify for such a privilege, the undertaking in question must fulfil two positive and two negative conditions:

its market share in the relevant market was below 5% at any time during the infringement of competition law;[161]

the application of the normal rules of joint and several liability would irretrievably jeopardise its economic viability and cause its assets to lose all their value;[162]

the SME has (not) led the infringement of competition law or has (not) coerced other undertakings to participate therein;[163]

the SME has (not) previously been found to have infringed competition law.[164]

4.3.2 *Justification of the Special Regime*

Interestingly enough, Directive 2014/104/EU does not give any explanation of why SMEs need to be treated in a special way. The *travaux préparatoires* of the Directive do not give much guidance either. The special rules concerning SMEs were

[160] This is implemented by Part 3 Section 12(1)(d) in connection with 12(3) and 12(5) of the UK Act, adding 'containing/inclusive' and 'derived' products; by § 33d(3) in connection with § 33d(4) of the GWB stating that the limitation is '*zur Höhe des Schadens … den dieses seinen unmittelbaren und mittelbaren Abnehmern oder Lieferanten verursacht hat*' and reminding that this limitation applies only to the damage caused to direct and indirect purchasers and providers. German rules include in addition subsidiary liability of SMEs for damages made to other actors, which is formulated in the same way as for leniency applicants, see § 33d(3) last sentence. A relevant implementation is introduced in France by Article L. 481-10(1) and (5) of the Code Commerce and in Poland by Article 5(1) in connection with Article 2(17) of the Polish Act.

[161] Article 11(3)(a) of Directive 2014/104/EU. This is implemented by Part 3 Section 12(1)(b) of the UK Act; by § 33d(3)(1) of the GWB; by Article L.481-10(2) of the Code de Commerce; by Article 5(1)(1) of the Polish Act.

[162] Article 11(3)(b) of Directive 2014/104/EU. This is implemented by Part 3 Section 12(1)(c) and Section 12(4) of the UK Act using exactly the same terms, however, adding that it needs to be accounted for 'the undertaking's other liabilities'; by § 33(d)(3)(2) of the GWB referring to the same terms '*seine wirtaschaftliche Lebensfähigkeit unwiderbringlich gefährden und seine Aktiva jeden Werts berauben würde*'; by Article L. 481-10(3) of the Code de Commerce referring to exactly the same terms '*compromettrait irrémédiablement sa viabilité économique et ferait perdre toute valeur à ses actifs*'; by Article 5(1)(2) of the Polish Act using exactly the same terms '*nieodwracalne zagrożenie dla ekonomicznej opłacalności jego działalności i skutkowałoby całkowitą utratą wartości jego przedsiębiorstwa*'.

[163] Article 11(4)(a) of Directive 2014/104/EU. This is implemented by Part 3 Section 12(2)(a) and (b) of the UK Act; by § 33d(5)(1) and (2) of the GWB; by Article L.481-10(4) of the Code de Commerce; by Article 5(2) of the Polish Act.

[164] Article 11(4)(b) of Directive 2014/104/EU. This is implemented by Part 3 Section 12(c) of the UK Act; by § 33d(5)(3) of the GWB; by Article L.481-10(4) of the Code de Commerce; by Article 5 (2) of the Polish Act.

proposed for the first time in the parliamentary discussions on the adoption of the Directive.[165]

4.3.2.1 The Case for the Protection of SMEs

As the idea of privileging SMEs appeared very late, it may be supposed that it was realised due to the political influence exercised on the Directive's drafters. Special treatment of SMEs has been on the top of EU and national political agendas for a long time. The European Commission has realised a comprehensive policy of supporting SMEs. It has adopted many acts, especially for SMEs, including the Small Business Act for Europe, Entrepreneurship Action Plan, and The Late Payment Directive.[166] The European Union is also not isolated in protecting SMEs. This is also encouraged by the OECD[167] and has also been realised in German antitrust law.[168]

One reason for treating SMEs differently is that they are vulnerable to committing antitrust infringements. Although *De Minimis* Notice, safe harbours in block exemption regulations and the *effect on trade* requirement limit the chances that SMEs will be found as infringing EU competition law, there are still matters in which such a finding is made. This is particularly true in the case of hard-core violations.[169]

This phenomenon can be explained by a multitude of reasons which all amount to the fact that SMEs have limited financial and human resources. Small and medium enterprises are more likely to behave negligently and engage in illegal practices in an unconscious way. Few employees run the entire business, and they are preoccupied by more fundamental concerns than antitrust compliance.[170] The Office of Fair Trading demonstrated that the more employees companies have, the

[165] Wils, 'Private Enforcement', 42.

[166] Communication from the Commission to the Council, the European Parliament, the European Economic and Social Committee and the Committee of the Regions, "Think Small First" – A "Small Business Act" for Europe, COM/2008/0394 final; Communication from the Commission to the European Parliament, the Council, the European Economic and Social Committee and the Committee of the Regions, Entrepreneurship 2020 Action Plan Reigniting the entrepreneurial spirit in Europe, COM/2012/0795 final; Directive 2011/7/EU of the European Parliament and of the Council of 16 February 2011 on combating late payment in commercial transactions, OJ L 48, 23.2.2011, pp. 1–10.

[167] See, for instance, OECD, 'SME and Entrepreneurship Outlook' (2005) available at https://oecd.org/cfe/smes/oecdsmeandentrepreneurshipoutlook-2005edition.htm, 17.

[168] Paragraph 3(2) of the GWB. See also Meinrad Dreherand Julia Körner, 'Germany' in Pranvera Këllezi, Bruce Kilpatrick and Pierre Kobel (eds.), *Antitrust for Small and Middle Size Undertakings and Image Protection from Non-Competitors* (Berlin: Springer, 2014), 130–131.

[169] In France, it is claimed that SMEs are frequently involved in cartels, see Mathilde Boudou, 'France' in Pranvera Këllezi, Bruce Kilpatrick and Pierre Kobel (eds.), *Antitrust for Small and Middle Size Undertakings and Image Protection from Non-Competitors* (Berlin: Springer, 2014), 106–108. See also Këllezi, Kilpatrick and Kobel, *Small and Middle Size Undertakings*, 3 *et seq.*

[170] OECD, 'Competition Policy', 264.

more knowledge of antitrust they have.[171] Small and medium enterprises also have limited capacity to pay for legal advice and defend themselves from allegations that they have violated antitrust law and their consequences. As mentioned by Wouter P. J. Wils, most companies applying for leniency are large enterprises, which can be explained by their more sophisticated legal strategy.[172]

Another reason to treat SMEs differently stems from the economic analysis of fault. The principle of economic analysis of fault is that only *optimal* care should be required by legal systems to prevent undesirable behaviours. Requiring the highest care is not efficient.[173] Optimal care should be determined by reference to the abilities of companies to provide for compliance.[174] This can be done, for instance, by classifying tortfeasors in separate groups.[175] Nowadays, no such differentiation is made. The economic analysis of fault gives, however, an indication that the standard of fault applied to SMEs is inappropriate. It may leave them with a Hobbesian choice: spending an extraordinary amount of funds for competition law compliance or paying an extraordinary fine for a potential breach of competition law.

Finally, Wouter P. J. Wils claims that SMEs need to be protected because antitrust liability may force them to leave the market.[176] He supports this reasoning with the fact that the EU already indirectly protects SMEs. The Commission's Guidelines on Fines provide that the fine should be capped at 10 per cent of the company's turnover and that the fine should be reduced if a company is unable to pay it.[177] These fining mechanisms protect SMEs insofar as their liability stays in proportion to their financial abilities. This eliminates a risk that a small company will be forced to leave the market only because of the imposed antitrust liability. Wouter P. J. Wils prolongs this reasoning to private law liability and claims that such a liability can be detrimental to the existence of SMEs. If SMEs are sued massively, their financial existence is endangered. The probability of such a situation occurring

[171] David Bailey, 'United Kingdom' in Pranvera Këllezi, Bruce Kilpatrick and Pierre Kobel (eds.), *Antitrust for Small and Middle Size Undertakings and Image Protection from Non-Competitors* (Berlin: Springer, 2014), 241 referring to Synovate, 'Competition Act and Consumer Rights' (April 2005) OFT 799, showing that among the enterprises consisting of 10–19 individuals 49 per cent of them were aware of the Competition Act, which contrasts with 80 per cent awareness declared by larger companies.

[172] Wils, 'Private Enforcement', 29.

[173] Michael Faure, 'Economic Analysis of Fault' in Pierre Widmer (ed.), *Unification of Tort Law: Fault* (Den Haag: Kluwer Law International, 2005), 313.

[174] Ibid., 317. See also Peter A. Diamond, 'Single Activity Accidents' (1974) *The Journal of Legal Studies*, 3, 107 *et seq*.

[175] Faure, 'Economic Analysis of Fault', 318–319.

[176] Wils, 'Private Enforcement', 29–30. Similarly also Advocate General Geelhoed in his Opinion in Case C-289/04 P, *Showa Denko KK v. Commission of the European Communities*, ECLI: EU:C:2006:52; Bovis and Clarke, 'Private Enforcement', 68; Müller-Graff, 'Kartellrechtlicher Schadensersatz', 702.

[177] Wils, 'Private Enforcement', 29–30.

is enhanced by the fact that most immunity recipients are large enterprises and they could be exempted from a large part of their own liability.[178]

4.3.2.2 The Case against the Protection of SMEs

However, there are serious reasons to claim that there is no place in Directive 2014/104/EU for protecting small and medium enterprises.[179]

First, the special treatment of SMEs runs contrary to the principle of equality.[180] Competition law applies equally to all undertakings and the size of a company, in terms of the number of employees, is not a feature that requires distinctive treatment in EU competition law. The Commission's fining policy does not change this finding. The rules on fines apply equally to all undertakings. For instance, even a large undertaking may find itself in a financial difficulty, which would be considered by the Commission under its inability to pay provisions.

Second, market-related objectives such as protection of the market structure cannot be realised with the means of private law. The Commission may account for such factors in its competition law enforcement policy as its mission is to ensure that markets function properly. Such an aim is very distant to private law. The function of claims for damages is to provide for restitution and compensation.[181] These functions are generally fulfilled without regard to the financial abilities of those concerned,[182] a fortiori without regard to the structure of the markets. Private law judges are also not qualified to decide market structure and competitiveness.

Third, although the arguments based on the economic analysis of fault are convincing, they cannot be applied until this theory becomes a letter of law.

This analysis shows that there is no place in the context of private law liability to protect SMEs. This should not be, however, considered a problem. There are other tools that can address the fact that SMEs are vulnerable to infringing antitrust law. For instance, some initiatives can be put in place to foster the general compliance culture among SMEs. State and trade organisations can launch information campaigns to increase the general awareness of competition law, and they can help SMEs resolve their competition law problems.

178 Ibid., 29.

179 Similarly Hösch, *Der schadensrechtliche Innenausgleich*, 375; Christian Steinle, 'Kartellschadensersatzrichtlinie – Auf dem Weg zum Sanktions-Overkill? (Gastkommentar)' (2014) 13 *Europäische Zeitschrift für Wirtschaftsrecht*, 482; Heike Schweitzer, 'Die neue Richtlinie für wettbewerbsrechtliche Schadensersatzklagen' (2014) 9 *Neue Zeitschrift für Kartellrecht*, 344; Thiede, 'Private Enforcement of Anti-trust Damages', 164–165.

180 On unequal treatment, see also Makatsch and Sascha Mir, 'EU-Richtlinie zu Kartellschadensersatzklagen', 11.

181 See Section 2.1.1.2.

182 Although in Germany and in Poland financial capacities have been considered in few contribution cases, see notes 147 and 155 in Chapter 3.

4.3.3 *Realisation of the Objectives*

From the outset, the idea of protecting SMEs with special rules of joint and several liability is flawed. The rules on SMEs will nonetheless be further scrutinised, and it is asked how the protection of SMEs is realised.[183]

4.3.4 *Practical Application*

4.3.4.1 Scope of the Modified Regime

Directive 2014/104/EU is praised for a clear definition of SMEs falling under specific rules of joint and several liability. Article 11(2) of the Directive defines small and medium undertakings by reference to Commission Recommendation 2003/361/EC.[184] According to Article 2(1) of the latter instrument, SMEs are companies with fewer than 250 employees, an annual turnover not exceeding EUR 50 million, and/or an annual balance sheet total below EUR 43 million.

4.3.4.2 Positive Conditions

In order to have the special system of joint and several liability applied, SMEs must meet two positive conditions.

The first condition is that their relevant market share is below 5 per cent. Although it is not a straightforward exercise to define markets,[185] in the case of follow-on actions the markets are already defined by the Commission and in the case of stand-alone claims historic case law facilitates defining markets.

The second condition requires that the application of joint and several liability 'irretrievably jeopardise the undertaking's economic viability and cause its assets to lose all their value'. These terms are difficult to interpret.[186] Most fundamentally, it is very rare for the companies' assets to lose all their value. Even if a company announces that it is going into insolvency, its assets still have some value and are used to pay for company debts. It is doubtful that Directive 2014/104/EU intended to set a threshold so high that it is impossible to meet. As a result, one can think that the

183 On practical application of the rules on joint and several liability for SMEs, see also Koenig, 'Making Contribution Work', 124–126.

184 Commission Recommendation 2003/361/EC of 6 May 2003 concerning the definition of micro, small and medium-sized enterprises, OJ L 124, 20.5.2003, pp. 36–41.

185 Schaper and Stauber, 'Gesamtschuld und Innenausgleich', 283–284; Schweitzer, 'Die Richtlinie für Schadensersatzklagen', 344.

186 This is not remedied by national implementations of Directive 2014/104/EU, which simply translated the term used by the Directive into national languages, see note 76. Critically also Thiede, 'Private Enforcement of Anti-trust Damages', 164–165; Thiede, 'Fine to Follow-On?', 251; Kersting, 'Die neue Richtlinie', 568; Kersting and Preuß, *Umsetzung der Kartellschadensersatzrichtlinie*, para. 122.

company's insolvency could in and of itself be an event that would trigger Article 11 of the Directive.[187] At this stage, the company is definitely not economically viable, and its assets are subjected to the insolvency proceeding. However, the moment of insolvency is not the only possible option. There is a chance that serious financial difficulties could jeopardise the undertaking's economic viability and the value of its assets. Due to the Directive's lack of specificity on how to understand Article 11(2)(b), it is difficult to predict the way this condition would be interpreted.[188]

The difficulties connected to this condition do not end at this point. Even if the benchmark is clear, it may be difficult to apply. For instance, if a decisive point is the company's insolvency, this insolvency must be forecasted. It must be asked whether the company will become insolvent as a result of claims for antitrust damages.[189] This requires a balancing of existing company assets, its ability to take liabilities and the size of future damages claims . This exercise is difficult, and its results are imprecise and uncertain.

Finally, it is difficult to see how this condition applies when the liability on SMEs is litigated and enforced gradually. It is easier to see that the economic existence of SMEs is endangered by high damages claimed in a collective action. However, it is more probable that claims for damages would be exercised individually and gradually given the lack of comprehensive rules on class actions in EU competition law. The SME cannot assess upfront that its civil law liabilities would jeopardise its economic viability. It does not have information on the number of antitrust victims, the amount of their claims, and the probability of being sued. It is, in fact, able to assess whether its insolvency comes only after a significant amount of such claims have been enforced. At this stage, the enterprise might, however, have already paid compensation to entities other than its direct and indirect contractors. It is thus difficult to see how this modified regime can be applied in practice.

4.3.4.3 Negative Conditions

Articles 11(4)(a) and 11(4)(b) of Directive 2014/104/EU provide for two negative conditions which, if fulfilled, deny the SME the right to rely on a modified regime of joint and several liability. These conditions refer to the SME's role in the cartel – ringleading and recidivism. The consideration of these conditions in Directive 2014/104/EU demonstrates that the EU legislator sought to exclude a more lenient

[187] In this line, Schaper and Stauber, 'Gesamtschuld und Innenausgleich', 283; Schweitzer, 'Die Richtlinie für Schadensersatzklagen', 343.

[188] In this line, Rust, 'Kartellverstoß und Gesamtschuld', 510; Müller-Graff, 'Kartellrechtlicher Schadensersatz', 702.

[189] Discussing past rather than future analysis, Schaper and Stauber, 'Gesamtschuld und Innenausgleich', 284; Schweitzer, 'Die Richtlinie für Schadensersatzklagen', 343.

treatment of undertakings that bear a relatively high share of culpability for the violation.

These conditions are easy to apply if the case is a follow-on one. Information about ringleading and recidivism is included in the Commission's infringement decision. In stand-alone claims, such information should also be easily accessible. It can be in the public domain (for instance, recidivism), or it can be delivered by the creditor as a part of establishing the infringer's fault.

The problem is the burden of proof. The Directive seems to require negative proof on the part of SMEs. As such a proof is impossible, it should be sufficient that SMEs only ascertain that negative conditions have not appeared[190] and that such findings are verified by the court.

4.3.4.4 External Aspect of Joint and Several Liability

Article 11(2) of Directive 2014/104/EU uses a similar term to limit SMEs' liabilities as that established in Article 11(4)(a) of the Directive concerning immunity recipients. Both provisions state that the protected entities are 'liable to own direct and indirect purchasers and providers'. As already identified above, this is an inappropriate term that gives rise to concerns regarding its application. As demonstrated, it seems that this term should limit the liability of an SME to the damage inflicted from the sales made by the SME to its direct and indirect contractors.

In contrast to the rules on immunity recipients, the limitation of an SME's liability to its own direct and indirect contractors is not coupled with its subsidiary liability to all antitrust victims. A lack of subsidiary liability has a negative impact on the principle of full compensation and is surprising given that Article 11(2) of Directive 2014/104/EU emphasises that the modifications made with respect to SMEs are 'without prejudice to the right of full compensation'. As a consequence, the drawback described here should be accounted for and remedied.

4.3.4.5 Internal Aspect of Joint and Several Liability

The limitation of liability made in Article 11(2) of Directive 2014/104/EU is laconic. It reads that 'the infringer is liable only to its own direct and indirect purchasers'. This wording is not clear whether the limitation of the liability applies with respect to the external relation (i), to the internal relation (ii) or to both of them (iii) to be stated.

For the application of the first option speaks the fact that the first option fulfils the aim sought by Article 11(2) of Directive 2014/104/EU.[191] One of the risks that SMEs face is that they would have to pay damages that exceed their financial capacity

[190] Kersting and Preuß, *Umsetzung der Kartellschadensersatzrichtlinie*, para. 119.

[191] For such an interpretation, Schaper and Stauber, 'Gesamtschuld und Innenausgleich', 284; Kersting and Preuß, *Umsetzung der Kartellschadensersatzrichtlinie*, para. 120.

regardless of their own liability share. Although an SME would normally have a right to limit its financial liability by claiming contribution from other debtors, this could happen too late and could not prevent its insolvency. From this standpoint, the limitation of liability is desired only in the external aspect of joint and several liability. Such a limitation would allow SMEs to defend themselves from lawsuits made from entities other than their direct and indirect contractors and have their final liability determined in contribution litigation.[192]

It would be implausible for the second option to be the aim of EU legislator. The limitation of liability in only the internal relationship does not solve the problem of an SME's incapability to pay damages to antitrust victims and the ability to bear the burden of massive litigation. The third option also seems to be unlikely. Article 11(2) of the Directive does not provide for the right to claim contribution in a special way. A systematic reading of the Directive encourages reliance on a regular rule to claim contribution without introducing a different treatment of SMEs.[193] The Directive provides for special regimes for contribution for those engaged in consensual dispute resolution, and for immunity recipients, it does not provide one for SMEs.

As a result, SMEs are liable internally according to the general rules on contribution. Externally, their liability is limited to their direct and indirect contractors. Such a solution is a balanced choice. Small and medium enterprises are protected from the risk that they could face unbearable initial liability if they become one of the central targets for massive antitrust litigation. However, in relation to other debtors, they remain liable according to their relative responsibility for the infringement.

4.3.5 *Conclusions and Recommendations*

The special regime of joint and several liability for SMEs rightfully faces criticism, and it is recommended to abolish it.

The modified regime for the liability of SMEs also raises many practical concerns. There are some gaps in Directive 2014/104/EU that cause interpretative difficulties and legal uncertainty. The criterion regarding an SME's loss of economic viability is difficult if not implausible to apply. This condition may turn the rules on joint and several liability of SMEs into a dead letter of the law.

4.4 CONCLUSIONS

The examination of the modifications to joint and several liability made in favour of those engaged in consensual dispute resolution, immunity recipients and small and medium enterprises has demonstrated that these rules are complex.

192 Against this view, Schaper and Stauber, 'Gesamtschuld und Innenausgleich', 284.
193 Similarly also Rust, 'Kartellverstoß und Gesamtschuld', 510.

The modifications to joint and several liability are not straightforward as they attempt to balance the protection of the chosen groups with other principles, such as the right to full compensation for creditors or the equal treatment of debtors.

Directive 2014/104/EU therefore raises many questions of interpretation and practical implementation. It is unclear how certain conditions for the application of special joint and several liabilities would apply and in consequence whether such regimes will ever be applied. In light of this, one should think of simplifying and making special regimes of joint and several liability more efficient.

5

Liability Sharing Agreements

The scrutiny of the legal framework for contribution claims in antitrust demonstrates that enforcing such claims in courts is a complex, uncertain and challenging task (see further in Section 6.1 in Chapter 6). This raises the question of what modifications are needed to improve the framework for claiming contribution (see Section 6.2 in Chapter 6). However, before reflecting on how to reform contribution claims, it is worth asking whether there are tools in the existing legal framework that can resolve the challenges connected to contribution litigation in antitrust.

A promising solution is to handle the problem of contribution in a contractual way. Antitrust infringers could conclude an agreement that would determine the amount of their relative liabilities regarding antitrust infringement ('liability sharing agreement', LSA).[1] For instance, if there are five antitrust infringers liable for EUR 10 million, the agreement can determine that each of them is liable for EUR 2 million or for a percentage equal to their market shares. Thanks to the LSA, antitrust infringers would have certainty on the way their relative liability is determined, which they do not have under the existing legal framework.

The freedom to determine relative shares of liability may yet be viewed reluctantly from a public policy perspective. Arguably, LSAs are part of anticompetitive collusion. They stabilise unlawful behaviour as well as jeopardise deterrence and the sanctioning policy of antitrust agencies.

The aim of this chapter is to investigate whether the contractual determination of contribution is allowed considering the public nature of competition law (Section 5.1). After having identified that LSAs are enforceable within certain limitations, it is asked what those negotiating LSAs must consider avoiding the

[1] Liability sharing agreements are also called *judgment sharing agreements* or just *sharing agreements*, see Leslie, 'Judgment-Sharing Agreements', 749; Yosef J. Riemer, 'Sharing Agreements among Defendants in Antitrust Cases' (1984) 52 *The George Washington Law Review*, 290.

agreements' invalidity (Section 5.2). The chapter then provides a conclusion (Section 5.3).

5.1 ARE LIABILITY SHARING AGREEMENTS ALLOWED IN EU COMPETITION LAW?

Liability sharing agreements are already used in US antitrust law, and there has been an initial discussion about whether to allow them also in the European Union. In contrast to the trend in the United States, the debate in the European Union has revealed a general reluctance towards LSAs.

5.1.1 *Liability Sharing Agreements in the United States*

Liability sharing agreements are recognised as valid in US antitrust law.[2] The no-contribution rule has forced antitrust infringers to seek ways in which they can redistribute liability that has been placed on only some of them. It has become increasingly frequent to rely on contractual arrangements to determine relative liability for any potential antitrust liability.[3] Despite some criticism,[4] the US courts and commentators approve the use of LSAs, noting that 'contractual contribution'[5] is a counterbalance to the negative effects of the no-contribution rule.

Liability sharing agreements have become a part of the US practice.[6] Whilst their content is generally unknown due to confidentiality, some practices have been revealed. It seems that LSAs are concluded before the antitrust liability has been established.[7] They determine relative liability on the basis of a specified benchmark, for instance, the parties' market shares.[8] Finally, they include additional provisions, such as arbitration, jurisdiction clauses,[9] and rules on how to settle with the creditor.[10]

2 *Cimarron Pipeline Constr. v. Nat'l Council on Comp. Ins.*, Civ. -89-822-T, 1992 U.S. Dist. LEXIS 18560 (W.D. Okla. 1992). See also Koeltl et al., *Manual for Complex Litigation*, 176 *et seq.*; Leslie, 'Judgment-Sharing Agreements', 750 *et seq.*

3 Riemer, 'Sharing Agreements', 290.

4 See in particular Leslie, 'Judgment-Sharing Agreements'.

5 ABA (1986), 19–20.

6 It is disputed whether this practice is common or moderate, given some difficulties in concluding LSAs. While it has been claimed that they are difficult to conclude due to differences between the entities engaged in negotiation, it has also been concluded that such agreements are fairly common. See Leslie, 'Judgment-Sharing Agreements', 755–756; Krüger, *Kartellregress*, 151; Körner, *Die Gesamtschuld im Kartellbußgeldrecht*, 25.

7 Leslie, 'Judgment-Sharing Agreements', 755.

8 See, for instance, United States District Court N.D. Illinois Eastern Division judgment of 11 April 1995 in Case 94 C 897, MDL 997, 1995 WL 221853, *In re Brand Name Pharm. Antitrust Litig.*, MDL 997, 1995 WL 234521 (N.D. Ill. 1995).

9 Leslie, 'Judgment-Sharing Agreements', 755.

10 Riemer, 'Sharing Agreements', 293.

5.1.2 *Distrust towards Liability Sharing Agreements in the European Union and Its Consequences*

Liability sharing agreements are new in EU antitrust law, and the author has no knowledge of such agreements being already concluded within the European Union. Liability sharing agreements may, however, appear with the increased amount of private antitrust litigation and uncertain rules on contribution.

There has been much hesitance about allowing LSAs in antitrust. The reasons are that LSAs can weaken the deterrent effect of antitrust liability.[11] In fact, they can be considered a part of antitrust violation,[12] in particular in cartel cases where they have a stabilising force.[13] The majority opinion is to allow LSAs only under certain circumstances[14] – most meaningfully, only *after* antitrust liability has been already established.[15]

The problem with such an approach is, however, that it is unlikely an LSA would be concluded after the antitrust violation is discovered. The diversity of the debtors' stakes is commonly known to impede concluding agreements regarding liability after such liability has materialised. Tortfeasors are reported to be unable to reach even agreements that deal with procedural matters such as referring adjudication of the dispute to arbitrators.[16] It would be surprising to see that in the competition law context, the parties are more successful than in other areas at concluding agreements when already facing liability.

The chances of a company signing an LSA when it is already facing a concrete antitrust liability are relatively low. It has been reported that LSAs occur only in narrowly defined circumstances, such as highly concentrated markets with few undertakings having similar characteristics.[17]

5.1.3 *The Case for Liability Sharing Agreements*

The low likelihood of concluding LSAs after liability has been established is prone to turn such agreements into a rare phenomenon. This raises the question of

[11] Weinhold, *Der Gesamtschuldnerausgleich*, 145; Krüger, *Kartellregress*, 156–158; Bieber, *Die gesamtschuldnerische Haftung*, 111.

[12] Weinhold, *Der Gesamtschuldnerausgleich*, 144–146; Krüger, *Kartellregress*, 154–157; Dreher, 'Die Haftungsverteilung', 156.

[13] Krüger, *Kartellregress*, 156; Dreher, 'Die Haftungsverteilung', 156.

[14] Weinhold, *Der Gesamtschuldnerausgleich*, 146; Körner, *Die Gesamtschuld im Kartellbußgeldrecht*, 205–208.

[15] Weinhold, *Der Gesamtschuldnerausgleich*, 146; Krüger, *Kartellregress*, 154; Dreher, 'Die Haftungsverteilung', 156.

[16] Gary B. Born, *International Arbitration: Law and Practice* (Alphen aan den Rijn: Kluwer Law International, 2012), 106; Joseph F. Morrissey and Jack M. Graves, *International Sales Law and Arbitration: Problems, Cases and Commentary* (Austin, Boston, Chicago, New York, The Netherlands: Wolters Kluwer Law and Business, 2008), 319.

[17] Krüger, *Kartellregress*, 151.

whether only allowing LSAs after the antitrust liability has been established is desirable under the current contribution regime. Liability sharing agreements have the potential to allow antitrust infringers to deal with contribution in a certain, simple and cost-saving way.

First, LSAs remedy the uncertainty inherent to the existing contribution framework. Those envisaging contributions currently cannot be sure on which basis such contribution would be considered, which criterion for dividing liability would be applied and how courts would handle the impact of competition law on contribution claims. Thanks to concluding LSAs, those considering contribution can shield themselves against these uncertainties and take control over the problem of contribution.

Second, an agreement on the proportions of relative liability makes securing contribution simple. By negotiating contribution rather than litigating it, parties to LSAs can decide the size of relative liability without disputing other issues (for instance, applicable law, burden of proof). The parties may also choose a criterion for dividing antitrust liability that is simple to manage. It has been reported that market shares are used as such a benchmark.[18] One can also think of other measures that are easy to apply, such as volumes of sales relating to the infringing product or *pro capita* division. If the parties can agree on how to divide their relative liabilities, they resolve a potentially complex dispute in a simple and efficient way.

Third, determining relative liabilities using a simple formula avoids many costs. A contractual agreement saves the costs of legal and economic assistance to define and support the companies' positions on various questions. Additionally and more fundamentally, it reduces the cost of such disputes to the justice system as a whole. It has been claimed by those supporting the no-contribution rule that a right to claim contribution should be rejected due to the costs borne by the public justice system. According to them, antitrust infringers are wrongdoers, and internal disputes among them should not be resolved by already busy courts.[19] Requiring public judges to resolve contribution disputes is a cost to society because other, more important cases are handled later.[20] Liability sharing agreements respond to this claim. They allow antitrust infringers to deal with the issue of contribution without relying on the public justice system. The majority of costs are placed on antitrust infringers themselves, as it is up to them to agree on contribution.

5.1.4 *Law on Liability Sharing Agreements*

The distrust towards LSAs is surprising from the policy standpoint and encourages a verification of the status of such agreements under existing law in the context of public and private antitrust enforcement.

[18] Riemer, 'Sharing Agreements', 293.

[19] See, for instance, Easterbrook, Landes and Posner, 'Contribution among Antitrust Defendants', 340–341; Cavanagh, 'Contribution, Claim Reduction', 1295.

[20] Ibid.

5.1.4.1 Public Enforcement

In the context of public antitrust enforcement, the CJEU acknowledged the existence of LSAs and implied that they should be respected:

> *where there is no contractual agreement* as to the shares to be paid by those held jointly and severally liable for payment of the fine, it is for the national courts to determine those shares.[21]

The CJEU expressed that only when there is no agreement on how to distribute antitrust liability, the courts have a responsibility to deal with the question of contribution.

The CJEU's sympathy towards the contractual determination of relative liability also demonstrates its laconism with respect to limitations to possible LSAs. This is striking given the context of the *Siemens Österreich* judgment, which was about joint and several liability imposed in the Commission's decision. One would imagine that contractual agreements on relative liabilities could potentially interfere with the Commission's decision to impose liability on given companies. The CJEU does not even name any concrete requirements that LSAs must meet, apart from their compliance with EU law, which is also required from courts dealing with contribution claims.[22]

5.1.4.2 Private Enforcement

In the private enforcement context, Directive 2014/104/EU stipulates nothing about the possibility of concluding LSAs. The Directive only states that

> [t]he determination of that share as the relative responsibility of a given infringer . . . is a matter for the applicable national law, while respecting the principles of effectiveness and equivalence.[23]

The Directive relies on national laws to provide for a framework to determine the shares in which infringers are individually liable.[24] It is then also up to national laws to answer the question of whether it is allowed to determine such shares in a contractual way. This question is answered positively by all of the researched jurisdictions.

Charles Mitchell reports that in England and Wales, contractual allocations of liability, including indemnity, are usually effective.[25] Section 7(3)(b) of the Contribution Act 1978 also allows for contracts in this respect. English law sets a

[21] CJEU, *Siemens Österreich*, para. 62.
[22] See Section 2.2.3.
[23] Recital 37 of Directive 2014/104/EU.
[24] See Section 3.1.1.
[25] Mitchell, *The Law of Contribution*, 188–190.

limitation that contractual determination of relative liabilities must be compliant with other areas of law. In this respect, it is claimed that LSAs cannot influence the rights of the creditor,[26] and generally public policy.[27]

In Germany, LSAs are also generally allowed.[28] They can cover both contribution and indemnity.[29] In addition, contractual determinations of contribution enjoy priority over other ways of determining relative liability.[30] They come before applying criteria established by law or criteria stemming from the circumstances of the case.[31] The limitation to LSAs is, however, their compliance with *bonos mores*[32] and *Treu und Glauben.*[33]

In France, it is reported that an agreement by which joint and several debtors share their debt is valid between them, although it cannot be claimed against the creditor.[34] The limitation to this is that in certain situations case law imposes additional requirements for debtors.[35] It also seems equally applicable to France that LSAs must be compliant with public policy and *bonos mores* under Article 6 of Code Civil.

In Poland, liability agreements are also allowed. It is claimed that the rules on contribution are *ius dispositive*, meaning that it is possible to derogate from them with a contractual agreement.[36] LSAs can concern both contribution and indemnity.[37] In Poland, LSAs also need to comply with the principle of *bonos mores* and public policy (*zasady współżycia społecznego*).

This short review reveals that contractual agreements on contribution are allowed in national laws. It is, however, disclaimed in all researched legal orders that there are certain limitations to the freedom to decide about relative liabilities. In England, the limitation relates to the protection of the creditor and public policy. In Germany, France, and Poland, LSAs must also be compliant with the principle of *bonos mores* and public policy. While the protection of the creditor can be accounted for in LSAs, public policy and *bonos mores* can be used against the LSAs in competition law. In order to establish whether LSAs dealing with antitrust

26 Ibid., 188.

27 Williams, *Joint Torts and Contributory Negligence*, 76; Mitchell, *The Law of Contribution*, 188, note 25.

28 Weinhold, *Der Gesamtschuldnerausgleich*, 143–144.

29 Ibid., 144.

30 Prediger, *Gesamtschuld*, 149. See also notes 143 and 157 in Chapter 3.

31 Dreher, 'Die Haftungsverteilung', 151. See also notes 143 and 157 in Chapter 3.

32 Rogers, 'Comparative Report', 297.

33 Körner, *Die Gesamtschuld im Kartellbußgeldrecht*, 206.

34 Cochet, 'La contribution', para. 23; Civ. I, 14.12.1964: D 1965, 95.

35 Cochet, 'La contribution', para. 23.

36 Karaszewski, '*Komentarz do Art. 441 Kodeksu cywilnego*', para. 10; Nesterowicz and Bagińska, 'Multiple Tortfeasors', 160.

37 Nesterowicz and Bagińska, 'Multiple Tortfeasors', 160.

liability are allowed, it is therefore necessary to discuss the arguments put forward to conclude that such agreements are against these principles.

5.1.5 *Arguments against the Use of Liability Sharing Agreements*

Public policy, *bonos mores* and *Treu und Glauben* are the concepts with which LSAs must be compliant in order to be enforceable. Much ink has been spent to define these notions and to demonstrate how they apply in different contexts.[38] Setting aside the precise definitions of these notions,[39] it may be safely assumed based on the CJEU's *Eco Swiss* judgment[40] that rules on competition are part of public policy and acting in line with them is also part of *bonos mores* and *Treu und Glauben*.[41]

As a result, special attention must be paid to all instances in which LSAs may be considered in breach of antitrust law themselves, may have positive impacts on anticompetitive behaviours and decrease the enforcement of competition law by reducing deterrence or discouraging settlements.

38 Various terms are also used, for instance, public order, *ordre public*, public good. See Philippe Malaurie, *L'Ordre Public et Le Contrat* (Reims: Editions Matot-Braine, 1953); Georges Ripert 'L'ordre public économique et la liberté contractuelle' in *Recueil d'études sur les sources du droit en l'honneur de François Gény* (Paris: Librairie du Recueil Sirey, 1934); W. S. M. Knight, 'Public policy of the English Law' (1922) 38 *Law Quarterly Review*, 379; Michael Howlett and Ben Cashore, 'Conceptualizing Public Policy' (2004) *Comparative Policy Studies*, 17; Katarzyna Kopaczyńska-Pieczniak 'Dobre obyczaje i zasady współżycia społecznego w prawie spółek handlowych' (2016) LXIII(2) *Annales Universitatis Mariae Curie-Sklodowska*, 93; Adam Łopatka and Zygmunt Ziembiński, 'Treść i Funkcja Zasad Współżycia Społecznego' (1957) 4/5 *Państwo i Prawo*, 802 ; Agnieszka Malarewicz-Jakubów, 'Klauzule Generalne i Zasady Słuszności' (2014) 17 *Białostockie Studia Prawnicze*, 145; Jan Mojak, 'Dobre Obyczaje w polskim prawie kontraktowym – wybrane zagadnienia' (2016) XXV. *Studia Iuridica Lublinensia*, 2, 161; Farshad Ghodoosei, 'The Concept of Public Policy in Law: Revisiting the Role of the Public Policy Doctrine in the Enforcement of Private Legal Arrangements' (2016) 94 *Nebraska Law Review*, 3, 685; Catherine Kessedjian, 'Public Order in European Law' (2007) 1 *Erasmus Law Review*, 1, 25; Heinrich Honsell, 'Die zivilrechtliche Sanktion der Sittenwidrigkeit' (1975) 30 *Juristen Zeitung*, 439; Gerhard Schricker, *Gesetzesverletzung und Sittenverstoß* (München: Beck, 1970); Gunther Teubner, *Standards und Direktiven in Generalklauseln* (Tübingen: Athenäum, 1971).

39 Ibid.

40 CJEU, Case C-126/97, *Eco Swiss China Time Ltd v. Benetton International NV*, ECLI:EU:C:1999:269, paras. 36–37 reads 'according to … Article 3(1)(g) EC, Article 81 EC [now Article 101 TFEU] … constitutes a fundamental provision which is essential for the accomplishment of the tasks entrusted to the Community and, in particular, for the functioning of the internal market. … It follows that where its domestic rules of procedure require a national court to grant an application for annulment of an arbitration award where such an application is founded on failure to observe national rules of *public policy*, it must also grant such an application where it is founded on failure to comply with the prohibition laid down in Article 85(1) of the Treaty'.

41 On the application of the public policy concept to competition law, see, for instance, Damien Geradin, 'Public Policy and Breach of Competition Law in International Arbitration: A Competition Law Practitioner's Viewpoint' (2016) 29 *TILEC Discussion Paper*, 1 *et seq*.

5.1.5.1 Liability Sharing Agreements Are Part of an Anticompetitive Agreement

The main allegation against LSAs is that they are in fact anticompetitive agreements and thus null and void under Article 101(2) of TFEU.[42] The following paragraphs verify this claim.

It can be asked whether LSAs can be themselves considered as anticompetitive agreements. The answer is negative. Anticompetitive agreements are agreements that have as an object or effect the prevention, restriction or distortion of competition.[43] Although there is no definition of what competition is, it is generally believed that it is the process by which commercial entities strive for customers.[44] Liability sharing agreements do not deal with such a process. Their object is legal liability and its distribution among those on which it has been imposed. This means that LSAs cannot prevent, restrict or distort competition and, because of that, fall outside Article 101(1) of TFEU.

Another way of looking at LSAs is to consider that although they are not inherently anticompetitive agreements, they are a part of a mechanism that enforces them and thus are null and void under Article 101(2) of TFEU.[45] Such an interpretation could be considered given the *AC-Treuhand* judgment.[46] The CJEU concluded that Article 101(1) of TFEU was breached by a company that was not present on the market in which the infringement occurred but was a consultancy firm that organised and helped enforce the cartel.[47] The case of LSAs is, however, different from the case of cartel enforcement agreements. Liability sharing agreements do not aim at enforcing anticompetitive violations, but they deal merely with the reality that *follows* the moment when the infringement has been established, has ceased and the legal liability for it has been imposed.

Finally, it may be claimed that LSAs may become a tool to commit antitrust infringements. Under the pretext of determining liability, negotiating parties may in fact exchange commercially sensitive information such as their turnover, pricing or

[42] Weinhold, *Der Gesamtschuldnerausgleich*, 144–145.

[43] David Bailey and Laura Elizabeth John, *Bellamy and Child: European Union Law of Competition* (Oxford: Oxford University Press, 2018), para. 2.085.

[44] Ibid., para. 2.086.

[45] The so-called consequential agreements or *Ausführungsverträge*. See CJEU, Case C-9/93, *IHT Internationale Heiztechnik GmbH and Uwe Danzinger v. Ideal-Standard GmbH and Wabco Standard GmbH*, ECLI:EU:C:1994:261, para. 59; CJEU, Case 28/77, *Tepea BV. v. Commission of the European Communities*, ECLI:EU:C:1978:133, para. 33; Komninos, *EC Private Antitrust Enforcement*, 157–158.

[46] CJEU, Case C-194/14 P, *AC-Treuhand AG v. European Commission*, ECLI:EU:C:2015:717 ('*AC-Treuhand*').

[47] GCEU, Case T-27/10, *AC-Treuhand AG v. European Commission*, ECLI:EU:T:2014:59, paras. 127–128 and CJEU, *AC-Treuhand*, paras. 35–39. Describing and criticizing such an operation Advocate General Wahl in his Opinion in Case C-194/14 P, *AC-Treuhand AG v. European Commission*, ECLI:EU:C:2015:717, paras. 61–76.

volumes. The parties may also try to use LSAs not only to divide existing or future liability but also to reach a wider arrangement and divide markets. Nonetheless, anticompetitive exchanges are not necessary elements of LSAs. Liability sharing agreements can become only a veil under which the anticompetitive agreement is concluded. If an LSA is inseverable with an anticompetitive agreement, it is null and void under Article 101(2) of TFEU. However, this cannot lead to finding that LSAs should be generally prohibited.

In conclusion, LSAs are not anticompetitive agreements by themselves as they do not relate to competition on any specific product market. In addition, they cannot be generally considered as agreements that enforce anticompetitive practices or a tool to undertake them. In principle, LSAs should be allowed as they fall outside Article 101(1) of TFEU.

5.1.5.2 Liability Sharing Agreements Stabilise Cartels

Even if LSAs are not considered as anticompetitive agreements, the argument continues that they may have a positive influence on cartels as they can stabilise them.

The cartel stabilisation claim relies on the assumption that trust between cartelists is a key element that allows for creating and maintaining cartels.[48] Christopher R. Leslie demonstrates that this trust is undermined by two mechanisms existing in US law: the public leniency programme[49] and sweetheart settlements[50] (the so-called 'private leniency programme'). Both leniency programmes allow antitrust infringers to be exempted from a part of private law liability[51] if they reveal antitrust activity and provide evidence that can be used against other antitrust infringers. The possibility of being partially exempted from private law liability creates a scenario similar to that present in the prisoner's dilemma. All cartelists are better off if they conceal the cartel. However, each of them is tempted to dismantle the cartel in order to benefit from the exemption from liability. Christopher R. Leslie claims that LSAs disrupt this scenario. Thanks to them, the future liability of cartelists is divided upfront and the reward that cartelists are offered in leniency programmes becomes meaningless as it will be shared between co-conspirators. On this basis, Christopher R. Leslie claims that by jeopardising the two leniency mechanisms, LSAs in fact stabilise cartels.[52]

[48] Leslie, 'Judgment-Sharing Agreements', 781.

[49] Ibid. See Section 4.2.3.2.

[50] Ibid. See Section 2.1.3.3.

[51] What is relevant in the case of the cartel stabilisation argument is only the liability for private law damages (and not public law sanctions). Liability sharing agreements consider only private law damages and not public law sanctions and can jeopardise only the discount that is given in the context of private antitrust enforcement.

[52] Leslie, 'Judgment-Sharing Agreements', 781 *et seq.*

This argument, although true in the US context, is likely to be invalid in the European Union.[53] This is because the EU lacks any leniency programmes akin to those discussed by Christopher R. Leslie.

Christopher R. Leslie speaks about two mechanisms that give cartelists a discount in their private law liability. The ACPERA gives leniency applicants a privilege in terms of criminal liability, the exemption from joint and several liability, and the reduction of treble damages to single ones.[54] Sweetheart settlements allow antitrust infringers to settle for a symbolic amount or an amount that is much lower than the liability that would have been established by the courts.[55] These two mechanisms give those who decide to reveal cartels generous reductions from expected private law liability. By contrast, in the European Union, there are no mechanisms that can give cartelists a comparable privilege in terms of private law liability.

As Section 4.2.3 demonstrates, public leniency programmes have been only minimally expanded in the course of private antitrust enforcement reform. In principle, leniency applicants can be exempted only from public law sanctions and are still liable for their private law liabilities. The privilege principally given by Directive 2014/104 is the reduction of immunity recipients' liability from the liability reflecting their relative responsibility for the infringement to the liability that they have towards their own direct and indirect contractors.[56] The difference between the regular share of liability and the liability limited to the damage made to direct and indirect contractors depends on the criterion used to divide the liability. It can be minimal or even non-existent if the value of sales, illicit gains or market shares criteria are used to determine relative responsibility for the infringement. Even if other criteria are adopted, such as fault, causation or *pro capita* division, it is still questionable whether the discount is sufficient to ensure an effective leniency programme (see Section 4.2.3). If there is no sufficient reward regarding private law liability, it is unlikely that the prisoner's dilemma setting would be created. A logical consequence of it is that LSAs cannot disturb a non-existing setting and in this way stabilise cartels.

Also, private leniency is unlikely to occur in the European Union. In the United States, it is common that those suffering antitrust damages settle for a low amount

[53] Adopting Christopher R. Leslie's argument in the EU context Krüger, *Kartellregress*, 158; Dreher, 'Die Haftungsverteilung', 156.

[54] Leslie, 'Judgment-Sharing Agreements', 781 *et seq*. See also Section 4.2.3.2.

[55] See Ibid.

[56] Directive 2014/104/EU introduced two modifications. In the external aspect, an immunity recipient is primarily liable to its direct and indirect purchasers/providers. Internally, contribution claims are generally capped to the damages sustained by the direct and indirect purchasers, regardless of the liability for umbrella claims. The privilege in the external aspect of liability does not decide about the final amount of liability that the immunity recipient bears but decides only who can bring forward claims for damages. As a result, the privilege regarding the external aspect of joint and several liability is not discussed here. For a relevant discussion of this aspect of leniency programmes, see Section 4.2.

with the first defendant in order to get evidence that they can use against other infringers. The amount of settlement is reduced from already trebled damages and not before detrebling, so the creditor's goal is to bring at least one antitrust infringement to the trial. The difference between damages paid by those who settled first and the infringer who was brought to trial is large and creates the so-called race to settle (see Section 2.1.3.3). This effect is unlikely to occur in the European Union. Since there are no treble damages, the assessment of liability is made with reference to the same benchmark – single damages – both in the courts and in settlements. Consequently, the difference between the settlement and the damages awarded by the court is likely to be much smaller in the European Union than in the United States (see also Section 4.1.4.3). The discount achieved in settlements is also unlikely to be larger because of the evidence that the creditor can possibly obtain from the settling debtor. In the European Union, many private actions for damages are follow-on claims[57] and creditors rely on the findings made by an antitrust agency.[58] Since the discount achieved in settlements does not seem to be the game changer, it is unlikely that private leniency programmes would appear. As indicated in the paragraph above, if a leniency programme is ineffective, LSAs cannot jeopardise it and in this way stabilise cartels.

Comparison between EU and US leniency programmes demonstrates that the cartel stabilisation argument has a different value in the EU and US contexts. In the current state of law, it is unlikely that EU leniency programmes will create the prisoner's dilemma, which could be possibly disrupted by LSAs. The cartel stabilisation argument is based on the premise that a sufficient discount is offered in private law liability. If this assumption falls away, the entire argument falls. Consequently, the cartel stabilisation argument should not be currently used to deny LSAs the validity in the European Union.

5.1.5.3 Liability Sharing Agreements Weaken Deterrence

Another reason to oppose LSAs is that they allegedly reduce the deterrent effect of antitrust liability. This argument was also formulated by Christopher R. Leslie and has been accepted in the EU context.[59]

First, Christopher R. Leslie claims that the 'sanction is reduced' due to LSAs. This is achieved through a division of overall liability (i)[60] and through a possibility to reduce the overall liability (ii).[61] The first effect shall now be illustrated. If the

[57] See note 215 in Chapter 2.

[58] See Article 9 of Directive 2014/104/EU.

[59] Leslie, 'Judgment-Sharing Agreements', 785 *et seq*. See also Weinhold, *Der Gesamtschuldnerausgleich*, 145; Krüger, *Kartellregress*, 158; Bieber, *Die gesamtschuldnerische Haftung*, 111.

[60] Ibid., 796–797.

[61] Ibid., 796.

liability for three entities held jointly and severally liable is 100, each of them can be called to pay 100 by the creditor. Given that in the United States there is no contribution, each infringer can be ultimately liable for 100. If expected profits from the infringement are 40 for each antitrust violator, it is unlikely that they would decide to enter into anticompetitive practice.[62] Liability sharing agreements change this calculation as they lower the maximal amount for which each antitrust infringer will be ultimately liable. Going back to the example above, if it is assumed that there is an LSA that stipulates that each antitrust infringer is liable for 33.(3), such a liability is not sufficient to prevent the violation that brings a profit of 40 to each wrongdoer. Regarding the second effect, Christopher R. Leslie argues that because each infringer has already assessed what its individual liability is, each of them is less likely to engage in the race to settle. This leads to a smaller aggregate value of settlements.[63]

Second, Christopher R. Leslie states that 'the probability of being held liable' for antitrust infringements drops with LSAs (iii). He relies on the cartel stabilisation argument and demonstrates that by having a negative impact on leniency, LSAs decrease the chances that anticompetitive agreements would be discovered and sanctioned.[64]

Finally, Christopher R. Leslie indicates that LSAs eliminate an element of 'uncertainty' regarding antitrust liability, which allows the conducting of a cost–benefit analysis with greater certainty than without such agreements (iv).[65]

Similarly as in the case of previous arguments, the interference between deterrence and LSAs must be looked at through the lens of EU competition law. This is in order to verify whether deterrence understood in the context of US law has the same meaning in EU law.

The first factor that LSAs are claimed to influence is the size of the sanction (i). In the European Union, the size of the sanction can also be influenced by division amongst multiple entities via the LSAs. As a result, it is at least *prima facie* possible that LSAs reduce the amount of liability of individual companies by spreading the antitrust fine amongst multiple entities. Although this is true, this argument has no effect in EU public competition law enforcement given that even without LSAs the Commission cannot provide for individual deterrence when applying joint and several liability. Section 2.1.2.1 above demonstrates that this is because joint and several debtors can choose which of them will pay the Commission's fine voluntarily. In order to provide for individual deterrence, the Commission must thus fine companies individually. If the Commission insists on imposing joint and several liability on several companies, it needs to be assumed that it also considers

[62] In this example, the impact of the probability of being held liable is disregarded.
[63] Leslie, 'Judgment-Sharing Agreements', 796.
[64] Ibid.
[65] Ibid., 800.

deterrence as achieved when entities held jointly and severally liable are treated as a collective. In such a scenario, LSAs have no influence on deterrence as it is achieved, regardless of which company ultimately bears liability and in which amount. What matters is that the collective as a whole satisfies the liability established by the Commission. Liability sharing agreements should be allowed in public antitrust enforcement on this basis.

As regards private antitrust enforcement, LSAs in theory can also jeopardise the deterrence of national judgments establishing private law liabilities for antitrust infringements. As Christopher R. Leslie explains, LSAs divide antitrust liability between several entities and therefore reduce the size of liability for each infringer. This argument, however, loses its validity if we consider the approach of the EU lawmaker towards deterrence in private law enforcement. Most fundamentally, in the European Union, deterrence is not achieved by the manipulation of the amount of liability. Any multiple and punitive damages are prohibited, and damages granted in private lawsuits need to exactly reflect the damage sustained by victims of antitrust violations. Deterrence is therefore achieved by the increase in detection and law enforcement rather than an imposition of liability on top of compensation.[66] While LSAs can indeed decrease the amount of the ultimate private law liability of an antitrust infringer, this does not interfere with this understanding of deterrence. In fact, LSAs can increase detection and law enforcement, which are paramount in the European Union. Pursuant to such agreements, those who so far escaped private law liability will also contribute to the payment of damages to those harmed by their actions. This undoubtedly increases the detection element of deterrence. Even if decreasing the size of sanctions is insisted upon in LSAs, this does not mean that they should be prohibited. Directive 2014/104/EU allows for contribution claims that reduce the size of private liability exactly in the same way LSAs do.[67] If the latter are allowed, there is no reason to reject LSAs.

This conclusion only holds true if LSAs are concluded between those held jointly and severally liable by the Commission. Spreading liability on a company not indicated by the Commission would interfere with its choice of those who need to bear liability and will reduce the amount of sanctions. This is due to the involvement of an additional entity with which the burden of the fine can be shared. Such a situation would inevitably reflect the problem discussed here and should be prohibited.

A second factor that works against LSAs is that they can reduce the size of the sanction due to a reduced number of settlements (ii). Such an argument has no place in the context of public antitrust enforcement. Public law liability is imposed exclusively by the Commission and national competition authorities. The

66 See Section 2.1.1.2.
67 See Article 11(5) of Directive 2014/104/EU.

settlements in their private law meaning are not part of this enforcement system.[68] The amount of antitrust fines is at the full discretion of the competition authority, which sets it on the basis of various criteria that are in no relation to LSAs (see Section 2.1.1.1). In private enforcement of EU competition law, LSAs are also unlikely to endanger settlements. First and foremost, in the European Union, there is no race to settle that LSAs could possibly eliminate. The impact of LSAs on settlements and thus the size of the sanction is not the same in the United States and in the European Union. Second, LSAs could in fact increase settlements in the European Union. Currently, settlements are not as frequent in the European Union as they are in the United States. The lack of a fixed legal criterion according to which the relative liability is established makes antirust infringers virtually unable to assess their liabilities and, on that basis, conclude settlements. By allowing LSAs, settlements could be actually increased. Antitrust infringers would have an effective tool to determine their shares of liability among themselves, which would make it easier for them to start to negotiate individual settlement agreements with victims of antitrust infringements.

The second and third factors that influence deterrence are the probability of being held liable (iii) and the reduction of certainty of who is going to be held liable (iv), which Christopher R. Leslie analyses on the basis of weakened leniency programmes. The argument relating to leniency programmes is inapplicable in the context of joint and several liability imposed in public antitrust enforcement. Leniency programmes are exclusively used in the case of cartels and are in no relation to the Commission's practice of fining companies on the basis of corporate and economic links that exist between them.[69] It is the Commission that determines the addressees of its decisions, and those fined have no influence on the Commission's choice.[70] Liability sharing agreements cannot impact the way the Commission decides who is liable, and they cannot give any security to who is going to be called by the Commission to be liable. Christopher R. Leslie's arguments are also not valid with respect to European private antitrust enforcement. As explained with respect to deterrence and settlements, LSAs in the European setting are likely to increase detection and the number of entities that are held liable for antitrust infringements. The increase in certainty is also a desired effect in the European Union given its positive impact on settlements. As there is no race to settle and

[68] Public enforcement provides for settlements, but they are considered a specific type of administrative procedure. For the settlement procedure, see, for instance, Kris Dekeyser and Christian Roques, 'The European Commission's Settlement Procedure in Cartel Cases' (2010) 55 *The Antitrust Bulletin*, 4, 819 *et seq.*; Kai Hüschelrath and Ulrich Laitenberger, 'The Settlement Procedure in the European Commission's Cartel Cases: An Early Evaluation' (2017) 5 *Journal of Antitrust Enforcement*, 3, 458.

[69] Para. 1 of 2006 Notice on Leniency.

[70] See notes 88–90 in Chapter 2.

therefore no private law leniency program in the European Union, the increased certainty on who is going to be held liable does not lead to negative externalities.

This analysis demonstrates that although the idea that LSAs weaken deterrence is intuitively appealing, this argument does not hold if applied rigorously in the framework of EU competition law enforcement. This justifies why the CJEU was not hesitant to acknowledge LSAs in the context of public antitrust enforcement. When private antitrust enforcement is concerned, the argument that LSAs would endanger deterrence is missed from the very beginning, as such a function is not envisaged in private antitrust enforcement. As a result, there are no deterrence-related obstacles that would prevent using LSAs.

5.1.5.4 Liability Sharing Agreements Have a Negative Influence on Settlements

Another claim against LSAs is that they reduce settlements. This argument has also been expressed with respect to the US framework.

According to the literature on US antitrust law, the effects of LSAs on settlements are five-fold. First, LSAs eliminate the race to settle (i).[71] They reduce the risk that a debtor may be called to pay treble damages for the entire damage by spreading the liability among all parties concluding the agreement. As the ultimate amount of liability is decided in the LSA, the moment in which settlements are concluded becomes irrelevant and thus the likelihood of a race to settle decreases dramatically. Second, LSAs can eliminate sweetheart settlements (ii).[72] The share of liability that each debtor is to bear is determined in the LSA. As a result, the advantages of concluding a sweetheart settlement are not kept by the entities concluding them but are spread according to the formula set in the LSA. This could discourage settling parties from giving the evidence against other co-debtors as a trade-off in order to conclude such deals. Third, LSAs can reduce the value of initial settlements by eliminating full settlements (iii).[73] One of the reasons is that LSAs clearly establish what the relative shares of the various debtors' liability are. This makes them likely to negotiate the settlement for only their own part of liability. Fourth, LSAs frequently include carve-out provisions that complicate negotiating the settlement (iv).[74] A carve-out guarantees that the creditor will not seek damages from non-settling

[71] Leslie, 'Judgment-Sharing Agreements', 769; Cavanagh, 'Contribution, Claim Reduction', 1327; Riemer, 'Sharing Agreements', 29.

[72] Leslie, 'Judgment-Sharing Agreements', 769, Riemer, 'Sharing Agreements', 29.

[73] Leslie, 'Judgment-Sharing Agreements', 770.

[74] Ibid., 771; Stephens Clay A. in 'Antitrust Damage Allocation. Hearings before the Subcommittee on Monopolies and Commercial Law of the Committee on the Judiciary' (1983 House of Representatives 118), 7. In the same line but putting emphasis on the unwillingness of creditors to settle with carve-outs, Riemer, 'Sharing Agreements', 306–307.

debtors with respect to the settling debtor's sales.[75] This is another element that needs to be negotiated in addition to the settlement amount, which complicates the entire negotiation process and makes it more difficult to reach an offer that satisfies both the terms of the LSA and the creditor's needs. Lastly, by reducing the size of the potential liability from treble damages to the liability share established in the LSA and complicating the process of concluding settlements, the incentives to conclude settlements decrease (v).[76]

Not all reasons expressed in the US literature are applicable in the EU context. Most essentially, it is unlikely that the phenomenon of the race to settle (i) and sweetheart settlements would occur in the European Union (see Section 4.1.4.3) (ii).

Additionally, the loss in the incentives to settle is much smaller in the European Union than in the United States (v). Currently, in the European Union, most settlements are likely to be only partial (iii) and include carve-out provisions (iv). This is because the rules regulating settlements in EU competition law provide for a comparable set of conditions to those brought in the United States by LSAs. The current law on settlements has in mind only partial settlements that are concluded with respect to the settling debtor's relative share of liability (see Section 4.1.4.2) and which lead to proportionate claim reduction (see Section 4.1.3). Such rules have the same effects as carve-out provisions and imply that in every settlement, parties must consider which share of the damage is included in the settlement and which sum corresponds to it. The problems mentioned in the United States will thus concern every settlement negotiated within the EU framework, regardless of whether there is an LSA or not.

In fact, the effect of LSAs on settlements can be positive in the EU setting. Given that the parties negotiating the settlement can strongly disagree on what the relative share of liability is (see Section 4.1.4), LSAs allow negotiating parties to have a clear view on the relative liability. This can enhance settlement negotiations as it provides the parties with some benchmark concerning their liability.

As a result, the arguments regarding the risk that LSAs pose to settlements are not equally valid in the United States and in the European Union. Due to different antitrust enforcement regimes, LSAs have very different impacts on the effectiveness of antitrust law in these two jurisdictions. Although it may seem counterintuitive, LSAs have positive effects on settlements in the European Union. They provide the negotiating parties with intelligence and information on the determination of the relative shares of liability subjected to the settlement. From the settlements' standpoint, LSAs should be welcomed.

[75] Section of Antitrust Law of the American Bar Association, *Contribution and Claim Reduction*, 19; Leslie, 'Judgment-Sharing Agreements' 770.

[76] Leslie, 'Judgment-Sharing Agreements', 771; Harold E. Kohn in 'Antitrust Damage Allocation. Hearings before the Subcommittee on Monopolies and Commercial Law of the Committee on the Judiciary' (1983 House of Representatives 118), 93.

5.1.6 *Conclusions*

The investigation of the arguments expressed against LSAs indicates that most of them have no place in the EU legal order. As such, LSAs cannot be considered anticompetitive agreements, have minimal impact on stabilising cartels, do not weaken deterrence and have a positive rather than negative impact on settlements. As a result, such agreements do not run against public policy and other general clauses that are present in national legal orders. In light of this, LSAs should generally be allowed.

5.2 PRECAUTIONS THAT NEED TO BE CONSIDERED WHILE CONCLUDING LIABILITY SHARING AGREEMENTS

Although LSAs should be generally admissible, the analysis undertaken above has indicated that they may be invalid under certain specific circumstances. In this light, it is important that companies envisaging LSAs acknowledge several limitations.

5.2.1 *In Which Cases Can LSAs Be Concluded?*

Liability sharing agreements can be concluded both in the context of public and private antitrust enforcement. In principle, they can be used for liability stemming from various types of anticompetitive agreements.

An exception to this principle may arise in the future for cartels, should effective leniency programmes exist. Due to the negative effect that LSAs have on leniency programmes, their use prior to the discovery of cartels may be excluded. Although this is currently not the case due to a minimal interference that exists between LSAs and current leniency programmes, this interference might be sufficient for the judges enforcing LSAs to hold such agreements in breach of Article 101(1) of TFEU.

5.2.2 *Who Can Conclude Liability Sharing Agreements?*

Liability sharing agreements are considered in this study only as a means to provide for contribution.[77] As a consequence, they should be enforced only if their parties are those who are jointly and severally liable for an antitrust infringement. In public

[77] Liability sharing agreements may also be considered risk sharing agreements or some kind of insurance, see, for instance, Leslie, 'Judgment-Sharing Agreements', 749; Jing Liu and Michael Faure, 'Risk-Sharing Agreements to Cover Environmental Damage: Theory and Practice' (2018) 18 *International Environmental Agreements: Politics, Law and Economics*, 2, 255 *et seq.*; Pedro Pita Barros, 'The Simple Economics of Risk-Sharing Agreements between the NHS and the Pharmaceutical Industry' (2011) 20 *Health Economics*, 4, 461 *et seq.*

antitrust enforcement, this would mean an agreement between the mother company or holding company and its subsidiary, or the seller and the acquirer of the business that infringed EU competition law. In private antitrust enforcement, LSAs can be concluded by the parties of an anticompetitive agreement.

It is not advisable to conclude LSAs with the entities that have not been held jointly and severally liable. This applies particularly in the context of public antitrust enforcement. The reason is that one of the priorities of public antitrust enforcement is deterrence. If another entity than the one identified by the Commission carries the ultimate burden of antitrust sanctions, this influences both the size of the sanction imposed by the Commission and the identification of who is liable for paying it. A liability sharing agreement involving an external party would contradict the decision on fines, the effectiveness of EU competition law and the Commission's decision on how to guarantee it. A liability sharing agreement would also change its character from an agreement on the distribution of relative liability between joint and several debtors to a risk-spreading or even an insurance agreement.[78]

5.2.3 *When Can Liability Sharing Agreements Be Concluded?*

The conclusion of LSAs can generally take place *before* and *after* the liability materialises. In the first case, LSAs consider potential liability. In the second case, they consider a liability that is about to be established or has already been established by the Commission, a court or by a consensual method of dispute resolution.

Those envisioning LSAs must realise that concluding them is much easier before than after the liability has materialised. It is very difficult to align their positions if a concrete liability has been already established. It is thus recommended to conclude LSAs before the liability has materialised.

Nonetheless, entering into LSAs at an early stage may also lead to some uncertainty. First, it has been demonstrated above that if such an agreement is concluded in the case of cartels, it can be unenforceable due to its effect on leniency programmes. Second, in the public enforcement context, it is difficult to define the entities that are likely to be held jointly and severally liable for the fine by the Commission. While it is easy to conclude LSAs between the seller and acquirer of the business that could trigger antitrust liability, it is more difficult to say which concrete companies within a single economic entity may be held liable for antitrust infringements.[79] As a result, some general clauses or conditions can be used to establish the parties to the LSA.

78 See Ibid.

79 See notes 88–90 in Chapter 2.

5.2.4 *How to Conclude Liability Sharing Agreements?*

As indicated in Section 5.1.5.1, there is a risk that LSAs could become a cover for anticompetitive agreements. It is thus necessary that LSAs deal exclusively with the question of the method to determine relative liabilities for a given potential antitrust liability. For instance, the LSA should principally focus on statements similar to this one:

> with respect to joint and several liability, the parties agree to individually bear a share of liability that is established on the basis of their shares in the market concerned in the agreement.

Special attention must be paid to any forward-looking statements that do not relate to the problem of liability. For instance, it is unacceptable to determine relative liability as a basis of dividing markets. This is clearly an anticompetitive agreement that is in breach of Article 101(1) of TFEU.

When negotiating the quota or benchmark that would be used to establish relative liability, the parties must be cautious not to reveal information that is commercially sensitive. The current data on turnover, profits and market shares may allow other companies to discover the involved companies' competitive strategies and align their behaviour accordingly.[80] The exchange of sensitive information is considered a breach of Article 101(1) of TFEU.

Finally, the parties must account for the question of the severability of LSAs from a broader anticompetitive agreement.[81] Severability is a matter of national law on the validity of contracts and cannot be discussed here.[82] It is nonetheless advised that the parties to an LSA approach the issue of severability proactively and ensure, in compliance with national laws, that LSAs are treated separately from a given antitrust agreement.

5.3 CONCLUSIONS

Liability sharing agreements have the potential to resolve the problems connected with complex and uncertain court enforcement of the right to claim contribution in antitrust. They should thus be allowed.

[80] On illegal exchange of information between competitors, see, for instance, OECD, 'Roundtable on Information Exchanges between Competitors under Competition Law, Note by the Delegation of the European Union' (27–28 October 2010) DAF/COMP/WD(2010)118; Kai-Uwe Kühn, *Information Exchanges among Firms and Their Impact on Competition* (Luxembourg: Official Publications of the European Communities, 1995); Daivis Švirinas, 'The Assessment of Information Exchange Agreements between Competitors from the Perspective of Competition Law of the EU and of the Republic of Lithuania' (2012) 19 *Jurisprudencija*, 1, 87.

[81] See Weinhold, *Der Gesamtschuldnerausgleich*, 144–145.

[82] CJEU, Case 319/82, *Kerpen and Kerpen*, ECLI:EU:C:1983:374, para. 11.

This must be done, however, within certain limitations dictated by compliance with the Commission's fining decisions and public policy rules. It is advised to conclude LSAs only under the condition that the parties to the agreement are jointly and severally liable for antitrust infringement; to conclude them before the antitrust liability has materialised; to limit the content of the agreement to the issue of dividing potential liability; and to prevent the exchange of commercially sensitive information.

Whilst LSAs should have a place in the contribution law framework, it remains a question of the future whether such agreements will enter into antitrust practice and be positively recognised by judges.

6

Conclusions and Recommendations

6.1 CONCLUSIONS DE LEGE LATA

Twelve years ago, Carsten Krüger stated that the complexity of contribution claims in antitrust and problems with their enforcement in Germany would make the right to contribution illusory.[1] This research has proven that the problems present in German law are ongoing. In addition, they are common to the law of at least three other EU Member States. In addition, these problems are not limited to private antitrust enforcement but are similarly valid for public antitrust enforcement. The investigation undertaken here demonstrates that the exercise of contribution claims is currently a complex and uncertain task, which may lead to an effective unenforceability of the right to claim contribution in antitrust.

Such a state is undesirable from the perspective of EU law that clearly supports the right to claim contribution in antitrust. It has been, however, established that the right to claim contribution is an EU policy choice rather than an automatic consequence of the fact that joint and several liability applies. This is because the external aspect of joint and several liability – a creditor's right to call any of the debtors to pay the fine or antitrust damages –is independent from the internal aspect of joint and several liability: claims for contribution that the debtors have against each other after having paid the debt.

The investigation has demonstrated that these two aspects of joint and several liability interfere differently with competition law. While the external effects of joint and several liability increase the effectiveness of EU competition law, the internal aspect of it – which encompasses contribution claims – has a limited impact on this principle. The principal reason is that the effectiveness of EU competition law is guaranteed before the contribution litigation has even started. As a result, it is justified that the European Commission's mandate to enforce competition law does

[1] Krüger, *Kartellregress*, 323.

not cover questions of the internal division of liability between joint and several debtors and that this matter is dealt with by national laws. Limiting interference between EU competition law and contribution claims leaves a lot of room for EU Member States to design the system of contribution in antitrust. This is restricted only by compliance with the Commission's decisions establishing antitrust liability and the principles of equivalence and efficiency.

It has been demonstrated that competition law challenges the traditional way of dealing with contribution claims. This is because of the complexity of antitrust law, different methods of enforcement and the potentially massive amount of contribution litigation. The attempt to apply a traditional legal framework to deal with such cases results in a very complex and uncertain litigation. In many legal orders, there are multiple legal bases and types of contribution claims. Some of them, such *as quiet time injunctions* in England and *Mitwirkung* and *Befreiung* claims in Germany, are unacceptable from the standpoint of the principle of effectiveness of EU competition law. In addition, national rules on contribution are often general rules that do not accommodate the needs of competition law. Even though there are positive developments in this respect, such as the adoption of a specific legal basis to claim contribution in antitrust in France, the relationship between modifications concerning competition law and general rules on contribution is unsettled. In addition, the most critical aspect of litigating contribution – the criteria used to apportion liability – are unsettled and not tailored to competition law. The jurisdictions that have been covered by this study provide for an open-ended catalogue of possible criteria and a large margin of discretion in deciding about their application. Such an approach is unacceptable in the context of antitrust as it may lead to incoherent results in which contribution liabilities stemming from the same factual set would be determined differently. The risk of incoherence was already observed by Justice Peter Roth: 'More claims are being brought on a weekly basis ... The question is not simply what is the "just and appropriate" way to handle the cases ... There are parallel issues across most of these claims ... [the objective should be to] achieve consistent outcomes. ... We need to be fair to all parties ... the CAT may need to take an "innovative" path to address issues heard in court'.[2]

Directive 2014/104/EU adds another level of complexity and uncertainty by introducing special regimes for joint and several liability. If one of the co-debtors receives immunity from fines, is an SME or has settled the creditor's claim in a consensual way, special rules on joint and several liability apply. These rules are different for each of these groups, and many questions on their practical application are raised. It is particularly questionable whether the reduction in the size of the liability for immunity recipients is sufficient, if complex rules on contribution are

[2] Simon Zekaria, 'Truck Cartel Disclosure "Slow" and "Difficult", UK Claimant Ryder Tells Competition Judge' (6 February 2020), *Mlex*, available at https://mlex.com/GlobalAdvisory/DetailView.aspx?cid=1160838&siteid=244&rdir=1.

justified, how to apply the rules on subsidiary liability and how to conclude settlements without having a clear benchmark of the relative liability determined by law.

Finally, the complexities of claiming contribution before national courts can be in theory avoided by concluding liability sharing agreements. Unfortunately, the opinion of the majority of scholars is that such agreements interfere with the current antitrust policy. If concluded before the antitrust liability materialises, such agreements are claimed to be a part of anticompetitive agreements or at least to stabilise cartels, weaken deterrence and have a negative impact on settlements. This position limits the potential that liability sharing agreements have in providing for a simple and efficient way of dealing with contribution.

In sum, the framework for contribution claims in antitrust is still in its early development. There is much insecurity related to substantive law on contribution. This may be a determining factor for a company's decision whether to engage or not in contribution litigation. In practice, it can mean that contribution claims will rarely be enforced. Since EU law is clear about providing the right to claim contribution in antitrust, this is an unacceptable situation. As a result, legislative intervention according to the solutions proposed below is needed.

6.2 CONCLUSIONS DE LEGE FERENDA

It is proposed that EU Member States adopt a special legal framework tailored to the needs of contribution claims in antitrust law.

First, it is advised to clearly state that antitrust infringers have the right to claim contribution in the context of EU competition law. Such a right does not interfere with the principle of effectiveness of EU competition law. It is limited only by the Commission's decision establishing antitrust infringement and the principles of effectiveness and equivalence.

Second, it is encouraged to adopt a simple unitary framework for contribution claims in antitrust. In order to achieve this, it is proposed to apply the same general rules for both contribution claims in public and private enforcement of EU competition law. Rules on contribution should be based on one type of claim in the form of a personal right to claim contribution. The right to claim contribution should be available as a partial contribution or indemnity, without introducing any separation between these two types of claims. This right should become available at the moment when the debtor pays a part of a debt exceeding its own share of liability. Any earlier exercise of such a right should be prohibited as interfering with the principle of effectiveness of EU competition law.

The criterion for determining internal liability should be based on a limited number of factors. A two-pillar rule is suggested. The primary rule should be division according to market shares. This criterion is objective and leads to coherent results if contribution is sought in many separate proceedings. It also is manageable. This criterion would find common application in most cases of private enforcement of EU competition law. A subsidiary rule is based on the principle of fault. This rule will apply in all cases in which market shares cannot be used. This is the case of vertical agreements and public enforcement. In the latter context, the criterion of fault is particularly valuable as it can remedy the Commission's sometimes unjustified fining policy. In order to limit legal uncertainty and incoherence of judgments adopted by different courts, this strict formula should always be applied, and no other criteria for apportioning liability should be used.

Furthermore, it is proposed to simplify the regimes of special joint and several liability. First, the privileged regime for SMEs must be abandoned as it complicates the system of liability without adequate justification. Second, clear rules on contribution should be provided with respect to immunity recipients and those engaged in consensual dispute resolution. Regarding immunity recipients, the rule that in the external dimension they are liable only to their own direct and indirect contractors should be maintained as it protects them from massive lawsuits. It should, however, be clearly stated that leniency applicants are indemnified internally. No subsidiary liability should be adopted. Regarding consensual dispute resolution, subsidiary liability should be avoided as well as it could jeopardise settlements. In addition, settlements should be recognised both in their partial and full forms. Furthermore, adopting a clear criterion for dividing liability according to market shares and fault should provide for clear benchmarks for discussing settlements and increase their rate.

Finally, liability sharing agreements should be generally allowed and excluded only in strictly limited circumstances. They are the simplest and the most effective tool for securing the right to contribution. Their fundamental advantage is that they guarantee contribution without reliance on public judicial resources. Since antitrust infringers are wrongdoers, this way of securing contribution should be preferred. With the public nature of competition law in mind, only the following limitations to LSAs should be currently considered: LSAs must be concluded exclusively between those jointly and severally liable for the infringement (i), and when negotiating an LSA, the parties must refrain from exchanging commercially sensitive information and deciding on other issues than antitrust liability (ii).

It has been claimed by many that contribution litigation is in itself complex, and it becomes even more challenging in the antitrust context. It is nonetheless hoped that this research clears up many unsupported claims made against the use of contribution in antitrust. It is also hoped that by introducing certain modifications to the traditional framework for contribution claims, such litigation will become simpler and more efficient. If EU Member States succeed in providing for an effective framework for claiming contribution, this could serve as an example for other countries that the contribution rule is feasible and can also be applied to antitrust law.

6.3 LOOKING AHEAD

The problem of contribution is new to competition law, and there are many uncertainties regarding the application of traditional frameworks on contribution in the antitrust context.

Many of the uncertainties described above are likely to be addressed soon due to the increased private enforcement of EU competition law. Claims for damages in the truck cartel are currently at an advanced stage. Many proceedings are taking place before the courts in Germany, the Netherlands and the United Kingdom. Joint and several liability is already used in these cases to direct the enforcement of claims for damages to desired jurisdictions, and some automobile manufacturers are more likely to face antitrust litigation than others. The increased contribution litigation is thus likely to appear with enhanced frequency in the coming years.

Upcoming litigation will give judges an opportunity to set precedents on the interference between EU competition law and contribution claims, as well as the way contribution claims should be enforced. Regarding the latter, judges will have particular control over the criteria that should be used in dealing with contribution in antitrust. It is hoped that this study will assist them in making reasoned choices.

The frequency of contribution claimed in courts will demonstrate how well the existing framework for dealing with contribution performs in the antitrust context. The future litigation will also give evidence about how successful Directive 2014/104/EU was in enhancing settlements and designing the rules protecting immunity recipients and small and medium enterprises. If the number of settlements starts to fall or the number of leniency applications takes a sudden drop, this will give the legislators empirical proof that modifications to the special regimes of joint and several liability are needed.

In light of this, the problem of contribution in antitrust law should continue to be analysed. Once they have had more experience in adjudicating contribution claims, the EU jurisdictions will have an opportunity to develop an efficient framework for dealing with claims for contribution in competition law. This can serve as an example that the right to claim contribution can feasibly apply to antitrust.

***

Bibliography

Aberle, Lukas, *Sanktionsdurchgriff und wirtschaftliche Einheit im deutschen und europäischen Kartellrecht* (Köln: Carl Heymanns Verlag, 2013)

Acton, Michael, 'Pirelli Challenges Cable Cartel Liability at EU's Top Court' (6 November 2019), *Mlex*, available at https://mlex.com/GlobalAdvisory/DetailView.aspx?cid=1140994&siteid=244&rdir=1

Ahrens, Börries, 'Gemeinschaftsunternehmen als wirtschaftliche Einheit' (2013) *Europäische Zeitschrift für Wirtschaftsrecht*, 899, available at https://beck-online.beck.de/Dokument?vpath=bibdata%2Fzeits%2Feuzw%2F2013%2Fcont%2Feuzw.2013.899.1.htm&anchor=Y-300-Z-EUZW-B-2013-S-899-N-1

Andreu, Lionel, *La réforme du régime général des obligations* (Paris: Dalloz, 2011)

Angland, Joseph, 'Joint and Several Liability, Contribution, and Claim Reduction' (2008), available at https://papers.ssrn.com/sol3/papers.cfm?abstract_id=1528007

Antitrust Modernization Commission, 'Report and Recommendations' (2007), available at https://govinfo.library.unt.edu/amc/report_recommendation/amc_final_report.pdf

Antoszek, Tomasz, 'Art. 441' in Maciej Gutowski (ed.), *Duże Komentarze Becka. Kodeks cywilny. Komentarz*, 2 vols. (Warszawa: C.H. Beck, 2016), vol. I

Ashurst, 'Study on the Conditions of Claims for Damages in Case of Infringement of EC Competition Rules' (2004), available at https://ec.europa.eu/competition/antitrust/actionsdamages/comparative_report_clean_en.pdf

Bailey, David, 'United Kingdom' in Pranvera Këllezi, Bruce Kilpatrick and Pierre Kobel (eds.), *Antitrust for Small and Middle Size Undertakings and Image Protection from Non-competitors* (Berlin: Springer, 2014)

Bailey, David and John, Laura Elizabeth, *Bellamy and Child: European Union Law of Competition* (Oxford: Oxford University Press, 2018)

Baker, John, 'The Use of Assumpsit for Restitutionary Money Claims 1600–1800' in Eltjo J. H. Schrage (ed.), *Unjust Enrichment: The Comparative Legal History of the Law of Restitution* (Berlin: Duncker and Humblot, 1999)

Baker, Lynn A., 'Mass Torts and the Pursuit of Ethical Finality' (2017) 85(5) *Fordham Law Review*, 2, 1943

von Bar, Christian and Clive, Eric M. (eds.), *Principles, Definitions and Model Rules of European Private Law. Draft Common Frame of Reference (DCFR)* (München and Oxford: Sellier European Law Publishers and Oxford University Press, 2009/2010)

(eds.), *Principles, Definitions and Model Rules of European Private Law. Draft Common Frame of Reference (DCFR). Full Edition*, 6 vols. (München: Sellier European Law Publishers, 2009), vol. I

Barbier de La Serre, Éric and Lagathu, Eileen, 'The Law on Fines Imposed in EU Competition Proceedings: On the Road to Consistency' (2014) 5 *Journal of European Competition Law and Practice*, 6, 400

Barennes, Marc, 'The Role of the Settlement Procedure and Leniency Programme in the European Commission's Fight against Cartels' in Vesna Tomljenović, Nada Bodiroga-Vukobrat, Vlatka Butorac Malnar and Ivana Kunda (eds.), *EU Competition and State Aid Rules. Europeanization and Globalization* (Berlin and Heidelberg: Springer, 2017)

Bargren, Paul, 'Joint and Several Liability: Protection for Plaintiffs' (1994) *Wisconsin Law Review*, 453

Barker, Kit and Steele, Jenny, 'Drifting towards Proportionate Liability: Ethics and Pragmatics' (2015) 74 *Cambridge Law Journal*, 1, 49

Barros, Pedro Pita, 'The Simple Economics of Risk-Sharing Agreements between the NHS and the Pharmaceutical Industry' (2011) 20 *Health Economics*, 4, 461

Bauer, Günter and Reisner, Nina, 'Erweiterte Zurechnung des Verhaltens Dritter bei der Festsetzung von Geldbußen im EG-Kartellrecht?' (2007) 8 *Wirtschaft und Wettbewerb*, 737

Baxter, William F., 'Antitrust Damage Allocation. Hearings before the Subcommittee on Monopolies and Commercial Law of the Committee on the Judiciary' (1983), House of Representatives 118, available at: https://babel.hathitrust.org/cgi/pt?id=pur1.32754077953184&view=1up&seq=3

'The Antitrust Equal Enforcement Act. Hearings before the Committee on the Judiciary' (1982), House of Representatives J-97-15, available at: https://www.justice.gov/sites/default/files/jmd/legacy/2013/10/07/hear-3359-1959.pdf

Bentele, Florian, *Gesamtschuld und Erlass* (Tübingen: Mohr Siebeck, 2006)

Bieber, Tobias, *Die gesamtschuldnerische Haftung für die Zahlung von Kartellbußen im EU-Recht* (Köln: Carl Heymanns Verlag, 2014)

Bien, Florian, 'Überlegungen zu einer haftungsrechtlichen Privilegierung des Kartellkronzeugen' (2011) *Europäische Zeitschrift für Wirtschaftsrecht*, 889

Bieniek, Gerard, 'Art. 415' in Bieniek Gerard, Ciepła Helena, Dmowski Stanisław, et al. (eds.), *Komentarz do kodeksu cywilnego. Zobowiązania*, 4 vols. (Warszawa: LexisNexis, 2011), vol. III

'Art. 441' in Bieniek Gerard, Ciepła Helena, Dmowski Stanisław, et al. (eds.), *Komentarz do kodeksu cywilnego. Zobowiązania*, 4 vols. (Warszawa: LexisNexis, 2011), vol. III

'Pojęcie regresu w prawie cywilnym' (1972) 6 *Nowe Prawo*, 889

'Solidarność; Regres' in Jacek Gudowski (ed.), *Komentarz do art. 441 Kodeksu cywilnego* (2013) *LEX*

Blair, Roger D. and Durrance, Christine Piette, 'Umbrella Damages: Towards a Coherent Antitrust Policy' (2018) 36 *Contemporary Economic Policy*, 2, 241

Blair, Roger D. and Sokol, D. Daniel (eds.), *The Oxford Handbook of International Antitrust Economics*, 2 vols. (New York: Oxford University Press, 2015), vol. I

Blöcker, Morten, *Die tätige Reue* (Baden-Baden: Nomos, 2000)

Blum, Ulrich, Steinat, Nicole and Veltins, Michael, 'On the Rationale of Leniency Programs: A Game-Theoretical Analysis' (2008) 25 *European Journal of Law and Economics*, 209

Bodenstein, Ines, 'Zurück zum bewährten Grundsatz: Wer handelt, haftet. Wegweisende Klärung zum Gesamtschuldnerausgleich bei Kartellgeldbußen durch den BGH in Sachen Calciumcarbid' (2015) *Neue Zeitschrift für Kartellrecht*, 141

Böhlke, Alexander, 'Die gesamtschuldnerische Verantwortlichkeit im EU-Wettbewerbsrecht' (2011) *Europäische Zeitschrift für Wirtschaftsrecht*, 781

Bonnecase, Julien, *La notion juridique de bonnes mœurs* (Paris: Études Capitant, 1939)

Boré, Jacques, 'La causalité partielle en noir et blanc ou les deux visages de l'obligation "in solidum"' (1971) 1 *La Semaine Juridique*, 2369

'Le recours entre coobligés in solidum' (1967) 1 *La Semaine Juridique*, 2126

Born, Gary B., *International Arbitration: Law and Practice* (Alphen aan den Rijn: Kluwer Law International, 2012)

Bosch, Wolfgang, 'Haftung für kartellrechtswidriges Handeln der Tochtergesellschaft – Neue Rechtslage nach dem Urteil in der Rechtssache Elf Aquitaine/Kommission?' (2012) 3 *Zeitschrift für Wettbewerbsrecht*, 368

'Verantwortung der Konzernobergesellschaft im Kartellrecht' (2013) 277 *Zeitschrift für das gesamte Handels- und Wirtschaftsrecht*, 454

Böttcher, Lars, '§ 421 BGB' in Harm-Peter Westermann, Barbara Grunewald and Georg Maier-Reimer (eds.), *Erman Bürgerliches Gesetzbuch* (Köln: OVS Verlag Dr. Otto Walter Schmidt, 2011)

'§ 426 BGB' in Harm-Peter Westermann, Barbara Grunewald and Georg Maier-Reimer (eds.), *Erman Bürgerliches Gesetzbuch* (Köln: OVS Verlag Dr. Otto Walter Schmidt, 2011)

Boudou, Mathilde, Charvoz, Laurence, de la Laurencie, Jean-Patrice, Sautel, Olivier and Sélinsky, Véronique, 'France' in Pranvera Këllezi, Bruce Kilpatrick and Pierre Kobel (eds.), *Antitrust for Small and Middle Size Undertakings and Image Protection from Non-Competitors* (Berlin: Springer, 2014)

Bougerol, Laetitia, 'La réforme de la solidarité passive, illusions perdues et incertitudes' (2016) 2 *Revue de Droit bancaire et financier*, 9

Bovis, Christopher H. and Clarke, Charles M., 'Private Enforcement of EU Competition Law' (2015) 36 *Liverpool Law Review*, 49

Boyce, Andrew, 'Truck Makers and AkzoNobel, Unilever, Others Dispute Damage Claim Time-frame in Dutch Court' (13 March 2020), *Mlex*, available at https://mlex.com/GlobalAdvisory/DetailView.aspx?cid=1170341&siteid=244&rdir=1

Braun, Dominik, *Das Konzept der gesamtschuldnerischen Verantwortlichkeit von Konzerngesellschaften im europäischen Wettbewerbsrecht* (Baden-Baden: Nomos, 2018)

Braun, Dominik and Kellerbauer, Manuel, 'Das Konzept der gesamtschuldnerischen Verantwortlichkeit von Konzerngesellschaften bei Zuwiderhandlungen gegen das EU-Wettbewerbsrecht – Teil 1' (2015) *Neue Zeitschrift für Kartellrecht*, 175

'Das Konzept der gesamtschuldnerischen Verantwortlichkeit von Konzerngesellschaften bei Zuwiderhandlungen gegen das EU-Wettbewerbsrecht – Teil 2' (2015) *Neue Zeitschrift für Kartellrecht*, 211

Bredenoord-Spoek, Marieke and Wesseling, Rein, 'Forum Shopping on the Dutch High Street. Jurisdiction Issues in Follow-on Litigation Cases', available at https://pure.uva.nl/ws/files/7171252/Paper_Wesseling_Bredenoord_Spoek_IBA_Competition_Law_Conference_Floren. . .pdf

Breit, William and Elzinga, Kenneth G., 'Antitrust Penalties and Attitudes towards Risk: An Economic Analysis' (1973) 86 *Harvard Law Review*, 4, 693

Bréna, Stéphane, *Les recours en contribution* (Montpellier: Université Montpellier 1, 2005)

Brenner, Steffen, 'An Empirical Study of the European Corporate Leniency Program' (2009) 27 *International Journal of Industrial Organization*, 6, 639

Brettel, Hauke and Thomas, Stefan, 'Unternehmensbußgeld, Bestimmtheitsgrundsatz und Schuldprinzip im novellierten deutschen Kartellrecht' (2009) 1 *Zeitschrift für Wettbewerbsrecht*, 25

Bronckers, Marco and Vallery, Anne, 'No Longer Presumed Guilty? The Impact of Fundamental Rights on Certain Dogmas of EU Competition Law' (2011) 34 *World Competition*, 4, 535

Bronett, Georg-Klaus de, 'Gesamtschuldnerische Geldbußen nach EU-Kartellrecht für Personen, die wettbewerbswidrig handelnden "wirtschaftlichen Einheiten" angehören' (2015) 3 *Europäisches Wirtschafts- und Steuerrecht*, 123

'"Unternehmen" als Wiederholungstäter im EU-Kartellrecht vor und nach der Akzo Nobel-Rechtsprechung des EuGH zum Unternehmensbegriff' (2014) 6 *Europäisches Wirtschafts- und Steuerrecht*, 313

Broulík, Jan, 'Two Contexts for Economics in Competition Law. Deterrence Effects and Competitive Effects' (2018) 17 *TILEC Discussion Paper*, 1

Brown, Adrian and Schonberg, Morris, 'Widening the Net: The General Court Extends the Principle of Successor Liability in EU Competition Law' (2013) 34(1) *European Competition Law Review*, 1

Buccirossi, Paolo, Ciari, Lorenzo, Duso, Tomaso, Spagnolo, Giancarlo and Vitale, Cristiana, 'Deterrence in Competition Law' (2009) 285 *GESY Discussion Paper*, 1

Buccirossi, Paolo, Marvão, Catarina M. P. and Spagnolo, Giancarlo, 'Leniency and Damages' (2015) 32 *Stockholm Institute of Transition Economics Working Paper*, 1

Buczkowski, Stefan, 'Z zagadnień regresu' (1952) 1 *Przegląd Ustawodawstwa Gospodarczego*, 43, 444

Bundeskartellamt, 'Bericht über die Tätigkeit in den Jahren 2003/2004', BT-Drs. 15/5790, 110

Buntscheck, Martin, 'Die gesetzliche Kappungsgrenze für Kartellgeldbußen. Bedeutung und Auslegung im Lichte der neuen Bußgeld-Leitlinien von Kommission und Bundeskartellamt' (2007) *Europäische Zeitschrift für Wirtschaftsrecht*, 423

Bürger, Christian, 'Die Haftung der Konzernmutter für Kartellrechtsverstöße ihrer Tochter nach deutschem Recht' (2011) 1 *Wirtschaft und Wettbewerb*, 130

'Unternehmensinterne Aufteilung einer Geldbuße der Kommission' (2015) *Wirtschaft und Wettbewerb*, 348

Buts, Caroline and Vanhaverbeke, Lynn, 'A Quantitative Analysis of the Efficiency of the EU's Leniency Policy' (2020) 1 *European Competition and Regulatory Law Review (CoRe)*, 12

Bydlinski, Peter, '§ 421 BGB' in Wolfgang Krüger (ed.), *Münchener Kommentar zum Bürgerlichen Gesetzbuch. Schuldrecht. Allgemeiner Teil*, 14 vols. (München: C.H. Beck, 2012), vol. II

'§ 423 BGB' in Wolfgang Krüger (ed.), *Münchener Kommentar zum Bürgerlichen Gesetzbuch. Schuldrecht. Allgemeiner Teil*, 14 vols. (München: C.H. Beck, 2012), vol. II

'§ 426 BGB' in Wolfgang Krüger (ed.), *Münchener Kommentar zum Bürgerlichen Gesetzbuch. Schuldrecht. Allgemeiner Teil*, 14 vols. (München: C.H. Beck, 2012), vol. II

Cabrillac, Rémy, *Droit des obligations* (Paris: Dalloz, 2016)

von Caemmerer, Ernst, (1968) 9 *Zeitschrift für Europarecht, Internationales Privatrecht und Rechtsvergleichung* 81

Cain, Oliver, and Carr, Danielle, 'Litigation and Enforcement in the UK (England and Wales): Overview' (2018), available at https://uk.practicallaw.thomsonreuters.com/7-502-0631?transitionType=DefaultandcontextData=(sc.Default)

Canenbley, Cornelis and Steinvorth, Till, 'Effective Enforcement of Competition Law: Is There a Solution to the Conflict between Leniency Programmes and Private Damages Actions?' (2011) 2 *Journal of European Competition Law and Practice*, 4, 315

Canin, Patrick, *Les actions récursoires entre coresponsables* (Paris: Litec, 1996)

Cannon, W. Stephen, 'The Administration's Antitrust Remedies Reform Proposal: Its Derivation and Implications' (1986) 55 *Antitrust Law Journal*, 1, 103

Carbonnier, Jean, *Droit civil. Les obligations*, 4 vols. (Paris: Presses Universitaires de France, 1992), vol. IV

Cartel Damages Claims, 'CDC's Claims against Kemira Aren't Time-barred, Dutch Court Rules' (4 February 2020), *Mlex*, available at https://mlex.com/GlobalAdvisory/DetailView.aspx?cid=1160399&siteid=244&rdir=1

Catala, Pierre, *Avant-projet de réforme du droit des obligations et de la prescription* (Paris: La Documentation française, 2006)

Cauffman, Caroline, 'The Interaction of Leniency Programmes and Actions for Damages' (2011) 34 *Maastricht European Private Law Institute Working Paper*, 181

Cavanagh, Edward D., 'Contribution, Claim Reduction, and Individual Treble Damage Responsibility: Which Path to Reform of Antitrust Remedies?' (1987) 40 *Vanderbilt Law Review*, 1277

Centre for European Policy Studies (CEPS), 'Making Antitrust Damages Actions More Effective in the EU: Welfare Impact and Potential Scenarios' (2007), available at https://ec.europa.eu/competition/antitrust/actionsdamages/files_white_paper/impact_study.pdf

Chabas, François, *L'influence de la pluralité de causes sur le droit à réparation* (Paris: Librairie générale de droit et de jurisprudence, 1967)

'Remarque sur l'obligation in solidum' (1967) 1 *Revue trimestrielle de droit civil*, 310

Chang, Howard F. and Sigman, Hilary A., 'Incentives to Settle under Joint and Several Liability: An Empirical Analysis of Superfund Litigation' (2000) 29 *The Journal of Legal Studies*, 1, 205

Chantepie, Gaël and Latina, Mathias, *La réforme du droit des obligations. Commentaire théorique et pratique dans l'ordre du Code civil* (Paris: Dalloz, 2016)

Chatterjee, Charles and Lefcovitch, Anna, *Alternative Dispute Resolution: A Practical Guide* (London and New York: Routledge, 2008)

Chen, Zhijun and Rey, Patrick, 'On the Design of Leniency Programs' (2013) 56 *The Journal of Law and Economics*, 4, 917

Chénedé, François, *Le nouveau droit des contrats et des obligations* (Paris: Dalloz, 2016)

Claudel, Emmanuelle, 'L'essor des sanctions en droit de la concurrence. Quelle efficacité ? Quelles garanties ?' (2014) 6 *Contrats Concurrence Consommation*, 13, 6

Cochet, Dorothée, 'La contribution à la dette des coobligés in solidum' (2004) 118 *Petites affiches*, 3

Competition Appeal Tribunal, 'JPMorgan, UBS, Barclays, Others Face Fresh Forex-rigging Lawsuit in UK, Court Filing Confirms' (20 December 2019), *Mlex*, available at https://mlex.com/GlobalAdvisory/DetailView.aspx?cid=1152433&siteid=244&rdir=1

'Prysmian Settles with Scottish Power, Other Suppliers in UK Cable-cartel Lawsuit' (30 July 2020), *Mlex*, available at https://mlex.com/GlobalAdvisory/DetailView.aspx?cid=1213902&siteid=244&rdir=1

Corgas-Bernard, Cristina, 'La pluralité de responsables en droit français et dans d'autres ordres juridiques nationaux' in G.R.E.R.C.A. (ed.), *Le droit français de la responsabilité civile confronté aux projets européens d'harmonisation* (Paris: Irjs editions, 2012)

Craig, Paul P., *EU Administrative Law* (Oxford and New York: Oxford University Press, 2012)

'Subsidiarity: A Political and Legal Analysis' (2012) 50 *Journal of Common Market Studies*, 1, 72

Crane, Daniel A., 'Optimizing Private Antitrust Enforcement' (2010) 63 *Vanderbilt Law Review*, 2, 675

Curry, Raper Kellie, Love, H. Alan and Shumway, C. Richard, 'Distinguishing the Source of Market Power' (2007) 89 *American Journal of Agricultural Economics*, 1, 78

Czachórski, Witold, 'Uwagi o rażącym niedbalstwie' in Jan Błeszyński (ed.), *Witold Czachórski. Wybór prac* (Warszawa: C.H. Beck, 2015)

Dąbrowa, Janina, *Wina jako przesłanka odpowiedzialności cywilnej* (Wrocław: Wrocławskie Towarzystwo Naukowe, 1968)

Danov, Mihail and Becker, Florian, 'Governance Aspects of Cross-Border EU Competition Actions: Theoretical and Practical Challenges' (2014) 10 *Journal of Private International Law*, 3, 359

Danov, Mihail, Becker, Florian and Beaumont, Paul, *Cross-border EU Competition Law Actions* (Oxford and Portland, OR: Hart Publishing, 2013)

Davidow, Joel, 'Recent Developments in US Antitrust' (2005) 28 *World Competition*, 3, 299

Davis, William Bruce, 'Multiple Defendant Settlement in 10b-5: Good Faith Contribution Bar' (1989) 40 *Hastings Law Journal*, 1253

Debroux, Michel, 'Sanctioning Cartels under EC Law: Definition and Consequences of Group Liability' (2008) 1 *Concurrences*, 42

Decocq, Georges, 'D'utiles précisions sur le régime de la solidarité pour le paiement d'une amende' (2014) 7 *Contrat Concurrence Consommation*, 165

Deguergue, Maryse, 'Causalité et imputabilité' (2013) 370–360 *JurisClasseur Responsabilité civile et Assurances*

Dejean de la Bâtie, Noël, 'Responsabilité délictuelle. Tome VI-2' in André Ponsard and Ibrahim Fadlallah (eds.), *Aubry et Rau, Droit Civil Français* (Paris: Librairies Techinques, 1989)

Dekeyser, Kris and Roques, Christian, 'The European Commission's Settlement Procedure in Cartel Cases' (2010) 55 *The Antitrust Bulletin*, 4, 819

Department for Business Innovation and Skills, 'Consultation: Implementing the EU Directive on Damages for Breaches of Competition Law' (January, 2016), available at https://assets.publishing.service.gov.uk/government/uploads/system/uploads/attachment_data/file/495757/BIS-16-6-consultation-implementing-the-EU-directive-on-damages-for-breaches-of-competition-law.pdf

Deutsche, Bahn, 'Deutsche Bahn Settles Damages Litigation with Lufthansa' (26 August 2019), *Mlex*, available at https://mlex.com/GlobalAdvisory/DetailView.aspx?cid=1123288&siteid=244&rdir=1

Diamond, Peter A., 'Single Activity Accidents' (1974) 3(1)*The Journal of Legal Studies*, 3

Dobbin, Robert F., 'Settlement of Private Antitrust Litigation Including Class Type Actions and Multiple Defendant Lawsuits' (1973) 34 *Ohio State Law Journal*, 513

Dohrn, Daniel, *Die Bindungswirkung kartellrechtlicher Entscheidungen der Kommission sowie deutscher und mitgliedsstaatlicher Kartellbehörden und Gerichte im deutschen Zivilprozess* (Köln: Carl Heymanns Verlag, 2010)

Domke, Martin, *Domke on Commercial Arbitration* (Eagan: West Group, 1984)

Dopuch, Nicholas, Ingberman, Daniel E. and King, Ronald R., 'An Experimental Investigation of Multi-defendant Bargaining in "joint and several" and Proportionate Liability Regimes' (1997) 23 *Journal of Accounting and Economics*, 189

Dougan, Michael, *National Remedies Before the Court of Justice. Issues of Harmonisation and Differentiation* (Oxford and Portland, OR: Hart Publishing, 2004)

Dreher, Meinrad, 'Die Haftungsverteilung bei der gesamtschuldnerischen kartellrechtlichen Schadenersatzhaftung' in Stefan Bechtold, Joachim Jickeli and Mathias Rohe (eds.), *Recht, Ordnung Und Wettbewerb: Festschrift Zum 70. Geburtstag Von Wernhard Möschel* (Baden-Baden: Nomos, 2011)

'Zum Ausgleich zwischen den Gesamtschuldnern (innerhalb eines Konzerns) einer Kartell-Geldbuße ("Calciumcarbid-Kartell II")' (2015) 7 *Entscheidungen zum Wirtschaftsrecht*, 231

Dreher, Meinrad and Körner, Julia, 'Germany' in Pranvera Këllezi, Bruce Kilpatrick and Pierre Kobel (eds.), *Antitrust for Small and Middle Size Undertakings and Image Protection from Non-Competitors* (Berlin: Springer, 2014)

du Chambon, Patrick Maistre, 'Régime de la réparation. Action en réparation. Parties à l'instance' (2016) *JurisClasseur Civil Code*, 220

Dubis, Wojciech in Edward Gniewek and Piotr Machnikowski (eds.), *Komentarze Kodeksowe. Kodeks Cywilny. Komentarz* (Warszawa: C.H. Beck, 2014)

Dugdale, Anthony M., 'The Civil Liability (Contribution) Act 1978' (1979) 42 *The Modern Law Review*, 2, 182

Dunleavy, Nathy, 'Contribution among Antitrust Defendants in English Law' (2009) 30 *European Competition Law Review*, 1, 22

Dunne, Niamh, 'Competition Law and Policy after Brexit' (2017) 24 *LSE Law Policy Briefing Series*, Brexit Special 4, 2

'The Role of Private Enforcement within EU Competition Law' (2014) 16 *Cambridge Yearbook of European Legal Studies*, 143

Dunz, Walter, 'Abwägungskriterien bei der Schadensausgleichung' (1964) 46 *Neue Juristische Wochenschrift*, 2133

Durner, Wolfgang, 'Die Unabhängigkeit nationaler Richter im Binnenmarkt – Zu den Loyalitätspflichten nationaler Gerichte gegenüber der EG-Kommission, insbesondere auf dem Gebiet des Kartellrechts' (2004) 4 *Zeitschrift Europarecht*, 547

Dybowski, Tomasz in Zbigniew Radwański (ed.), *System Prawa Prywatnego. Prawo zobowiązań – część ogólna*, 21 vols. (Warszawa: C.H. Beck and Instytut Nauk Prawnych Polskiej Akademii Nauk, 2002), vol. II

Dzikiewicz, Lech, 'O pojęciu winy i jej trzech odmianach' (1977) IV *Państwo i Prawo*, 87

Easterbrook, Frank H., 'The Antitrust Equal Enforcement Act. Hearings before the Committee on the Judiciary' (1982), House of Representatives J-97-15, available at: https://www.justice.gov/sites/default/files/jmd/legacy/2013/10/07/hear-3359-1959.pdf

Easterbrook, Frank H., Landes, William M. and Richard, A. Posner, 'Contribution among Antitrust Defendants: A Legal and Economic Analysis' (1980) 23 *The Journal of Law and Economics*, 2, 331

Ebert, Ina, *Pönale Elemente im deutschen Privatrecht* (Tübingen: Mohr Siebeck, 2004)

Eckert, Jörn, 'Sittenwidrigkeit und Wertungswandel' (1999) 199 *Archiv für die civilistische Praxis*, 3, 337

Ehmann Horst, *Die Gesamtschuld* (Heidelberg: Inaugural-Dissertation, 1971)

Eilmansberger, Thomas, 'The Green Paper on Damages Actions for Breach of the EC Antitrust Rules and Beyond: Reflections on the Utility and Feasibility of Stimulating Private Enforcement through Legislative Action' (2007) 44 *Common Market Law Review*, 431

Elzinga, Kenneth G., 'The Goals of Antitrust: Other than Competition and Efficiency, What Else?' (1977) 125 *University of Pennsylvania Law Review*, 1191

Emiliou, Nicholas, *The Principle of Proportionality in European Law: A Comparative Study* (London and Cambridge, MA: Kluwer Law International, 1996)

Enneccerus, Ludwig and Lehmann, Heinrich, *Recht der Schuldverhältnisse* (Tübingen: Mohr, 1958)

European Commission, 'Antitrust: Commission Fines Google €4.34 billion for Illegal Practices Regarding Android Mobile Devices to Strengthen Dominance of Google's Search Engine' (18 July 2018) IP/18/4581

'Antitrust: Commission Fines Scania €880 million for Participating in Trucks Cartel' (27 September 2017) IP/17/3502

'Antitrust: Commission Fines Truck Producers € 2.93 billion for Participating in a Cartel' (19 July 2016) IP/16/2582

European Group on Tort Law, *Principles of European Tort Law: Text and Commentary* (Wien and New York: Springer, 2005)

Fabian, Claus-Peter, *Schädigermehrheit und Regreß im internationalen Umwelthaftungsrecht unter besonderer Berücksichtigung des anglo-amerikanischen Rechts* (Frankfurt am Main: Peter Lang, 1999)

Fasoula, Vasiliki, 'Extending the Principle of Economic Continuity to Private Enforcement of Competition Law. What Lies Ahead for Corporate Restructuring and Civil Damages Proceedings after Skanska? Case Comment to the Judgment of the Court of Justice of 14 march 2019 Skanska Industrial Solutions and others (Case C-724/17)' (2019) 20 *Yearbook of Antitrust and Regulatory Studies*, 259

Faure, Michael, 'Economic Analysis of Fault' in Pierre Widmer (ed.), *Unification of Tort Law: Fault* (Den Haag: Kluwer Law International, 2005)

Feltovich, Nick and Hamaguchi, Yasuyo, 'The Effect of Whistle-Blowing Incentives on Collusion: An Experimental Study of Leniency Programs' (2018) 84 *Southern Economic Journal*, 4, 1024

Feunten, Tristan, 'Industry-wide Trucks Cartel Face Massive Legal Claim in UK Tribunal' (30 July 2018), *Weightmans*, available at https://weightmans.com/media-centre/news/industry-wide-trucks-cartel-facing-massive-legal-claim-in-uk-tribunal/

Ford, Sarah, 'Claims for Contribution in Competition Damages Actions: The Impact of the EU Damages Directive' (2015) 36 *European Competition Law Review*, 8, 327

Frenz, Walter and Lülsdorf, Tanja, 'Kontinuität und Zurechnung im Kartellrecht' (2012) 12 *Europäisches Wirtschafts- und Steuerrecht*, 504

Frese, Michael, *Sanctions in EU Competition Law: Principles and Practice* (Oxford and Portland, OR: Hart Publishing, 2014)

Fritzsche, Alexander, Klöpper, Carsten and Walter, Schmidt Miriam, 'Die Praxis der privaten Kartellrechtsdurchsetzung in Deutschland – Teil 1: Aspekte des kartellrechtlichen Schadensersatzanspruchs' (2016) *Neue Zeitschrift für Kartellrecht*, 412

Galand-Carval, Suzanne, 'Fault under French Law' in Pierre Widmer (ed.), *Unification of Tort Law: Fault* (Den Haag: Kluwer Law International, 2005)

Gamble, Rorger, 'The Cartel Penumbra: Where Public and Private Enforcement Policies Intersect' (2013) 42 *Common Law World Review*, 23

Gänswein, Olivier, 'Gesamtschuldnerausgleich unter Kartellbeteiligten: Bestimmung des Haftungsanteils und Verjährung der Ausgleichsansprüche' (2016) *Neue Zeitschrift für Kartellrecht*, 50

Garlicki, Stanisław, 'Glosa do orzeczenia Sądu Najwyższego z dn. 21.11.1967 r.' (1969) 1 *Orzecznictwo Sądów Polskich i Komisji Arbitrażowych*, 342

Gebauer, Martin, '§ 423 BGB' in Thomas Pfeiffer (ed.), *Soergel Bürgerliches Gesetzbuch Schuldrecht*, 3 vols. (Stuttgart: Kohlhammer, 2009), vol. III

'§ 426 BGB' in Thomas Pfeiffer (ed.), *Soergel Bürgerliches Gesetzbuch Schuldrecht*, 3 vols. (Stuttgart: Kohlhammer, 2009), vol. III

Gehrlein, Markus, '§ 421 BGB' in Heinz Georg Bamberger and Herbert Roth (eds.), *Kommentar zum Bürgerlichen Gesetzbuch*, 3 vols. (München: C.H. Beck, 2012), vol. I

'§ 426 BGB' in Heinz Georg Bamberger and Herbert Roth (eds.), *Kommentar zum Bürgerlichen Gesetzbuch*, 3 vols. (München: C.H. Beck, 2012), vol. I

Gelmini, Francesca, 'Brexit: The Future of Private Antitrust Enforcement in the UK' (20 December 2017), *European Future*, available at https://europeanfutures.ed.ac.uk/brexit-the-future-of-private-antitrust-enforcement-in-the-uk/

Geradin, Damien, 'Public Policy and Breach of Competition Law in International Arbitration: A Competition Law Practitioner's Viewpoint' (2016) 29 *TILEC Discussion Paper*, 1

Geradin, Damien and Grelier, Laurie-Anne, 'Cartel Damages Claims in the European Union: Have We Only Seen the Tip of the Iceberg?' in Nicholas Charbit and Elisa Ramundo (eds.), *William E. Kovacic. An Antitrust Tribute. Liber Amicorum*, 2 vols. (New York: Institute of Competition Law, 2014), vol. II

Geradin, Damien and Sadrak, Katarzyna, 'The EU Competition Law Fining System: A Quantitative Review of the Commission Decisions between 2000 and 2017' in Nicolas Charbit, Carolina Malhado and Ellie Yang (eds.), *Douglas H. Ginsburg. An Antitrust Professor on the Bench. Liber Amicorum*, 2 vols. (New York: Concurrences, 2018), vol. I

Geradin, Damien, Stephan Andreas and Argenton, Cedric, *EU Cartel Law and Economics* (Oxford: Oxford University Press, 2020)

Geulette, Alexandre, 'La solidarité pour le paiement des amendes en droit de la concurrence de l'Union' (2014) 2 *Revues des Affaires européennes*, 433

Ghodoosei, Farshad, 'The Concept of Public Policy in Law: Revisiting the Role of the Public Policy Doctrine in the Enforcement of Private Legal Arrangements' (2016) 94 *Nebraska Law Review*, 3, 685

Ginsburg, Douglas H., 'Comparing Antitrust Enforcement in the United States and Europe' (2005) 1 *Journal of Competition Law and Economics*, 3, 427

Ginsburg, Douglas H. and Wright, Joshua D., 'Antitrust Sanctions' (2010) 6 *Competition Policy International*, 2, 3

Glaßer, Heinrich, *Der Gesamtschuldnerausgleich zwischen deliktisch haftenden Schuldnern* (München: VVF, 1995)

Glöckner, Jochen, 'Individualschutz und Funktionenschutz in der privaten Durchsetzung des Kartellrechts – Der Zweck heiligt die Mittel nicht; er bestimmt sie!' (2007) 5 *Wettbewerb in Recht und Praxis*, 490

Götte, Wulf, *Gesamtschuldbegriff und Regressproblem* (Bonn: Ludwig Rührscheid, 1974)

Gould, John P., 'The Economics of Legal Conflicts' (1973) 2 *The Journal of Legal Studies*, 2, 279

Grangeon, Julie, 'La directive relative aux actions en réparation à la suite d'une pratique anticoncurrentielle: révolution ou évolution du private enforcement dans l'Union ?' (2015) 101 *Revue Lamy droit des affaires*, 59

Grundmann, Stefan, '§ 276 BGB' in Wolfgang Krüger (ed.), *Münchener Kommentar zum Bürgerlichen Gesetzbuch. Schuldrecht. Allgemeiner Teil I*, 14 vols. (München: C.H. Beck, 2019), vol. II

Grzybowski, Stefan, 'Roszczenia zwrotne w prawie alimentacyjnym a problem nieprzenaszalności roszczeń alimentacyjnych' (1956) 1 *Nowe Prawo*, 41

Guttso, Laura, 'I'm an Immunity Applicant, Get Me Out of Here: Joint and Several Liability Revisited' (2014) 7 *Global Competition Litigation Review*, 2, 94

Hamman, Hartmut, *Das Unternehmen als Täter im europäischen Wettbewerbsrecht* (Pfaffenweiler: Centaurus, 1992)

Harrington, Joseph E. Jr, 'Optimal Corporate Leniency Programs' (2008) 56 *The Journal of Industrial Economics*, 2, 215

Harrison, Farin, 'The Practical Antitrust Implications of Tomorrow: Brexit Day', (30 January 2020), *Kluwer Competition Law*, available at https://competitionlawblog.kluwercompetitionlaw.com/2020/01/30/the-practical-antitrust-implications-of-tomorrow-brexit-day/

Haus, Florian C., 'Die Entscheidung des BGH im Fall Calciumcarbid – (nicht nur) Regeln für den Innenregress bei gesamtschuldnerischer Bußgeldhaftung' (2015) *Der Konzern*, 114

Havu, Katri, 'EU Law in Member State Courts: 'Adequate Judicial Protection' and Effective Application – Ambiguities and Nonsequiturs in Guidance by the Court of Justice?' (2015) 8 *Contemporary Readings in Law and Social Justice*, 1, 158

Hawk, Barry E., *Common Market and International Antitrust: A Comparative Guide* (New York and Washington: Aspen Law and Business, 1990)

Hay, Bruce and Rosenberg, David, '"Sweetheart" and "Blackmail" Settlements in Class Actions: Reality and Remedy' (2000) 75 *Notre Dame Law Review*, 1377

Hazelhorst, Monique, 'Private Enforcement of EU Competition Law: Why Punitive Damages Are a Step Too Far' (2010) 4 *European Review of Private Law*, 757

Heck, Philipp, *Grundriß des Schuldrechts* (Tübingen: Mohr, 1929)

Heidel, Ulrich, *Die Auswirkungen von Haftungsbeschränkungen auf die Entstehung von Gesamtschuldverhältnissen unter besonderer Berücksichtigung versicherungsrechtlicher Probleme* (Heidelberg: Dissertation, 1975)

Heinichen, Christian, *Unternehmensbegriff und Haftungsnachfolge im Europäischen Kartellrecht* (Baden-Baden: Nomos, 2010)

Heinrichs, Helmut, '§ 249 BGB' in Peter Bassenge, Gerd Brudermüller, Uwe Diederichsen, Wolfgang Edenhofer, Helmut Heinrichs, Andreas Heldrich, Hans Putzo, Hartwig Sprau and Heinz Thomas Walter Weidenkaff, Palandt. Bürgerliches Gesetzbuch (München: C.H. Beck, 2004)

Hilgenfeld, Mario, 'HeidelbergCement Settles German Cement-cartel Damages Claims with CDC' (13 August 2019), *Mlex*, available at https://mlex.com/GlobalAdvisory/DetailView.aspx?cid=1120911&siteid=244&rdir=1

Hilgenfeld, Mario and Hirst, Nicholas, 'Lufthansa, Deutsche Bahn settle air-cargo Damages Litigation' (26 Autust 2019), *Mlex*, available at https://mlex.com/GlobalAdvisory/DetailView.aspx?cid=1123289&siteid=244&rdir=1

Hinloopen, Jeroen, 'An Economic Analysis of Leniency Programs in Antitrust Law' (2003) 4 *De Economist*, 415

Hocquet-Berg, Sophie, 'Affaire du « Distilbène » : une importante avancée en matière d'indemnisation des victimes' (2009) 44 *La Semaine Juridique Edition Generale*, 381

Hofstetter, Karl and Ludescher, Melanie, 'Fines against Parent Companies in EU Antitrust Law: Setting Incentives for "Best Practice Compliance"' (2010) 33 *World Competition*, 1, 55

Hölzel, Norman, *Kronzeugenregelungen im Europäischen Wettbewerbsrecht* (Halle: Universitätsverlag Halle-Wittenberg, 2011)

Honoré, Anthony Maurice, *International Encyclopedia of Comparative Law: Torts. Causation and Remoteness of Damage*, 17 vols. (Tübingen: Mohr, 1971), vol. XI

Honsell, Heinrich, 'Die zivilrechtliche Sanktion der Sittenwidrigkeit' (1975) 30 *Juristen Zeitung*, 439

Hontebeyrie, Antoine, 'Pluralité de sujets : altération et complications' (2015) 249 *Droit et Patrimoine. Dossier*, 46

'Quelques incidences de la réforme du droit des obligations en matière de responsabilité civile' (2015) 249 *Droit et Patrimoine. Dossier*, 54

'Régime général des obligations : l'essentiel d'une réforme substantielle' (2015) 249 *Droit et Patrimoine. Dossier*, 33

Hösch, Antonia, *Der schadensrechtliche Innenausgleich zwischen Kartellrechtsverletzern* (Baden-Baden: Nomos, 2015)

Howlett, Michael and Cashore, Ben, 'Conceptualizing Public Policy' (2004) *Comparative Policy Studies*, 17

Hubert, Patrick and Combet, Marie-Laure, '*Total SA and Elf Aquitaine* SA: A Missed Opportunity to Shed More Light on Joint and Several Liability' (2015) 6 *Journal of European Competition Law and Practice*, 9, 653

Hüffer, Uwe, *Der Rückgriff gegen den deliktisch handelnden Schädiger bei Entschädigungsleistungen Dritter* (Heidelberg: Carl Winter Universitätsverlag, 1970)

Hüschelrath, Kai and Laitenberger, Ulrich, 'The Settlement Procedure in the European Commission's Cartel Cases: An Early Evaluation' (2017) 5 *Journal of Antitrust Enforcement*, 3, 458

Hviid, Morten and Medvedev, Andrei, 'The Role of Contribution among Defendants in Private Antitrust Litigation' (2008) 8 *CCP Working Paper*, 3, 1

Idot, Laurance, 'Responsabilité des sociétés mères' (2016) 8–9 *Europe*, 1

Inderst, Roman and Thomas, Stefan, *Schadensersatz bei Kartellverstößen* (Düsseldorf: Handerlsblatt Fachmedien, 2015)

Infantino, Marta and Zervogianni, Eleni, *Causation in European Tort Law* (Cambridge: Cambridge University Press, 2017)

Janka, Sebastian Felix, 'Parent Liability and Claims for Recovery between Joint and Several Debtors According to EU Antitrust Law' (2014) 35 *European Competition Law Review*, 12, 594

Jędrejek, Grzegorz, 'Polski Kodeks Zobowiązań z 1933 Roku. Powstanie, źródła, znaczenie dla Europejskiego prawa obligacyjnego' (2001) XI *Roczniki Nauk Prawnych*, 1, 47

Jędrzejewska, Maria, *Współuczestnictwo Procesowe* (Warszawa: Wydawnictwo Prawnicze, 1975)

Jolowicz, John Anthony, 'Procedure and Substance – Apportionment of Damages' (1988) 47 (1)*The Cambridge Law Journal*, 32

Jones, Alison, 'The Boundaries of an Undertaking in EU Competition Law' (2012) 8 *European Competition Journal*, 2, 301

Jourdain, Patrice, 'Droit à réparation. Lien de causalité. Détermination des causes du dommage' (2013) *JurisClasseur Civil Code*, 160

'Droit à réparation. Responsabilité fondée sur la faute. Notion de faute: fautes qualifiées' (2017) *JurisClasseur Civil Code*, 120–220

'Droit à réparation. Responsabilité fondée sur la faute. Applications de la notion de faute: imprudences et négligences ; fautes commises à l'occasion d'un contrat' (2017) *JurisClasseur Civil Code*, 130–410

'Les recours en contribution' (2015) 9 *Responsabilité civile et assurance*, 16

'Pour un réexamen du droit de recours en contribution' (2009) 3 *Responsabilité civile et assurances*, 3

Jüchser, Alexander, 'Gesamtschuldnerausgleich zwischen Mutter- und Tochtergesellschaft im Falles Schadensersatzes' (2012) 10 *Wirtschaft und Wettbewerb*, 1048

Jürgens, Robert and Seeliger, Daniela, 'Die geplante Neufassung der Kronzeugenregelung der Europäischen Kommission' (2006) 8 *Europäisches Wirtschafts- und Steuerrecht*, 337

Jurkowska-Gomułka, Agata, *Publiczne i prywatne egzekwowanie zakazów praktyk ograniczających konkurencje: w poszukiwaniu zrównoważonego modelu współistnienia*

(Warszawa: Wydawnictwo Naukowe Wydziału Zarządzania Uniwersytetu Warszawskiego, 2013)

Kahan, Marcel, 'The Incentive Effects of Settlements under Joint and Several Liability' (1996) 16 *International Review of Law and Economics*, 389

Kalben, Jonas von and Sekunde, Alexander, 'Relative Responsibility of Joint and Severally Liable Units in Public and Private Enforcement of EU Competition Law – What Role for Economic Criteria?' (2016) 37 *European Competition Law Review*, 1, 1

Kaliński, Maciej, *Szkoda na mieniu i jej naprawienie* (Warszawa: C.H. Beck, 2011)

Kaplan, Larry S., 'From Contribution to Good Faith Settlements: Equity Where Are You?' (1984) 49 *Journal of Air Law and Commerce*, 771

Karaszewski, Grzegorz, '*Komentarz do art. 441 Kodeksu cywilnego*' (2014) *LEX*

Kasiński, Tadeusz, 'Roszczenia regresowe z art. 441 para 3 kodeksu cywilnego' (1972) 9 *Nowe Prawo*, 387

Katt, Mareen, *Die Gesamtschuldnerische Haftung des Kronzeugen* (Tübingen: Mohr Siebeck, 2019)

Kellerbauer, Manuel and Weber, Olaf, 'Die gesamtschuldnerische Haftung für Kartellgeldbußen und ihre Grenzen: Das Urteil Siemens VA Tech' (2011) 17 *Europäische Zeitschrift für Wirtschaftsrech*, 666

Këllezi Pranvera, Kilpatrick Bruce and Kobel Pierre (eds.), *Antitrust for Small and Middle Size Undertakings and Image Protection from Non-Competitors* (Berlin: Springer, 2014)

Kelly, Molly, 'Settling for Settlement: The European Commission's New Cartel Settlement Procedure' (2010) 9 *Washington University Global Studies Law Review*, 699

Kern, Christoph, 'Private Law Enforcement versus Public Law Enforcement' (2007) 12 *Zeitschrift für Zivilprozess International*, 351

'Restrukturierung als "private enforcement"' in Boris Paal, Dörte Poelzig and Oliver Fehrenbacher (eds.), Festschrift für Werner F. Ebke (Münich: C.H. Beck 2021)

Kersting, Christian, 'Die neue Richtlinie zur privaten Rechtsdurchsetzung im Kartellrecht' (2014) 6 *Wirtschaft und Wettbewerb*, 564

'Die Rechtsprechung des EuGH zur Bußgeldhaftung in der wirtschaftlichen Einheit' (2014) 12 *Wirtschaft und Wettbewerb*, 64, 1156

'Gesamtschuldnerausgleich bei Kartellgeldbußen' (2016) *Neue Zeitschrift für Kartellrecht*, 147

'Liability of Sister Companies and Subsidiaries in European Competition Law' (2020) 41 *European Competition Law Review*, 125

'Perspektiven der privaten Rechtsdurchsetzung im Kartellrecht' (2008) 3 *Zeitschrift für Wettbewerbsrecht*, 252

'Removing the Tension between Public and Private Enforcement: Disclosure and Privileges for Successful Leniency Applicants' (2014) 5 *Journal of European Competition Law and Practice*, 1, 2

Kersting, Christian and Preuß, Nicola, *Umsetzung der Kartellschadensersatzrichtlinie (2014/104/EU). Ein Gesetzgebungsvorschlag aus der Wissenschaft* (Baden-Baden: Nomos, 2015)

Kessedjian, Catherine, 'Public Order in European Law' (2007) 1 *Erasmus Law Review*, 1, 25

Keuk, Brigitte, 'BGB §§ 426, 633, 634, 635, 638, 242' (1972) 17 *Juristen Zeitung*, 525

Kirgis, Paul F., 'Apportioning Tort Damages in New York: A Method to the Madness' (2001) 75 *St. John's Law Review*, 427

Kirst, Philipp and Bergh, Roger Van den, 'The European Directive on Damages Actions: A Missed Opportunity to Reconcile Compensation of Victims and Leniency Incentives' (2016) 12 *Journal of Competition Law and Economics*, 1

Klein, Alfred, 'Istota solidarności biernej a stosunki prawne odpowiedzialności' in Zbigniew Radwański (ed.), *Studia z prawa zobowiązań* (Warszawa and Poznań: Polskie Wydawnictwo Naukowe, 1979)

Klerman, Daniel, 'Settling Multidefendant Lawsuits: The Advantage of Conditional Setoff Rules' (1996) 25 *The Journal of Legal Studies*, 1, 445

Knight, W. S. M., 'Public Policy of the English Law' (1922) 38 *Law Quarterly Review*, 379

Koch, Jens, 'Der kartellrechtliche Sanktionsdurchgriff im Unternehmensverbund' (2007) 171 *Zeitschrift für das gesamte Handels- und Wirtschaftsrecht*, 554

'Rechtsdurchsetzung im Kartellrecht: Public vs. private enforcement: Auf dem Weg zu einem level playing field?' (2013) 68 *Juristen Zeitung*, 390

Köhler, Helmut, 'EU-Kartellgeldbußen gegen Mutter- und Tochtergesellschaft: Gesamtschuldnerische Haftung und Ausgleich im Innenverhältnis' (2011) 3 *Wettbewerb in Recht und Praxis*, 277

'Kartellverbot und Schadensersatz' (2004) *Gewerblicher Rechtsschutz und Urheberrecht*, 99

Koenig, Carsten, 'Making Contribution Work: The Liability of Privileged and Non-privileged Injurers in EU Competition Law' (2018) 14 *European Competition Journal*, 110

Kohn, Harold E., 'Antitrust Damage Allocation. Hearings before the Subcommittee on Monopolies and Commercial Law of the Committee on the Judiciary' (1983) House of Representatives 118

Kokott, Juliane, 'Zur Haftung von Muttergesellschaften, die Walter Selbst nicht wirtschaftlich tätig sind für Kartellverstöße von Tochtergesellschaften' (2013) *Neue Zeitschrift für Kartellrecht*, 28

Kokott, Juliane and Dittert, Daniel, 'Die Verantwortlichkeit von Muttergesellschaften für Kartellvergehen ihrer Tochtergesellschaften im Lichte der Rechtsprechung der Unionsgerichte' (2012) 7–8 *Wirtschaft und Wettbewerb*, 670

Komisja, Kodyfikacyjna and Podkomisja Prawa, o Zobowiązaniach, *Uzasadnienie Projektu Kodeksu Zobowiązań. Zeszyt* 4, 2 vols. (Warszawa: Wydawnictwo Urzędowe Komisji Kodyfikacyjnej, 1934), vol. I

Komisja, Kodyfikacyjna and Podsekcja III, Prawa Cywilnego, *Projekt prawa o zobowiązaniach. Zeszyt* 4, 2 vols. (Warszawa: Wydawnictwo Urzędowe Komisji Kodyfikacyjnej, 1932), vol. I

Komisja, Kodyfikacyjna, *Uzasadnienie projektu kodeksu zobowiązań* (Warszawa: Komisja Kodyfikacyjna Rzeczpospolitej Polskiej, 1939)

Komninos, Assimakis P., *EC Private Antitrust Enforcement. Decentralised Application of EC Competition Law by National Courts* (Oxford and Portland, OR: Hart Publishing, 2008)

Koniak, Susan P. and Cohen, George M., 'Under Cloak of Settlement' (1996) 82 *Vanderbilt Law Review*, 1051

Kopaczyńska-Pieczniak, Katarzyna, 'Dobre obyczaje i zasady współżycia społecznego w prawie spółek handlowych' (2016) LXIII(2) *Annales Universitatis Mariae Curie-Sklodowska*, 93

Körner, Julia, *Die Gesamtschuld im europäischen Kartellbußgeldrecht* (Köln: Carl Heymanns Verlag, 2016)

Kornhauser, Lewis A. and Revesz, Richard L., 'Settlements under Joint and Several Liability' (1993) 68 *New York University Law Review*, 427

'Multidefendant Settlements: The Impact of Joint and Several Liability' (1994) 23 *The Journal of Legal Studies*, 1, 41

'Sharing Damages among Multiple Tortfeasors' (1989) 98 *Yale Law Journal*, 5, 831

Kornhauser, Lewis A. and Takeda, Keith T., 'N-Defendant Litigation and Settlement: The Impact of Joint and Several Liability' (2008) 109 *New York University Law and Economics Working Papers*, 1

Kosik, Jan, 'Glosa do orzeczenia Sadu Najwyższego z dn. 14.03.1964 r.' (1965) 5 *Orzecznictwo Sądów Polskich i Komisji Arbitrażowych*, 329

Krüger, Carsten, 'Der Gesamtschuldnerausgleich im System der privaten Kartellrechtsdurchsetzung' (2012) 1 *Wirtschaft und Wettbewerb*, 6

'Die haftungsrechtliche Privilegierung des Kronzeugen im Außen- und Innenverhältnis gemäß dem Richtlinienvorschlag der Kommission' (2013) *Neue Zeitschrift für Kartellrecht*, 483

'Überlegungen zur Gesamtschuld von Kartellmitgliedern im System der privaten Kartellrechtsdurchsetzung. Einer für alle, alle gegen einen?' in Peter Oberender (ed.), *Private und öffentliche Kartellrechtsdurchsetzung* (Berlin: Duncker and Humblot, 2012)

Kartellregress (Baden-Baden: Nomos, 2010)

Kuhlmann, Jens, *Rückgriffsgrundlagen bei Gesamtschuld, Bürgschaft und Schadensversicherung in Deutschland, England und Schweden* (Berlin: BMV Berliner Wissenschafts-Verlag, 2005)

Kühn, Kai-Uwe, *Information Exchanges among Firms and Their Impact on Competition* (Luxembourg: Official Publications of the European Communities, 1995)

Kuijpers, Matthijs, Tuinenga, Stefan, Wisking, Stephen, Dietzel, Kim, Campbell, Suzy, and Fritzsche, Alexander, 'Actions for Damages in the Netherlands, the United Kingdom, and Germany' (2015) 6 *Journal of European Competition Law and Practice*, 2, 1

La Rocca, Laura, 'The Controversial Issue of the Parent-company Liability for the Violation of EC Competition Rules by the Subsidiary' (2011) 2 *European Competition Law Review*, 68

Laina, Flavio and Bogdanov, Aleko, 'The EU Cartel Settlement Procedure: Latest Developments' (2017) 8 *Journal of European Competition Law and Practice*, 5, 333

Laitinen, Klas, *Multi-party and Multi-contract Arbitration Mechanisms in International Commercial Litigation. A study on Institutional Rules of Consolidation, Joinder, and Intervention from a Finnish Perspective* (2013), available at https://helda.helsinki.fi/bitstream/handle/10138/44922/klaslaitinenprogradu.pdf?sequence=2

Lande, Robert H., 'The Role of Private Enforcement within EU Competition Law' in Albert A. Foer and Jonathan W. Cuneo (eds.), *The International Handbook on Private Enforcement of Competition Law* (Cheltenham and Northampton: Edward Elgar Publishing, 2010)

Landes, William M., 'An Economic Analysis of the Courts' (1971) 14 *The Journal of Law and Economics*, 1, 61

Laufenberg, Christoph von, *Kartellrechtliche Konzernhaftung* (Berlin: Duncker and Humblot, 2018)

The Law Commission, *Working Paper No 59 Contribution* (London: Her Majesty's Stationery Office, 1975)

Le Tourneau, Philippe, *Droit de la responsabilité et des contrats* (Paris: Dalloz, 2012)

Le Tourneau, Philippe and Julien, Jérôme, 'Solidarité' (2013) *Répertoire de droit civil Dalloz*

Leczykiewicz, Dorota, 'Private Party Liability in EU Law: In Search of the General Regime' in Catherine Barnard and Okeoghene Odudu (eds.), *The Cambridge Yearbook of European Legal Studies. Volume 12, 2009-2010* (Oxford and Portland, OR: Hart Publishing, 2010)

Leonardo, Armati, '*Siemens Österreich*, *Areva* and *Alstom*: Joint and Several Liability in the Gas-insulated Switchgear Cartel' (2015) 6 *Journal of European Competition Law and Practice*, 1, 26

Leslie, Christopher R., 'Judgment-Sharing Agreements' (2009) 58 *Duke Law Journal*, 747

Lettl, Tobias, 'Der Schadensersatzanspruch gemäß § 823 Abs 2 BGB i. V. mit Art. 81 Abs. 1 EG' (2003) 167 *Zeitschrift für das gesamte Handels- und Wirtschaftsrecht*, 473

Lewaszkiewicz-Petrykowska, Biruta, 'Wina jako podstawa odpowiedzialności z tytułu czynów niedozwolonych' (1969) *Studia Prawno-Ekonomiczne*, 87

Wyrządzenie szkody przez kilka osób (Warszawa: Wydawnictwo Prawnicze, 1978)
Lianos, Ioannis, 'The Principle of Effectiveness, Competition Law Remedies and the Limits of Adjudication' (2014) 6 *CLES Research Paper Series*, 3
Liu, Jing and Faure, Michael, 'Risk-sharing Agreements to Cover Environmental Damage: Theory and Practice' (2018) 18 *International Environmental Agreements: Politics, Law and Economics*, 2, 255
Longchamps de Bérier, Roman, *Polskie Prawo Cywilne. Zobowiązania*, 5 vols. (Lviv: Księgarnia Wydawnictwa Gybrynowicz i Syn, 1938), vol. II
Lopatka, John E., 'Missed Opportunity: The Enforcement Recommendations of the Antitrust Modernization Commission' (2008) 53 *Antitrust Bulletin*, 663
Lowe Philip, Marquis Mel and Monti Giorgio (eds.), *European Competition Law Annual 2013: Effective and Legitimate Enforcement of Competition Law* (Oxford and Portland, OR: Hart Publishing, 2016)
Ludwichowska-Redo, Katarzyna, 'Basic Questions of Tort Law from a Polish Perspective' in Helmut Koziol (ed.), *Basic Questions of Tort Law from a Comparative Perspective* (Wien: Jan Sramek Verlag, 2015)
Łopatka, Adam and Ziembiński, Zygmunt, 'Treść i Funkcja Zasad Współżycia Społecznego' (1957) 4(5) *Państwo i Prawo*, 802
Magnus, Ulrich, 'Multiple Tortfeasors under German Law' in W. V. Horton Rogers (ed.), *Unification of Tort Law: Multiple Tortfeasors* (Den Haag: Kluwer Law International, 2004)
Magnus, Ulrich and Seher, Gerhard, 'Fault under German Law' in Pierre Widmer (ed.), *Unification of Tort Law: Fault* (Den Haag: Kluwer Law International, 2005)
Maier-Rigaud, Frank and Schwalbe, Ulrich, 'Quantification of Antitrust Damages' in David Ashton and David Henry (eds.), *Competition Damages Actions in the EU. Law and Practice* (Chelentham and Northampton: Edward Elgar Publishing, 2013)
Makatsch, Tilman and Sascha, Mir Arif, 'Die neue EU-Richtlinie zu Kartellschadensersatzklagen – Angst vor der eigenen "Courage"?' (2015) *Europäische Zeitschrift für Wirtschaftsrecht*, 7
Malarewicz-Jakubów, Agnieszka, 'Klauzule Generalne i Zasady Słuszności' (2014) 17 *Białostockie Studia Prawnicze*, 145
Malaurie, Philippe, Aynes, Laurent and Stoffel-Munck, Philippe, *Droit civil. Les obligations* (Paris: Defrénois, 2004)
Malaurie, Philippe, *L'Ordre Public et Le Contrat* (Reims: Editions Matot-Braine, 1953)
Mansdörfer, Marco, 'Das Modell der Verbandshaftung im europäischen Kartellbußgeldrecht' (2011) *Europäische Zeitschrift für Wirtschaftsrecht*, 214
Marcus Stanley, Koeltl John G., Motz J. Frederick, Rosenthal Lee H., Sanders Barefoot, Birnbaum Sheila, Ray Frank A. and Smith Fern M. (eds.), *Manual for Complex Litigation* (Washington: Federal Judicial Center, 2004)
Marek, Wojciech, 'Roszczenia regresowe z art. 441 k.c.' (1974) 3 *Nowe Prawo*, 287
Marshall, Robert C., Marx, Leslie M. and Samkharadze, Lily, 'Dominant-Firm Conduct by Cartels' (15 February 2011), available at https://capcp.la.psu.edu/papers/2011/dominantfirm.pdf (last visited 09.12.2017)
Martin, Didier R., 'Article 1310 : l'obligation solidaire' (2015) 3 *Revue de contrats*, 799
Marx, Leslie M., Mezzetti, Claudio and Marshall, Robert C., 'Antitrust Leniency with Mutliproduct Colluders' (2015) 7 *American Economic Journal: Microeconomics*, 3, 205
Mäsch, Gerald, 'Innenausgleich bei gesamtschuldnerisch festgesetzter Kartellbuße der EU-Kommission – „Calciumcarbid"' (2012) *Gewerblicher Rechtsschutz und Urheberrecht Praxis im Immaterialgüter und Wettbewerbsrecht*, 268

'Private Ansprüche bei Verstößen gegen das europäische Kartellverbot – „Courage" und die Folgen' (2003) 5 *Zeitschrift Europarecht*, 825

Mazeaud, Henri, Mazeaud, Léon, Mazeaud, Jean and Tunc, André, *Traité théorique et pratique de la responsabilité civile délictuelle et contractuelle*, 3 vols. (Paris: Montchrestien, 1958), vol. II

Medicus, Dieter, *Bürgerliches Recht* (Köln, Berlin, Bonn, München: Vahlen, 2002)

Meier, Sonja, *Gesamtschulden* (Tübingen: Mohr Siebeck, 2010)

Mestre, Jacques, 'La pluralité d'obligés accessoires' (1981) *Revue trimestrielle de droit civil*, 1

Meyer-Lindemann, Hans Jürgen, Wartenburg, Clemens Graf York von and Kafetzopoulos, Andreas, 'Private Equity Investors Are Not Immune to Antitrust Risks in the European Union' (2014) 35 *European Competition Law Review*, 8, 367

Meyring, Bernd, 'Uferlose Haftung im Bußgeldverfahren?' (2010) 2 *Wirtschaft und Wettbewerb*, 157

Mignot, Marc, 'Commentaire article par article de l'ordonnance du 10 fevrier 2016 portant réforme du droit des contrats, du régime general et de la preuve des obligations (VIII)' (2016) 80 *Petites affiches*, 4

'Plaidoyer pour l'abrogation de l'article 1216 du Code civil' (2006) 27 *Revue Lamy Droit civil*, 27

'Régime général des obligations. Pluralité de sujets de l'obligation. Principe de division' (2017) *JurisClasseur Civil Code*, 10

'Régime général des obligations. Pluralité de sujets d'obligation. Obligation solidaire' (2017) *JurisClasseur Civil Code*, 20

Les obligations solidaires et les obligations in solidum en droit privé français (Paris: Dalloz, 2002)

Milewska, Aleksandra, 'Solidarna odpowiedzialność sprawców naruszenia prawa konkurencji przewidziana w projekcie ustawy o roszczeniach o naprawienie szkody wyrządzonej przez naruszenie prawa konkurencji z 7 lutego 2017 r. – aspekt podmiotowy' (2017) 1 *internetowy Kwartalnik Antymonopolowy i Regulacyjny*, 6, 58

Miskolczi Bodnár, Péter and Szuchy, Robert, 'Joint and Several Liability of Competition Law Infringers in the Legislation of Central and Eastern European Member States' (2017) 15 *Yearbook of Antitrust and Regulatory Studies*, 85

Mitchell, Charles, *The Law of Contribution and Reimbursement* (Oxford: Oxford University Press, 2002)

Modzelewska de Raad, Małgorzata, 'Consensual Dispute Resolution in the Damages Directive. Implementation in CEE Countries' (2017) 15 *Yearbook of Antitrust and Regulatory Studies*, 49

Mojak, Jan, 'Dobre Obyczaje w polskim prawie kontraktowym – wybrane zagadnienia' (2016) XXV *Studia Iuridica Lublinensia*, 2, 161

Montesa, Aitor and Givaja, Ángel, 'When Parents Pay for Their Children's Wrongs: Attribution of Liability for EC Antitrust Infringements in Parent-Subsidiary Scenarios' (2006) 29 *World Competition*, 4, 555

Morrissey Joseph F. and Graves Jack M. (eds.), *International Sales Law and Arbitration: Problems, Cases and Commentary* (Austin, Boston, Chicago, New York, The Netherlands: Wolters Kluwer Law and Business, 2008)

Motta, Massimo and Polo, Michele, 'Leniency Programs and Cartel Prosecution' (2003) 21 *International Journal of Industrial Organization*, 347

Müller-Graff, Peter-Christian, 'Kartellrechtlicher Schadensersatz in neuer Versuchsanordnung' (2015) 179 *Zeitschrift für das gesamte Handels- und Wirtschaftsrecht*, 691

Nagy Csongor, István, 'The New Hungarian Rules on Damages Caused by Horizontal Hardcore Cartels: Presumed Price Increase and Limited Protection for Whistleblowers – An Analytical Introduction' (2011) 32 *European Competition Law Review*, 2, 63

Napel, Stefan and Oldehaver, Gunnar, 'Kartellschadensersatz und Gesamtschuldnerausgleich – Ökonomisch faire Schadensaufteilung mit dem Shapley-Wert' (2015) *Neue Zeitschrift für Kartellrecht*, 135

Nehl, Hanns Peter, 'Anmerkung' (2013) 14 *Europäische Zeitschrift für Wirtschaftsrecht*, 554

Nelken, David, 'Using the Concept of Legal Culture' (2004) 29 *Australian Journal of Legal Philosophy*, 1

Nesterowicz, Mirosław and Bagińska, Ewa, 'Multiple Tortfeasors under Polish Law' in W. V. Horton Rogers (ed.), *Unification of Tort Law: Multiple Tortfeasors* (Den Haag: Kluwer Law International, 2004)

Newman, Matthew, 'EU Cartel Busters Start at Least Three own-initiative Probes as Leniency Candidates Dry up, Madero Says' (12 July 2019), *Mlex*, available at https://mlex.com/GlobalAdvisory/DetailView.aspx?cid=1111720&siteid=244&rdir=1

Odudu, Okeoghene and Bailey, David, 'The Single Economic Entity Doctrine in EU Competition Law' (2014) 51 *Common Market Law Review*, 1721

OECD, 'Competition Policy: Promoting Efficiency and Sound Markets' (2012), available at https://oecd.org/cleangovbiz/toolkit/50037123.pdf

'Roundtable on Information Exchanges between Competitors under Competition Law, Note by the Delegation of the European Union' (27–28 October 2010), DAF/COMP/WD(2010)118

'SME and Entrepreneurship Outlook' (2005), available at https://oecd.org/cfe/smes/oecdsmeandentrepreneurshipoutlook-2005edition.htm

OFT, 'Private Actions in Competition Law: Effective Redress for Consumers and Business' (April 2007) OFT 916

Ohanowicz, Alfred, 'Glosa do orzeczenia Sądu Najwyższego z dn. 23.01.2957 r.' (1958) 2 *Orzecznictwo Sądów Polskich i Komisji Arbitrażowych*, 139

Olejniczak, Adam, 'Art. 441' in Andrzej Kidyba (ed.), *Kodeks cywilny. Komentarz. Zobowiązania. Część ogólna*, 4 vols. (Warszawa: Wolters Kluwer Polska, 2014), vol. III

Opper, Kai-Uwe, *Die gesamtschuldnerische Bußgeldhaftung für Kartellverstöße innerhalb eines Konzerns* (Baden-Baden: Nomos, 2016)

Ota, Shozo, 'The Fairness and the Efficiency of the Compensation System: An Economic Analysis of the Tort Theories' (1987) 7 *International Review of Law and Economics*, 229

Pauer Nada, Ina, *The Single Economic Entity Doctrine and Corporate Group Responsibility in European Antitrust Law* (New York: Wolter Kluwer Law and Business, 2014)

Peter, Josefa F. and Wagener, Dominique S., 'Anmerkung' (2013) 7 *Europäische Zeitschrift für Wirtschaftsrecht*, 268

Peyer, Sebastian, 'Compensation and the Damages Directive' (2015) 15 *Centre for Competition Policy Working Paper*, 10, 1

'Myths and Untold Stories – Private Antitrust Enforcement in Germany' (2010) *Centre for Competition Policy Working Paper*, 10–12, 1

Pimont, Sébastien and Roux-Sibillon, Eric, 'Les dispositions du projet de réforme du droit des obligations relatives aux obligations plurales' (2015) 47 *La Semaine Juridique Notariale et Immobliere*, 1218

Piszcz, Anna and Wolski, Dominik, *Implementation of the EU Damages Directive in Central and Eastern European Countries* (Warsaw: University of Warsaw Faculty of Management Press, 2017)

Pitsch, Johannes, 'Kein Rückgriff der Muttergesellschaft gegen die Tochtergesellschaft wegen kartellrechtlicher Geldbuße (Calciumcarbid-Kartell)' (2011) *Gesellschafts- und Wirtschaftsrecht*, 192

Polden, Donald J. and Sullivan, E. Thomas, 'Contribution and Claim Reduction in Antitrust Litigation: A Legislative Analysis' (1983) 20(1) *Harvard Journal on Legislation*, 397

Polinsky, A. Mitchell and Shavell, Steven, 'Contribution and Claim Reduction among Antitrust Defendants: An Economic Analysis' (1981) 33 *Stanford Law Review*, 3, 447

'The Optimal Trade-off between the Probability and Magnitude of Fines' (1979) 69 *American Economic Review*, 880

Ponsoldt, James F. and Terry, Benjamin H., 'Contribution in Civil Antitrust Litigation: The Emerging Consensus in Legal Literature' (1981) 38 *Washington and Lee Law Review*, 2, 315

Prediger, Bernhard, *Zur Auslegung und Anwendung der Regelungen im BGB über die Gesamtschuld* (Frankfurt am Main: Peter Lang, Europäische Hochschulschriften, 1988)

Pree, Jolling K. de and Molin, Stefan C. H., 'Shareholder Liability for Joint Venture Infringements in the European Union' (2011) 34 *Fordham International Law Journal*, 3, 431

Radwański, Zbigniew and Olejniczak, Adam, *Zobowiązania – część ogólna* (Warszawa, C.H. Beck, 2016)

Ranouil, Marine, *Les recours entre coobligés* (Paris: Bilbliothèque de l'IRJS – André Tunc, 2014)

Raynaud, Pierre, 'La nature de l'obligation des coauteurs d'un dommage : obligation "in solidum" ou solidarité ?' in *Mélanges dédiés à Jean Vincent* (Paris: Dalloz, 1981)

Reasoner, Harry M., 'Prepared Statement of Harry M. Reasoner' (14 July 2005), available at https://govinfo.library.unt.edu/amc/commission_hearings/pdf/Reasoner.pdf

Regnier, Lukas, 'Cartel Damages Actions in German Courts: What the Statistics Tell Us' (2020) 11 *Journal of European Competition Law & Practice*, 1–2, 72

Reich, Norbert, 'Horizontal Liability in EC Law: Hybridization of Remedies for Compensation in Case of Breaches of EC Rights' (2007) 44 *Common Market Law Review*, 705

Riemer, Yosef J., 'Sharing Agreements among Defendants in Antitrust Cases' (1984) 52 *The George Washington Law Review*, 289

Riley, Alan, 'Beyond Leniency: Enhancing Enforcement in EC Antitrust Law' (2005) 28 *World Competition*, 3, 377

Ripert, Georges, 'L'ordre public économique et la liberté contractuelle' in *Recueil d'études sur les sources du droit en l'honneur de François Gény* (Paris: Librairie du Recueil Sirey, 1934)

Ritter, Jan-Stephan, 'Private Durchsetzung des Kartellrechts – Vorschläge des Weißbuchs der Europäischen Kommission' (2008) 7 *Wirtschaft und Wettbewerb*, 773

Rogers, W. V. Horton, 'Causation under English Law' in Jaap Spier (ed.), *Unification of Tort Law: Causation* (Den Haag: Kluwer Law International, 2000)

'Comparative Report on Multiple Tortfeasors' in W. V. Horton Rogers (ed.), *Unification of Tort Law: Multiple Tortfeasors* (Den Haag: Kluwer Law International, 2004)

'Fault under English Law' in Pierre Widmer (ed.), *Unification of Tort Law: Fault* (Den Haag: Kluwer Law International, 2005)

'Multiple Tortfeasors under English Law' in W. V. Horton Rogers (ed.), *Unification of Tort Law: Multiple Tortfeasors* (Den Haag: Kluwer Law International, 2004)

Rossi, Lucia Serena and Casolari, Federico, *The Principle of Equality in EU Law* (Cham: Springer International Publishing, 2017)

Rostron, Allen, 'Beyond Market Share Liability: A Theory of Proportional Share Liability for Nonfungible Products' (2003) 52 *UCLA Law Review*, 151

Roth, Hans-Peter, 'Für 10% Gesamtumsatzgrenze einer Geldbuße ist jeweilige Konzernzugehörigkeit maßgeblich' (2014) *Gesellschafts- und Wirtschaftsrecht*, 439

Roth, Wulf-Henning, 'Effet utile im europäischen Kartellrecht' (2013) 3 *Wettbewerb in Recht und Praxis*, 257

Rother, Werner, 'Die "vorwiegende Verursachung"' (1983) 33 *Versicherungsrecht*, 793

Rüßmann, Helmut, '§ 421 BGB' in Markus Junker (ed.), *Juris Praxis Kommentar – BGB. Schuldrecht*, 6 vols. (Saarbrücken: juris, 2010), vol. II(1)

'§ 426 BGB' in Markus Junker (ed.), *Juris Praxis Kommentar – BGB. Schuldrecht*, 6 vols. (Saarbrücken: juris, 2010), vol. II(1)

'Die Abgrenzung der Gesamtschuld von anderen Schuldnermehrheiten – BGHZ 59, 97' (1974) *Juristische Schulung*, 292

Rust, Ulrich, 'Kartellverstoß und Gesamtschuld – Bestandsaufnahme und Ausblick' (2015) *Neue Zeitschrift für Kartellrecht*, 502

Rzetecka-Gil, Agnieszka, 'Warunki odpowiedzialności solidarnej za szkodę. Komentarz do art. 441 Kodeksu cywilnego' (2011) *LEX*

Safjan, Marek, 'Art. 441' in Krzysztof Pietrzykowski (ed.), *Kodeks cywilny. Komentarz*, 2 vols. (Warszawa: C.H. Beck, 2011), vol. I

Savey-Casard, Paul, 'Le repentir actif en droit pénal français' (1972) 3 *Revue de science criminelle et de droit pénal comparé*, 515

Savigny Friedrich, Karl von, *Das Obligationenrecht als Theil des heutigen Römischen Rechts*, 2 vols. (Berlin: Bei Zeit und Comp., 1851), vol. I

Schaper, Hanno and Stauber, Peter, 'Ausgewählte Themen des neuen Kartellschadensersatzrechts – Schadensersatz, Abwälzung, Gesamtschuld und Innenausgleich' (2017) *Neue Zeitschrift für Kartellrecht*, 279

Schmidt, Walter, *Gesamtschuld und Gesamtschuldregress* (Köln: Inaugural-Dissertation, 1973)

Schneider, Hans-Helmut, 'Art. 16 VO 1/2003' in Günter Hirsch, Frank Montag and Franz Jürgen Säcker (eds.), *Münchener Kommentar. Europäisches und Deutsches Wettbewerbsrecht. Kartellrecht, Missbrauchs- und Fusionskontrolle*, 2 vols. (München: C.H. Beck, 2007), vol. I

Schnelle, Ulrich, 'Die Aufteilung von Bußgeldern im Konzern' (2015) 4 *Wirtschaft und Wettbewerb*, 332

Schreiber, Till and Savov, Vasil, 'Kone v. Commission: Umbrella Damages Claims' (2014) 5 *Journal of European Competition Law and Practice*, 8, 548

Schricker Gerhard, *Gesetzesverletzung und Sittenverstoß* (München: Beck, 1970)

Schwalbe, Ulrich and Höft, Jan, 'Ausgestaltung von Kronzeugenprogrammen und private Kartellrechtsdurchsetzung' in Stefan Bechtold, Joachim Jickeli, Mathias Rohe (eds.), *Recht, Ordnung und Wettbewerb – Festschrift zum 70. Geburtstag von Wernhard Möschel* (Baden-Baden: Nomos, 2012)

Schweitzer, Heike, 'Die neue Richtlinie für wettbewerbsrechtliche Schadensersatzklagen' (2014) 9 *Neue Zeitschrift für Kartellrecht*, 335

Schwenke, Hendrik, 'Die Richtlinie für private Kartellschadensersatzklagen und der Gesamtschuldnerausgleich: Wie kann Art. 11 v. ins deutsche Recht umgesetzt werden?' (2015) *Neue Zeitschrift für Kartellrecht*, 383

Section of Antitrust Law of the American Bar Association, 'Report on Contribution and Claim Reduction' (14 December 2005), available at https://americanbar.org/content/dam/aba/administrative/antitrust_law/at-comments/2005/12-05/contribution_claim_comm.pdf

Antitrust Evidence Handbook (Chicago: American Bar Association Publishing, 2016)
Contribution and Claim Reduction in Antitrust Litigation (Chicago: American Bar Association Publishing, 1986)

Seegers, Martin, 'Interaction of the Rules on Joint and Several Liability and Settlements under the EU Directive on Damage Actions' (2014) 7 *Global Competition Litigation Review*, 3, 140

Selb, Walter, *Schadensbegriff und Regreßmethoden* (Heidelberg: Carl Winter Universitätsverlag, 1963)

Siakka, Tatiana, 'Case C-724/17 Vantaan kaupunki v. Skanska Industrial Solutions: Transposition of the Concept of an "Undertaking" into Civil Damages Actions' (2019) 10 *Journal of European Competition Law & Practice*, 8, 479

Silbye, Frederik, 'A Note on Antitrust Damages and Leniency Programs' (2012) 33 *European Journal of Law and Economics*, 691

Silver, Charles and Baker, Lynn Anne, 'Mass Lawsuits and the Aggregate Settlement Rule' (1997) 32 *Wake Forest Law Review*, 733

Singer, Linda R., *Settling Disputes: Conflict Resolution in Business, Families, and the Legal System* (Boulder, San Francisco, Oxford: Westview Press, 1994)

Sitarz, Olga, 'Active Repentance as an Instrument of Criminal and Penal Policy' (2009) 31 *Archiwum Kryminologii*, 159

Slim, Hadi, 'Approche comparative de la faute dans la responsabilité civile extra-contractuelle' (2003) 6 *Responsabilité civile et assurance*, 18

Śmieja, Andrzej, 'Art. 441' in Adam Olejniczak (ed.), *Prawo zobowiązań – część ogólna. System Prawa Prywatnego*, 21 vols. (Warszawa: C.H. Beck, 2014), vol. VI

Sośniak, Małgorzata, 'Elementy winy nieumyślnej w prawie cywilnym' (1975) 68 *Prace Naukowe Uniwersytetu Śląskiego*, 151

Sousa, Ferro Miguel, 'Antitrust Private Enforcement and the Binding Effect of Public Enforcement Decisions' (2019) 2 *Market and Competition Law Review*, 3, 51

Spagnolo, Giancarlo, 'Divide et impera: Opimal leniency programs' (2004) 4840 *CEPR Discussion Paper*, 1

Spier, Kathryn E., 'A Note on Joint and Several Liability: Insolvency, Settlement, and Incentives' (1994) 23 *Journal of Legal Studies*, 55

Stamm, Jürgen, *Regreßfiguren im Zivilrecht. Eine Rückbesinnung auf die Gesamtschuld unter Neubewertung des Zessionsregresses gemäß § 255 BGB und der Drittschadensliquidation* (Berlin: Duncker and Humblot, 2000)

Stanevičius, Mantas, '*Portielje*: Bar Remains High for Rebutting Parental Liability Presumption' (2014) 5 *Journal of European Competition Law and Practice*, 1, 24

Stanley, Timothy James, 'An Analysis of the Rules of Contribution and No Contribution for Joint and Several Liability in Conspiracy Cases' (1994) 35 *Santa Clara Law Review*, 1, 1

Steel, Sandy, *Proof of Causation in Tort Law* (Cambridge: Cambridge University Press, 2015)

Stefanicki, Robert, 'Civil Law Remedies for Violation of Competition Law' (2012) 4 *European Review of Contract Law*, 400

Stefano, Gianni de, 'General Court Rules on Successor Liability and Apportionment of Group Liability in the Gas Insulated Switchgear Cartel' (2011) 2 *Journal of European Competition Law and Practice*, 4, 344

Steinle, Christian, 'Kartellschadensersatzrichtlinie – Auf dem Weg zum Sanktions-Overkill? (Gastkommentar)' (2014) 13 *Europäische Zeitschrift für Wirtschaftsrecht*, 481

Stephan, Andreas, 'An Empirical Assessment of the European Leniency Notice' (2008) 5 *Journal of Competition Law and Economics*, 3, 537

Stephens, Clay A., 'Antitrust Damage Allocation. Hearings before the Subcommittee on Monopolies and Commercial Law of the Committee on the Judiciary' (1983), House of Representatives 118

Stockmann, Kurt, 'Ziele und Zielkonflikte bei Kartellsanktionen' in Ingo Brinker, Dieter H. Scheuing and Kurt Stockmann (eds.), *Recht und Wettbewerb. Festschrift für Rainer Bechtold zum 65. Geburtstag* (München: C. H. Beck, 2006)

Švirinas, Daivis, 'The Assessment of Information Exchange Agreements Between Competitors from the Perspective of Competition Law of the EU and of the Republic of Lithuania' (2012) 19 *Jurisprudencija*, 1, 87

Sychowicz, Marek 'Art. 441' in Gerard Bieniek, Helena Ciepła, Stanisław Dmowski, Jacek Gudowski, Krzysztof Kołakowski, Marek Sychowicz, Tadeusz Wiśniewski and Czesława Żuławska (eds.), *Komentarz do kodeksu cywilnego. Zobowiązania*, 6 vols. (Warszawa, LexisNexis, 2010), vol. III

Synovate, 'Competition Act and Consumer Rights' (April 2005) OFT 799

Szpunar, Adam, 'Glosa do orzeczenia Sądu Najważniejszego z dn. 16.10.1958 r.' (1960) 1 *Orzecznictwo Sądów Polskich i Komisji Arbitrażowych*, 6

'Glosa do orzeczenia Sądu Najwyższego z dn. 21.11.1967 r.' (1968) 11 *Orzecznictwo Sądów Polskich i Komisji Arbitrażowych*, 486

'The Law of Tort in the Polish Civil Code' (1967) 16 *The International and Comparative Law Quarterly*, 1, 86

'Roszczenia regresowe Zakładu Ubezpieczeń' (1974) XII *Studia Prawno-Ekonomiczne*, 29

Tangdham, Krisadhikhun, *The Potential Civil Liability of Innocent Subsidiaries as a Consequence of the Notion of undertaking in EU Competition Law an Implication from the Recent Case Skanska* (Lund: Lund University, 2020)

Teff, Harvey, '"Market Share" Liability: A Novel Approach to Causation' (1982) (31) *The International and Comparative Law Quarterly*, 4, 840

Temple, Lang John, 'How Can the Problem of the Liability of a Parent Company for Price Fixing by a Wholly-owned Subsidiary Be Resolved?' (2014) 37 *Fordham International Law Journal*, 5, 1481

Tereszkiewicz, Piotr, 'Solidarność dłużników w świetle europeizacji prawa obligacyjnego' in Joanna Haberko, Adam Olejniczak, Agnieszka Pyrzyńska and Dorota Sokołowska (eds.), *Współczesne problemy prawa zobowiązań* (Poznań: Wolters Kluwer Polska, 2014)

Terré, François, *Pour une réforme du droit de la responsabilité civile* (Paris: Dalloz, 2011)

Teubner, Gunther, *Standards und Direktiven in Generalklauseln* (Tübingen: Athenäum, 1971)

Thiede, Thomas, 'Fine to Follow-on? Private Anti-trust Actions in European Law' (2017) 5 *China-EU Law Journal*, 233

'Private Enforcement of Anti-trust Damages in Europe. A Germanic Perspective on Directive 2014/104/EU' (2016) *ELTE Law Journal*, 147, available at: https://eltelawjournal.hu/private-enforcement-anti-trust-damages-europe-germanic-perspective-directive-2014104eu/

Thoma, Kerstin, *Der internationale Regress. Formen und Gerichtszuständigkeit – unter Berücksichtigung des deutschen, österreichischen, schweizerischen und französischen materiellen Regressrechts* (Hamburg: Verlag Dr. Kovač, 2007)

Thomas, Stefan, 'Die Gesamtschuld im EU-Kartellbußgeldrecht – die Kommission als "juristischer Pascha"?' in Stefan Bechtold, Joachim Jickeli, Mathias Rohe (eds.), *Recht,*

Ordnung und Wettbewerb – Festschrift zum 70. Geburtstag von Wernhard Möschel (Baden-Baden: Nomos, 2012)

'Guilty of a Fault That One Has Not Committed. The Limits of the Group-Based Sanction Policy Carried out by the Commission and the European Courts in EU-Antitrust Law' (2012) 3 *Journal of European Competition Law and Practice*, 1, 11

'Konzernprivileg und Gemeinschaftsunternehmen – Die kartellrechtliche Beurteilung konzerninterner Wettbewerbsbeschränkungen mit Gemeinschaftsunternehmen' (2005) 3 *Zeitschrift für Wettbewerbsrecht*, 236

Till, Ernest, *Polskie prawo zobowiązań. Część ogólna. Projekt wstępny z motywami* (Lviv: Komisja Kodyfikacyjna Rzeczpospolitej Polskiej, 1923)

Vecchio, Karoline Del, 'German Sugar Cartelists Fail to Settle with Food Makers, Will Face Court Ruling' (12 July 2019), *Mlex*, available at https://mlex.com/GlobalAdvisory/DetailView.aspx?cid=1111634&siteid=244&rdir=1

United Nations Conference on Trade and Development, 'Appropriate Sanctions and Remedies, Sixth United Nations Conference to Review All Aspects of the Set of Multilaterally Agreed Equitable Principles and Rules for the Control of Restrictive Business Practices' (8–12 November 2010), TD/RBP/CONF.7/5, available at https://unctad.org/en/Docs/tdrbpconf7d5_en.pdf

United States Congress, 'Antitrust Damage Allocation. Hearings before the Subcommittee on Monopolies and Commercial Law of the Committee on the Judiciary' (1983 House of Representatives 118)

'The Antitrust Equal Enforcement Act. Hearings before the Committee on the Judiciary' (1982), House of Representatives J-97-15

United States Government Accountability Office, 'Criminal Cartel Enforcement. Stakeholder Views on Impact of 2004 Antitrust Reform Are Mixed, but Support Whistleblower Protection' (2011), GAO-11-619

United States Department of Justice, 'The Modern Leniency Program after Ten Years – A Summary Overview of the Antitrust Division's Criminal Enforcement' (12 August 2003), *Justice News*, available at https://justice.gov/atr/speech/modern-leniency-program-after-ten-years-summary-overview-antitrust-divisions-criminal

'Public and Private Antitrust Enforcement in the United States' (11 February 2004), *Justice News*, available at https://justice.gov/atr/file/517756/download

Vetu, F., 'Application de la responsabilité civile pour faute à la violation du droit des pratiques anticoncurrentielles' (2003) 48(II) *La Semaine Juridique Edition Génerale*, 10183

Vincent, Jean, 'L'extension en jurisprudence de la notion de solidarité passive' (1939) 38 *Revue trimestrielle de droit civil*, 601

Viney, Geneviève, 'Apres la réforme du contrat, la nécessaire réforme des textes du Code civil relatifs à la responsabilité' (2016) 4 *La Semaine Juridique Edition Generale*, 99

Virgo, Graham, 'Contribution Revisited' (2008) 67 *The Cambridge Law Journal*, 2, 254

Vogenauer Stefan and Weatherill Stephen (eds.), *General Principles of Law: European and Comparative Perspectives* (Oxford and Portland, OR: Hart Publishing, 2017)

Vormizeele, Philipp Voet van, 'Die EG-kartellrechtliche Haftungszurechnung im Konzern im Widerstreit zu den nationalen Gesellschaftsrechtsordnungen' (2010) 9 *Wirtschaft und Wettbewerb*, 1008

Völzmann-Stickelbrock, Barbara, '§ 421 BGB' in Barbara Dauner-Lieb, Thomas Heidel and Gerhard Ring (eds.), *Nomos Kommentar. BGB Schuldrecht*, 8 vols. (Baden-Baden: Nomos, 2014), vol. II(1)

'§ 423 BGB' in Barbara Dauner-Lieb, Thomas Heidel and Gerhard Ring (eds.), *Nomos Kommentar. BGB Schuldrecht*, 8 vols. (Baden-Baden: Nomos, 2014), vol. II(1)

'§ 426 BGB' in Barbara Dauner-Lieb, Thomas Heidel and Gerhard Ring (eds.), *Nomos Kommentar. BGB Schuldrecht*, 8 vols. (Baden-Baden: Nomos, 2014), vol. II(1)

Wagener, Hans-Markus, 'Follow-up to Skanska – The "Implementation" by National Courts So Far' (2019) 10 *Neue Zeitschrift für Kartellrecht*, 535

Wagner, Gerhard '§ 823 BGB' in Mathias Habersack (ed.), *Münchener Kommentar zum Bürgerlichen Gesetzbuch. Schuldrecht. Besonderer Teil III*, 14 vols. (München: C.H. Beck, 2013), vol. V

Wagner-von Papp, Florian, 'Der Richtlinienentwurf zu kartellrechtlichen Schadensersatzklagen' (2009) 11 *Europäisches Wirtschafts- und Steuerrecht*, 445

Weinhold, Janine, *Der Gesamtschuldnerausgleich zwischen den Kartellmitgliedern* (Frankfurt am Main: PL Academic Research, Europäische Hochschulschriften, 2015)

Widmer, Pierre, 'Comparative Report on Fault as a Basis of Liability and Criterion of Imputation' in Pierre Widmer (ed.), *Unification of Tort Law: Fault* (Den Haag: Kluwer Law International, 2005)

Williams, Glanville Llewelyn, *Joint Torts and Contributory Negligence* (London: Stevens and Sons Limited, 1951)

Wils, Wouter P. J., 'Leniency in Antitrust Enforcement: Theory and Practice' (2007) 30 *World Competition*, 1, 25

'Optimal Antitrust Fines: Theory and Practice' (2006) 29 *World Competition*, 2, 183

'Private Enforcement of EU Antitrust Law and Its Relationship with Public Enforcement: Past, Present and Future' (2017) 40 *World Competition*, 1, 3

'The Relationship between Public Antitrust Enforcement and Private Actions for Damages' (2009) 32 *World Competition*, 1, 3

'The Undertaking as Subject of E.C. Competition Law and the Imputation of Infringements to Natural or Legal persons' (2000) 25 *European Law Review*, 99

'The Use of Leniency in EU Cartel Enforcement: An Assessment After Twenty Years' (2016) 39 *World Competition*, 327

Wish, Rirchard and Bailey, David, *Competition Law* (New York: Oxford University Press, 2012)

Wolski, Dominik, 'Solidarna odpowiedzialność naruszycieli' in Tadeusz Skoczny (ed.), *Prawo konkurencji. 25 lat* (Warszawa: Wolter Kluwers Polska, 2015)

Wright, Richard W., 'Allocating Liability among Multiple Responsible Causes: A Principled Defense of Joint and Several Liability for Actual Harm and Risk Exposure' (1988) 21 *UC Davis Law Review*, 1141

Wurmnest, Wolfgang, 'Schadensersatz wegen Verletzung des EU-Kartellrechts. Grundfragen und Entwicklungslinien' in Oliver Remien (ed.), *Schadensersatz im europäischen Privat- und Wirtschaftsrecht* (Tübingen: Mohr Siebeck, 2012)

'Zivilrechtliche Ausgleichsansprüche von Kartellbeteiligten bei Verstößen gegen das EG-Kartellverbot' (2003) *Recht der internationalen Wirtschaft*, 896

Ysewyn, Johan and Kahmann, Siobhan, 'The Decline and Fall of the Leniency Programme in Europe' (2018) 1 *Concurrences*, 44

Zandler, Dieter, 'Die wirtschaftliche Einheit als Normadressat im Kartellbußgeldrecht' (2016) *Neue Zeitschrift für Kartellrecht*, 98

Zekaria, Simon, 'Truck Cartel Disclosure "slow" and "difficult", UK Claimant Ryder Tells Competition Judge' (6 February 2020), *Mlex*, available at https://mlex.com/GlobalAdvisory/DetailView.aspx?cid=1160838&siteid=244&rdir=1

'Visa, WH Smith Settle Antitrust Claim Over Card Fees' (9 July 2019), *Mlex*, available at https://mlex.com/GlobalAdvisory/DetailView.aspx?cid=1110490&siteid=244&rdir=1

'Wallenius Wilhelmsen Data Provides "smoking gun" in Car-shipper Operations, Daimler Tells UK Judge' (5 May 2020), *Mlex*, available at https://mlex.com/GlobalAdvisory/DetailView.aspx?cid=1184384&siteid=244&rdir=1

Zelek, Mariusz, 'Art. 415' in Maciej Gutowski (ed.), *Duże Komentarze Becka. Kodeks cywilny. Komentarz. Art. 1-449* (Warszawa: C.H. Beck, 2016), vol. I

Zhou, Wanli, 'The Effects of Joint and Several Liability Rule on Collusion and Antitrust Settlement' (2015) 4 *The Bonn Journal of Economics*, 1, 76

Zimmer, Daniel J. and Paul, Thomas, 'Kartellbußgeldrechtliche Haftung und Haftungsbefreiung im Konzern' (2007) 9 *Wirtschaft und Wettbewerb*, 970

Zingales, Nicolo, 'European and American Leniency Programmes: Two Models towards Convergence?' (2008) 5 *The Competition Law Review*, 1, 5

Index

Absicht, 128
Acquis Group, The, 55
action
  mandati, 96
  negotiorum gestorum, 96
AC-Treuhand, 214
adequate (*Adäquanz*), 135
Advocate General (AG), 57, 111
Akzo Nobel, 20
aminobutanol, 14
Antitrust Criminal Penalty Enhancement and Reform Act, The (ACPERA), 187–188, 216
Antitrust Modernization Commission, The, 43
  96th, 97th and 98th Congress Sessions, 40
ArcelorMittal, 15, 20, 80, 81
Arques, 50, 68
as quiet time injunctions, 228
association of undertaking, 9, 76
Ausgleichsklage, 6, 102
Austrian banks, 26
aute d'imprudence ou de negligence, 129
Autoliv, 13, 20

Bahn, Deutsche, 166
bedingter Vorsatz, 129
Befreiung, 66, 98, 101, 105, 158, 228
benefits, 35–36, 89, 133, 139, 153, 166, 168, 179, 190, 194
Bieber, Tobias, 26, 28, 54
bonos mores, 212–213
Brexit, 5
Brook's Wharf and Bull Wharf Ltd v. Goodman Bros, 113
Bundesgerichtshof (BGH), The, 50, 69–70, 102–103, 106, 128, 153
Bürgerliches Gesetzbuch (BGB), The, 37
  § 254, 69
  § 254(1), 119, 121–122
  § 42, 94
  § 421, 29
  § 426, 102, 107, 119
  § 426(1), 34, 69, 94, 98, 100, 102, 106, 108, 114
  § 426(2), 94, 100, 108, 114
  § 840(1), 29

Caemmerer, Ernst von, 35
Calcium carbide, 49–50, 68–70, 102–103, 122, 125, 152, 154
cartel, *Cement*, 183
CAT, The, 228
causation (*przyczynić się*), 120
CDC, 176
Cemex, 184–185
circumstances of the case (*okoliczności*), 120
claimant, The, 6
claims, *Mitwirkung*, 67
Code Civil (CC), The, 90
  Article 6, 212
  Article 134, 108
  Article 1213 (old version), 38
  Article 1251(3) (old version), 38
  Article 1317, 96, 108, 114
  Article 1346, 34, 95, 103, 114
Code de Commerce, The, 96
  Article L. 481-489, 96, 99, 102–103, 108, 120, 159–160
Commercial Solvens (CSC), The, 14, 22. *See also* CSC-ICI-Group, The
Commission Communication, The, 193

Commission Guideline on Fines, The, 130, 154–155
Commission Recommendation 2003/361/EC, 202
Article 2(1), 202
Commission's Guidelines on Fines, The, 9, 10, 46, 130, 140, 141, 143, 153, 154, 155, 200
companies, 18
company, holding, 21–22, 26, 50, 148, 224
company, sister, 21–22
Competition Act 1998, The, 5
Competition Appeal Tribunal, The, 80
consensual dispute resolution, 29, 162–163, 166–167, 205, 224, 230
Contribution Act 1978, The, 38, 89, 92, 100–101, 106
Section 1, 101
Section 2(1), 92
Section 2(2), 97
Section 3, 29
Section 7(3)(b), 211
corporate group, 15, 19, 26, 50, 111–112, 131–132, 141
Cour de Cassation of 11 July 1892, The, 29
Courage, 11
Court of Justice of the European Union (CJEU), The, 11, 15, 17, 19–20, 22–24, 26–28, 32, 49–50, 52, 55, 57–58, 60, 67–76, 83, 87, 104, 110, 128, 150–151, 211, 213–214, 221
court, private, 2
CSC-ICI-Group, The, 14
Cyprus, 5

damage, 101
de effuses ve deiectis, 37
De Minimis Notice, 199
debt, The, 6, 93, 101, 103
deterrence, 9–10, 13, 24, 26, 28, 31, 36, 40, 42, 44–45, 47, 52, 61, 63–65, 67–70, 72–74, 112, 133, 139, 153–154, 181, 186, 193, 207, 213, 218–221, 223–224, 229
Deutche Telekom AG, 73
Directive 2014/104/EU, 3, 5, 12, 28–29, 31, 45, 48, 53, 60, 62, 71, 73–74, 83, 86–87, 96, 99, 101, 106–107, 118–120, 124, 155, 159, 162–163, 166, 168, 174, 177, 179, 181, 185, 188–192, 194–195, 197–198, 201–203, 205, 211, 216, 219, 228, 231
11(4)(a), 196
Article 1(1), 17, 32
Article 2(15), 194
Article 3, 12
Article 3(3), 44
Article 11, 29, 33, 55, 203
Article 11(1), 13, 28, 62, 73, 83
Article 11(2), 197, 202, 204–205
Article 11(2)(b), 203
Article 11(4)(1), 188
Article 11(4)(a), 180, 203
Article 11(4)(b), 180, 203
Article 11(5), 53, 58, 62, 83, 180, 195–196
Article 11(6), 181, 195–196
Article 19(3), 172
Recital 48, 166
Recital 5, 166
Directorate-General for Competition (DG COMP), The, 190
Distilbène (DES), 146
Dittert, Daniel, 55
doctrine, economic continuity, 22, 25, 63–65, 76, 111, 148
doctrine, single economic entity, 19, 20–21, 25, 68, 111
dolus directus, 128, 134
dolus eventualis, 129
Duncan, Fox and Co v. North and South Wales Bank, 97, 104
Düsseldorf, The Appellate Court in, 177
Dyckerhoff, 185

Easterbrook, Frank H., 41
economic continuity, 16, 24, 26, 32, 73, 82, 110
economic successor, 23
Eco Swiss, 213
effect on trade, 199
effectiveness of EU competition law, 23, 25, 31, 52, 54, 58, 60–64, 66–69, 82–83, 105, 116, 160, 224, 227, 229
effets principaux, 90
ei incumbit probatio qui dicit, 195
Enactments (Amendment)) Regulations 2017, 2017 No. XXXX, The, 5
England and Wales. *See also* UK
antitrust issues, 100
contribution, 92, 113
divide contribution, 101
indemnity, 104
joint and several liability, 29. *See also* liability, joint and several
law analysis, 91
public story, 212
record damages, 1
subrogation, 103
subrogation claim, 107
English Contribution Act, The
Section 1, 34
entry fee, 10
erga omnes, 80
Esso, 171
European Commission (Commission), The, 3–4, 9–10, 12, 14–16, 18–20, 22–28, 31–33, 45–47,

49–58, 61, 63–65, 67–84, 86, 101, 103–104, 106, 109–110, 113, 116, 131, 133, 140, 142–143, 145, 147–150, 153–158, 161, 167, 177–178, 182–184, 188–190, 192, 194, 199, 201–202, 204, 211, 218–220, 224, 226–227, 229–230
European Group on Tort Law, The, 55
ex turpi causa, 89
ex turpi causa non oritur action, 89

Fahrlässigkeit, 129
fairness, 36–37, 39–40, 42–43, 57, 122, 134, 142, 151–152, 158
fault (*wina*), 120
faute inexcusable, 129
faute intentionelle, 128
faute légère, 129
faute lourde, 129
Finnboard, 15
FOREX, 174, 189
fortiori, 27
forum shopping, 30
foundation, 21, 81
France
  contribution, 114
  joint and several liability, 29. *See also* liability, joint and several
  record damages, 1
  subrogation, 103
  subrogation claim, 108
full settlements', 174

gains, illicit, 142
general clause, 223
General Court of the European Union (GCEU), The, 18, 51–52, 55, 58
general deterrence, 10
general regime, 162
Generics, 77
Germany
  antitrust issues, 100
  contribution, 114
  discussion to introduce contribution claim, 38
  joint and several liability, 29. *See also* liability, joint and several
  record damages, 1
  subragation, 103, 108, 114
gesamtschuldnerische Haftung, 5
Gesetz gegen Wettbewerbsbeschränkungen (GWB), The, 28, 94, 96, 100, 102, 107, 163, 171, 180, 181, 198, 199
Gigaset, 50
Google, 10
Gosselin Group NV, 75–76

Green Paper, The, 12, 30, 179, 190, 191
grobe Fahhrlässigkeit, 129
gross negligence, 129
Groupe Gascogne, 27

HeidelbergCement, 176, 185
Höfner, 17
Holcim, 185
Hungary, 191

immunity recipient, 3, 29, 162, 179–181, 183–188, 191–197, 201, 204–205, 216, 228, 230–231
in dubio pro reo, 56
indemnify, 133
individual deterrence, 10
injunctions, *quia timet*, 67
inpari delicto, 40
inrfringed norm (*Schutzzweck der Norm*), 135
internal relationship, 83
International Removal Services, 75, 77
Ireland, 5
Istituto Chemioterapico Italiano (ICI), *See also* CSC-ICI-Group, The
ius dispositive, 212

Johnson and Johnson, 14, 26
just and recommended, 39
Justinian's Novellea 99, The, 37, 89

Kendrion, 21, 76, 104
KNP BT, 26
Kodeks Cywilny (k.c.), The, 90, 93
  Article 376, 122
  Article 441, 93
  Article 441(1), 29
  Article 441(2), 34, 92, 98, 100, 102, 106, 108, 114, 120, 122
  Article 441(3), 97–98, 114, 120
Kokott, Juliane, 54–55
Körner, Julia, 26, 54
Krüger, Carsten, 138, 227

la solidarité, 38
Lafarge, 185
Landes, William M., 41
Landesgericht (LG) München, 50, 68–69
law, private, 9
legal Pascha, the (*juristischer Pascha*), 30
legal tradition, 4
  Central and Eastern European legal orders, 4
  common law, 4
  Germanic legal orders, 4
  Napoleonic legal orders, 4
leichte Fahrlässigkeit, 129

lekkomyślność, 129
leniency programme, 180–181, 184, 187, 190, 192, 215, 217, 220–221, 223
Leslie, Christopher R., 215–220
Lettl, Tobias, 44
lex specialis, 93
Liability Sharing Agreement (LSA), The, 207–225, 230
liability, bottom-up, 22
liability, individual, 77
liability, joint and several, 1–6, 8, 11, 13–16, 18–20, 22–39, 44, 46–48, 52–57, 59, 61–73, 75, 77, 82–83, 85, 89–90, 93, 100–101, 104–106, 110–111, 115–116, 123, 131–133, 136, 142, 150, 153, 156–158, 161–164, 167–169, 172, 174, 178–181, 184–185, 187–192, 194, 197–198, 202–203, 205, 211, 216, 218, 220, 225, 227–228, 230–231
liability, parental, 22
liability, subsidiarial, 22
liability, top-down, 22
liability. joint and several, 82, 146
Lufthansa, 166
Lundbeck, 76, 147

Manfredi, 11, 62
Manheim Regional Court, The, 176
materially involved, 25
McClory, 43
Mengozzi, Advocate General (AG), 52, 54, 56–57
Mercedes Benz Trucks España SL (Mercedes), 32
Merck KGaA, 77
Merryweather, the, 37, 89
Mitchell, Charles, 211
Mitwirkung, 66, 68, 101, 105, 158, 228
Mitwirkunganspruch, 98
model, Shapley, 138
multiple and punitive damages, 219

Napel, Stefan, 137
nature of the matter (*Natur der Sache*), 35
negligence, 134
Netherlands
  claims for damages, 30
  obstructing exports of new motor vehicles, 15
  private enforcement, 12
  record damages, 1
niedbałość, 129
Nitropopan, 14
non qui negat, 195
non-consensual dispute resolution, 163
Note, Leniency, 182
Novartis, 146

nulla crimen sine culpa, 157
nulla poena sine lege, 56
Nuova Magrini Galileo S.p.a., 51

O'Higgins, Michael, 174
Oberlandesgericht (OLG), The, 50
  OLG München, The, 69
obligation in solidum, 6, 38, 106
Occupant Safety Systems, The, 13, 20, 143
odpowiedzialność proporcjonalna, 6
odpowiedzialoność solidarna, 6
Office of Fair Trade (OFT), The, 191, 199
Oldehaver, Gunnar, 137
Opel, 15
Organisation for Economic Co-operation and Development, The (OECD), 199
Otis, 60

person, private, 9
personal claim (*Ausgleichspflicht*), 94
personal liability, 23, 26, 56
Pitruzella, Advocate General (AG), 22, 31–32, 71–74, 106
Poland
  contribution, 114
  indemnity, 104
  joint and several liability, 29. *See also* liability, joint and several
  subrogation claim, 108
Posner, Richard A., 42
Prawo Zobowiązań, 90
Pre-Insulated Pipe Cartel, 23–24
presumption, 20, 63
prima facie, 2, 49, 218
private enforcement, 4–5, 9, 11–14, 24, 28, 30–33, 44–45, 46–49, 53, 55–58, 61–62, 66, 70–71, 74, 80, 82–84, 86–87, 99–103, 106–114, 116–118, 125–128, 131, 141, 145, 150, 153, 156, 157–161, 174, 177, 179, 183–184, 188–190, 192–193, 210–211, 216, 218–221, 223–224, 227, 229–231
private equity investor, 21
private law, 54, 190, 193, 201, 220–221
private law antitrust liability, 1
private law damage, 111, 133, 183, 191
private law liability, 44, 71, 183, 185, 187, 189, 192, 197, 200–201, 215–217, 219
private lawsuit, 113, 165, 189
private leniency programme, 215–217
private liability, 185, 187, 190, 219
Professional Beauty Supply, 40
proportional liability, 6, 31, 33, 35, 146
proportionate claim reduction, 168
public court, 166
public domain, 204

public fine, 184, 190
public interest, 1
public justice system, 210
public law, 70, 216
public law liability, 103, 185, 190, 219
public law nature, 69–70
public leniency programme, 215–216
public nature of competition law, 207, 230
public penalty, 190
public policy, 207, 212–213, 223, 226
punitive function, 11–12
punitive role, 11

quia timet, 66, 68, 105

Raw tobacco – Spain, 21, 25
rażące niedbalstwo, 129
recours en contribution, *See also recours*
regres
  sensu largo, 102, 106
  sensu stricto, 93, 106
Regulation 1/2003, The, 50, 61
  Article 16, 79
  Article 23(2), 17, 27, 52, 76
  Article 23(2)(a), 128
  Article 23(b), 72
  Recital 30, 50
remedy, private, 11
res judicata, 82
responsabilité proportionnelle, 6
Roman times, 37
roszczenia regresowe, *See also regres*
Roth, Peter, justice, 228
roulette, 38
Royal Mail, 80

Sasol, 18, 171
Savigny, Friedrich Karl von, 39
scenario, counterfactual, 140
Schneider Electric SA, 51
Schwenk, 185
settlement, Mary-Carter, 165
Shell, 171
Siemens, 15, 22, 27–28, 48, 50–60, 67–75, 77, 79, 83, 86, 104, 110, 116, 118, 128, 150, 211
single economic entity, 16, 18–20, 22, 24, 63, 82, 110–111, 142, 224
Skanska, 12, 32, 44, 71, 73, 83, 110–111
SKW, 50
slight negligence, 129
Slovak Telecom, 27, 73
small and medium enterprise (SME), 3, 197–205, 228, 230
  Entrepreneurship Action Plan, 199
  Late Payment Directive, The, 199
  Small Business Act for Europe, The, 199
solidarité, 5, 90, 106
Spain
  record damages, 1
Stichting Administratiekantoor Portielje, 75
Study Group on the European Civil Code, The, 55
subrogation (*Legalzession*), 94
Sumal, 15, 32, 71–72, 111, 113, 132
sweetheart settlements, 215, 222

Teilschuld, 6
Telekom AG, 73
Texas Industries, 1, 2, 40, 44, 146
tort law, 12, 29, 31, 33, 46, 62, 66, 68, 105, 122, 150, 193–194
Tortfeasors Act 1935, The, 38, 89
transfer of business, 23
travaux préparatoires, 198
Treaty on the Functioning of the European Union (TFEU), The, 214
  Article 101 4, 9, 17, 32, 44, 50, 61, 72, 79, 136
  Article 101(1), 214, 223, 225
  Article 101(2), 214–215
  Article 102, 9, 79
  Article 105(2), 9
  Article 299(2)(1), 18
Treu und Glauben, 212–213
Tribunal de commerce de Grenoble, The, 51
truck cartel, 1–2, 32, 34, 189, 231
  DAF, 1–2, 189
  Daimler, 1–2, 32, 34, 189
  Iveco, 1–2, 34, 189
  MAN, 1–2, 189
  UK Truck Cartel, *See also* UKTC
  Volvo Group, 1–2, 189
types of damages, 12

UCB Pharma, 146
UKTC v. Iveco and Daimler, 1–2, 34
Umstände, 121
unclean hands, 40
undertaking, 9–10, 13, 16–19, 23, 25, 27–28, 32, 51–52, 54–55, 57, 61, 63–65, 68, 73, 76, 80, 82, 102, 105, 111, 118, 125, 129, 132, 136–137, 141, 143–145, 148, 152–153, 157, 178, 180, 185, 198, 201–204, 209
Uniform Contribution Among Tortfeasors Act 1939, The, 38
United States
  antitrust enforcement, *See also* US
  antitrust law, 165, 208

United States (cont.)
  antitrust scholar and practitioner, 48
  contribution claim, 38
  debate on contribution claims, 44
  leniency programme, 187
  no-contribution system, 39
  private enforcement, 44
  public enforcement, 45
  US Senate, The, 43
unlawful profits, 24, 28

Versalis, 27
verursacht, 121
Verursachung, 107
Volkswagen, 78–79
Vorsatz, 128

White Paper, The, 11–12, 29, 30, 179, 191, 192, 196
Whitham v. Bullock, 6, 92, 97
Wils, Wouter P. J., 190, 200

zamiar
  bezpośredni, 128
  ewentualny, 129
Zurich Club, The, 81

For EU product safety concerns, contact us at Calle de José Abascal, 56–1°, 28003 Madrid, Spain or eugpsr@cambridge.org.

www.ingramcontent.com/pod-product-compliance
Lightning Source LLC
LaVergne TN
LVHW011525200926
848484LV00001B/151

* 9 7 8 1 1 0 8 8 3 9 3 1 0 *